ITALIAN SMALL ARMS
of the First and Second World Wars

ITALIAN SMALL ARMS

OF THE FIRST AND SECOND WORLD WARS

RALPH RICCIO

Schiffer Publishing Ltd
4880 Lower Valley Road • Atglen, PA 19310

DEDICATION

This book is dedicated first to my wife, Charlene, who continues not only to put up with my passion for writing, but who has taken an active part in helping with various aspects of the writing and proofing. It is also dedicated to our children: John, Stephen, Carla and Jennifer; their spouses: Lisa, Lucy, Jeremy and Fazl; and our grandchildren: Alexis, Ashley, Garrett, Etienne, Marley, Asher and Sebastian.

Library of Congress Control Number: 2014930256

Printed in China
ISBN: 978-0-7643-4583-8

We are interested in hearing from authors with book ideas on related topics

Published by Schiffer Publishing Ltd.
4880 Lower Valley Road
Atglen, PA 19310
Phone: (610) 593-1777
FAX: (610) 593-2002
E-mail: Info@schifferbooks.com.

Visit our web site at:
www.schifferbooks.com
Please write for a free catalog.
This book may be
purchased from the publisher.
Try your bookstore first.

CONTENTS

Chapter 1: PISTOLS

Chapter 2: RIFLES

Chapter 3:
SUBMACHINE GUNS

Chapter 4:
MACHINE GUNS

APPENDICES

PREFACE

The first somewhat meager draft of this book was written more than thirty-five years ago, when I was stationed with the U.S. Army in Italy and had access to the Beretta Arms Museum and to the military museum at Rovereto. I managed to collect a number of photographs, which at the time I thought would enable me to write a fairly comprehensive history of Italian small arms used during World War II. The inevitable moves that are part and parcel of military life, plus family obligations and other interests, led to abandonment of the project until late-2011 when, after having completed a number of other books, I happened to find a copy of the original manuscript and the photographic documentation. That led to renewed research and an expanded scope for the book; the Internet made it possible to achieve what I could never have dreamed of more than three decades ago by enabling me to correspond easily with arms experts, museums, and a host of other individuals and organizations in Italy that provided information and images for the project.

ACKNOWLEDGMENTS

In addition to documentary sources that provided material for this book, a great number of individuals and organizations provided unique and priceless information, advice, and photographs. Although everyone's contribution was important and answered some usually obscure question or filled some gap, a number of individuals merit special recognition and thanks, because of their continued direct interest and participation and because of the quality and volume of information or images they provided.

Ruggero Filippo Pettinelli, co-author of the comprehensive Italian book on the Carcano, was extremely generous in providing information not expressly contained in his book, as well as providing images from his personal collection. His patience in answering what at times seemed a stream of questions I posed via E-mail was more than could be reasonably expected.

Leonardo M. Antaris, MD, an acclaimed firearms author himself, was unbelievably responsive to my request for images of Italian pistols from his superb personal collection. Dr. Antaris gave much of his time in phone calls and E-mails and spared no effort in providing me with outstanding professional quality photographs that easily equal the incomparable quality of those in his own books.

Fred Ellingsen, a friend, fellow gun enthusiast, and accomplished photographer who critiqued an early draft of the book and who, more importantly, over the course of seveal sessions photographed most of the weapons from my collection to their best advantage.

Dott. Marco Leonardi Scomazzoni (Conservatore, Museo storico italiano della Guerra, Rovereto) and **Dott. Davide Zendri** of the Museo storico italiano della Guerra, who graciously and patiently acceded to a deluge of requests for information and who provided photographs of unique weapons from the extensive collection of Italian Military History Museum in Rovereto.

Paolo Silvano, of the Armeria Berrone in Alessandria, Italy, who I had the good fortune to stumble across by an unimaginable stroke of luck while making more or less random phone calls to gun shops in Italy in the hopes of ferreting out information on an Italian designer Giulio Sosso. Silvano, a consummate gentleman, was helpful and enthusiastic, and provided a significant amount of documentation on Sosso, some based on personal knowledge.

John Moss, an acknowledged ammunition expert, who not only provided authoritative information on Glisenti cartridges, but who furnished a number of excellent images of Beretta and Glisenti pistols.

Jon Cohen was gracious and generous in sharing information concerning the specialized field of cartridge collecting, but also provided access to his extensive collection and allowed me to photograph the entire range of cartridges produced and used by the Italians in both World Wars.

Luca Vallebona, of Armeria Black Hills, Genova, who, in the final weeks of preparation, provided a treasure trove of pictures and information on toy carbines as well as pictures of various Beretta pistols with unique markings.

Giovanni Chegia, author and manager of www.il91.it, a website dedicated to the Carcano rifle, whose meticulous research and willingness to share his extensive knowledge have made it possible to include details on the Carcano found in no other source.

Gianluigi Usai, who graciously offered to his in-depth knowledge of Italian pistols and submachine guns, proofread my draft text, and saved me from embarrassment by pointing out a number of factual errors.

Steve Woodrum, a dedicated collector of unusual Carcano variants and of Bodeo revolvers, who seemed to always be able to provide images of one-of-a-kind markings or specimens.

Bob Biondi, Doug Congdon-Martin, Ian Robertson, and the staff at Schiffer Publishing for their patience with numerous photo shoots and more than a few questions about style and format.

Jarno Antonelli (Fabbrica d'Armi Pietro Beretta)
Russ Arendell
Etienne Ayoub
Vittorio Balzi
Alessandro Baratta (Fabbrica d'Armi Pietro Beretta)
Corrado Barbieri
Professore Giovanni Barozzi (Provveditore, Museo storico italiano della Guerra)
Scott Benedict (Pre98 Vintage Military and Collectible Firearms)
Bruno Benvenuti
Silvia Bertelli (Centro Studi e Ricerche Storiche sull'Architettura Militare del Piemonte)
John Bill
Bradley Bloom
Stefano Cacciani (Armeria Delven, Roma)
Cesare Calamandrei
Tenente Colonnello Filippo Cappellano (Ufficio Storico, Stato Maggiore Esercito)
Tenente Colonnello Cesare Cavallari (Fabbrica Armi Esercito – Terni)
Signora Luisella Ceretta (Città di Avigliana)
Antonio Ciavoni

Ron Clarin Collectors Firearms, Houston, Texas
David Condon, Inc. (Middleburg, VA)
James Cook (Vermont gunbroker)
Augusto Costantino (Centro Storico Fiat)
Joe Cox (Old State Stuff)
Chief Warrant Officer Giuseppe de Finis (Embassy of Italy, Office of the Defense Attaché and Defense Cooperation)
Larry Eisel (Eisel Armory)
Viviana Facchini (Banco Nazionale di Prova)
Ing. Costantino Fiocchi (Giulio Fiocchi, Lecco)
John Freudenthal (Lazy J's)
Alden Gainey
Joel Genaw
Ing. Antonio Girlando (Direttore, Banco Nazionale di Prova)
Franceso Giubilei (KME Group SpA)
Amedeo Gnutti (Eredi Gnutti Metalli S.p.A)
Pavel Gorecky (American Embassy, Prague)
Daniele Guglielmi
Zachary Hein (CZ-USA)
John Holbert (Riverside Gun Shop)
Paolo Iannarone
Victor Katerinich
Aleš Kratochvil
Simonetta Leonetti (Centro Sportivo Villaggio Breda)
Liberty Tree Collectors, Corinth, Maine
Emanuele Marcianó
Ed Mattioli
Ian McCollum (Forgotten Weapons)
Alberto Miorandi (Consigliere, Museo storico italiano della Guerra)
M. Mondini (Musei d'Arte e Storia, Brescia)
Ugo Muffolini (Beretta USA)
Museo Torino (Torino), Curators
Northeast Firearms, Inc., Honesdale, PA
Antonio Oropesa (Fabbrica d'Armi Pietro Beretta)
Claudio Pergher (Gruppo Modellistico Trentino)
Mike Petrozello (Shooting Gallery Books)
Ruggero Pettinelli
Maria Nisi Pignato
Rodolfo Redolfi (Redolfi Armi, Manerbio, Brescia)
Liisa Rutanen (Assistant, Office of the Defense, Military and Air Attaché, Embassy of Finland,)
Remo Sabatini (Polo di Mantenimento delle Armi Leggere, Terni)
Tristana Serino (Embassy of Italy, Office of the Defense Attaché and Defense Cooperation)
Chris Shanahan
Alberta Simonis (Archivio e Centro Storico Fiat)
Caroline Simms (National Firearms Museum)
Alberto Simonelli
Jan Skramoušský (Military Museum Prague) (Vojenský Historický Ústav Praha)
Stabilimento Militare Spolette, Torre Annunziata
COL Patrick Sullivan (DATT, USDAO Prague)
Marco Taesi (Communication & Press Office, Eredi Gnutti Metalli S.p.A)
Tenete Colonnello Roberto Tarquini (Polo di Mantenimento delle Armi Leggere, Terni)
Enrico Tempini (Tempini S.p.A., Brescia)
Dennis Todd
Brigadier General Pietro Tornabene (Embassy of Italy, Office of the Defense Attaché and Defense Cooperation)
Renzo Turco (Museo della Meccanica e del Cuscinetto-Villar Perosa)
Ken and Erica Turner (Orchard's Pawn Shop)
Ufficio Storico dello Stato Maggiore Esercito, Rome
Dr. Astrid M.S. Vallati (DocAV on Gunboards.com), Brisbane, Australia
Serena Vanessa (Armeria Berrone)
Keith Versaw
Alessandro Viti (Fabbrica d'Armi Pietro Beretta)
Frank Walters (Deland Military Collectibles)
COL Charles Wilson (ARMA, USDAO Prague)
Woodin Laboratory, Tucson, Arizona
Col. Antonio Zarcone (Capo Ufficio, V Reparto Affari Generali – Ufficio Storico, Stato Maggiore dell'Esercito)

INTRODUCTION

There are very few books in the English language dealing specifically with Italian small arms that were used in World War I and World War II, and these largely are confined to just a few books on the Carcano Model 1891 rifle and Beretta pistols. Occasional magazine articles address various individual Italian small arms, often superficially, and—in common with some of the books—are marked by truly atrocious misspellings of Italian names, words, or weapons designations. There has, however, been no book in English that examines Italian military small arms in a comprehensive manner. There are two noteworthy books in English that deal with Beretta pistols: *Modern Beretta Firearms*, by Gene Gangarosa Jr., and *Beretta Automatic Pistols: The Collector's and Shooter's Comprehensive Guide*, by J.B. Wood, both of which provide very good background and reference information on the Berettas. *The Carcano: Italy's Military Rifle*, by Richard Hobbs, is a generally accurate and informative treatment of Carcano rifles, although unfortunately, Hobbs' book has some erroneous information that, by virtue of the fact that until just very recently it was the only English-language book on the subject, has been taken as gospel by many. In 2012, a rather well researched book dedicated to the Carcano, *Italy's Battle Rifle, Story of the Mannlicher-Carcano Series of Rifles*, by Russ Arendell and Steve Woodrum, was published. Overall, it is quite a comprehensive work by two dedicated collectors and authors. Until relatively recently, there had been a somewhat similar phenomenon in Italian coverage of the subject, but fortunately, since the 1990s a number of books have been written in Italian that have done much to fill in the lack of documentation that existed. The best and most informative of these are: *I mitra italiani 1915-1991* by Vittorio Balzi, which covers Italian submachine guns; *Le armi della fanteria italiana 1919-1945* by Nicola Pignato and Filippo Cappellano, which is a comprehensive treatment of weapons used by Italian infantry; *1891: il fucile degli italiani* by Bruno Di Giorgio and Ruggero Filippo Pettinelli, which is a superb in-depth work on Italy's iconic Model 1891 Carcano rifle; and *Le cinque vite della Glisenti 1910* by Emanuele Marcianó and Adriano Simoni, a more than adequate coverage of the Glisenti pistol.

This book describes all small arms produced in Italy from handguns to machine guns chambered for rifle-caliber cartridges used by the Italian armed forces during both World Wars, as well as prototype and limited production weapons manufactured in Italy during the period from the early-1930s through the war years. The developmental history of each weapon is provided as far as possible, and emphasis is placed on identification and description of variants where applicable, but technical and engineering details such as method of operation and disassembly procedures generally are not provided.

In addition to weapons designed and produced in Italy, weapons that were purchased on a contract basis or that were captured and generally issued to colonial or second-line units and those that were used by the Italian armed forces subordinate to the Germans or Allies subsequent to the armistice of 8 September 1943 are covered briefly in an appendix.

The nomenclature used throughout the book follows Italian nomenclature as closely as possible. The heading given for each weapon will bear the most commonly used Italian designation, but variants of the designation will also be specified in the text. In most cases the English equivalent of the Italian heading will appear on the first line of the text.

Undoubtedly, comparison of the material presented in this book with information contained in other English-language works will reveal discrepancies, in some cases to the extent that virtually contradictory information will be encountered. Also, some gaps may be encountered in the general format of the book itself; this is in most cases explained by the fact that accurate information is not available on many weapons, as records, both factory and government, were lost or destroyed during the war or during the period of administrative chaos immediately following the war.

ITALIAN WEAPON DESIGNATIONS

The Italians used several variations of words, numbers and abbreviations to designate their weapons. The word *modello* (model), followed by two, three or four numbers to denote the year of adoption of a weapon, is normally used to designate or identify a weapon. However, *modello* may begin with a lower case or upper case letter and be abbreviated as Mod. or mod.; the year of adoption may be either the full four digits (e.g., 1934) or the last two digits of the year (e.g., 91) or, less frequently, the last three digits of the year. Yet another variation is to use just the full or partial year designation, without any form of the word *modello* (e.g., Beretta 1934, or *fucile 91*). Modifications to a basic weapon were referred to by numbers separated by an oblique, such as the 91/38, indicating the basic Model 1891 rifle whose modified form was adopted in 1938. To add further to the welter of designation possibilities, the modified 1891 rifle adopted in 1941 was known simply as the *modello 41* rather than the 91/41. It should be noted that when referring to a weapon's caliber, the Italians use the Continental system of designating a fractional number by using a comma between the whole number and the fractional part of the number, e.g., 7,35mm rather than the English system that uses a full stop, or period, between the numbers, e.g., 7.35mm. However, there are exceptions to this rule, as for example on the caliber indication stamped on buttstocks of 7.35mm rifles which uses the period rather than the comma.

The year date shown on Italian weapons produced during the 1930s and 1940s was commonly expressed in Arabic numerals denoting the Christian year as well as in Roman numerals denoting the year according to the Fascist calendar. The Fascist calendar's base date was 28 October 1922, which commemorated Fascism's rise to power in Italy. Because of the discrepancy between the beginning dates for the two calendars (1 January for the Christian calendar and 28 October for the Fascist), weapons produced in November and December of a normal calendar year would reflect the successive Fascist era year, e.g., a weapon produced in 1942 would be marked with the 1942 Christian date throughout the year but would be marked with the Fascist year XX from January to October, and XXI in November and December.

CHAPTER 1: PISTOLS

During both World War I and World W ar II Italian military forces used a fairly wide variety of pistols ranging from the Model 1874 Chamelot-Delvigne revolver to the Beretta Model 1934 and Model 1935 semi-automatic pistols; many of the pistols that saw service in World War I, such as the Bodeo Model 1889 and Glisenti Model 1910, continued to be issued during World War II. In addition to regulation weapons produced by the Italians themselves, there were a few types used during World War I that were manufactured under license in Spain, as well as Spanish designs that were bought to supplement the Italian pistols. Adding further to the pistol inventory were substantial numbers of pistols and revolvers acquired as war reparations from Austria-Hungary following World War I. There was also a profusion of non-regulation sidearms in use because of the fact that although Italian officers were issued with personal sidearms by the government, they were also free to purchase and carry the personal sidearm of their own particular liking. This latter option was responsible for creating the situation in which during World War II officers carried pistols that ranged from 6.35mm (.25 caliber) to 9mm *corto* (.380 ACP) in caliber, even though by 1942 the only sidearms officially recognized in the Italian Army inventory were the Model 1889 revolver (types A and B) and the Beretta Model 1934 pistol.

It is generally conceded that Italian service pistols manufactured by the firm of Pietro Beretta were well-designed, well-made, well-finished and reliable weapons. References to other Italian sidearms, however, and in particular to the Model 1889 Bodeo revolver, are not always so flattering, although it should be recognized that many of these negative observations are not put into proper perspective. Although there has been some suggestion that the Model 1889 revolver was an anachronism in World War II, in fact it was no more of an anachronism than were the Webley revolvers originally adopted by the U.K. in 1887, or the French M1873 revolvers still in service at that time.

PISTOLA A ROTAZIONE MODELLO 1874

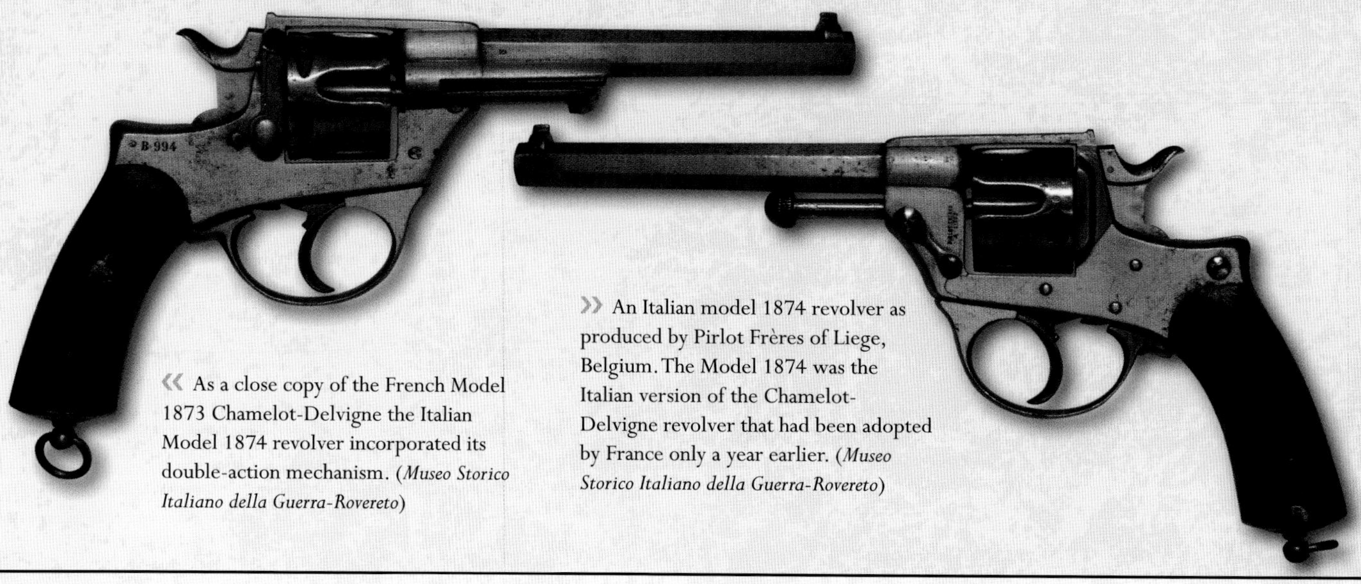

« As a close copy of the French Model 1873 Chamelot-Delvigne the Italian Model 1874 revolver incorporated its double-action mechanism. (*Museo Storico Italiano della Guerra-Rovereto*)

» An Italian model 1874 revolver as produced by Pirlot Frères of Liege, Belgium. The Model 1874 was the Italian version of the Chamelot-Delvigne revolver that had been adopted by France only a year earlier. (*Museo Storico Italiano della Guerra-Rovereto*)

In 1874 Italy made the decision to adopt the French Chamelot-Delvigne Model 1873 revolver to replace its obsolete Lefauchaux service revolver; the Italian version was designated the Model 1874 and was almost identical to the French version which had a solid frame and swing-out cylinder. It was not officially adopted by Italy until 22 March 1876, even though Glisenti and the Brescia Arsenal had produced a number of the revolvers that were issued for trail purposes to ten Italian cavalry regiments in 1875. Subsequently, issue of the Model 1874 was extended to infantry and alpine officers and later to the *Carabinieri* as well. The earliest Model 1874 revolvers were not blued but were issued in the white; later revolvers were blued, and at least some of the early ones were blued during arsenal refurbishment. Although the Model 1874 was supplanted and replaced by the Bodeo Model 1889 revolver beginning in 1889, it remained in Italian service throughout the 1911-1912 campaign in Libya against the Ottoman Turks and continued to serve throughout World War I. The Model 1874 was also issued in limited numbers during World War II. ■

PISTOLA A ROTAZIONE MODELLO 1874

Designer: J. Chamelot and Henri Gustave Delvigne
Manufacturers: Fabbrica d'Armi Brescia; Siderurgica Glisenti; Pirlot Frères, Liege
Caliber: 10.35mm
Cartridge: 10.4x22mm Italian Ordnance
Operating system: Double action, revolver
Overall length: 290mm (11.42")
Barrel length: 160mm (6.30")
Weight: 1.15 kg (2.54 lbs)
Front sight: Blade
Rear sight: Notch in top strap
Muzzle velocity: 252 m/sec (825 fps)
Feed system: 6 shot cylinder

PISTOLA A ROTAZIONE MODELLO 1889

Despite its age and despite the fact that some excellent Beretta pistols were available, the Model 1889 revolver was still an official sidearm of *Regio Esercito* (Royal Army) and *Carabinieri* during World War II. It resembles the earlier *pistola a rotazione modello 1874*, which in turn was based on the French Chamelot-Delvigne design, but it is smaller and its design is different. In 1886 Carlo Bodeo, a gunmaker from Naples, was issued a patent for what was essentially an improved version of the *modello 1874*. The resulting revolver is commonly referred to in Italy as the Bodeo, although the official designation is the *pistola a rotazione modello 1889*. Production began in 1889 and continued on until possibly as late as 1932, with a total of about 200,000 being produced; in addition to being produced by a number of different firms in Italy itself, during World War I it was also produced by three firms in Spain. The Model 1889 was the most widely issued handgun in the Italian Army between the

A 1933 replacement barrel on a Model 1889 revolver; the significance of the letter F to the right of the date is unknown. (*Author's collection*)

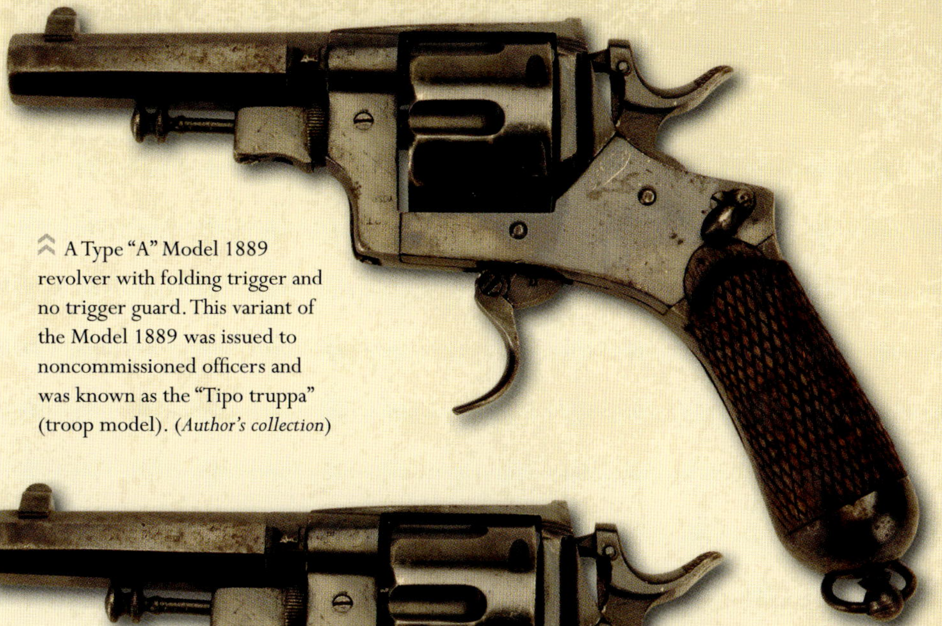

A Type "A" Model 1889 revolver with folding trigger and no trigger guard. This variant of the Model 1889 was issued to noncommissioned officers and was known as the "Tipo truppa" (troop model). (*Author's collection*)

Partially struck manufacturer's marking and only partially legible date on a Brescia produced Model 1889 revolver. (*Author's collection*)

A Model 1889 Type "A" revolver with trigger folded. Despite its age, the Bodeo was a solid and reliable weapon and was used through World War II. (*Author's collection*)

A Type "B" Model 1889 revolver, issued to officers. This particular revolver was manufactured by the government arsenal in Brescia. (*Aleš Kratochvil*)

Right side view of a 1926 Bodeo with Arabic markings on the frame. (*Courtesy Steve Woodrum*)

The Arabic marking on the frame of this Model 1889 revolver is believed to indicate that it was in service with the Egyptian police. (*Courtesy Steve Woodrum*)

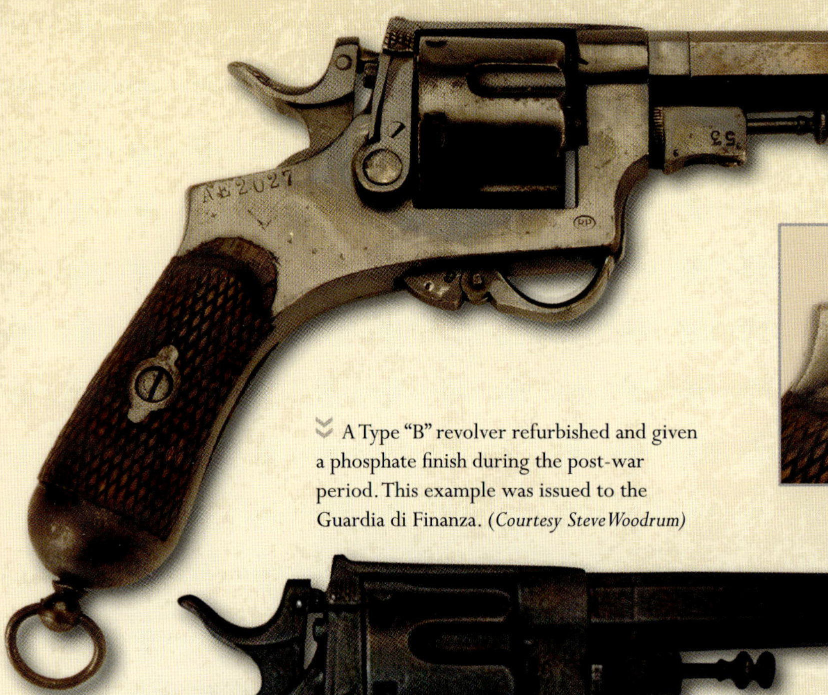

Right side view of the Bodeo with trigger folded in the forward position. (*Author's collection*)

The serial number on Bodeo revolvers was on the right side of the frame. Bodeo revolvers may also be encountered with assembly numbers on the barrel and other parts. (*Author's collection*)

A Type "B" revolver refurbished and given a phosphate finish during the post-war period. This example was issued to the Guardia di Finanza. (*Courtesy Steve Woodrum*)

This Model 1889 bears a profusion of markings including the Savoy crest, the Guardia di Finanza marking, repair date, inspector's initals, and the maker's logo. (*Courtesy Steve Woodrum*)

A Modello 1889 Tipo "B" alleggerita, manufactured by Metallurgica Bresciana già Tempini (MBT). This variant of the Bodeo was characterized by its short barrel. (*Aleš Kratochvil*)

Probable assembly numbers on a Bodeo Model 1889 revolver. (*Author's collection*)

Inspector's stamp on the right side of the frame of a Bodeo revolver. (*Author's collection*)

Detail of the open loading gate on a Model 1889 revolver. (*Author's collection*)

two World Wars. In 1922, a modified version of the Model 1889 that allowed more rapid cartridge extraction and reloading was tested but was not adopted for several reasons, including cost and performance issues.

The 1889 is a double-action weapon with a solid frame, hammer block safety, rod ejector and loading gate on the right-hand side, somewhat similar in many respects to the Russian Nagant M1895. Three basic versions of the Bodeo revolver were made. The first, designated the type "A" – and also as the *Tipo Truppa* (Troop Type) – which was issued to NCOs and other ranks, was characterized by a folding trigger and the absence of a trigger guard; the exterior of the barrel was octagonal. The second, designated as the type "B" – and also as the *Tipo Ufficiali* (Officer Type) – was issued to officers and had a standard trigger and trigger guard. The third type, known as the *B alleggerita* ("lightened B") was basically the same as the type "B", but differed in that its barrel was shorter and was tapered, rather than being octagonal as on the types "A" and "B". All three types had checkered walnut grips. Many variations in manufacture may be encountered among the various producers. Finish generally was not up to the usual Italian standards, but the weapon nevertheless was strong, reliable and was appreciated for its stopping power; it remained in use by the *Carabinieri* and *Guardia di Finanza* until the 1950s. Reflecting the Italian obsession with food, because of its configuration the Bodeo was nicknamed the *coscia d'agnello*, or "leg of lamb" by the Italians.

The serial number was on the right side of the frame, above the grip; a mark consisting of the letters RE (*Regio Esercito*) surmounted by a crown also was on the left frame, in front of the cylinder; manufacturer's markings were on the left side of the frame on some specimens, above the trigger and in front of the cylinder. Numbered assembly markings may be encountered on the barrel and small parts. ■

PISTOLA A ROTAZIONE MODELLO 1889

Designer: Carlo Bodeo
Manufacturers: MIDA (già Castelli), Brescia; N & V Castelli, Brescia; Toschi-Castelli; Siderurgica Glisenti, Brescia; Fabbrica d'Armi di Brescia; Fabbrica d'Armi Metallurgica Bresciana; Bernardelli; and possibly Fabbrica d'Armi Pietro Beretta. The Mod. 1889 was also produced in Spain by Arizmendi y Goenaga, Eulogio Arostegui and Antonio Errasti (all located in Eibar).
Caliber: 10.35mm
Cartridge: 10.4x22mm Italian Ordnance
Operating system: Double action, revolver
Overall length: 235mm (9.25") type "A"; 211mm (8.3") type "B alleggerita"
Barrel length: 114mm (4.5") type "A"; 90mm (3.6") type "B alleggerita"
Weight: 0.91 kg (2 lbs) type "A"
Front sight: Inverted V with bead
Rear sight: V notch cut in frame
Muzzle velocity: 252 m/sec (825 fps)
Feed system: 6 shot cylinder

PISTOLA AUTOMATICA MODELLO 1899 TIPO "REGIA MARINA" *(Mauser-Selbstladepistole C96)*

The Mauser C96 semi-automatic pistol, chambered for the proprietary Mauser 7.63x23mm cartridge, had been developed in 1896, and was offered commercially by Mauser. In 1899, the Italian *Regia Marina* (Italian Royal Navy) adopted the C96, and its order for 5,000 pistols marked the first major military contract for that pistol as well as the first adoption of a semi-automatic pistol by a military organization. The C96 adopted by the Italian Navy differed from the commercial version in a number of respects: the receiver was "slab-sided," lacking the milling cuts characteristic of the commercial Mausers, and it had a large "ring" hammer. In Italian service the C96 was designated *pistola automatica Mod. 1899 tipo "Regia Marina"* (Model 1899 automatic pistol, Royal Navy type). The *Regia Marina* guns had their own serial number range that ran from 1 through 5000. There is reason to believe that the C96 was also issued to some *Guardia di Finanza* (Finance Guard) units, but it is not certain if these were part of the Navy contract or were purchased separately. A number of C96s were issued to Italian aviators during World War I as well, but the details of their procurement are not known. There is some speculation that the C96 pistols issued to the aviators were the pre-war Commercial

PISTOLA AUTOMATICA MOD. 1899 TIPO "REGIA MARINA" (ITALIAN) MAUSER-SELBSTLADEPISTOLE C96 (CONSTRUKTION 96) (GERMAN)

Designer: Fidel, Friedrich and Josef Feederle
Manufacturers: Mauser Werke, Oberndorf-am-Neckar
Caliber: 7.63mm
Cartridge: 7.63x23mm Mauser
Operating system: Short recoil
Overall length: 312mm (12.28")
Barrel length: 140mm (5.51")
Weight: 1.3 kg (2.87 lbs) unloaded
Front sight: Inverted V
Rear sight: V-notch rear tangent adjustable to 1,000 meters
Muzzle velocity: 425 m/sec (1394 fps)
Feed system: 10-round fixed staggered row magazine

version, not flatsides. In some cases the aviators used guns that were taken from captured enemy fliers; Italy's most famous World War I flying ace, Francesco Baracca, carried a C96 retrieved from an Austrian reconnaissance aircraft downed in 1917. Despite the Italian Navy's purchase of 5,000 Brixia Model 1913 pistols to replace the Mauser, the C96 remained in service until the 1920s, when it was finally replaced by Beretta pistols. ■

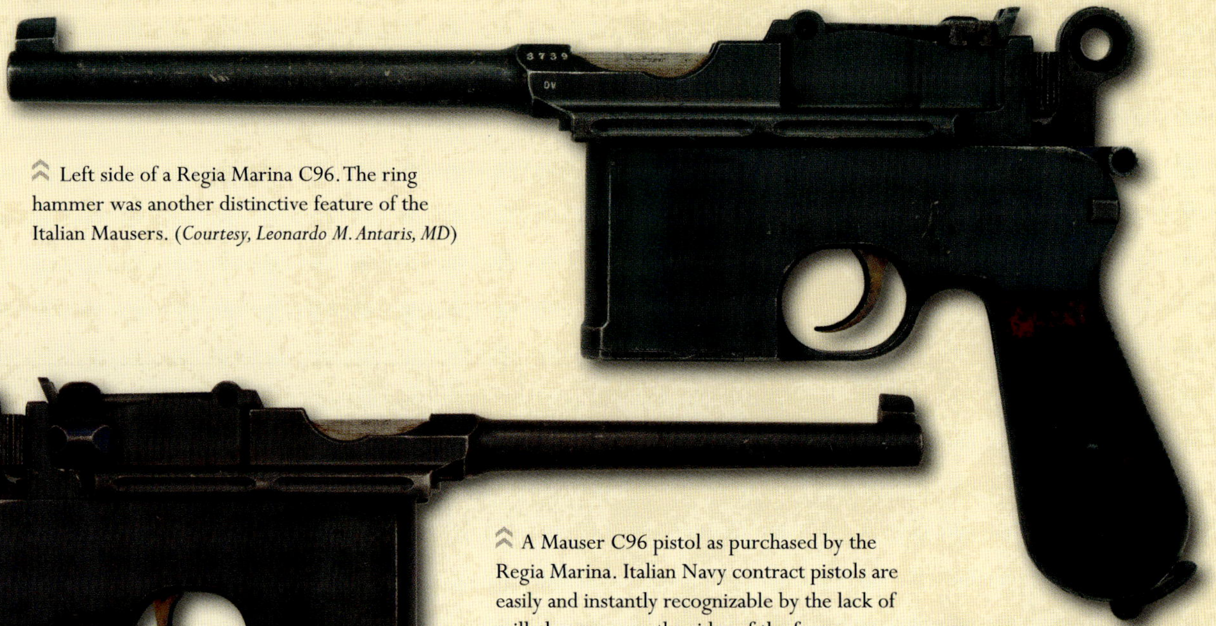

Left side of a Regia Marina C96. The ring hammer was another distinctive feature of the Italian Mausers. *(Courtesy, Leonardo M. Antaris, MD)*

A Mauser C96 pistol as purchased by the Regia Marina. Italian Navy contract pistols are easily and instantly recognizable by the lack of milled grooves on the sides of the frame. *(Courtesy, Leonardo M. Antaris, MD)*

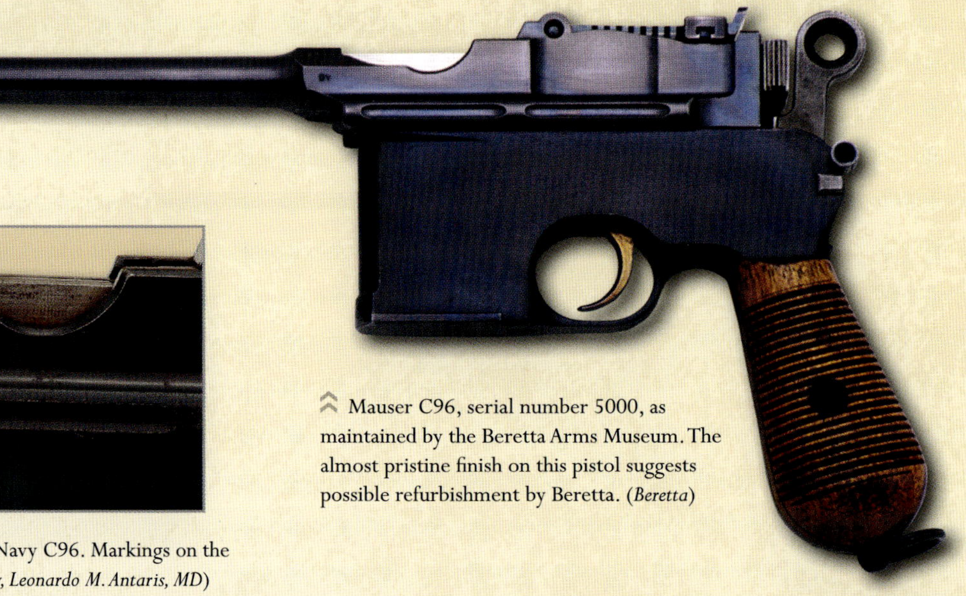

Mauser C96, serial number 5000, as maintained by the Beretta Arms Museum. The almost pristine finish on this pistol suggests possible refurbishment by Beretta. *(Beretta)*

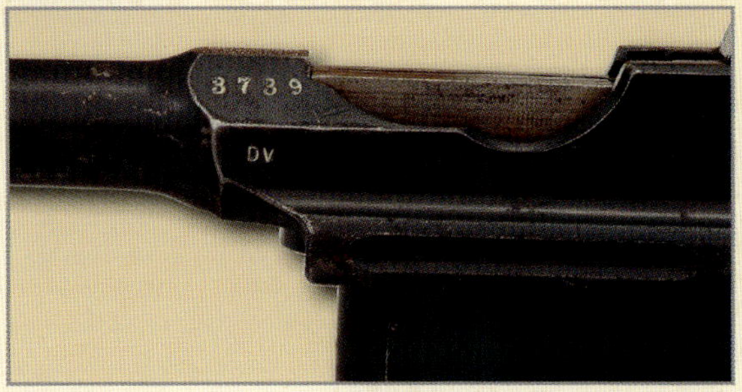

Detail of serial number of an Italian Navy C96. Markings on the Italian C96 pistols were sparse. *(Courtesy, Leonardo M. Antaris, MD)*

PISTOLA AUTOMATICA MODELLO 1910 *(Glisenti)*

There has been more than a little confusion concerning the Glisenti and the later Brixia pistols, not the least of which stems from the fact that the pistol was designed by Revelli, patented by Glisenti – but never actualy produced by that firm – and then manufactured by Metallurgica Bresciana giá Tempini. The very recent book by Marcianò and Simoni which focuses on the background, design, development and production of the Glisenti/Brixia has done much to dispel erroneous assumptions and information about the Glisenti pistols. To the wholly uninitiated, the Glisenti instantly evokes comparison to the German P.08 Luger, and in fact has been referred to in English language sources as the "Italian Luger," and in Italian sources as the "poor man's Luger," although Marcianò and Simoni suggest that it might be better described as the "Luger of the well-to-do" as compared to the "Luger of the rich" being the P.08 itself. However, aside from its general external appearance the Glisenti has little in common with the Luger. It is a locked-breech pistol, and while it is also in 9mm caliber and its cartridge dimensions are compatible with those of the 9mm Parabellum, the 9mm Glisenti cartridge is a much lower powered cartridge to enable the pistol to withstand the firing stresses. Firing standard 9mm Parabellum ammunition, or even worse, the Italian Fiocchi 9M38 9mm round, in a Glisenti is dangerous and potentially catastrophic.

Right side view of a 1910 Glisenti showing serial number, inspector's stamp, and Fabbrica Armi Brescia logo and year. This is an early production pistol with the Bakelite grips. (*Courtesy, Leonardo M. Antaris, MD*)

A 1910 Glisenti. Although it bore a superficial resemblance to the German P.08 Luger, it was a totally different design and fired a much weaker 9mm cartridge than did the Luger. (*Courtesy, Leonardo M. Antaris MD*)

Detail of the stowage position for the Glisenti takedown tool. (*Courtesy, Leonardo M. Antaris, MD*)

PISTOLA AUTOMATICA MODELLO 1906

Designer: Bethel Abiel Revelli
Manufacturer: Metallurgica Bresciana giá Tempini
Caliber: 7.65mm
Cartridge: 7.65x22 Parabellum
Operating system: Locked breech, single action
Overall length: 220mm (8.7 inches)
Barrel length: 120mm (4.72 inches)
Weight: .83 kg (1.8 lbs)
Front sight: Barleycorn
Rear sight: V notch
Muzzle velocity: 365 m/sec (1200 fps)
Feed system: 8 round detachable box magazine

PISTOLA AUTOMATICA MODELLO 1910

Designer: Bethel Abiel Revelli
Manufacturer: Metallurgica Bresciana giá Tempini
Caliber: 9mm
Cartridge: 9x19mm Glisenti
Operating system: Locked breech, single action
Overall length: 206mm (8.1 inches)
Barrel length: 95mm (3.7 inches)
Weight: .80 kg (1.76 lbs)
Front sight: Barleycorn
Rear sight: V notch
Muzzle velocity: 320 m/sec (1050 fps)
Feed system: 7 round detachable box magazine

In 1887, upon the death of Francesco Glisenti the family company, which was essentially an ironworks, passed into the hands of Alfredo Glisenti who in 1900 founded the Siderurgica Glisenti and who was the moving force behind the idea of developing and producing an automatic pistol. Glisenti engaged the services and talent of Bethel Abiel Revelli who by 1903 had designed a semi-automatic pistol chambered for a 7.65mm cartridge and that was clearly influenced by the Mauser C96 pistol – indeed, one version of the pistol had the forward mounted magazine characteristic of the C96, and the rectangular bolt of the Glisenti with its distinctive cocking knob wings is unmistakably copied from that of the C96. At an unspecified date, but probably in 1905, a prototype of the Glisenti was produced which was quite similar to the Model 1905/1906 and was characterized by wooden grips and a slightly longer barrel than the definitive Model 1910. Also in 1905, the Fabbrica d'Armi Glisenti filed a patent for a semi-automatic pistol whose shape and mechanical layout were similar to those of the later Model 1910. In 1906 Glisenti tooled up for manufacture of the pistol, but that same year Alfredo Glisenti died and was never to see the practical realization of his desire to develop an automatic pistol. After Alfredo's death, in March 1907 Siderurgica Glisenti sold its weapons sector – the Fabbrica d'Armi Glisenti – and manufacturing rights for the pistol, which by this time was referred to as the *Sistema Glisenti*, or Glisenti System, to Metallurgica Bresciana giá Tempini (MBT) which had previously manufactured some components of the Glisenti pistol on a subcontract basis. As a historical sidelight, there is strong evidence that Metallurgica Tempini had close ties to Ludwig Loewe and consequently to DWM in Germany; in fact, it appears that DWM was a majority shareholder in Metallurgica Tempini.

The Model 1905 was a locked breech weapon chambered for the 7.65mm Parabellum cartridge and was tested at the *Scuola Centrale di Fanteria* (Central Infantry School) in Parma; during the tests a number of structural shortcomings were noted, especially in the frame and the left hand side plate. The tests also showed the need for a

« A later production model of the Glisenti 1910 fitted with wooden grips. Wooden grips were adopted because the early Bakelite grips were prone to cracking and breaking. (*Courtesy, Leonardo M. Antaris, MD*)

» The safety on the rear of a Glisenti Model 1910. (*Courtesy, Leonardo M. Antaris, MD*)

» Detail of the serial number and manufacturer's marking on a Glisenti Model 1910. (*Courtesy, Leonardo M. Antaris, MD*)

» Sideplate of an early Glisenti. Like almost every small part of the Glisenti, the sideplate bore the serial number and, in this case, an inspector's mark as well. (*Courtesy, Leonardo M. Antaris, MD*)

A

B

Images A & B
Late production Glisenti Model 1910 with magazine. (*Courtesy, Leonardo M. Antaris, MD*)

The Glisenti's serial number was in an unusual position, on the front of the Glisenti's trigger guard. (*Courtesy, Leonardo M. Antaris, MD*)

The takedown tool for a Glisenti Model 1910 pistol. (*Courtesy, Leonardo M. Antaris, MD*)

Detail of the ornate MBT logo on the top of the Glisenti barrel extension. (*Courtesy, Leonardo M. Antaris, MD*)

more powerful cartridge, which led to development of the 9mm Glisenti which was dimensionally identical to the 9mm Parabellum (9x19). However, in 1905 the Ministry of War decided to adopt the Model 1905, subject to further testing, and indicated a desire to acquire 30,000 pistols to issue to officers. Further tests were carried out using an initial lot of about 100 pistols, still in 7.65mm; an estimated total of between 150 and 200 Model 1906 pistols, as the pistol came to be known, are believed to have been produced, making it a quite rare pistol. Between 1906 and 1910 the definitive Model 1910 evolved, based on modifications requested by the Ministry of War (to increase the caliber to 9mm) and by suggestions made by the test commission at the Infantry School in Parma. It is interesting to note that, apparently to avoid any semblance of a conflict of interests, Revelli was not anxious to to claim paternity of the pistol as he was a chief consultant to the army inspectorate that was to make of the barrel extension are the serial number consisting of a letter prefix over a number one to four digits long, as well as, enclosed in a circle, the letters FAB surmounted by a crown, with the year of manufacture underneath. To the left of that circle was a smaller oval bearing the letters TM, indicating the inspector (in this case, Mario Turani). The TM inside the oval also appeared on the bottom left side of the magazine. Although not considered a marking as such, it appears that on early production Model 1910 pistols the inside surfaces of the left hand sideplate were meticulously finished with a machined jeweled finish and could be encountered with the finish left in the white or blued.

» A partially disassembled Glisenti with magazine inserted. The takedown tool is not present in its retaining slot. (*Courtesy, Leonardo M. Antaris, MD*)

the decision on adopting the new pistol. Aside from the change in caliber the chief differences between the Model 1906 – the pistol is referred to variously as the Model 1905, the Model 1905/6, and the model 1906 – and the Model 1910 are the safety on the left side consisting of a lever that blocks the firing pin, the shape of the ejection port, the longer and thinner profile barrel, and the absence of the safety on the rear of the bolt. Except for those differences, the Model 1906 and Model 1910 were mechanically identical; from the point of view of external aesthetics, the most obvious difference between the two was that the grips on the Model 1906 were checkered ebonite grips, while those of the Model 1910 bore a prominent crest of the House of Savoy. Because the ebonite grips did not stand up well in use, later production pistols were fitted with checkered wood grips that were much stronger.

Markings on the Model 1910 consisted of a very ornate MBT logo on the top of the receiver, and on the right side

Precise figures for the number of Glisentis produced are not available, as the records of both Siderurgica Glisenti and Metallurgica Bresciana giá Tempini have long since been destroyed. However, based on serial number extrapolations, about 33,000 are believed to have been produced between 1909 and 1911 or 1912. ■

PISTOLA MODELLO 1913 *(Brixia)*

Although the Brixia Model 1913 pistol bears a close external resemblance to the Glisenti Model 1910 it is a considerably different pistol in a number of respects. That the Model 1913 – probably better known as the Brixia, which was the Latin name for Brescia – was directly derived from the Glisenti Model 1910 is obvious and unquestionable. The Model 1913 reflected a drastic rework of the 1910; not a single part of the Brixia is interchangeable with those of the Glisenti. Although mechanically the Brixia and the Glisenti are identical in their operating systems, they differ both aesthetically and structurally.

A close comparison of the two pistols reveals that the Brixia's lines are somewhat cleaner and less cluttered and are much more slab-sided. Somewhat less evident is the absence of the front grip safety, which was eliminated on the Brixia. Internally, those parts that were not eliminated were redesigned, simplified, and strengthened on the Brixia; one of the most significant changes was the complete redesign and strengthening of the left sideplate. The grips are configured differently, and while still bearing a smaller

Brixia Model 1913 right side view. There are no markings on this side of the frame or barrel extension; the grips are impressed with the House of Savoy crest and the letters MBT (Metallurgica Bresciana Tempini) beneath it. (*Courtesy, Leonardo M. Antaris, MD*)

The Brixia with the sideplate removed, providing an excellent view of the many small parts that are numbered. (*Courtesy, Leonardo M. Antaris, MD*)

Savoy crest, also include the identifying letters MBT on the right grip. The magazines also are different and are not interchangeable with those of the Glisenti Model 1910.

The Model 1913 was developed for the *Regia Marina*, which ordered a total of 5,000; the Model 1913 was intended to replace the Navy's 5,000 Mauser C96 pistols. The first 2,500 pistols were delivered in late 1913, and the remaining 2,500 in early-1914. An estimated 200-300 Brixias were made for the civilian market. Markings include a flowery MBT logo within a circle stamped on the top of the barrel extension and the serial number on the front of the trigger guard; almost all other parts are marked with the serial number, and the inspector's proof mark consisting of two initials surmounted by a crown are on the left of the frame behind the trigger guard. *Regia Marina* pistols bore serial numbers consisting of one to four digit numbers (1 to 1000) preceded by a letter (A through E); pistols for the civilian market had only a number without a letter prefix or suffix. ■

PISTOLA MODELLO 1913 "BRIXIA"

Designer: Bethel Abiel Revelli (via the Glisenti Model 1906 and 1910)
Manufacturer: Metallurgica Bresciana giá Tempini
Caliber: 9mm
Cartridge: 9x19 Glisenti
Operating system: Locked breech, single action
Overall length: 206mm (8.1 inches)
Barrel length: 95mm (3.7 inches)
Weight: .95 kg (2.1lbs)
Front sight: Barleycorn
Rear sight: V notch
Muzzle velocity: 320 m/sec (1050 fps)
Feed system: 7 round detachable box magazine

A Brixia Model 1913 pistol; the Brixia was a close cousin of the Glisenti Model 1910 pistol but presented a much cleaner appearance. *(Courtesy, Leonardo M. Antaris, MD)*

Following the practice established on the Glisenti pistols, the serial number was stamped on the front of the Brixia trigger guard. *(Courtesy, Leonardo M. Antaris, MD)*

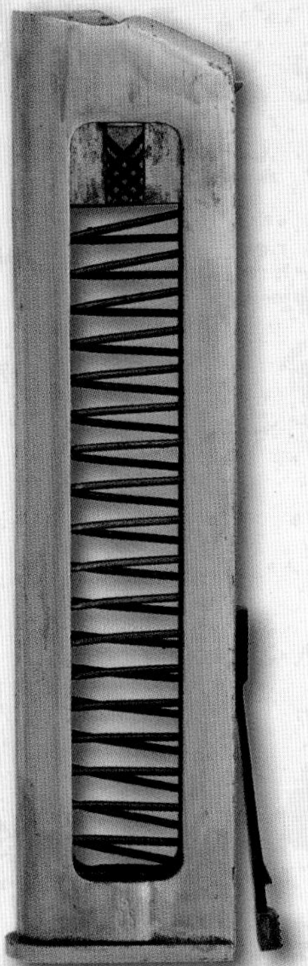

The Brixia magazine, a single row type that held seven 9mm Glisenti cartridges. *(Courtesy, Leonardo M. Antaris, MD)*

Top view of the Brixia 1913, with the ornate MBT logo on the top of the receiver which is uncluttered by any other type of marking. *(Courtesy, Leonardo M. Antaris, MD)*

The small proof and inspector's marks on the trigger guard are the only markings on the side of the frame on the Brixia pistols. *(Courtesy, Leonardo M. Antaris, MD)*

PISTOLA BREVETTO 1915, CALIBRO 9MM GLISENTI

The Beretta Model 1915 pistol was the first of a very successful line of semi-automatic pistols designed by Tullio Marengoni although Marengoni is also quite justly remembered for the design of the Beretta Model 1938 submachine gun. The Model 1915 was intended to replace the Glisenti Model 1910 pistol which was much too expensive and complicated to manufacture. As a consequence, simplicity was stressed in the manufacture of the 1915. Marengoni undoubtedly was aware of the design characteristics and technical features of other automatic pistols being produced at the time; not surprisingly, the Model 1915 incorporates features introduced by Browning and to a lesser extent by Mauser. However, Marengoni's Model 1915 was not merely a plagiarized copy of other automatics, but was a skillful blend of various features that were incorporated with his own innovations that resulted in a design that continued to be refined in an evolutionary process lasting almost twenty

Top view of a Beretta Model 1915. The Model 1915 featured a separate top-mounted ejection port, a front blade sight that was integral to the slide, and a dovetail mounted rear sight. (*Courtesy, Leonardo M. Antaris, MD*)

Except for the inspector's mark on the tang, the right side of the Model 1915 was bereft of markings. (*Courtesy, Leonardo M. Antaris, MD*)

Detail of the frequently encountered PS marking on the right tang of an early Model 1915 pistol. (*Courtesy, Leonardo M. Antaris, MD*)

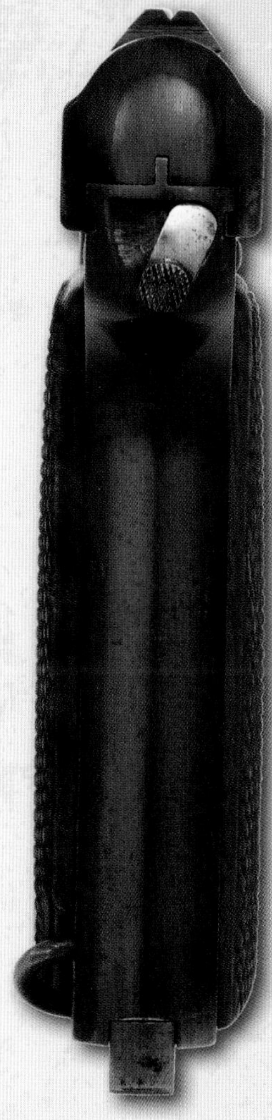

Rear view of a Model 1915 pistol showing the hammer-block safety on the rear of the frame. (*Courtesy, Leonardo M. Antaris, MD*)

The chief visual difference between the 9mm and the 7.65mm Model 1917 versions were the grips, which were checkered on the 9mm version and vertically grooved on the Model 1917. The magazine is an early type with six holes; the later type was open and exposed most of the magazine spring. (*Courtesy, Leonardo M. Antaris, MD*)

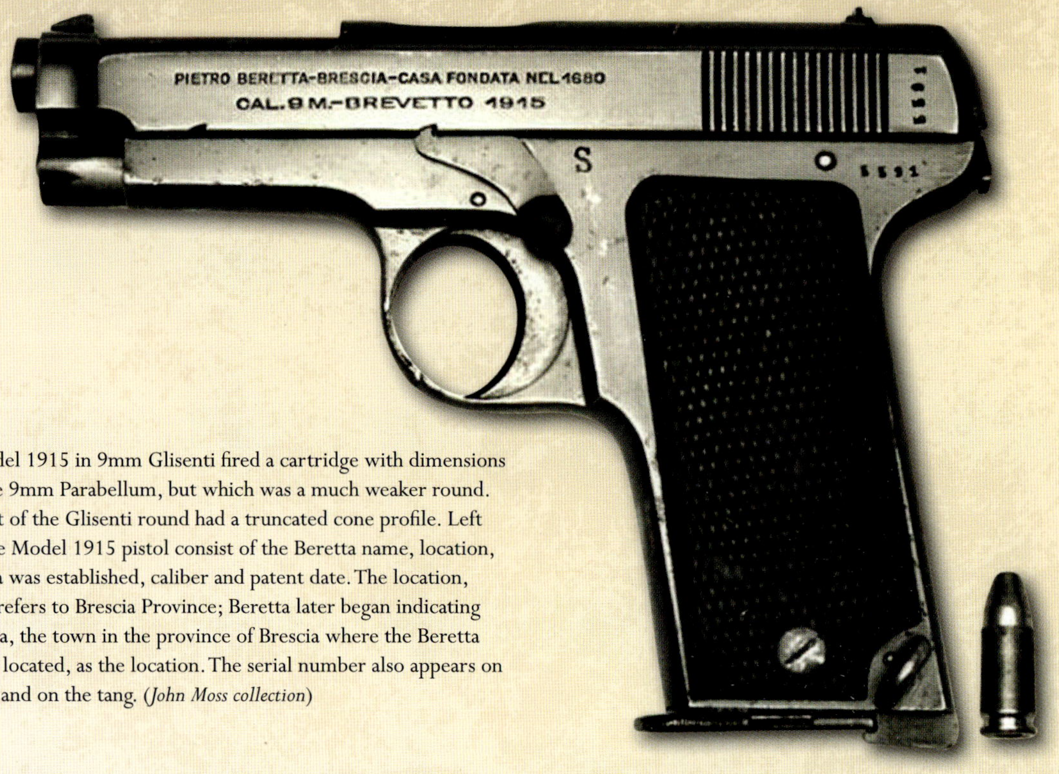

» The Beretta Model 1915 in 9mm Glisenti fired a cartridge with dimensions similar to that of the 9mm Parabellum, but which was a much weaker round. As shown, the bullet of the Glisenti round had a truncated cone profile. Left side markings on the Model 1915 pistol consist of the Beretta name, location, the year that Beretta was established, caliber and patent date. The location, Brescia, apparently refers to Brescia Province; Beretta later began indicating Gardone Val Trompia, the town in the province of Brescia where the Beretta plant was physically located, as the location. The serial number also appears on the rear of the slide and on the tang. (*John Moss collection*)

PISTOLA BREVETTO 1915

Designer: Tullio Marengoni
Manufacturer: Fabbrica d'Armi Pietro Beretta, Gardone Val Trompia
Caliber: 9mm Glisenti
Cartridge: 9x19mm Glisenti
Operating system: Simple blowback; single action
Overall length: 170mm (6.69")
Barrel length: 94mm (3.7")
Weight: .85 kg (1.87 lbs)
Front sight: Blade, integral with slide
Rear sight: Fixed V notch
Muzzle velocity: 266 m/sec (875 fps)
Feed system: 7 round detachable box magazine

years, culminating in the iconic Beretta Model 1934 and Model 1935 pistols.

Mechanically, the Model 1915 was a straight blowback pistol with no locking system, with a heavy buffer spring cushioning the recoil impact on the frame. Internally, the barrel was fixed to the frame by means of a vertical stud and was removed by lifting straight up with the slide latch in the "safe" position and the slide locked open. The Model 1915 also had a separate hammer-block safety at the rear. Simplicity was enhanced by using a solid frame instead of the side plate construction that was used on many automatic pistols at the time. The forward portion of the slide was marked by a cutout as well as a separate ejection port on the top of the slide. One of the features of the Model 1915 that would carry over to all of the Berettta pistols designed by Marengoni was the front sight that was an integral part of the slide rather than being a more traditional separate dovetailed sight. The chief recognition features of the Model 1915 were its round trigger guard, nearly straight grip, checkered wooden grips, and the absence of an external hammer.

Markings on the left side of the slide read PIETRO BERETTA – BRESCIA – CASA FONDATA NEL 1680 on one line, with a line below that reading CAL. 9M. – BREVETTO 1915. On early production versions the first line was enclosed by inverted commas. The serial number was stamped horizontally on the left upper rear of the frame, and vertically on the left rear of the slide behind the slide serrations. The serial number, either full or the last three or four digits, also appeared on a number of other parts, including the barrel, trigger bar, sear, sear plate, spring guide, firing pin, extractor, ejector, manual safety, rear safety, magazine catch, and grips. The first 4,000 or so pistols were marked IF within an oval on the right tang; subsequent pistols usually bore the letters PS within an oval on the right tang. The letters PS were an inspector's initials; the initials IF could also be encountered.

The Model 1915 was furnished almost exclusively to the *Regio Esercito*; the first contract for 5,000 pistols was dated 11 November 1915, exactly three years before World War I ended. This contract was followed by two subsequent contracts for 5,000 each, and a final contract for only 300 pistols. Another 200-300 were produced for the civilian market for a total of 15,500-15,600 Model 15 pistols. Production ceased in 1918 and the Model 15 is believed to have remained in service until the mid-1930s, but was kept in storage until 1943 when it was offered to sale to officers at a modest price. ■

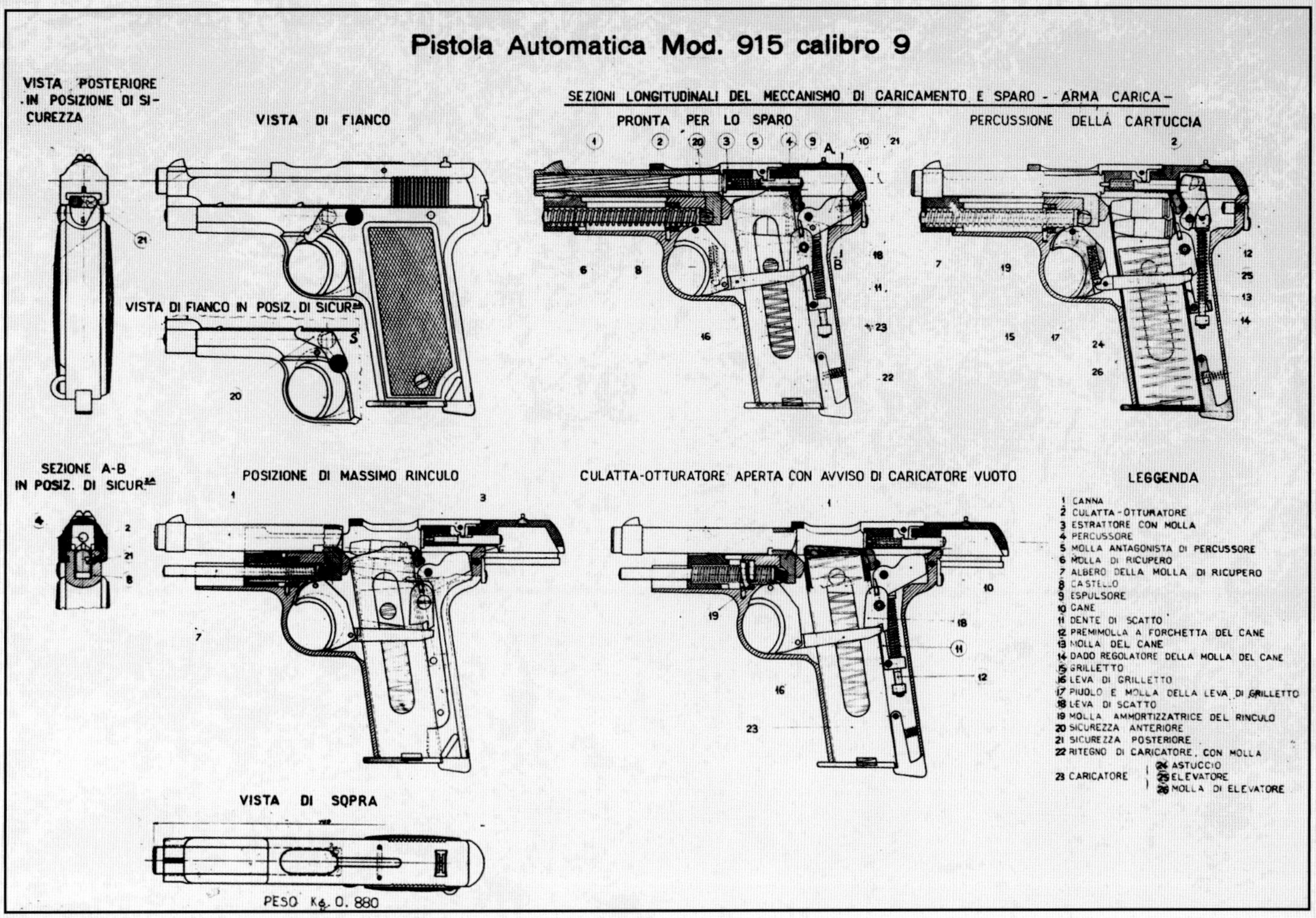

Longitudinal sectional drawings of the Beretta Model 1915 pistol in 9mm Glisenti caliber showing loading and firing mechanisms. (*Beretta*)

PISTOLA BREVETTO 1915 MOD. 1917, CALIBRO 7.65 BROWNING

The Brevetto 1915, Mod. 1917 might be considered as a stop-gap pistol adopted by the Italian Army because the 7.65mm version of the Model 1915 was less expensive than the 9mm Glisenti Model 1915. The prototype of the pistol was presented on 5 July 1917, and was accepted for service on 14 September of that year. A contract for 10,000 7.65mm pistols was signed shortly thereafter, and the first pistol is believed to have been delivered on 30 December 1917 (#16000). With the end of World War I in November 1918 (#54000), the need for additional pistols no longer existed and military deliveries ceased in March 1919 (#60183). Production of the Mod. 1917 for the civilian market, however, continued until about 1921. Total production of the Mod. 1917 was somewhere around 56,000.

As a derivative of the Model 1915, the Mod. 1917 is quite similar to the Model 1915 but there are notable mechanical and aesthetic differences. The smaller caliber resulted in a dimensionally smaller pistol, but magazine capacity was increased to eight rounds because of the smaller cartridge. The ejector, buffer spring, and rear safety of the Model 1915 were also

PISTOLA BREVETTO 1915, MOD. 1917

Designer: Tullio Marengoni
Manufacturer: Fabbrica d'Armi Pietro Beretta, Gardone Val Trompia
Caliber: 7.65mm (.32 ACP)
Cartridge: 7.65x25mm Browning
Operating system: Simple blowback; single action
Overall length: 150mm (5.9")
Barrel length: 85mm (3.34")
Weight: .57 kg (1.25 lbs)
Front sight: Blade, integral with slide
Rear sight: Fixed V notch
Muzzle velocity: 266 m/sec (875 fps)
Feed system: 8 round detachable box magazine

dispensed with. Compared to the Model 1915, aside from its overall shorter length, external differences included a somewhat longer milled cut at the forward end of the bottom of the slide and grips that were a bit more ornate than those on the Model 1915. The Mod. 1917 wood grips had an oval at the top which incorporated the Pietro Beretta "PB" monogram, with vertical grooves below.

Markings on the 7.65mm Mod. 17 on the left slide flat read PIETRO BERETTA – BRESCIA – CAL. 765 – BREVETTO 1915, all on a single line. The designation Mod. 17 was not indicated. The serial number was stamped horizontally on the left upper rear of the frame and vertically on the left rear of the slide behind the slide serrations. Various inspector marks are found on the right tang, consisting of two letters or initials, usually in an oval (PS) but sometimes in a rectangle with concave corners (AB and DR). A very small number of Mod. 17s bore the *Regia Marina* mark on the left frame, above the trigger guard; the marking consisted of an anchor flanked by the letters R and M, all within an oval. In 1940 Finland acquired 1,500 Mod. 17 pistols which were marked with the Finnish Army mark consisting of the letters SA within a rectangle with rounded corners; the mark was applied to the left side of the frame above the trigger guard as well as on the magazine floorplate. ■

» A Beretta Model 1917 in 7.65mm (.32 ACP). The early Beretta pistols were marked "Brescia" rather than "Gardone Val Trompia." The grips on the 7.65mm version of the pistol were vertically grooved, and the grip screws were in a different position than on the 9mm version of the pistol. *(Beretta)*

PISTOLA BREVETTO 1915-19 MODELLO 1922, CALIBRO 7.65 BROWNING

This pistol, clearly based on the Model 1915, differs from the Model 1915 in two major respects: its barrel was no longer attached to the frame by means of a stud, but rather by a grooved block which mated with channels in the receiver, and the cutout on the slide was elongated so that the separate ejection port was eliminated. This elongated cutout, which had already been experimented with on the 6.35mm Beretta pistols, has remained a hallmark characteristic of almost all subsequent Beretta pistols. The rear sight was also integrated with the slide rather than being dovetailed and thus was not adjustable for windage. The wooden grips were also replaced by pressed steel grips that presented an appearance very similar to the wooden grips of the 1915 model, except that the PB logo at the top was much more distinct than that on the wooden grips. The 1915-19 also introduced the extension of the magazine floorplate. At the time of its introduction in early 1922, the pistol was known as the "Pistola Brevetto 1915-19," ("Pistol Patent 1915-19), but the designation later was changed to Modello 1922.

Markings on the Model 1922 consisted of the serial number on the right side of the slide forward of the slide serrations and on the right side of the frame above the trigger. The left side of the slide was marked PISTOLA AUT. – BERETTA 765 BREV. – 1915-1919. Some of those pistols were delivered to the *Regia Marina* and may show the Navy specific acceptance mark (RM with anchor) on both sides of the frame. Based on the serial number range, about 43,000 Model 1922 pistols were produced between 1922 and 1932. ■

PISTOLA MODELLO 1922

Designer: Tullio Marengoni
Manufacturer: Fabbrica d'Armi Pietro Beretta, Gardone Val Trompia
Caliber: 7.65mm Browning (.32 ACP)
Cartridge: 7.65x25mm Browning
Operating system: Simple blowback; single action
Overall length: 150mm (5.9") **Barrel length:** 84mm (3.3")
Weight: .61 kg (1.35 lbs)
Front sight: Fixed blade interal with slide
Rear sight: Fixed V notch integral with slide
Muzzle velocity: 297 m/sec (975 fps)
Feed system: 8 round detachable box magazine

The Beretta Model 1922 introduced the elongated slide cutout that has remained a characteristic feature of Beretta pistols since that time. A further modification to the slide was incorporation of the rear sight as an integral part of the frame, replacing the earlier dovetailed rear sights used on Beretta pistols. *(Courtesy, Leonardo M. Antaris, MD)*

The Italian Navy left no doubt as to ownership of the Model 1922 pistols in its inventory. In addition to the Regia Marina anchor symbol on the right tang, the same symbol was stamped on the left side of the frame over the trigger guard. *(Courtesy, Leonardo M. Antaris, MD)*

Detail of the Regia Marina marking consisting of an anchor flanked by the letters R and M within an oval, on the tang of a Model 1922 pistol. *(Courtesy, Leonardo M. Antaris, MD)*

The Beretta Model 1922 was designated by Beretta as the Brevetto 1915-1919, but later became known as the modello 1922. It introduced the pressed metal grips with the PB logo at the top. This pistol has the Regia Marina marking on the slide above the trigger guard. *(Courtesy, Leonardo M. Antaris, MD)*

PISTOLA BREVETTO 1915-19 MODELLO 1923, CALIBRO 9 GLISENTI

The Model 1923 pistol introduced another of the incremental changes that ultimately led to the definitive and iconic Model 1934: it was the first of the Beretta pistols to appear with the external ring hammer. It was chambered for the 9mm Glisenti round that was the official round used in Italian automatic pistols of the era and because of the relatively high power of the round the pistol was fitted with a fiber disc to absorb recoil, performing the same function as the buffer spring on the Model 1915. Despite Pietro Beretta's assertion that the Model 1923 was capable of firing all types of 9x19mm ammunition, in fact firing standard Parabellum ammunition was hazardous and foolhardy. Although there seem to be no documented cases of injuries due to firing higher powered rounds in the Model 1923, there is at least one reported instance of a cracked hammer due to use of inappropriate ammunition. In addition to the standard version, there was also a version that had grooves milled into the base of the butt which accepted a special metal strut and leather holster stock, but how many of that version were made is undocumented (one source mentions 100 examples). Model 1923 pistols for the civilian market had smooth walnut burl grips with a small metal inset with the PB logo near the bottom of the grips, while military issue pistols had pressed steel grips with the PB logo in an oval at the top of the grips.

In 1935 the *Milizia Forestale* (Forestry Militia) purchased

Right side view of the Model 1923 pistol. The pressed steel grips sported a prominent Beretta PB logo. (*Courtesy, Leonardo M. Antaris, MD*)

Serial numbers on the Model 1923 pistols began with 300000, but a defective die caused the second digit appear to be a C rather than a zero (0). (*Courtesy, Leonardo M. Antaris, MD*)

The standard military version of the Beretta Model 1923; the Model 1923 was the first of the Beretta pistols to have the exposed ring hammer. (*Beretta*)

A Regio Esercito marked Model 1923 with the bottom of the frame cut for the optional holster shoulder stock. (*Courtesy, Leonardo M. Antaris, MD*)

Detail of the attachment slots and lugs for the stock holster. (*Courtesy, Leonardo M. Antaris, MD*)

250 Model 1923 pistols, followed by a purchase of 3,000 by the Italian Army in 1936. Sales to the Italian military and paramilitary forces were rather modest as by 1936 the Model 1934 was available and quickly became the pistol of choice for the Italian military. Previous to the 1936 Italian Army purchase there had been substantial foreign sales of the pistol; Bulgaria had purchased 4,000 of the Model 1923 in 1926, and in 1933-34, the Argentine Provincial Police had ordered a lot of 600. In 1931 a small lot of 25 was sold to the Turkish Navy as well. A total of about 10,400 Model 1923 pistols were produced, and the pistol served with the Italian Army until 1945.

Markings followed the familiar pattern with the serial number on the right hand side of the slide and frame and the Beretta markings on the left slide flat as well as the last four digits on the rear of the barrel. In accordance with Beretta practice the Model 1923 pistols were assigned a new serial number series beginning with 300000, but because of a damaged die the first two characters of the serial number on most if not all Model 1923 pistols appeared to be 3C rather than 30. Pistols in Italian service bore the designation PISTOLA BERETTA – 9m BREV. 1915-1919 – Mo 1923; the pistols for Argentina were marked as POLICIA DE LA PROVINCIA DE BUENOS AIRES on one line, and on the line below it PISTOLA BERETTA – 9*m* BREV. 1915-1919 – Mo 1923. Italian Army pistols bore the letters RE surmounted by a crown on the left rear of the frame. ■

PISTOLA MODELLO 1923

Designer: Tullio Marengoni
Manufacturer: Fabbrica d'Armi Pietro Beretta, Gardone Val Trompia
Caliber: 9mm
Cartridge: 9x19mm Glisenti
Operating system: Simple blowback; single action
Overall length: 163mm (6.42")
Barrel length: 98mm (3.86")
Weight: .88 kg (1.94 lbs)
Front sight: Blade, integral with slide
Rear sight: Fixed V notch, integral with slide
Muzzle velocity: 305 m/sec (1000 fps)
Feed system: 8 round detachable box magazine

PISTOLA BREVETTO 1915-19 MODELLO 1931, CALIBRO 7.65 BROWNING

The Model 1931 was very similar to the preceding Model 1922 pistol, but like the earlier Model 1922 was chambered for the 7.65mm (.32 Auto) round. Compared to the Model 1922 it incorporated a number of mechanical changes including elimination of the fiber recoil buffer, a slightly enlarged trigger guard, and a longer 180o swing for the safety lever. Dimensionally the Model 1931 was smaller than the Model 1923 and its external configuration was altered somewhat with a longer tang and a straight profile slide top so that it assumed an appearance very similar to that of the later definitive Model 1934. The earliest production version of the Model 1931 had short wooden grips that left much of the disconnector exposed; the grips were lengthened after about the first thousand pistols. The *Regia Marina* received the first Model 1931 in September 1931 and by June 1934 had taken delivery of 3,250 of the pistols. Other users of the Model 1931 were the *Milizia Nazionale della Strada* (National Road Militia) which bought 150 in August 1933, and the *Milizia Forestale* which acquired a small lot; a limited number were absorbed by the civilian market. The Navy version had walnut grips and an inset medallion that had the figure of an anchor between the letters R M on it.

Beretta made a number of minor modifications to the back strap, trigger, magazine release and lanyard loop ring of the Model 1931 that led to redesignating the pistol as the Model 1932 (not to be confused with the 9mm *corto* Model 1932, which was dimensionally different). Further minor improvements led to another redesignation as the Model 1934 (again, not to be confused with the Model 1934 in 9mm *corto*), but it is unknown how many of either the 7.65mm Model 1932 and Model 1934 pistols were made. Total production of Model 1931 pistols, including the 7.65mm Model 1932 and Model 1934 variants, is estimated at about 10,000.

Model 1931 serial numbers began with 400000 and serial number placement followed the established pattern, i.e., on the right side slide flat and the right frame above the trigger. The left side flat bore the marking PISTOLA BERETTA 765 BREV. 1915-1919 – Mo 1931. Some later pistols may have the last digit of the 1931 date overstruck by either a 2 or a 4, but specific information as to the number range of these pistols is scant, nor is it clear if all of the modified pistols were marked with the last digit of 2 or 4, as appropriate. ■

PISTOLA MODELLO 1931

Designer: Tullio Marengoni
Manufacturer: Fabbrica d'Armi Pietro Beretta, Gardone Val Trompia
Caliber: 7.65mm Browning
Cartridge: 7.65x25mm Browning
Operating system: Simple blowback; single action
Overall length: 150mm (6")
Barrel length: 85mm (3.35")
Weight: .61 kg (1.34 lbs)
Front sight: Blade integral with slide
Rear sight: Fixed V notch, dovetailed
Muzzle velocity: 251 m/sec (825 fps)
Feed system: 8 round detachable box magazine

« Detail of the commercial proof marks of the Banco di prova di Gardone (Gardone proof house) on the tang of a Model 1931 pistol. *(Courtesy Luca Vallebona, Armeria Black Hills)*

» A 7.65mm Beretta Model 1931 pistol with the PB logo inset on the grips. The magazine floorplate is an early flat type. *(Courtesy Luca Vallebona, Armeria Black Hills)*

Right side view of a Model 1931 Regia Marina issue pistol. *(Courtesy, Leonardo M. Antaris, MD)*

Markings on the Model 1931 pistol. *(Courtesy Luca Vallebona, Armeria Black Hills)*

A Model 1931 top view; the rear sight is dovetail mounted. (*Courtesy, Leonardo M. Antaris, MD*)

A Beretta Model 1931 Navy pistol with the long wood grips. (*Courtesy, Leonardo M. Antaris, MD*)

Markings on the tang of this Model 1931 include the inspector's initial and the Regia Marina mark consisting of a shield divided into four quadrants. (*Courtesy, Leonardo M. Antaris, MD*)

A Navy issue Beretta Model 1931 pistol with the characteristic Navy medallion inset in the wood grips. The grips are the early short type. (*Beretta*)

Detail of the Regia Marina medallion inset on the grip of a Model 1931 pistol. (*Courtesy, Leonardo M. Antaris, MD*)

PISTOLA BREVETTO 1915-19 MODELLO 1932, CALIBRO 9 CORTO

The Beretta Model 1932 pistol was the direct precursor of the iconic Model 1934 pistol, differing chiefly in its grips and slide markings from the Model 1934. The burl grips have the PB medallion inset, and the slide markings reflect the caliber as 9mm corto. (*Beretta*)

The Model 1932 pistol was the immediate precursor of the Model 1934 and might be considered as a transitional or limited production weapon; it was chambered for the 9mm *corto* (9mm short, or .380 ACP) round that would be used for the Model 1934. Initial trials of 25 Model 1932 pistols were carried out in October 1932, and in September 1933 the Fabbrica d'Armi Regio Esercito, Terni, received nine of the pistols for further testing. In March 1934 a contract for 650 Model 1932 pistols (the Model 1934 designation was not adopted until the following month, in April) was let by the *Regio Esercito*; the contract was however, suspended until late 1935 due to issues regarding the type of safety the pistol should have (trigger or firing pin); ultimately, the trigger safety as originally designed was retained. The version of the Model 1932 with the slide-mounted firing pin safety is extremely rare, with perhaps only a dozen or so actually produced.

The Model 1932 pistol itself is quite rare; there is some divergence of opinion as to how many examples were made, but the in-depth research by Menchini and Taviani suggests strongly that somewhat less than 100 were produced before the pistol morphed into the Model 1934. The earliest model of the Model 1932 had the short wooden grips that were chartacteristic of the early production version of the 7.65mm Model 1931, but these were replaced by longer grips on the later version. Beretta made a series of changes and improvements to the 1932 that soon led to the definitive Model 1934, described in detail in the following entry.

The Model 1932 initiated the 500000 serial number range that continued on into the Model 1934. Serial numbers were located as on the Model 1931; the slide markings were BERETTA – Cal 9 CORTO – BREV. 1915-1919 – Mo 1932. ■

PISTOLA MODELLO 1932

Designer: Tullio Marengoni
Manufacturer: Fabbrica d'Armi Pietro Beretta, Gardone Val Trompia
Caliber: 9mm
Cartridge: 9x17mm Browning Short
Operating system: Simple blowback; single action
Overall length: 150mm (6")
Barrel length: 86.5mm (3.4")
Weight: 660 kg (1.46lbs)
Front sight: Blade, integral with frame
Rear sight: Fixed V notch, dovetailed
Muzzle velocity: 251 m/sec (825 fps)
Feed system: 7 round detachable box magazine

PISTOLA MODELLO 1934, CALIBRO 9 CORTO

Unquestionably the best known and most common Beretta military pistol is the iconic Model 1934. The weapon originally was developed for Italian police agencies, but its use was soon extended to the Italian armed forces as well. It was a very popular weapon not only with the Italians but with German and Allied troops as well as it was light, handy, and functioned well under varied climatic conditions, proving itself in Italian service from

North Africa to Russia. For American GIs, it was a very desirable war trophy, and as a result the Model 1934 is readily available on the collector market in the U.S.

In the early-1930s it became obvious to Italian authorities that the pistols such as the Model 1889, the Glisenti and some of the early Berettas then issued to the armed forces and police agencies were not up to contemporary standards and were no longer adequate for military requirements. It required no extraordinary effort for Marengoni, who had conceived and designed Beretta's pistol line beginning with the Model 1915, to take the design a step further than the Model 1931 by adopting the 9x17 (.380 ACP) round, known and referred to in Italy as the 9mm *corto* (9mm short), resulting in the Model 1932 which except for its grips and slide markings was identical to the Model 1934. Notable features introduced on the Model 1934 were the half-cock safety and the steel-backed Bakelite grips (known as "filbak" in Italian). The simple single action design lacked features such as a magazine disconnector and cartridge indicator found on contemporary German pistols, but the simple design and few working parts eliminated the need for many complicated milling operations, enabling it to be easily mass produced. In addition, the Model 1934 is rugged and well built, is easy to maintain, and is very reliable. Most knowledgeable firearms experts acknowledge the Model 1934 to be an extremely well designed and engineered pistol whose reliability is enviable. These positive attributes are offset to some extent by the fact that the 9mm Short cartridge is somewhat underpowered for a military pistol, and extracting an empty magazine, whose follower holds the slide open after the last round is fired, does not lend itself well to quick magazine changes under combat conditions. Most examples of this pistol were well finished, but examples produced during the latter stages of the war may be encountered with very rough exterior finishing, although fit and tolerances of the mechanical components continued to remain high, allowing reliable functioning.

The first contract for the Model 1934 pistol as such was signed in 1935, for 1,000 pistols to be issued to the *Pubblica Sicurezza* police force. In March 1936 an order for 250 Model 1934 pistols was placed by the *Milizia Portuaria* (Port Militia), shortly followed in June 1936 by the first sizeable Italian Army contract for 150,000 Model 1934 pistols even though the Model 1934 was not officially adopted in service until 16 October 1936. Between 1938 and 1940 the Italian Army placed two other contracts, one for 80,000 and one for 165,000 pistols. Subsequent orders went to equip all three military services; monthly production figures varied considerably; during the second half of 1942 production ran between 3,000 to 10,000 Model 34 pistols per month, and the figures for early 1943 were 9,000 in January, 4,000 in February, and 23,000 in March. Each pistol was issued with a leather holster and two magazines; officers were issued a brown holster, while NCOs and other ranks were issued a grey-green (*grigio-verde*) holster; *Carabinieri* personnel were issued a black holster.

Although basic markings on the Model 1934 are somewhat consistent, there are many variations and nuances that can be encountered. For pistols in Italian service, markings on the left side of the frame above the grip tang indicate the arm of service. Army issue pistols were marked with the letters RE, for *Regio Esercito* (Royal Army); Navy pistols bore the letters RM for *Regia Marina* within a circle, with an anchor between the letters R and M, or a shield divided into four quadrants, and air force issue pistols bore the letters RA for *Regia Aeronautica* (Royal Air Force) with an eagle surmounted by a royal crown. The marking for the *Milizia Forestale*, and later the *Guardia Forestale* (Forestry Guards) had an eagle and crown and two crossed axes. The serial number was on the right side of the slide and frame, as well as on the barrel. The left side of the frame bore the maker's name, caliber, model number (1934), and the Italian word "Brevettato" (patented), or its abbreviated form, "Brevet." on one line, and a second line reflecting the place of manufacture (Gardone V.T.) and the year of manufacture. A curious (and presumably unique and rare) example of an early production Model 1934 has recently come to light in which the word for patented has been factory stamped as BREVETTAT, missing the final O. In addition to being marked with the year of production in Arabic numerals, the year of production is also shown in

THE 9MM CORTO CARTRIDGE

The 9x17 Browning Short, or .380 ACP cartridge, referred to as the 9mm *corto* in Italian, was chosen by the Italians in order to ease logistic problems by adopting a standard pistol cartridge for the armed forces. At the time that the 9mm *corto* was introduced there were at least five different handgun calibers in use by Italian military forces, including 6.35mm, 7.63mm (by the Navy only), 7.65mm, 9mm Glisenti, and 10.35mm. Although adopting yet another cartridge type to alleviate the problem was an apparent anachronism, the wisdom of adopting the 9mm *corto* was vindicated as during the war, although the supply system still had to stock all of the previously mentioned calibers to some extent, the Beretta Model 1934 was the most widely produced and issued Italian pistol of World War II. One might be tempted to argue that not long after adoption of the 9mm *corto* the Italians further exacerbated their ammunition problems by adopting the 9mm Parabellum (or 9M38) cartridge for their submachine guns and that it would have been much more sensible if they had adopted a pistol chambered for the 9mm Parabellum round rather than the 9mm *corto*, but all considered, given the evolutionary path of the Beretta semi-auto pistols, adoption of the 9mm *corto* round was a reasonable choice.

Detail of the IV U acceptance mark on the right tang of a Model 1934 pistol. The mark on this pistol was only partially struck, as the left portion of the oval and the letter I are missing. (*Author's collection*)

A 1942 Model 1934 with the crown over RE army marking on the tang. The Roman numeral XX indicates the 20th year of Fascist rule, i.e. 1942, as indicated in Arabic numerals. (*Courtesy Luca Vallebona, Armeria Black Hills*)

The IV U version of the 4 UT marking appears on the tang of this Model 1934 pistol. (*Author's collection*)

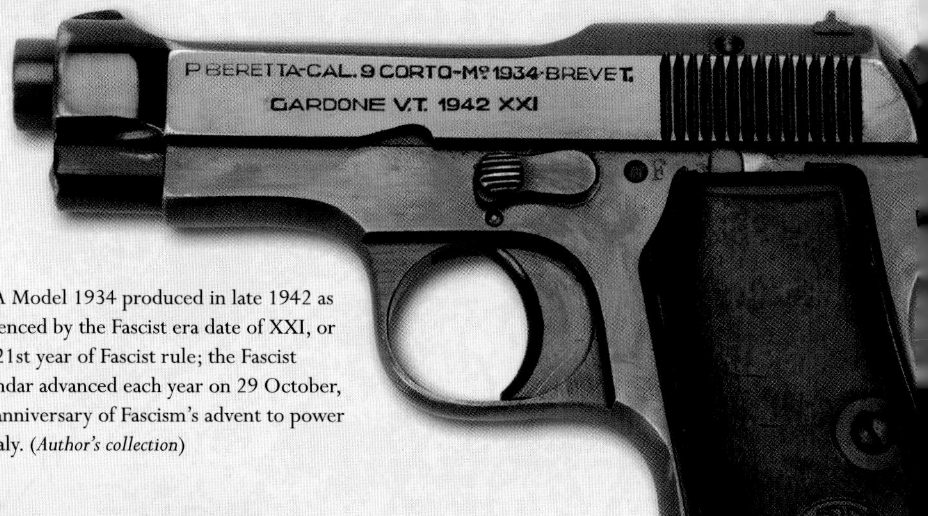

A Model 1934 produced in late 1942 as evidenced by the Fascist era date of XXI, or the 21st year of Fascist rule; the Fascist calendar advanced each year on 29 October, the anniversary of Fascism's advent to power in Italy. (*Author's collection*)

Close-up view of the incompletely struck IV U acceptance mark. (*Author's collection*)

A Model 1934 pistol whose RE mark has been double struck. (*Author's collection*)

The classic Beretta Model 1934 pistol in 9mm corto (.38 ACP). The marking on the tang – the letters RE surmounted by a royal crown – indicate that this was an Army issued pistol. (*John Moss collection*)

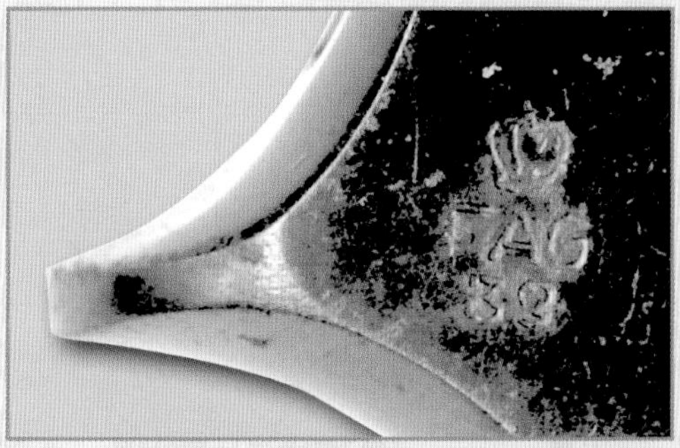

Detail of the inspector's mark on the tang of a Model 1934. This particular mark is unusual in that the letters FAG proofing by the Fabbrica d'Armi Gardone and is stamped 1939, while the slide is marked 1940. (*John Moss collection*)

Detail of the crown over RE marking on the right tang of a 1942 Model 1934 pistol. (*Courtesy Luca Vallebona, Armeria Black Hills*)

Markings on the right side of the Model 1934 included the serial number on both the slide and frame, and an inspector's mark on the tang. (*John Moss collection*)

The IV U stamp on this 1942 Model 1934 pistol was applied upside down. (*Courtesy Luca Vallebona, Armeria Black Hills*)

BERETTA PISTOL SERIAL NUMBERS

The serial number range for early Model 1934 pistols was a continuation of the 500000 block that had begun with the Model 1932. When serial number 999999 was reached, rather than continuing on with a seven-digit serial number, Beretta began numbering its Model 1934s with an F prefix; there seems to be no explanation as to why the initial letter prefix was an F rather than an A. The F and G blocks were followed by AA and BB suffix blocks. The C block began in 1946, and post-war blocks continued through the alphabet until the H block. The last Model 1934 pistols, issued to the *Guardia di Finanza* in 1980, bore a T prefix. Total production of the Model 1934 was 1,080,000.

An MVSN (Volunteer Militia) trooper with a holstered Beretta pistol; he is also armed with a dagger and is carrying either a Model 91/24 or Model 91/28 carbine. (*SME, via Andrea and Antonio Tallillo*)

Roman numerals according to the Fascist calendar in which 1923 was year I. Very few pistols with serial numbers with an AA suffix, produced between April and July 1944, were issued to the air force of the Fascist *Repubblica Sociale Italiana* (Italian Social Republic). Guns in the BB suffix range, produced from August 1944 to January 1945, were finished only in a very summary fashion on the exterior, in the so-called "wartime finish." There were no markings on the slide, and sometimes only the caliber and serial number appeared on the frame.

After Italy signed an armistice with the Allies in September 1943 the Beretta plant, which was located in northern Italy under German control, continued to make the Model 1934 for use by German forces; one source cites a figure of 53,725 Model 1934 pistols produced under German control. Many of the pistols produced under German control bore the marking 4UT (for *4o Ufficio Tecnico di Controllo Armi e Munizioni* – the 4th Technical Office for Arms and Munitions Inspection), which was responsible for acceptance of many, but apparently not all, Italian weapons from 1941 through the period of the Italian Social Republic, or R.S.I. This mark was usually on the right tang. Contrary to widely held belief, the 4UT, also at times noted as IV U, was not a German-run agency or the Italian equivalent of the *Waffenamt*. A number of the pistols, however, did also bear the German WaA 162 *Waffenamt*, some with and some without a circled swastika. The German designation for the Model 1934 was P671(i). Use of the Fascist era date in Roman numerals was also discontinued after July 1943.

The Model 1934 enjoyed modest export success. In 1940 Romania placed an order for 61,000 of the pistols, but ultimately only 37,000-40,000 were delivered. Sources differ as to the dates of production for the Romanian order; some say production was limited to 1941 while others cite dates from 1940 to 1942. The only differences between the standard Italian pistol and the Romanian version was that the caliber marking on the slide appears as 9 *Scurt* (9 Short) in Romanian, and the Fascist date in Roman numerals is omitted.

Another fairly small order for the Model 1934 was made by Finland. In July 1941 the Finns ordered 500 Model 1934 pistols that were not delivered until April 1943; all apparently were issued to the Civil Guard (*Suojeluskuntain Yliesikunta*). These pistols, marked Sk.Y, serial numbered 0100-0597, are quite rare. An additional order for the Model 1934 was placed, possibly for 1,000 examples, for use by the Finnish Army, and were marked SA (*Suomen Armeija*). There are other estimates as to how many Model 1934 were sold to Finland, ranging from a low of 900 to a high of 1400.

PISTOLA MODELLO 1934

Designer: Tullio Marengoni
Manufacturer: Fabbrica d'Armi Pietro Beretta, Gardone Val Trompia
Caliber: 9mm
Cartridge: 9x17mm Browning Short (.380 ACP)
Operating system: Simple blowback; single action
Overall length: 150mm (6")
Barrel length: 86.5mm (3.4")
Weight: .66 kg (1.46 lbs)
Front sight: Blade, integral with frame
Rear sight: Fixed V notch, dovetailed
Muzzle velocity: 240 m/sec (787 fps)
Feed system: 7 round detachable box magazine

There is vague and unsubstantiated reference to Model 1934 pistols having been provided to Bulgaria and Poland as well as the suggestion that some Model 1934 and Model 1935 pistols were sold to Japan, sent out aboard either Italian or Japanese submarines, but never reached Japan.

In addition to military export sales, the Model 1934 was exported to Germany commercially where it was marketed by the firm of Gustav Genschow whose trademark was GECO. The left-hand side of the slides on GECO pistols lacked the standard Beretta markings, which instead appeared in an abbreviated format on the frame itself; the serial number appeared in the normal location on the right-hand side of the slide and frame. The left tang carried civilian proof marks as well as the year below the proof marks, and the right tang was marked with a stylized GECO logo. ■

A

B

Images A, B & C Complete Model 1934 rig, consisting of pistol, holster, and two magazines, as originally delivered by Beretta to the Italian Army. (*Author's collection*)

A Beretta 1934 in its issue holster, complete with spare magazine. Brown holsters were issued to officers and to the Carabinieri, while NCOs and other ranks were issued grey-green holsters. (*John Moss collection*)

C

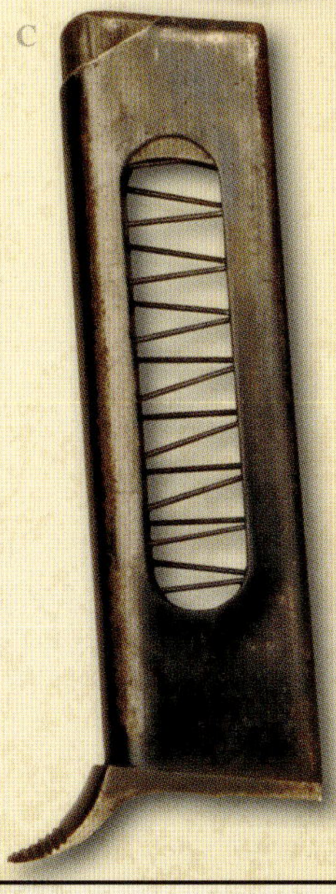

›› By 1944 the quality of exterior finish of Beretta pistols had dropped considerably as shown on this Model 1934 with the "wartime finish" produced after August 1944. (*Author's collection*)

‹‹ A late-1944 Model 1934 pistol with a BB suffix serial number. (*Author's collection*)

From late-1943 onwards the Roman numeral designation denoting the Fascist year was dropped from the slide markings, as on this 1944 Model 1934. (*Author's collection*)

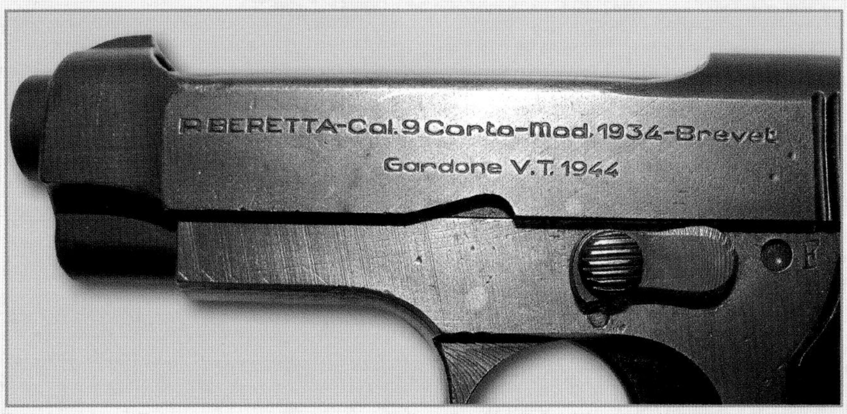

›› Detail of barrel marking on a Model 1934. (*Author's collection*)

PISTOLA MODELLO 1935, CALIBRO 7.65 BROWNING

The Model 1935 is commonly thought of as a modified Model 1934, differing chiefly in its caliber. In actuality, the Model 1935 was more of a direct lineal descendant of the 7.65mm Model 1931 pistol, which had been the basis for the Model 1932 and 1934 pistols. The Model 1935 incorporated all of the improvements and modifications that had been made to the Model 1931, as well as other features such as the half-cock hammer that had been introduced on the Model 1934. The Model 1935 was a logical companion to the Model 1934 as the 7.65mm, or .32 ACP, was a very popular caliber and was initially aimed at the civilian market, though it was later adopted for police and military use as well. A limited number of the Model 1935 was produced with a light alloy frame, probably limited to the 1936-1937 timeframe.

When production of the Model 1935 began, fit and finish were kept to very high standards, as was typical for Beretta products. However, once the war began and progressed, standards for fit remained high but the quality of the finish of the Model 1935 pistol deteriorated significantly, as also was the case with the Model 1934, and examples produced towards the end of the war were very crudely finished. Except for a small lot of possibly around 1,000 produced by Armaguerra in Cremona, probably all of which were produced in 1944, none of the Model 1935 pistols were subcontracted but were produced by Beretta at Gardone. Some barrels during the latter part of the war were manufactured by F.N.A., and may show the F.N.A. factory mark on one side.

Among the Italian military forces the Model 1935 was favored by the *Regia Aeronautica* and the *Regia Marina*, although they were also purchased by the *Regio Esercito* and the *Milizia Forestale*. The Model 1935 was also sold to a number of foreign customers and countries, including Iraq,

A civilian Model 1934 exported to Germany. Note the absence of the normal Beretta markings on the slide and the information limited to the Beretta name and caliber designation on the frame itself. (*Courtesy Luca Vallebona, Armeria Black Hills*)

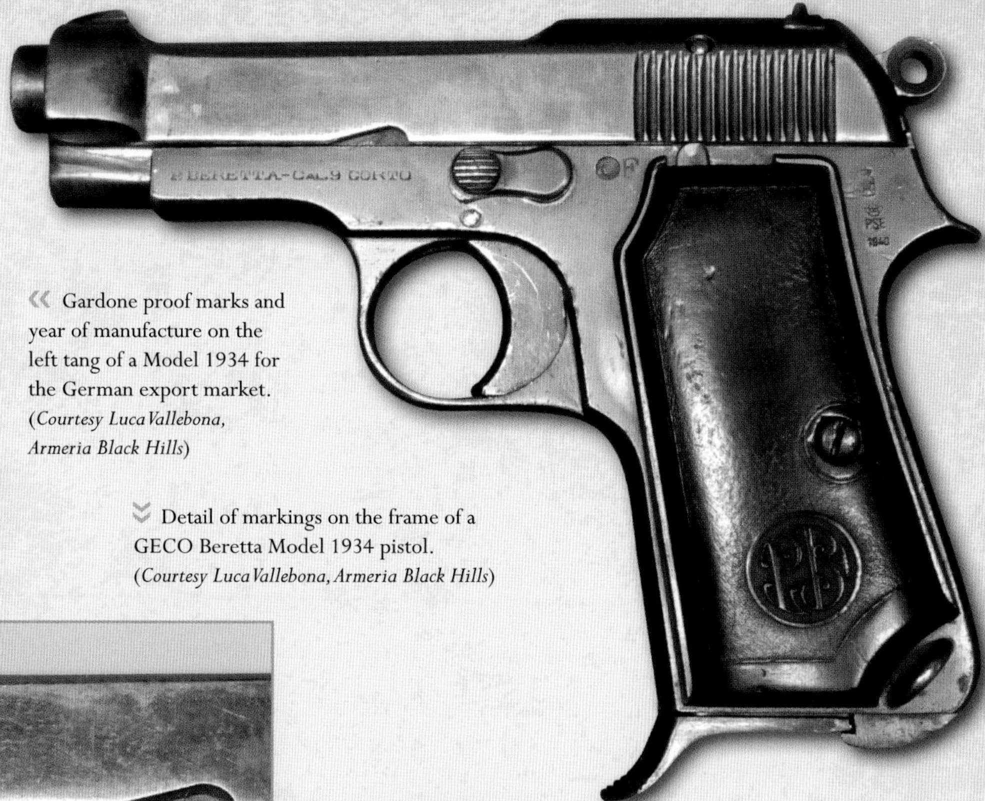

Gardone proof marks and year of manufacture on the left tang of a Model 1934 for the German export market. (*Courtesy Luca Vallebona, Armeria Black Hills*)

Detail of markings on the frame of a GECO Beretta Model 1934 pistol. (*Courtesy Luca Vallebona, Armeria Black Hills*)

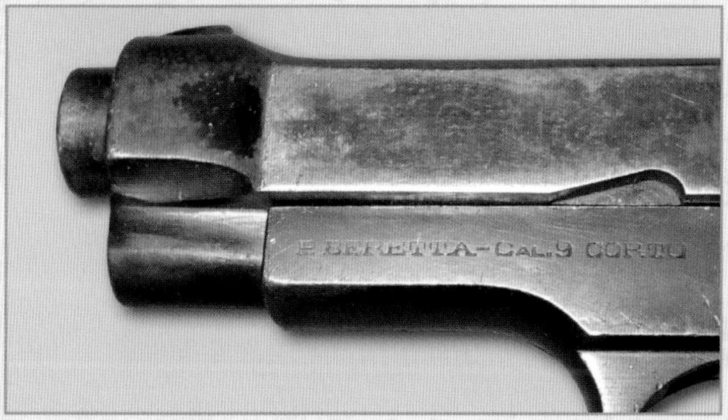

The GECO logo on the right tang of a Beretta Model 1934 produced in 1940. (*Courtesy Luca Vallebona, Armeria Black Hills*)

Japan, Bulgaria and Poland, presumably in small quantities, and to Finland. The Finns supposedly ordered 4,000 Model 1935 pistols, although there is doubt and confusion as to how many were actually delivered, with estimates ranging from 3,100 to 4,100 having made their way to Finland. After September 1943, the Model 1935 continued to be produced for the Germans until 1945; between 1 October 1943 and 31 October 1944 53,725 Model 35 pistols were produced for the Germans. The Germans seemed to have had a preference for the 7.65mm Beretta pistol, possibly because of the many other pistols in their inventory chambered for the same round.

An estimated 200,000-201,000 Model 1935 pistols were produced between 1935 and the end of the war; this included about 115,000 produced under German supervision in 1944 and 1945. The Model 1935 remained in production after the war; the last Model 1935 was produced in April 1967 with an H prefix. The Model 1935 remained in Italian service with police agencies until the 1980s. The total number of Model 1935

PISTOLA MODELLO 1935

Designer: Tullio Marengoni
Manufacturer: Fabbrica d'Armi Pietro Beretta, Gardone Val Trompia; Armaguerra, Cremona
Caliber: 7.65mm
Cartridge: 7.65x25mm Browning (.32ACP)
Operating system: Simple blowback; single action
Overall length: 148mm (5.8")
Barrel length: 85mm (3.4")
Weight: .620 kg (1.36 lbs)
Front sight: Blade, integral with slide
Rear sight: Fixed V notch, dovetailed
Muzzle velocity: 265 m/sec (870 fps)
Feed system: 8 round detachable box magazine

A roughly finished 1944 production Beretta Model 1935 marked with the 4 UT acceptance stamp on the tang. Although late war Beretta pistols were either roughly or only semi-finished externally, all critical functioning components continued to be well finished, and the pistols still performed reliably. The barrel on this pistol has been left in the white. (*Author's collection*)

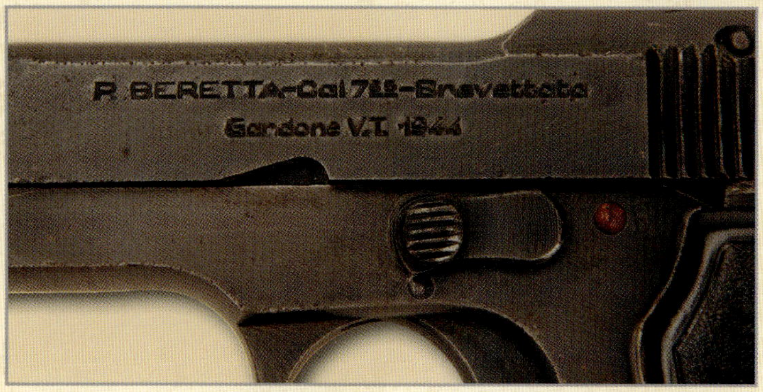

The Fascist date indication in Roman numerals has been dropped on this 1944 Model 1935. This pistol exhibits some surface pitting, but the rough wartime finish is also clearly evident. (*Author's collection*)

A 1944 Model 1935 manufactured by Armaguerra. This is quite a rare specimen, as only about 1,000 are believed to have been produced, all with a G prefix. Note the rough wartime finish underneath the bluing, especially on the frame. (*Courtesy Bradley Bloom*)

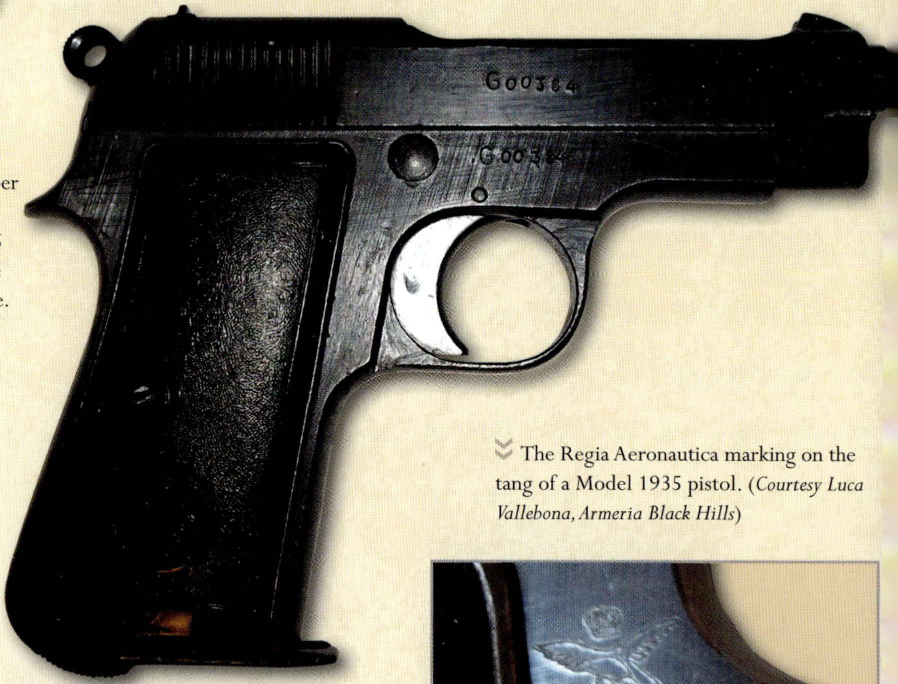

This 1944 Model 1935 still bears the serial number on the slide and frame; very late war Model 1935 pistols dispensed with the serial number on the slide. (*Author's collection*)

The Regia Aeronautica marking on the tang of a Model 1935 pistol. (*Courtesy Luca Vallebona, Armeria Black Hills*)

Detail of slide markings on a Model 1935 pistol produced by Armaguerra. *Courtesy Bradley Bloom*)

Markings on this 1942 Model 1935 pistol reflect yet another variation in lettering style found on Beretta pistols; this pistol is believed to have been a Navy issue pistol, although it does not bear specific Regia Marina markings. (*Courtesy Luca Vallebona, Armeria Black Hills*)

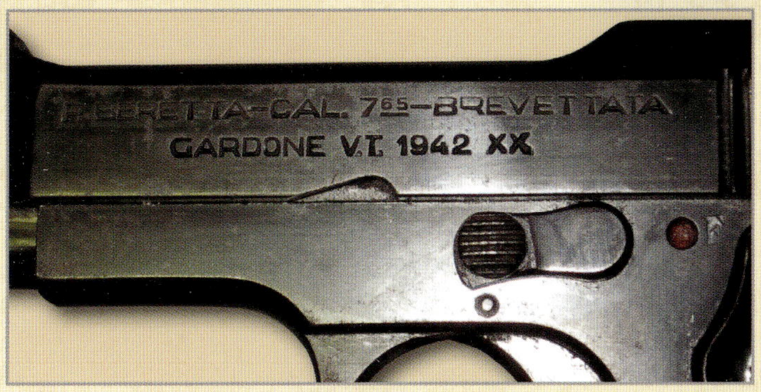

Example of a pre-war finished Model 1935 pistol with Regia Aeronautica markings. (*Courtesy Luca Vallebona, Armeria Black Hills*)

Left side view of the Armaguerra Model 1935; machining marks are quite visible on the frame. Presumably the grips were supplied by Beretta, as they bear the PB logo. (*Courtesy Bradley Bloom*)

Detail of the Armaguerra serial number; the leading zeroes, especially on the slide, are canted at a noticeable angle. (*Courtesy Bradley Bloom*)

The Model 1934 magazine on the left has a solid 1st type floorplate; there were also two other types of solid or milled floorplates. The Model 1934 magazine in the middle has a stamped sheet metal 1st type floorplate, and the Model 1935 magazine on the left has a stamped 2nd type floorplate. (*Author's collection*)

Detail of the 4 UT stamp on the left tang of a 1944 Model 1935. The 4 UT mark could also be expressed as IV U, as pictured in the section describing the Beretta Model 1934 pistol. (*Author's collection*)

Complete slide markings on a 1936 Model 1935 pistol. (*Courtesy Luca Vallebona, Armeria Black Hills*)

Images A & B A Model 1935 pistol, top, and a Model 1934 pistol, bottom. Externally the two pistols are virtually indistinguishable except for their slide markings. (*Author's collection*)

pistols produced between 1935 and the end of production in 1967 is estimated to be 525,000.

Markings on the Model 1935 followed the same convention as on the Model 1934, except for the caliber marking, which was indicated as CAL 765. As with the Model 1934, the late wartime 7.65mm pistols often lacked slide markings, along with being very roughly finished on the exterior. Model 1935 pistols produced by Armaguerra had five-digit serial numbers with a G prefix; the left side of the slide was marked Pistola Beretta Cal. 7,65 M.35 on one line, with a second line reading S.A. Armaguerra-Cremona-1944. ■

PISTOLA SOSSO MOD. 1941, CALIBRO 9 LUNGO

In 1934 Giulio Sosso designed and developed his first pistol, an advanced double action locked breech design that had a unique 19-round magazine. It is not certain as to what facility actually manufactured the early Sosso pistol; both sides of the slide bore the inscription Giulio SOSSO Torino, but neither photographs of the pistol or a 1937 catalog gave any indication of the actual

« This photograph from the FNA brochure for the Sosso pistol shows a soldier aiming a Sosso pistol fitted with the shoulder stock holster. The curve of the ammunition pouch suggests that it holds spare magazines for the Sosso. Interestingly, the soldier is wearing the old style Model 1915 Adrian helmet rather than the standard Model 1933 helmet that was almost universally issued by the time this photograph was taken. (*Courtesy Paolo Silvano, Armeria Berrone*)

This gold engraved Sosso pistol belonged to Aimone Savoia Aosta, Duke of Spoleto, who also held the title of Grand Admiral of the Italian Navy. The pistol and partially filled magazine rest on a World War II Italian podium flag that has the House of Savoy crest embroidered on it. Other items complementing the pistol are a matched pair of admiral's shoulder tabs, a Regia Marina officer's cap badge, and a bronze medal called the "Medal of Honor for Long Navigation" (Medaglia d'onore per lunga nvaigazione). (*Courtesy, Leonardo M. Antaris, MD*)

manufacturing facility. However, the gun proved too expensive to manufacture, and accordingly Sosso developed a new version with the same locking mechanism, a more rounded slide, and an alloy frame that did not work out satisfactorily. Small numbers of the second model Sosso were manufactured from 1938 to 1940. Sosso then developed an improved all steel model which he offered unsuccessfully to Walther in Germany. Externally, the Sosso, with its rounded forward portion of the slide and barrel bushing lock, was quite similar in appearance to the Spanish Astra series of tubular slide pistols and like the Astra its recoil spring fit over the barrel. This version went into production at the F.N.A. Brescia factory in 1941. It fired a 9mm Parabellum cartridge, referred to in Italy as the 9mm *lungo* (9mm long). Two variants were produced; the first was a military model with a lanyard ring and a metal frame holster that could be attached as a stock, and the second was a commercial version that lacked the lanyard ring and could not accept a stock. The magazine was a highly unusual design that held 20 rounds in what was described as an "endless belt" magazine; an additional round in the chamber brought total ammunition capacity to 21 rounds, making it a very early high capacity magazine pistol. This pistol was quite large and heavy, weighing in at almost four pounds loaded – almost a pound and a half heavier than the Colt 1911A1 – and was also about an inch longer than the Colt. The Italian Army reportedly ordered about a hundred, but the Sosso in either version is an extremely rare pistol by any measure. ■

PISTOLA SOSSO MOD. 1941, CAL. 9 LUNGO

Designer: Giulio Sosso
Manufacturer: Fabbica Nazionale d'Armi, Brescia
Caliber: 9mm
Cartridge: 9x19mm Parabellum
Operating system: Locked breech, single action
Overall length: 242mm (9.5")
Barrel length: 150mm (5.9")
Weight: 1.51 kg (3.32 lbs) empty; 1.755 kg (3.9 lbs) loaded
Muzzle velocity: 395 m/sec (1295 fps)
Feed system: 20 rounds in an "endless belt" magazine

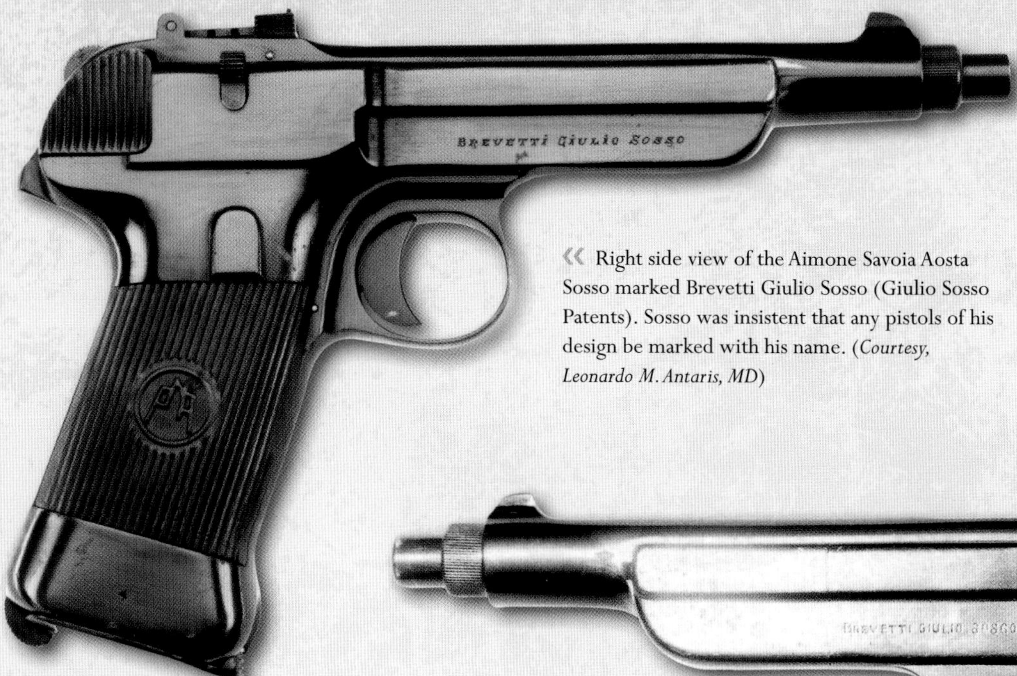

Right side view of the Aimone Savoia Aosta Sosso marked Brevetti Giulio Sosso (Giulio Sosso Patents). Sosso was insistent that any pistols of his design be marked with his name. (*Courtesy, Leonardo M. Antaris, MD*)

The 9mm Sosso pistol bore a strong external resemblance to the earlier Astra tubular slide pistols because of the rounded contour of the forward portion of the slide and the barrel bushing lock. The date 1941 is visible under magnification, between the proof marks and the safety lever which is in the Fire position (F denotes Fuoco, or Fire.) This pistol is marked Brevetti Giulio Sosso above the trigger guard. Note also the ring hammer. (*Author's files*)

The Sosso pistol engraved expressly for Aimone Savoia Aosta, Duke of Spoleto, who was the cousin of King Victor Emmanuel III. The left sideplate is inlaid in gold with a crown and the highly stylized initials of Aimone Savoia Aosta. The frame is marked Fabbrica Nazionale d'Armi Brescia, as well as bearing proof marks and the year of manufacture, 1942. (*Courtesy, Leonardo M. Antaris, MD*)

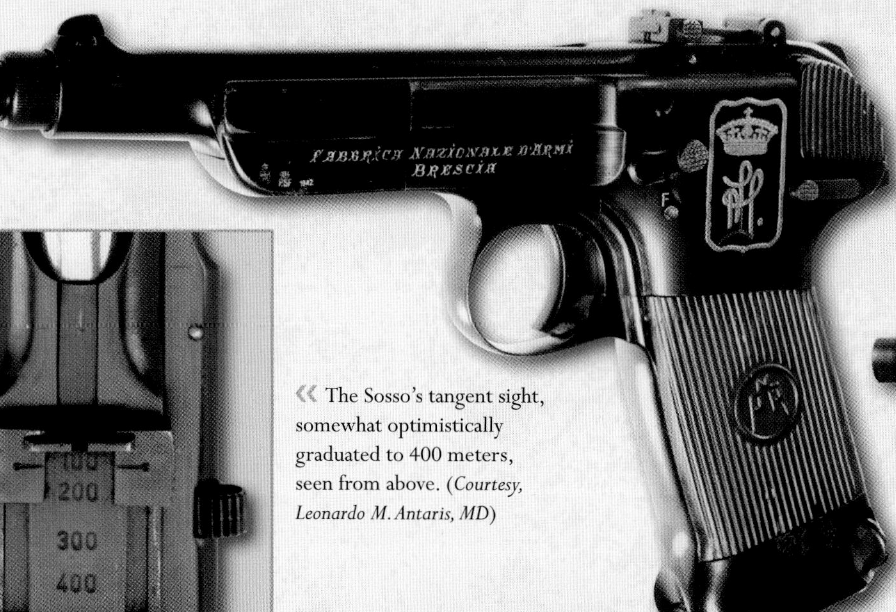

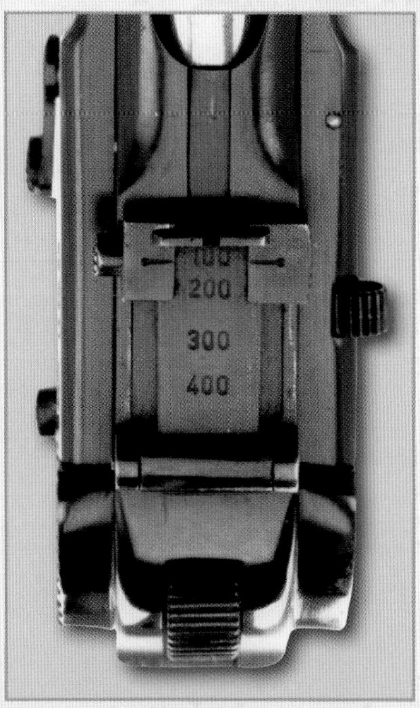

The Sosso's tangent sight, somewhat optimistically graduated to 400 meters, seen from above. (*Courtesy, Leonardo M. Antaris, MD*)

The Sosso pistol with its shoulder holster stock attached. (*Courtesy Paolo Silvano, Armeria Berrone*)

The Sosso pistol in its holster which also doubled as a carbine-type stock. *(Courtesy Paolo Silvano, Armeria Berrone)*

The Sosso pistol and its unique 21-round "endless belt" magazine. (*Courtesy, Leonardo M. Antaris, MD*)

Detail of the Aimone Savoia Aosta inlay; the tangent sight is also clearly visible. (*Courtesy, Leonardo M. Antaris, MD*)

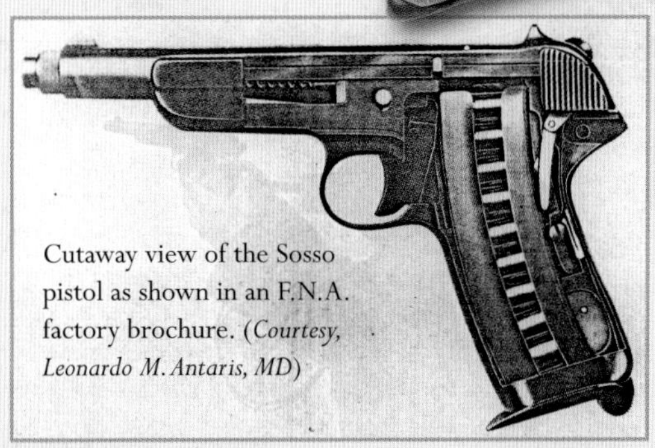

Cutaway view of the Sosso pistol as shown in an F.N.A. factory brochure. (*Courtesy, Leonardo M. Antaris, MD*)

The military version of the Sosso pistol as illustrated in a F.N.A. catalogue. The pistol has a lanyard ring and the grips have vertical grooves and the F.N.A. logo impressed directly into the grip material. The back strap is grooved to accept a shoulder stock. (*Courtesy Paolo Silvano, Armeria Berrone*)

The commercial version of the Sosso pistol from the same catalogue. This pistol does not have the lanyard ring, and the grips are checkered, with the F.N.A. logo on this model also including the word BRESCIA. (*Courtesy Paolo Silvano, Armeria Berrone*)

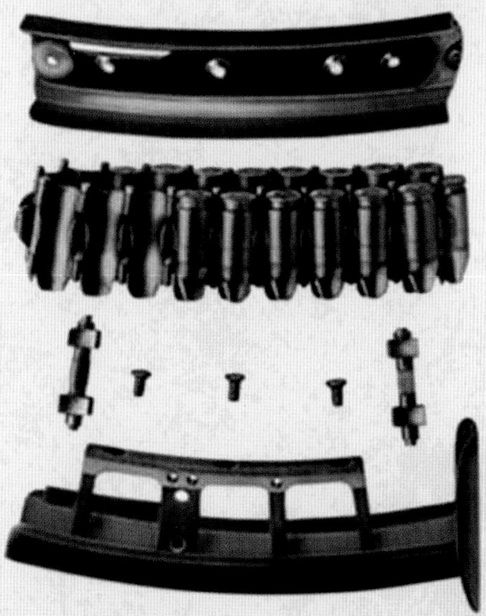

Component parts of the Sosso "endless belt" magazine. (*Courtesy Paolo Silvano, Armeria Berrone*)

PROTOTYPE & EXPERIMENTAL PISTOLS

During the inter-war period there were some private initiatives to develop and offer a new pistol for Italian military use. FIAT submitted at least two prototype pistols in 1921 and 1922, in 1923 the prolific Bethel Abiel Revelli offered a pistol (not a revolver) with six barrels, in the late-1920s the Terni Arsenal submitted a 7.5mm pistol of its own design, and in 1930 Galesi of Brescia presented a 7.65mm pistol that was not favorably received. Once the war had begun the Italians did not devote much effort to developing new pistols. Aside from the 9mm Parabellum Sosso pistol described above, the only other attempt at developing a 9mm Parabellum pistol was undertaken by Beretta, not in response to any stated Italian Army requirement, but rather to meet a Romanian requirement.

PISTOLA MODELLO 1920 *(Brixia)*

The Brixia Model 1920, with its long barrel, seems to have been an attempt by MBT to interest the *Regia Marina* in a long-barrelled version of the Model 1913; the Navy, however, never placed an order for the weapon. The Model 1920, which at times is also referred to as the Model 1923, was slightly improved with respect to the Model 1913, mainly by replacing flat springs with coil springs, but mechanically was essentially the same as the Model 1913. The chief difference was in the length of its barrel, and consequent greater overall length. Barrel length was increased by 80mm (about 3.2 inches), and overall length by 82mm (about 3.25 inches). The rear sight on the Model 1920 was an almost identical copy of that of the Mauser C96. The magazine was slightly different than that of the Model 1913, and the grips were wood with vertical grooves. The Model 1920 had a lug on the back strap that enabled a combination holster and wooden shoulder stock almost identical to that of the Mauser C96 to be fitted. It is not clear how many Model 1920 pistols were produced, but it seems to have been produced on a very limited prototype basis; two known prototypes bear the serial numbers 2 and 6. ■

PISTOLA MODELLO 1920 "BRIXIA"

Designer: Bethel Abiel Revelli (via the Glisenti Model 1906 and 1910)
Manufacturer: Metallurgica Bresciana Tempini
Caliber: 9mm
Cartridge: 9x19 Glisenti
Operating system: Simple blowback; single action
Overall length: 288mm (11.3")
Barrel length: 175mm (6.9")
Weight: 1.12 kg (2.46 lbs)
Front sight: Barleycorn
Rear sight: Tangent, graduated from 100 to 1000 meters
Muzzle velocity: Unknown
Feed system: 7 round detachable box magazine

A standard Brixia Model 1913 pistol (bottom), and a long-barrelled Model 1920 prototype with adjustable rear sight. Aside from the length of the barrel and the rear sight, the Model 1920 also has a differently configured lower grip frame and has wooden grips rather than the standard composition grips. (*Editoriale Olimpia*)

PISTOLA MODELLO 1938, CAL. 9 LUNGO

Beretta Model 1938, serial number 3.L, is maintained by the Beretta Museum in Gardone Val Trompia. (*Beretta*)

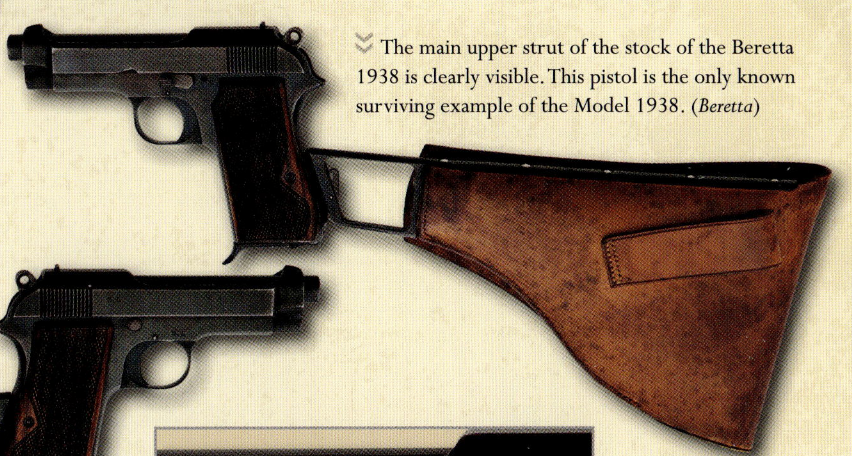

The main upper strut of the stock of the Beretta 1938 is clearly visible. This pistol is the only known surviving example of the Model 1938. (*Beretta*)

The Beretta Model 1938 with combination holster/should stock attached. Its configuration is nearly identical to that of the Model 1934. (*Beretta*)

Detail of slide marking on the Model 1938 pistol, showing the caliber as 9 lungo (9mm Parabellum) and model designation as Mod 1938. (*Beretta*)

The Beretta Model 1938 was produced in response to a 1938 Romanian request for a pistol chambered for the increasingly popular 9mm Parabellum round. It was no challenge for Marengoni to design a pistol based on the Model 1923 and Model 1934 and chambered for the 9x19 Parabellum cartridge, but negotiations between Beretta and the Romanians see-sawed until 1940 by which time the international situation had changed drastically and Beretta was having difficulty in obtaining enough raw materials to satisfy even Italian needs. At one point the Romanians expressed a desire for 100,000 of the Model 1938 (also referred to as the Model 1940), but a deal was never concluded with the Romanians, nor apparently was the Italian military interested in the weapon, and only a handful of experimental and prototype models were made. As might be expected, the Model 1938 retained the layout and external appearance of Marengoni's other pistols and looked very much like a beefed-up Model 1934, which in essence it was. The back strap had a milled slot that allowed a shoulder stock holster to be attached. One surviving example, serial numbered 3 L, is in the Beretta arms museum; the suffix L may have stood for *lungo* (long), in reference to the 9mm Parabellum round which the Italians referred to as 9mm *lungo*. Historically, the Model 1938 was the first Beretta pistol to be chambered for the 9x19mm Parabellum round and set the stage for later development of the Model 1951 and of the hugely successful Beretta Model 92, adopted by the U.S. military in 1985 as the M9. ■

PISTOLA MODELLO 1938

Designer: Tullio Marengoni
Manufacturer: Fabbrica d'Armi Pietro Beretta, Gardone Val Trompia
Caliber: 9mm
Cartridge: 9x19 Parabellum
Operating system: Locked breech, single action
Overall length: 178mm (7.0")
Barrel length: Not available
Weight: .995 kg (2.19 lbs)
Front sight: Blade, integral with frame
Rear sight: Fixed V notch, dovetailed
Muzzle velocity: 320 m/sec (1050 fps)
Feed system: 7 round detachable box magazine

CHAPTER 2: RIFLES

Essentially, all of the rifles used by the Italian armed forces during World War II were derivatives of the 6.5mm World War I vintage Model 1891 bolt-action rifle although exceptionally a few models of completely different rifles could be encountered. However, it would be erroneous to assume that the Italian Army was content to go to war in the late-1930s with the Model 91 series even though the weapon had proven itself well in World War I. In fact, in 1932 the Italian Army Staff undertook studies to determine a suitable replacement for the Model 91 rifle as it was felt that the 6.5mm cartridge was no longer adequate when compared to the 8mm Mauser and the .303 British. The result was that in 1938 the 7.35x51 cartridge was adopted and production was begun of the Model 91/38 short rifle and of the 91/38 carbines, all in 7.35mm. About 645,000 91/38 rifles, TS carbines and cavalry carbines were manufactured in 7.35mm, and after it was decided in view of the circumstances to retain only the 6.5mm weapons in order to avoid the chaos of utilizing two different calibers concurrently, new production of the Model 38 family was continued in 6.5mm for a total of about 2,154,000 weapons. The weapon produced in the highest number during the war years was the 6.5mm 91/38 cavalry carbine – over 1.6 million produced – followed by the Model 41 rifle, of which over 900,000 were produced. Because of its longevity and the number of variants produced, well over 9.5 million Carcanos were produced between 1893 and 1944.

The Carcano family of rifles was marked by simplicity and functionality, but the weapons were made of high quality materials and were robust, reliable and accurate. Perhaps it is fair to describe them as utilitarian, devoid of unnecessary refinement. The Carcano design itself was technically innovative and incorporated features that were advanced or even ground-breaking at the time of their introduction; among these features were gain twist rifling and controlled feed (which was not adopted by Mauser until 1896). Criticisms of the Carcano action as being weak or of the quality of materials being poor are simply unfounded. The standards of finish were appropriate for military weapons that were expected to see hard use in the field; most metal surfaces were blued, but bolts and some small parts such as the trigger, sear and follower were left in the white; stocks were nicely contoured and finished.

The system of identifying and marking Carcanos might best be described as a two-tier system of primary and secondary markings. The primary markings consisted of fairly standardized and generally obligatory markings consisting of the serial number, manufacturer, date and steel supplier indicated on the barrel and on the buttstock; the serial number appeared only on the barrel and until 1919 on the bolt as well, but no other parts bore the serial number. Essentially, the Italians carried the principle of interchangeability to its logical extreme: if parts were fully interchangeable, there was no need to number them to an individual rifle. The secondary markings consisted of various numbers, letters, or combinations representing assembly numbers, inspector codes, subcontractor codes, or manufacturers codes or logos that could be applied to almost any small part or to the stock. There seems to have been no clear pattern or consistency as to which small parts were marked and which were not; small parts markings might best be described as chaotic. The only general rule with respect to the markings on small parts is that there are no identifiable rules.

Some English language authors infer, if not actually state, that the Carcano rifle family was basic and simple because Italian recruits and soldiers were not capable of using anything much more sophisticated. While this may appeal to the stereotype of Italian soldiers still held by some authors and readers, it is a stereotype with little or no validity and the design of the rifle, as far as this author has been able to determine, was not influenced by any consideration of the mechanical aptitude of the average Italian conscript of the time. At the time of its design the Carcano Model 1891 was fully competitive with contemporary bolt action military rifles, so one could argue that at the time of its introduction the average Italian soldier was no more or less proficient in handling a bolt action rifle than were French, German, Russian or British soldiers. The Carcano made its debut at the same time as the Russian Mosin-Nagant Model 1891 and slightly later than the French Lebel and Berthier rifles, and less than a decade before introduction of the German Mauser Gewehr 98. Its most serious shortcomings compared to those rifles were its relatively small caliber and ballistic characteristics, but even those factors should be viewed in perspective as a number of nations, including Japan, Greece, Romania, Holland, Norway, Sweden and Portugal all used rifles in 6.5mm, although the Carcano bullet was the lightest used by any nation. Forwarding to World War II, when the Carcano could be considered in some respects to be outdated (but more or less on a par with the Japanese Arisaka Model 38), probably the worst that could be said about the Carcano was that it remained in service too long and its caliber was no longer totally adequate for World War II requirements in the North African, European and Russian theaters where it was up against weapons using more potent cartridges that enabled targets to be engaged at longer ranges.

It is almost surprising that Italy did not enter the war with a semi-automatic rifle in light of the fact that as early as the late-1800s Italian gun designers had begun to experiment with and develop semi-automatic rifles. In 1870 Colonel Gaspare Freddi put forth a proposal to transform a Vetterli 1870 rifle into a semi-automatic weapon, developing several prototypes, and in 1900 designed a completely new semi-automatic rifle that, however, apparently never made it past the prototype stage. Another early Italian initiative aimed at developing a semi-automatic rifle was the rifle developed by another Italian officer, Amerigo Cei-Rigotti, who took out a number of patents relating to a semi-automatic design between 1895 and 1911. The Cei-Rigotti represented a ground-breaking design in many respects, but due to the combination of its innovative design and a number of teething problems it never reached series production. Its short stroke gas operating system was similar to that used later in the U.S. M1 carbine. An undetermined number of the rifles were built by Glisenti, some chambered for the Italian 6.5mm Mannlicher-Carcano round and some for the Swiss 7.5mm round, and fed by 10, 20 or 50 round detachable box magazines. A number of other semi-automatic designs surfaced in the interwar years, among them the Terni Modello 21 (an attempt to adapt the existing Model 1891 rifles as a semi-automatic); the Genovesi modified Terni rifle (a similar attempt at converting the Model 1891 to a semi-automatic), an almost unknown 1925 prototype by Meccanica Bresciana già Tempini, and the gas operated 6.5mm *fucile automatico sperimentale* (experimental automatic rifle), developed for the Italian Navy, only two examples of which are known to exist. Breda developed a gas operated semi-automatic rifle in 1931, the Breda PG, a small number of which were sold to Costa Rica, but the Italian Army was not interested in a gas operated weapons; Breda subsequently offered a series of rifles in 7.35mm using a short recoil system – the CR 31/37, CR 3, CR 5, and CR 29 – in the 1938 timeframe, but these did not meet Italian Army requirements. Work continued on developing a rifle adequate for military use; the text covers the Pavesi, Beretta, Breda, Scotti and Armaguerra rifles in detail. All of these programs ultimately led the Italian Army to decide to adopt the Revelli Model 1939 (Armaguerra) semi-automatic rifle in the newly adopted 7.35mm caliber, but the outbreak of the war earlier than Italy had anticipated completely upset plans to re-equip Italian forces with the 7.35mm 91/38 bolt action weapons and the Revelli semi-automatic. It is also of interest to note that the factory that had been purpose built in Cremona to manufacture the Revelli Model 1939 had barely been completed at the time of the decision, and instead of producing the 7.35mm semi-automatic rifle as had originally been intended, was used for the manufacture of the Model 41 bolt-action rifle in 6.5mm. ■

FUCILE MODELLO 1891

The *fucile modello 1891* was officially adopted by the Italian Army in March 1892 as a successor to the 10.4mm Vetterli and Vetterli-Vitali rifles that had been standard issue until then. The Model 91 was the standard issue Italian infantry weapon in World War I and was used in World War II to some extent as well – during World War I the government armory at Terni alone produced 2,063,750 Model 91 rifles. The weapon is commonly known as the "*modello 91*," or even more simply as "*il 91*" in Italy, but is also referred to as the Carcano, Mannlicher-Carcano, or Parravicino-Mauser by many non-Italian sources. These various designations stem from the fact that the rifle, which was designed in 1891, has a Mauser type (cock on opening) bolt system that was developed by Salvatore Carcano, uses a Mannlicher feed system, and was adopted by a small arms commission that was headed by General Gustavo Parravicino.

Prompted by introduction of the Lebel 8x50R smokeless powder cartridge by France in 1886, in 1888 the Italian Minister of War charged the army's Small Arms Commission to study adoption of a new rifle to replace the 10.4mm 1870/87 Vetterli-Vitali service rifle. Early experiments by the commission were oriented towards calibers ranging from 7.5mm to 8mm and used barrels in those calibers mated to a Vetterli action. However, the commission's secretary, Major Antonio Benedetti, proposed adoption of a smaller caliber, between 6mm and 6.5mm. This proposal is said to have been motivated at least in part by the memory of the annihilation of some 500 Italian troops at Dogali, Eritrea, in January 1887. The Italians, armed with the Vetterli and 80 rounds of ammunition per man, accounted for some 1,500 Eritreans before their ammunition ran out and they were overwhelmed. Major Benedetti apparently reasoned that had a smaller cartridge been in use the troops could have carried much more ammunition and might have survived the battle. It is also interesting to note that prior to adoption of the Model 91 Italian Army authorities went to extremes that in retrospect appear to have been unwarranted in order to avoid disclosure of the caliber of the weapon – at the time the adoption of a caliber as small as 6.5mm for military use was considered by the Italians to be revolutionary – and were even more jealous in guarding information concerning gain twist rifling for the weapon. Benedetti's views prevailed and on 18 April 1890 the 6.5mm caliber was officially

A quiet moment in prepared trench positions, 1917. The Model 1891 was very effective when firing from prepared positions, where its long barrel was an advantage in aimed fire. (*SME via Andrea and Antonio Tallillo*)

The Model 1891 rifle was the standard Italian rifle during World War I and soldiered on in various versions into World War II. As with most rifles of the World War I era it had a straight bolt handle and a very long barrel. (*Giovanni Chegia collection*)

established as the caliber to be adopted; at the same time, competition was opened for selection of a new rifle in that caliber. The first fifteen designs submitted by Italian and foreign contenders were all rejected and by the end of 1890 a further ten entries had been submitted. The testing revealed problems with jacket separation, and Major Garelli – who had succeeded Benedetti – proposed that gain twist riling be adopted to remedy the problem. Tests continued with an astounding number of entries between 1890 and early 1891 – some 45 in addition to the earlier entries – but none proved suitable, so yet another competition was held with entries to be submitted by the end of December 1891. The contenders were narrowed down to two: Rifle No. 1, presented by the Torino Arsenal, and Rifle No. 2, presented by the Terni and Torre Annunziata Arsenals. After several modifications, these became Rifle No. 1 *bis* and Rifle No. 2 *bis*. The Torino rifle, 1 *bis*, which had a Mauser-type bolt with two front locking lugs, a Mannlicher feed system, and a safety designed by Carcano, was judged the winner and was adopted on 29 March 1892. Although the rifle was designated the *fucile modello 1891*, production of the rifle did not actually began until early 1893.

Mechanically, the Model 1891 was an extremely simple weapon, and had many features in common with the German *Gewehr 1888* (or Gew. 88) rifle. It had a tubular split-bridge receiver, a cock on opening bolt with two frontal locking lugs and a bolt handle that acted as a safety lug, and a six-round Mannlicher-style clip that was symmetrical and could be inserted either end up in the clip housing. As on the Gew. 88, a catch in the front of the trigger on the magazine housing allowed the rifleman to release the clip and any remaining cartridges upward through the open action; when the last cartridge is stripped from the clip the

FUCILE MODELLO 1891

Designer: Salvatore Carcano
Manufacturers: Fabbrica d'Armi Terni (1892-1941); Fabbrica d'Armi Brescia (1895-1897); Fabbrica d'Armi Torino (1892-1900); Fabrica d'Armi Roma (1917-1918); Fabbrica d'Armi Torre Annunziata (1894-1900); MIDA Brescia (1916-1918); Fabbrica d'Armi Pietro Beretta (1937-1940)
Caliber: 6.5mm
Cartridge: 6.5x52mm Mannlicher-Carcano
Overall length: 1288mm (50.7")
Barrel length: 780mm (30.7")
Rifling: RH gain twist, 483mm (19") at breech, 203mm (8") at muzzle
Weight: 3.9 kg (8.6 lbs) walnut, 3.95 kg (8.7 lbs) beech
Front sight: Barleycorn
Rear sight: Quadrant with V notch, adjustable to 2000 meters
Muzzle velocity: 700 m/sec (2135 fps)
Feed system: 6 round integral box using six-round Mannlicher-Carcano clips

SNIPER RIFLES

The crossed rifle symbol on a Model 91/28 carbine manufactured by Terni in 1929. The symbol can be encountered in a number of different positions and locations on the barrel chamber. (*Author's collection*)

The Italians are not particularly well known for use of sniper rifles, but during World War I the Model 91 initially was fitted with a French Scheibler 4X telescope, offset mounted on the left to allow clearance for the six-round stripper clip to be inserted. Later, Italian 4X scopes manufactured by La Filotecnica of Milano were used. The Filotecnica scopes were mounted directly above the chamber and reloading required that the scope be removed in order to insert a new six-round clip. In both types of scoped rifles the bolt handles were turned down to allow bolt clearance. Following World War I experimentation with scopes continued and the Galileo and Salmoiraghi optics companies produced small lots that were fitted on a trial basis on Model 1891 rifles as well as on Model 38 and Model 41 rifles, but actual use of scoped sniper rifles during World War II seems to have been very limited. In 1939 there appear to have been only 122 scoped rifles in the entire Italian Army inventory, and orders were given to distribute the entire lot to terriorial units in northern Italy for use by *Guardia alla Frontiera* (Border Guard) units. In March 1941 there was an urgent request for 40 scoped rifles to be sent to snipers in Albania, but the ultimate disposition of this request was not indicated by the source document. One reference indicates that in May 1942 there were 119 Model 1891 rifles with scopes in the army's inventory. There are some claims in both Italian and English-language publications that snipers were issued with rifles that had been identified during the proofing process as being especially accurate and were marked on one of the barrel facets with a symbol consisting of crossed rifles surmounted by two concentric circles and a dot representing a target. This is a totally incorrect interpretation of the "crossed rifles" symbol, which in reality indicates that the rifle – or carbine, which is hardly a sniper's weapon – was one of 10% selected at random from the production line to be disassembled and then reassembled to ensure that the parts fit correctly; five rounds were then fired from a bench rest at 200 meters to ensure that the weapon functioned satisfactorily and grouped the shots within certain acceptable parameters. The 6.5mm Model 38 rifle fitted with a cheap commercial 4X scope that was used to kill President John F. Kennedy on 22 November 1963 provides a sad historical footnote regarding Italian sniper rifles. ■

The Roma Arsenal produced an estimated 233,000 Model 1891 rifles from 1917 to 1918. The year of production is indicated by the last three digits, 918. Roma production rifles were identified by an OR (Officine Roma) prefix to their serial numbers. (*Giovanni Chegia collection*)

A field stripped Carcano bolt. The components consist of the firing pin, firing pin spring, safety catch, cocking piece, cocking piece nut, and bolt body. (*Author's collection*)

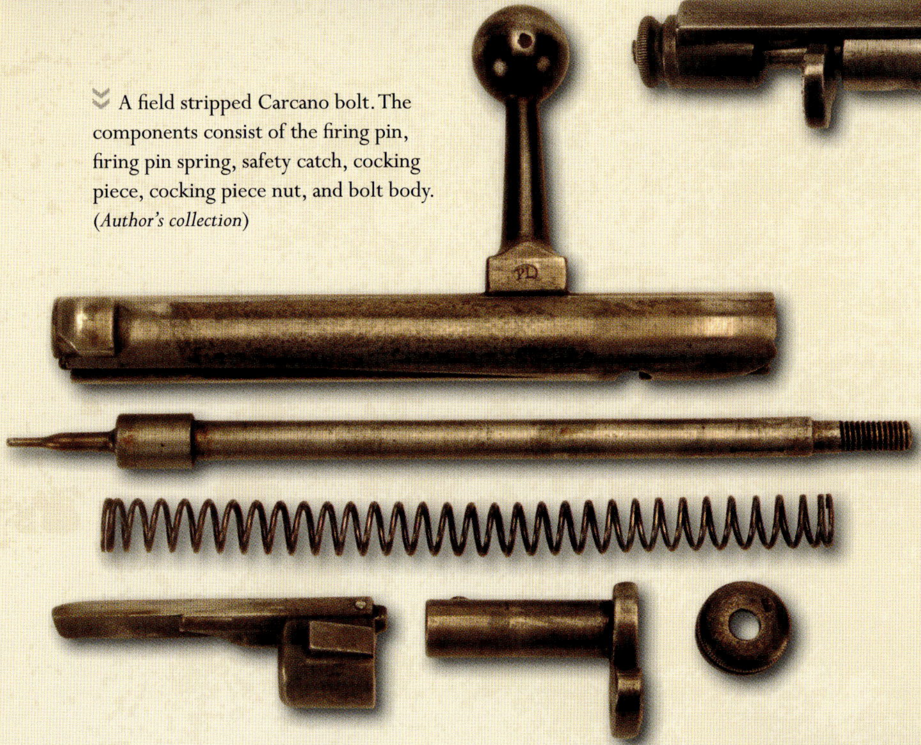

The markings on the barrel of this Model 1891 rifle tell an interesting story. The barrel is a Terni barrel produced in 1897, but the serial number ORW 1722 is for a rifle made by the Arsenale di Roma in 1918. The stock is marked as having been repaired in 1931 at Terni; apparently during the repair process the original Rome Arsenal barrel was replaced by a serviceable Terni barrel whose serial number was replaced by that of the original Arsenale di Roma weapon. (*Author's collection*)

The rear sight on the Model 1891 rifle was a quadrant sight graduated from 600 to 2000 meters. When the sight was flipped fully forward the combat sight was set for 300 meters. (*Author's collection*)

The hallmark feature of the Carcano rifle was its bolt, designed by Salvatore Carcano. (*Author's collection*)

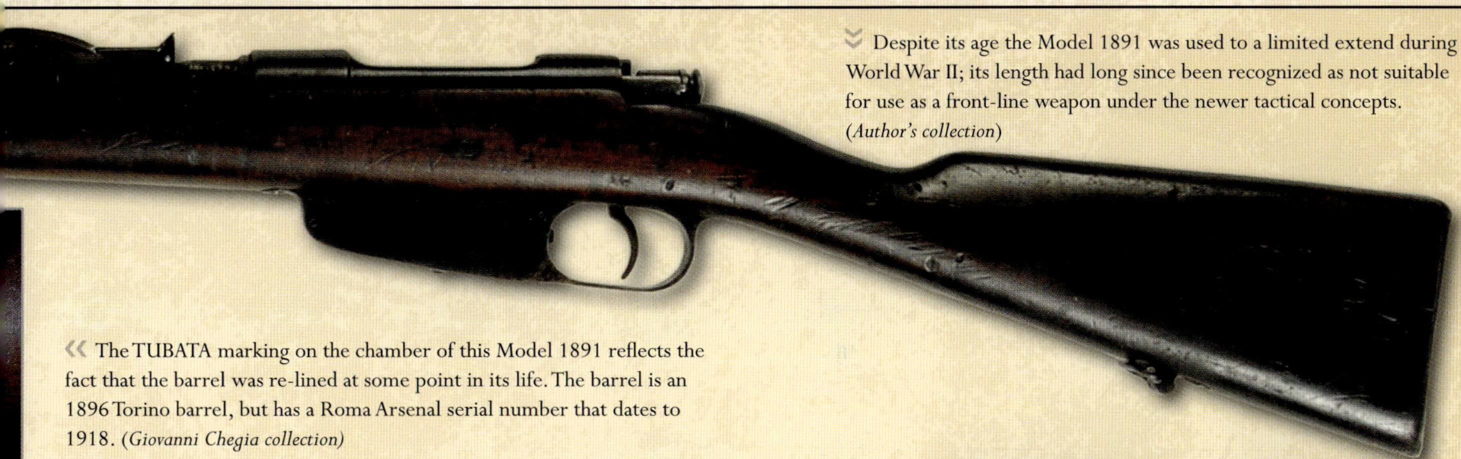

Despite its age the Model 1891 was used to a limited extend during World War II; its length had long since been recognized as not suitable for use as a front-line weapon under the newer tactical concepts. (*Author's collection*)

The TUBATA marking on the chamber of this Model 1891 reflects the fact that the barrel was re-lined at some point in its life. The barrel is an 1896 Torino barrel, but has a Roma Arsenal serial number that dates to 1918. (*Giovanni Chegia collection)*

Images A & B Comparison of a Carcano bolt, top, and a Mauser Kar98k bolt. The Carcano, finished in the white, is characterized by its extreme simplicity and its dual locking lugs; the Mauser is a much more elegant and complicated assembly. (*Author's collection*)

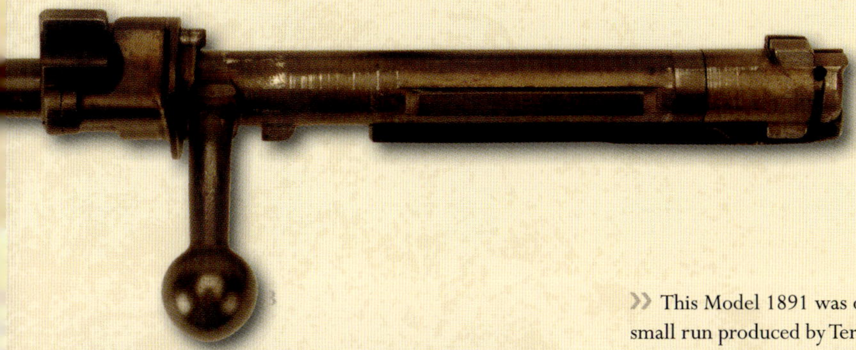

Detail of the different slot configurations on Model 1891 bolts. (*Author's collection*)

This Model 1891 was one of a small run produced by Terni in 1933; in 1918 production of the Model 1891 rifle ceased, but between 1932 and 1936 Terni resumed production on a very modest scale. (*Author's collection*)

One of the lowest volume producers of the Model 1891 was MIDA Brescia, accounting for an estimated 129,000 rifles manufactured between 1916 and 1918; this example was produced in 1917, indicated by the last two digits of the year stamped on the chamber flat. (*Courtesy Steve Woodrum*)

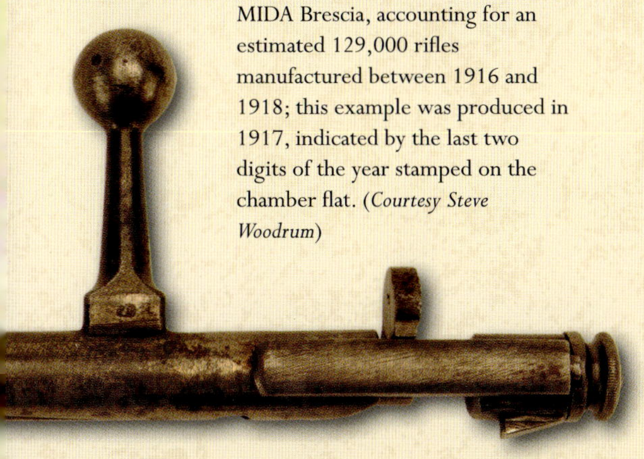

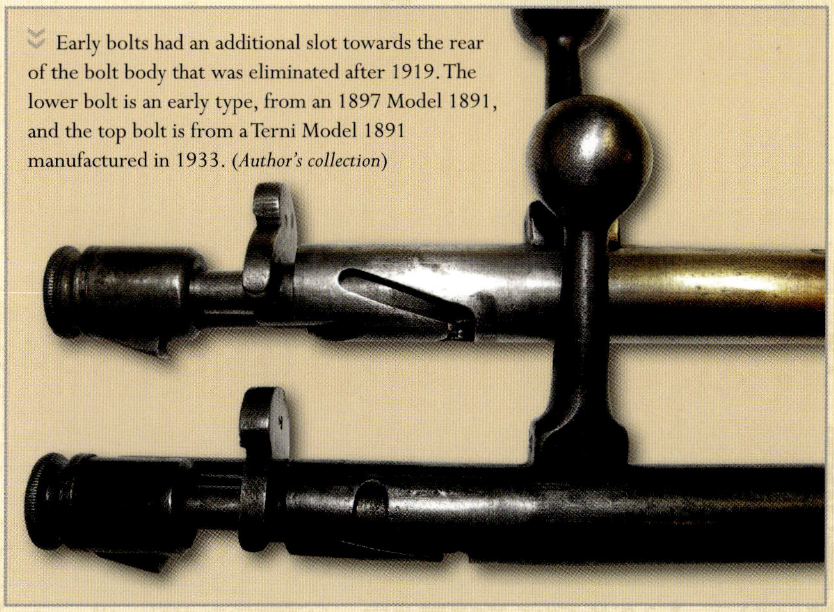

Early bolts had an additional slot towards the rear of the bolt body that was eliminated after 1919. The lower bolt is an early type, from an 1897 Model 1891, and the top bolt is from a Terni Model 1891 manufactured in 1933. (*Author's collection*)

An Italian infantryman in the mountains during the winter of 1916; his Model 1891 rifle is complete with unsheathed bayonet. (*SME via Andrea and Antonio Tallillo*)

An Italian sentry standing guard along the coast, armed with a Model 1891 rifle. A Breda 1930 light machine gun is resting on the ground to his left. (*Bruno Benvenuti*)

empty clip is automatically ejected from the bottom of the magazine housing. One notable and significant difference was that the Carcano bolt body was a one-piece unit milled out from the rear to accept the firing pin mechanism, making it simpler and stronger than the bolt with a separate bolt head used on the Gew. 88. The safety was somewhat cumbersome and consisted of a flat ear attached to the bolt sleeve that had to be pushed in and rotated upward to the left, while holding the bolt handle down, to lock the firing pin and bolt. One of the breakthrough features of the Model 1891 was that its four-groove barrel used progressive, or gain twist, rifling, with 483mm (19 inches) at the breech end, increasing to 203mm (8 inches) at the muzzle.

For purposes of identification and recognition a number of features of the Model 91 should be noted as they differ in the successive derivative weapons described later and serve as points of comparison. The bolt of the Model 91 had a straight bolt handle. On rifles manufactured prior to 1913 the extractor was positioned in a slot underneath the right-hand locking lug, whereas on rifles manufactured beginning in 1913 the right-hand lug was solid and the extractor was located on the upper part of the bolt. The breech end of the barrel corresponding to the chamber exterior flares out and is cut into five facets. These facets bear the initials of the factory supplying the barrel blank, the year of manufacture, the arsenal of manufacture, serial number of the rifle, and proof marks. On rifles manufactured subsequent to 1937, however, this portion of the barrel is tapered rather than being faceted. Until 1919 the bolt also bore the serial number on the upper bolt flat. Serial numbers were allocated in blocks, normally with one or two letter prefixes followed by up to four digits (up to 9999). Until about 1935 Terni rifles were marked simply as TERNI; in 1935 and 1936 the marking consisted of the letters RE (for *Regio Esercito*) surmounted by a royal crown, as well as the word TERNI.

Rifles manufactured at the Brescia, Torino, Torre Annunziata and Roma arsenals bore the inscriptions BRESCIA, TORINO, TORRE ANNUNZIATA and ROMA, respectively. MIDA Brescia rifles were marked MIDA BRESCIA, and Beretta rifles were marked BERETTA GARDONE. An interesting characteristic of the Model 1891 rifles manufactured by Beretta was that, in addition to exhibiting the usual high standard of finish associated with Beretta products, the bolt and the rear sight base were sometimes case hardened.

The quadrant rear sight is fixed to the barrel by two screws. The sight base itself has an integral notch sight set for 300 meters; in order to be used, it requires that the sight leaf itself is flipped fully forward and rests in the notch in the upper handguard. When the leaf is in the normal down position it is set for 450 meters and is used for distances ranging from 400 to 500 meters. The sight ramps used in conjunction with the leaf are graduated from 600 to 2000 meters. The front sight of the Model 91 was mounted either on a ferrule (Torino and Terni arsenals) or on a sight base welded on the barrel (Brescia and Torre Annunziata arsenals). In both cases, it was adjustable for windage.

The stock was a straight grip type and had no finger grooves. Stocks were made of either walnut or beech; the Torino, Brescia, and Torre Annunziata arsenals used beech exclusively, while rifles produced by the Terni arsenal used both types of wood. The forearm of the stocks of Terni rifles were also one centimeter shorter than those produced in the other arsenals with the result that whereas with a fixed bayonet the bayonet crossguard was flush with the end of the muzzle on other Model 91s, on those produced at Terni the muzzle protruded one centimeter beyond the crossguard. A wooden handguard ran from in front of the rear sight to a single spring retained barrel band; a muzzle band with bayonet lug was attached to the forearm by a screw. A channel in the forearm under the barrel accommodated a full length cleaning rod. Until about 1898 the stock was fitted with a full width reinforcing bolt that was replaced by an internal reinforcing lug on later production rifles. The left hand side of the stock close to the butt end bore fairly elaborate manufacturer's markings, usually in a circle or oval, but the Terni marking could also be encountered within a hexagon. The serial number also appeared on the buttstock. The buttplate of the Model 1891, affixed by two screws, was solid, with no checkering, and rather roughly finished; internally, it had a stiffening rib that ran full length from top to bottom.

The first documented use of the Model 1891 was, rather sadly, to confront citizens in Milan who had taken to the streets to protest an almost two-fold increase in the price of bread in 1898. Italian light infantry troops armed with the Model 1891 fired on the crowd, killing about 100 and wounding a similar number.

» Italian infantrymen armed with the Model 1891 rifle during the battle for the hill of Montello in Treviso Province in 1918. (*SME via Andrea and Antonio Tallillo*)

Signal Corps troops laying cable in North Africa in 1941, armed with the venerable Model 1891 rifle. (*Cronache della Guerra, Tuminelli Editore, via Andrea and Antonio Tallillo*)

The more conventional baptism of fire, in military operations, took place during the Italo-Turkish War of 1911-1912, when the Italians fought against the Ottoman Turks in what is now Libya and in the Dodecanese Islands. During the brief course of that conflict production of the Model 1891 at the Terni arsenal rose from 540 a month to 2,500 a month.

The Model 1891 rifle was the standard issue long arm of the Italian infantry during World War I; the derivative *moschetto modello 1891* was issued primarily to *bersaglieri* (light infantry), cavalry, artillery, and engineer units. Total production of the Model 1891 rifle is believed to be about 3,587,600, almost all of which were produced between 1893 and 1918. The arsenal at Terni was the largest producer, accounting for something more than 2,000,000 rifles during World War I. The Model 1891 served the Italian Army well between 1915 and 1918 and performed creditably against its primary adversaries, the Steyr-Mannlicher 8x50mmR M1895 straight-pull bolt action used by the Austro-Hungarian forces, and the 7.92x57mm bolt action German Mauser *Gewehr 1898*; the main disadvantage of the Model 1891 compared to those two rifles was the relative lack of range and stopping power of its 6.5mm cartridge, which was partially offset by its greater magazine capacity of six rounds compared to the five rounds of the Steyr-Mannlicher and Mauser.

During World War I the Italians re-lined the barrels of a fairly large number of Model 1891 rifles whose barrels had been badly worn. Replacing the worn barrel linings of artillery pieces was an established practice, and in 1916 the Italians began to apply a similar principle to rifle barrels by inserting a sleeve to convert the 10.35mm Vetterli-Vitali rifles to 6.5mm. Re-lining the Model 1891 barrels, however, called for re-lining the barrel in the original caliber, which was accomplished by boring out the original barrel and force fitting a steel rod into the resulting tube. The rod was then bored and rifled just as it was in making a new barrel. The process, developed by a technician named Salerno, is called *tubatura* (tubeing) in Italian, and rifles thus modified were marked on the upper facet of the barrel chamber with the word TUBATO or TUBATA. The different spellings, i.e., masculine and feminine word forms in Italian, can be explained by the fact that the masculine form *tubato* would refer to repairing the rifle (*fucile*) itself, which is masculine, whereas the feminine form *tubata* would refer to relining the barrel (*canna*), which is feminine. The designation may also be encountered on Model 91/24 carbines whose barrels had previously been re-lined on the original rifle. DiGiorgio and Pettinelli estimate that somewhere around 80-81,000 rifles were thus reconditioned.

In mid- to late-1917 two interesting modifications were proposed for the Model 1891. The first was for a 25-round removable magazine developed by a Major Saccani of the Terni Arsenal, based on a German magazine reported by the Italian intelligence service; following successful testing, 500 were ordered from Terni. The second proposed modification was to replace the magazine and trigger housing with a simplified combination made of stamped and welded sheet steel; Terni was authorized to produce 10,000 on a test basis. Actual examples of these modifications, however, are not known to have survived.

Because of the availability of large numbers of the Model 1891 it also saw limited service during World War II, supplementing other shorter weapons in the Carcano family that had been developed subsequent to World War I. The Terni Arsenal resumed production of the Model 1891 between 1932 and 1936 for a total of about 120,000 rifles, and then produced another very small lot in 1941. Somewhat curiously Beretta, which had not manufactured the Model 1891 rifle during World War I when it had manufactured carbines only, produced some 22,000 Model 1891 rifles between 1937 and 1940.

Serial number ranges were quite varied. Brescia Arsenal rifles had suffixes AA through AF; Torino Arsenal rifles used blocks O through U, OO and OP, U, V, OQ through OU, and EH through EM; Torre Annunziata rifles used blocks W through Z, UR through UZ, and VV through VX; Rome Arsenal rifles used blocks OR-A through OR-Y; Terni Arsenal, which manufactured the huge majority of the Model 1891, used a bewildering number of blocks with both single letter and two letter prefixes, number/letter prefixes, and, in 1935, numbers up to six digits with no prefix; MIDA rifles used A through N; Beretta rifles were in the A and B blocks only, with weapons not accepted for military use bearing only one through four digits.

While certainly not without its shortcomings, especially when compared to bolt-action rifles that appeared subsequently, or even more unjustly, when compared to semi-automatics, the Model 91 (and its derivatives) was a reliable, accurate weapon. Much of the criticism leveled against it is unfounded or undeserved. The Italians like to point out that with respect to its accuracy, in June 1969 in a shoot-off between a Model 91 with a modified front sight and a Parker-Hale rear peep sight against a match grade Beretta manufactured M-1 Garand on a 300 meter range, the same shooter achieved a higher score with the Model 91 than he did with the Garand (491 versus 482). ■

MOSCHETTO MODELLO 1891, CAL. 6.5 MOSCHETTO MODELLO 91/38, CAL. 7.35 MOSCHETTO MODELLO 91/38, CAL. 6.5

This carbine is sometimes referred to in Italian as the *moschetto da cavalleria*, or the *91 cavalleria* (cavalry carbine, or 91 cavalry), and is commonly referred to in English language publications as the cavalry carbine, but strictly speaking those designations are incorrect: the official designation of the carbine was simply the *moschetto modello 1891* (Model 1891 carbine). The carbine was issued not only to cavalry units, but to *bersaglieri* cyclist troops, *Carabinieri*, artillery, engineers, the M.V.S.N. (*Milizia Volontaria per la Sicurezza Nazionale* – National Security Volunteer Militia) and to Libyan paratrooper units. Three basic versions of this weapon were produced, although within these versions there were a number of variants.

The earliest version, whose adoption on 9 June 1893 was ratified 15 July 1893, utilized the principal components of the Model 1891 rifle, but differed in its shortened barrel, extremely abbreviated stock, modified rear sight, and turned down bolt handle. A distinctive feature of the carbine was a permanently attached triangular spike bayonet that folded back under the barrel when not in use. A number of different locking systems for the bayonet were used on successive versions, the earliest type being a spring-loaded latch on the bayonet itself, a second type with a two-position locking lever on the bayonet support, and a final version with a locking button. The very first models of the carbine had a transversal stock bolt forward of the clip housing similar to those found on Mauser weapons, but this was soon dispensed with. Early models also lacked the handguard, but by 1916 field experience led to the addition of a handguard in order to avoid causing burns to the hands of soldiers who grasped the barrel that became hot after firing. The addition of the handguard required a slightly redesigned front band that had a lip on the rear of its upper surface that held the forward edge of the handguard in place. In keeping with the intended use by cavalry troopers, the sling was side mounted rather than bottom-mounted as on the Model 1891 rifle; there was a sling bar on the left side of the front band, and a sling well with a sling bar secured by two screws on the left side of the buttstock. A two-piece cleaning rod was carried in a butt trap. The rear sight was similar to that on the *fucile modello 1891* except that the sight ramps were graduated from 450 to 1500 meters rather than up to 2000 meters; with the sight assembly flipped forward the combat sight was set for 300 meters as it was on the rifle.

A mountain artillery gunner next to a mountain howitzer; a moschetto mod. 91 with its bayonet extended is slung over his shoulder. (*Pignato collection*)

MOSCHETTO MODELLO 1891; MOSCHETTO MODELLO 91/38

Designer: Modification of the 1891 rifle designed by Salvatore Carcano
Manufacturers: Fabbrica d'Armi Brescia (1893-1919); F.N.A. Brescia (1932-1944); Fabbrica d'Armi Terni (1935-1938); Fabbrica d'Armi Pietro Beretta (1935-1943); SFARE Gardone Val Trompia (1935-1943)
Caliber: 6.5mm or 7.35mm
Cartridge: 6.5x52mm Mannlicher-Carcano; 7.35x51mm
Overall length: 919mm (36.2") with bayonet folded; 1263mm (49.7") with bayonet extended
Barrel length: 451mm (17.8")
Rifling: RH gain twist, 390mm at breech and 190mm at muzzle (6.5mm versions); 240mm constant for 7.35mm version; 215mm constant for 6.5mm Model 38
Weight: 3.16 kg (6.95 lbs) with walnut stock; 3.32 kg (7.3 lbs) with beechwood stock
Front sight: Barleycorn
Rear sight: Quadrant with V notch, or fixed notch, depending on version
Muzzle velocity: 661 m/sec (2169 fps) 6.5mm; 740 m/sec (2428 fps) 7.35mm
Feed system: 6 round integral box using six-round Mannlicher-Carcano clips

The *moschetto modello 91/38, cal. 7.35* differed from the earlier model, apart from its caliber, in that it had constant rather than gain twist rifling, and its rear sight was a simple fixed notch type set for 200 meters. The exterior of the barrel corresponding to the chamber was also conical rather than pentafaceted. All new production carbines in 7.35mm were fitted with the late type bayonet catch with the locking button. Some 6.5mm carbines were rebored to 7.35mm and fitted with the fixed rear sight, but the

« A rare specimen of a Model 1891 carbine with Napoleone e Vittorio Castelli (NVC - B) markings; the serial number on this carbine suggests that it was from the block assigned to the Brescia Arsenal in 1916. (*Courtesy Steve Woodrum*)

The model 1891 cavalry carbine was a drastically shortened version of the Model 1891 rifle, had a turned down bolt handle and adjustable rear sights, later replaced by a fixed rear sight. It still serves with Carabinieri units in a ceremonial role. (*Editoriale Olimpia*)

» The 6.5mm caliber marking on the fixed rear sight of a Gardone 91/38 cavalry carbine. This 6.5mm fixed rear sight continued the practice that began with adoption of the fixed rear sight for 7.35mm weapons. (*Author's collection*)

» Left side view of the cavalry carbine showing side-mounted sling attachments. The cavalry carbine was never issued with bottom mounted sling swivels. (*Author's collection*)

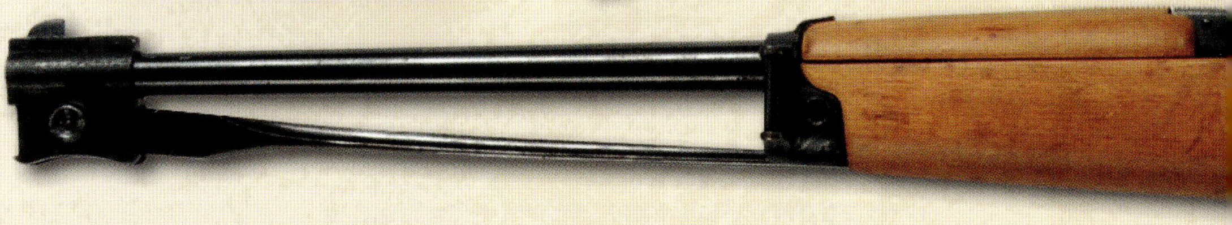

« The markings on this 6.5mm moschetto 91/38 manufactured by Gardone depart from the norm, as the year of manufacture and manufacturer's designation are omitted from the normal barrel markings and only the serial number is shown. Gardone manufactured the majority of 6.5mm Model 91/38 carbines during World War II, producing well over one million between 1940 and 1943. (*Author's collection*)

The 6.5mm Model 91/38 carbines produced by F.N.A. Brescia reverted to the old style adjustable rear sight rather than retaining the fixed sight that had been introduced on the 7.35mm Model 91/38; essentially they were configured like the pre-7.35mm Model 91 carbines. (*Author's collection*)

The year of manufacture on the Gardone carbine is marked on the underside of the receiver ring. Curiously, the year shown is 1941 even though the serial number of this weapon indicates that it was manufactured in 1943. (*Author's collection*)

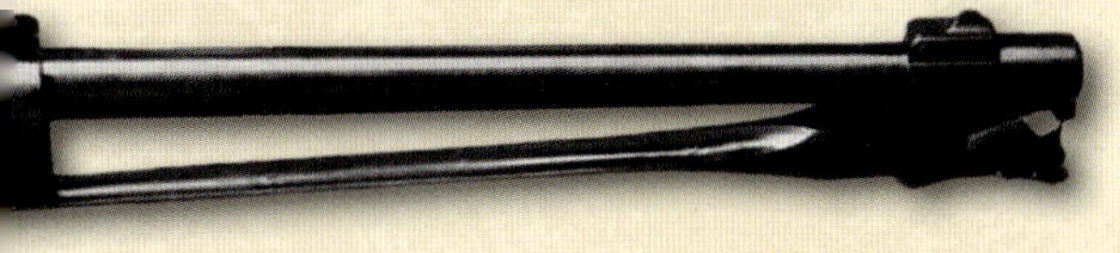

The definitive type push-button lock and release mechanism for the folding bayonet. (*Author's collection*)

A Model 91/38 cavalry carbine with its graceful triangular bayonet extended. (*Author's collection*)

With the short lived introduction of the 7.35mm cartridge the Model 1891 cavalry carbines chambered in that caliber were fitted with fixed sights; the fixed sights were retained on the 6.5mm Model 91/38 carbines that replaced the 7.35mm version. (*Author's collection*)

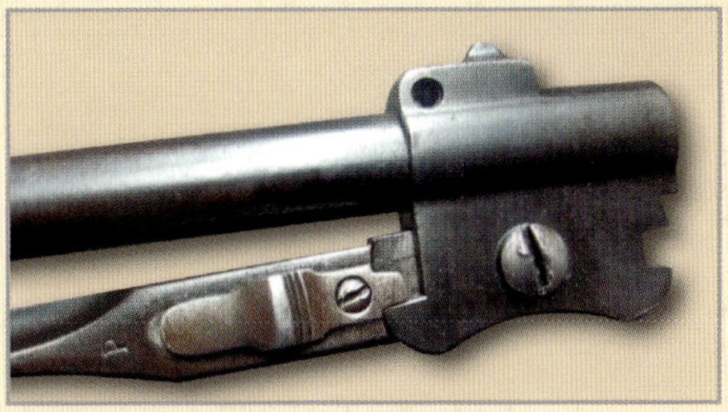

The early type double lever bayonet latch on a 1905 Brescia cavalry carbine. (*Courtesy Larry Eisel, Eisel Armory*)

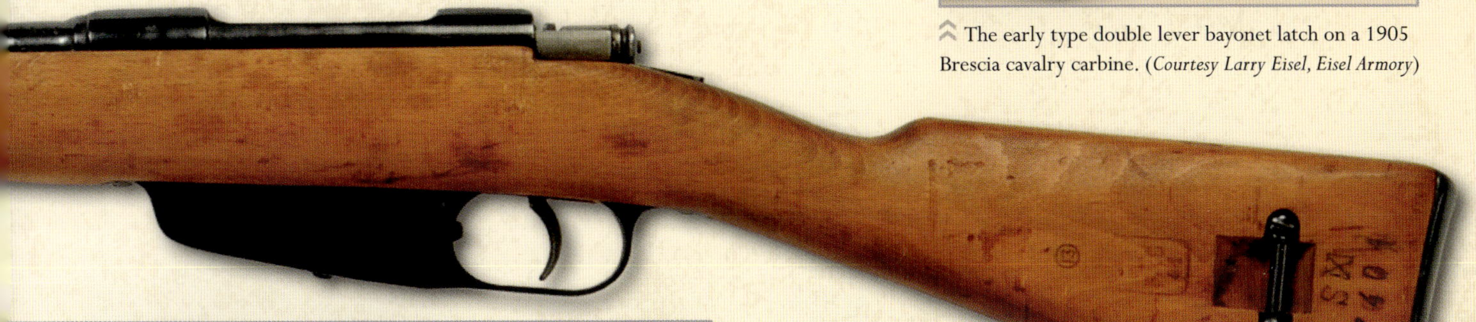

F.N.A. reverted to the old style adjustable rear sight on the 6.5mm Model 91/38 cavalry carbine, while other manufacturers retained the fixed rear sight that had been introduced on the 7.35mm weapons. (*Author's collection*).

A moschetto mod. 91 cavalry carbine with the distinctive permanently attached folding triangular bayonet with a sliding lock, recognizable as an early version as it lacks the upper hand guard added on later models. (*Alberto Simonelli and Giovanni Chegia*)

bayonet catch may be one of the earlier types.

When it was decided to standardize production on 6.5mm weapons, production of the *moschetto modello 91/38* again resumed in 6.5mm; the fixed rear sight was retained, except for the carbines produced by F.N.A. Brescia which reverted to the quadrant sight graduated from 300 to 1500 meters; the fixed sight used by other producers was set for 300 meters. The barrel had 215mm constant twist rifling. Of all of the small arms produced during the war years, the 6.5mm 91/38 carbine was produced in larger numbers than any other weapon, to the tune of about 1,618,000 copies between 1940 and 1943, and was widely distributed to all types of troops. Shortly after the end of World War I the army hierarchy had come to realize that the length of the Model 1891 rifle was excessive for current and developing requirements, and that even though ballistic performance was not equal to that of the full length rifle the carbine was otherwise light, extremely easy to carry and handle, reliable and effective. The decision to focus the bulk of production effort on this carbine between 1940 and 1944 also may have been influenced by cost and raw material availability considerations; with its short barrel, compared to other weapons in the Carcano family this weapon required the least amount of steel to produce (the integral folding bayonet eliminated the need for a separate costlier bayonet and scabbard as well), and the abbreviated stock likewise required considerably less wood than a more conventional length stock.

One seldom encountered version of the *moschetto modello 1891* was the *moschetto 1891 per moschettieri del Duce* (Model 1891 carbine for the Duce's musketeers). This variant was produced and issued exclusively to a somewhat *ad hoc* honor guard for Mussolini that assembled only for ceremonial occasions. An estimated 200 examples were made in 1935; the entire lot may have been produced by the SFARE Gardone Val Trompia. The weapon was a standard *moschetto modello 1891* with some distinguishing features: the bolt, trigger, magazine housing, front barrel band, buttplate and rear sling swivel were nickel plated, the receiver chamber had the Fascist lictor symbol and the word DUX stamped on it and filled with silver wire, and the stock was stained or painted black. The remaining metal parts were in what appears to be a standard finish.

In 1939 Beretta produced a series of specially engraved Model 91 carbines for Amedeo II of Savoy (the Duke of Aosta), serially numbered from C8000 to C8100. The receivers on all of the carbines were engraved and gold plated, triggers were gold plated. Magazine housings were also engraved and finished in a highly polished blue. The stocks were select walnut and bore the Duke of Aosta's monogram and crest inlaid in silver near the butt, and some stocks bore additional silver inlays on the sides. It is not clear if some of these carbines were used by the Duke's personal bodyguard and others were intended to be given as gifts. Amedeo was Viceroy of Ethiopia and led the Italian defense against the British in 1941, most famously at Amba Alagi. Following the Italian capitulation many of these engraved carbines were seized by the British forces, and of those some eventually found their way to museums or private collections in England and South Africa. Only about 40 are estimated to have survived, of which only four or five are in Italy.

Manufacturer's markings varied according to the period of production and the weapon variant. The Terni-produced *moschetto 1891* bore the inscription TERNI; all *modello 38* versions had the royal crown surmounting the letters RE over TERNI in a concave arrangement. F.N.A. Brescia carbines were marked with F.N.A.-BRESCIA over a crown-surmounted RE, or without the crown/RE, or marked F.N.A. followed by a crowned RE followed by BRESCIA. Gardone Val Trompia 6.5mm carbines bore the inscription GARDONE over V.T and a crowned RE; Model 38 carbines in 7.35mm and 6.5mm were marked GARDONE V.T. on one line. Beretta carbines in 6.5mm were marked BERETTA over GARDONE, with a crowned RE at a right angle under GARDONE; the Model 91/38 carbines in 7.35mm and 6.5mm were marked BERETTA over GARDONE.

The serial number convention varied from model to model. The original 6.5mm models manufactured between 1893 and 1938 normally had a one or two letter prefix followed by a one to four digit number; many blocks were duplicated by the various manufacturers. Brescia Arsenal number blocks ran from A through Z, and from AA through AD; Terni Arsenal blocks ran from A through at least Q, and then switched to 1A through 1G; SFARE Gardone number blocks were A through Q; F.N.A. Brescia blocks were A through G; Beretta blocks were A through F. Similarly, blocks were repeated for the 7.35mm Model 38 version of the carbine: SFARE Gardone blocks were A through H; Terni blocks were A through D and P through S; Beretta used blocks A through G; F.N.A. used only the H block. Finally, when production of the Model 91/38 carbine reverted to 6.5mm, a new convention was adopted, generally using a two letter prefix: SFARE Gardone used blocks R through Z, and QA through QZ, RA through RZ, SA through SZ, and TA through TX; F.N.A. Brescia used XF through XZ and YA through YQ; Beretta used UF through UZ.

Although no longer a standard issue weapon, the *moschetto modello 91* is still used by the *Carabinieri* for ceremonial occasions and parades when the vintage *Carabinieri* uniform is worn.

Although arguably not as elegant, the *moschetto 1891* compares closely to the Mauser designed Swedish M1894 carbine. The M1894 is also a 6.5mm weapon (6x55mm) with a 449mm long barrel, only slightly longer with an overall length of 950mm, and somewhat heavier at 3.4 kg. ■

» A bersagliere on watch at an Italian position in front of Sollum, armed with a Model 91 cavalry carbine with bayonet extended. Behind him is another soldier armed, interestingly, with a captured British Enfield. (*Istituto Nazionle per le relazioni culturali con l'estero 2584*)

MOSCHETTO MODELLO 1891 PER TRUPPE SPECIALI; MOSCHETTO MODELLO 1891 PER TRUPPE SPECIALI MODIFICATO; MOSCHETTO MODELLO 91/28 PER TRUPPE SPECIALI; MOSCHETTO MODELLO 91/38 PER TRUPPE SPECIALI, CAL. 7.35; MOSCHETTO MODELLO 91/38 PER TRUPPE SPECIALI, CAL. 6.5

Although production of the *moschetto modello 1891 per truppe speciali* (Model 1891 carbine for special troops) began in 1898, it was not officially adopted for service until 6 January 1900. Aside from its official designation, the carbine was referred to as the *modello 91 TS* or the *moschetto TS*. The bolt, receiver, and barrel were identical to those of the *moschetto modello 1891* (the Model 91 cavalry carbine). As with the cavalry carbine a number of basic versions existed, with minor variations encountered within the separate versions.

The moschetto TS issued to troops during the large-scale Italian Army maneuvers held in Sicily in 1938. (*L'Illustrazione Italiana, 1938, via Andrea and Antonio Tallillo*)

The term "special troops" in the designation of the TS carbine essentially referred to all troops such as artillery, engineers, alpine supply units (mule handlers), etc. who were not issued either the Model 1891 rifle or the *moschetto 1891*; it did not imply any type of elite unit as an English reader might suspect or assume. TS carbines were also issued to the *Regia Marina*, the *San Marco* Naval Infantry Battalion, the Forestry Militia, and the MVSN (*Milizia Volontaria per la Sicurezza Nazionale*).

The chief differences between the *modello 91 TS* and the Model 91 rifle were that the barrel, stock, and cleaning rod were shortened, the bolt handle was turned down, and the rear sight was the same as that of the *moschetto modello 1891* carbine; the front sight was the same type as on the early Model 1891 rifles consisting of an integral sight base with a dovetailed sight blade, but the extended front sight base also acted as a stop for the bayonet ring. The buttplate, although similar in configuration to that of the cavalry carbine, did not have the butt trap for the segmented cleaning rod, as the *moschetto per TS* had a one-piece cleaning rod under the barrel. Over the span of its production history, a number of variants were produced. The first version of the TS carbine had a transversal stock bolt that went completely through the stock and had exposed ends. Possibly as early as 1898 the full length stock bolt was eliminated and replaced by an internal stock lug; this modification was retrofitted to existing carbines, which meant that new stocks had to be fitted. In January 1913, along with all other Model 91 rifles and derivatives, a new bolt with a repositioned extractor was introduced on newly manufactured TS carbines. In 1916 the original type of front band was replaced by a new band that had a modified configuration to retain the handguard. Both types of early bands had a transversal bayonet lug that required a special bayonet that was not compatible with that of the Model 1891 rifle. In 1920 the early front band was replaced by a new front band whose bayonet lug was the same as that used on the Model 1891 rifle, as well as adding the same

DISTINGUISHING FEATURES, MOSCHETTO 91 PER TRUPPE SPECIALI SERIES & MOSCHETTO 91/24

MODEL DISTINCTIVE FEATURES

Moschetto Modello 1891 Per Truppe Speciali carbine style adjustable rear sight; upper band only; transversal bayonet lug; front sight on integral base;bottom-mounted sling swivels.

Moschetto Ts Modificato carbine style adjustable rear sight; upper band and lower band; standard bayonet lug; front sight on integral base; sling swivels could be either bottom mounted, side mounted, or both.

Moschetto 91/28 carbine style adjustable rear sight; upper band and lower band; standard bayonet lug; front sight on ferrule; bottom mounted and side mounted sling swivels or bars.

Moschetto 91/38 Per Truppe Speciali, Cal. 7.35 fixed rear sight; CAL 7.35 stamped on rear sight; upper band and lower band; standard bayonet lug; front sight on ferrule; bottom mounted and side mounted sling bars.

Moschetto 91/38 Per Truppe Speciali, Cal. 6.5 fixed rear sight; CAL 6.5 stamped on rear sight; upper band and lower band; standard bayonet lug; front sight on ferrule; bottom mounted sling swivels and side mounted sling bars.

Moschetto Modello 91/24 rifle-style adjustable rear sight; upper band and lower band; standard bayonet lug; front sight on ferrule; bottom mounted sling swivels and side mounted sling bars ■

The moschetto modello 1891 per truppe speciali (Model 1891 carbine for special troops) was issued largely to artillery and engineer units. Shown with its bayonet is the "first type" with a transversal bayonet lug on the front band. (*Editoriale Olimpia*)

An Italian anti-tank gun crew in action. The ammunition bearer in the foreground has a moschetto TS slung over his back. (*Pignato collection*)

type of second barrel band as used on the Model 1891 rifle, allowing the same bayonet to be used on both types of weapon. This version was known as the *moschetto TS modificato*, or *moschetto TSM*, but was not officially designated as such. During the same general timeframe, or to be more exact, in August 1921, the sling attachment points were altered. The original TS carbines had bottom-mounted sling swivels under the rear portion of the buttstock and under the front band. However, as early as 1907 there were many complaints from artillery troops that carrying the carbine in the slung position led to injuries to the back caused by the magazine housing and requested that arrangements be made for side-mounted sling attachment points like those on the cavalry carbine. In a typical bureaucratic response to the request the highest staff echelons told the artillerymen to stack their arms close to the guns they were serving with the inference, although not stated, to quit their griping. However, it would seem that the gunners, undeterred by the official rebuff and still unhappy with bruised backs, continued to offer their "suggestions," and in 1921 the side mounts were authorized, but only for carbines issued to artillery troops; when fitting the side mounts, the bottom mounts were to be removed. In 1929 the modification was extended to all TS carbines that had the second barrel band. There were still other variations on the sling mount theme, as non-artillery TS carbines without the rear band were also authorized to be fitted with the modification that had been authorized in 1921, but still retaining the bottom-mounted sling swivels.

Between 1898 and 1919, the only arsenal that produced the *moschetto per truppe speciali* was the Brescia Arsenal; official production ceased completely at the end of 1919. However, in the 1920s requirements began to surface for additional small arms, witnessing introduction of the *moschetto 91/24* (see separate entry), as well as resumption of production by a number of other arsenals and private firms of the *moschetto per truppe speciali* in 1928. The chief difference between the *moschetto 91/28*, as it was unofficially known, and the earlier versions was that the front sight was altered; the early type integral sight base was replaced by a ferrule with a dovetail for the front sight. Production of the 91/28 was continued by some manufacturers until 1938 when the changeover was made to the new 7.35mm round. Between 1938 and 1940 about 51,000 of the 7.35mm version, known as the *moschetto 38 TS calibro 7.35mm*, were produced. The 7.35mm carbines consisted of both remanufactured and newly manufactured weapons; remanufacturing consisted of reboring the barrels to 7.35mm with constant twist rifling, and replacing the quadrant rear sight with a fixed sight set for 200 meters, on which the new caliber (cal. 7.35) was stamped; the caliber was also stamped on the left-hand side of the buttstock. Remanufactured carbines retained both the bottom-mounted and side-mounted sling attachments, but newly manufactured carbines (with

» Comparison of the front bands mounted on the early type Model 91 TS carbine and a TS modificato. (*Author's collection*)

« Detail of the early front band, seen from the bottom. A very shallow ridge on the inside of the bayonet lug yoke mated with the slot cut in the front band, providing a modicum of strength for the whole assembly. (*Author's collection*)

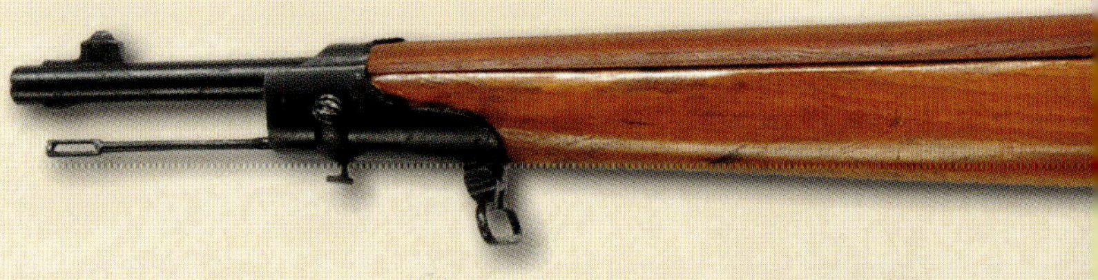

« Detail of the early type TS front band with the transversal bayonet lug. Also note the extended front sight base and the small lug below that acted as a stop for the bayonet ring. (*Author's collection*)

The first type Model 91 TS carbine with its distinctive single front band and transversal bayonet lug. (*Author's collection*)

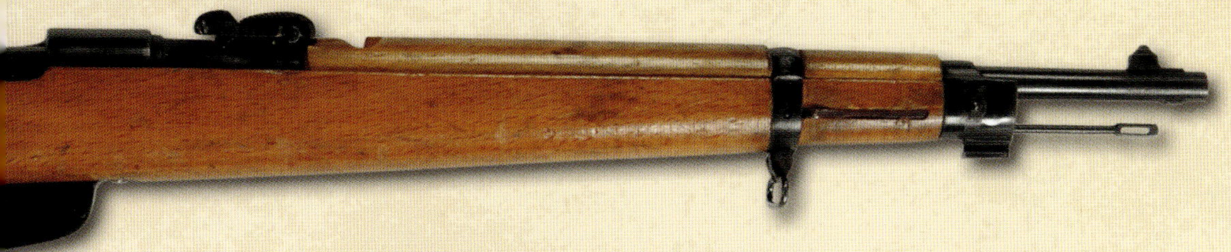

A moschetto TS modificato, with the modified front band with standard bayonet lug that replaced the early transversal lug. (*Author's collection*)

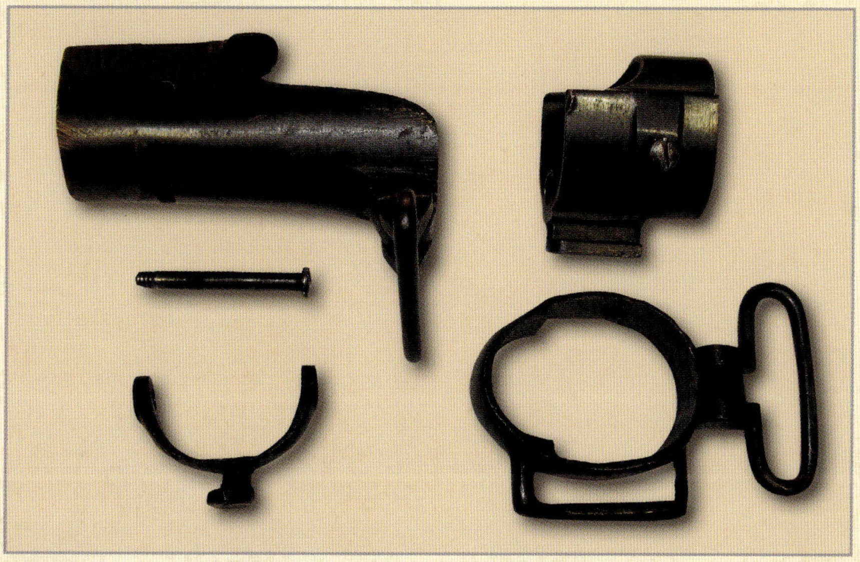

The front band on the early moschetto TS, to the left in the photograph, consisted of a nose cap with attached sling swivel, and a separate yoke with the bayonet lug; the yoke fit over the front band and was secured by a single screw. To the right are the front band and rear band of the moschetto TS modificato (the TSM); the front band incorporated the bayonet lug, and the rear band had a side mounted sling bar and a bottom mounted sling swivel. (*Author's collection*)

This left side view of the early Model 91 TS carbine illustrates the lack of side-mounted sling attachment points, which led to persistent demands by users for a side-mounted version. (*Author's collection*)

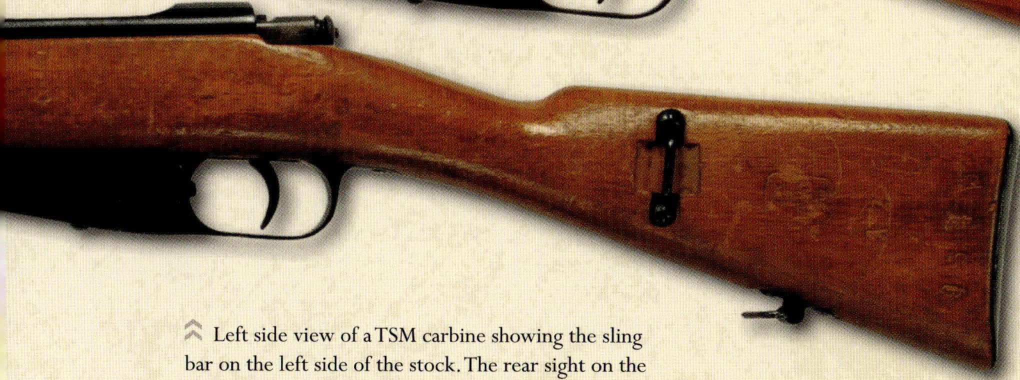

Left side view of a TSM carbine showing the sling bar on the left side of the stock. The rear sight on the TS and TSM carbines was similar to that used on the cavalry carbine. (*Author's collection*)

A 6.5mm Model 91/28 TS carbine manufactured by Terni in 1929. The front sight was mounted on a ferrule rather than on an integral sight base on the barrel. (*Author's collection*)

The rarest of the 91/28 carbines were those produced by Metallurgica Bresciana già Tempini, or MBT. Less than 4,000 were produced and are rarely encountered. (*Courtesy Steve Woodrum*)

The sight on the TS carbine was similar to that on the cavalry carbine and was graduated from 600 to 1400 meters. (*Author's collection*)

Model 91/28 carbines were fitted with bottom mounted sling swivels as well as with side mounted slide bars. (*Author's collection*)

The rear sight leaf on this Model 91/28 TS carbine supplied to Bavaria after World War II was removed and the rear sight notch was altered as shown. (*Author's collection*)

Pietro Lorenzotti Model 91/28 carbines, produced in 1930 and 1931, bore serial numbers with a PL prefix. Lorenzotti produced only slightly more than 10,000 carbines before being succeeded by Fabbrica Nazionale d'Armi, Brescia; the scarce Lorenzotti marked carbines are sought after by collectors. (*Courtesy Steve Woodrum*)

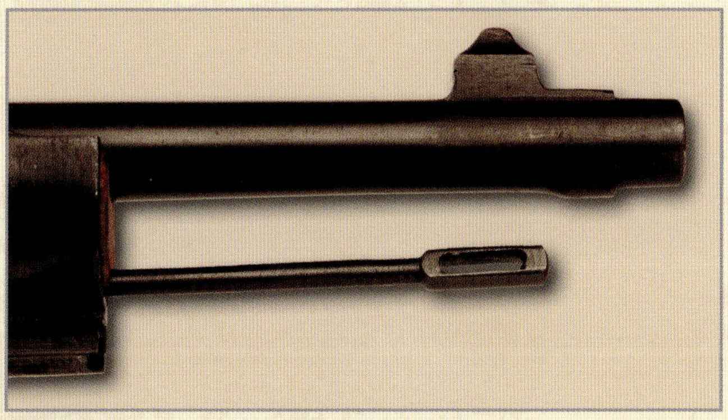

Detail of the front sight on a moschetto TS modificato; the sight was mounted on a sight base on the barrel rather than on a ferrule. (*Author's collection*)

The sling bar on this Terni 91/28 carbine refurbished in 1938 at Gardone is the type approved in July 1929 for use on the moschetto TS and had no ferrule. The sling bar was recycled and used when the carbine was refurbished and fitted with a new stock. (*Author's collection*)

The quadrant rear sight on a TS carbine shown in its normal position. When folded forward to rest in the recess in the hand guard the battle sight was set for 300 meters. (*Author's collection*)

The moschetto modello 91/38 per truppe speciali chambered for the 7.35mm round was recognizable by its fixed rear sight, but otherwise was a TS modello 91/28. (*Author's collection*)

New production Model 91/38 TS carbines in 7.35mm such as this one were fitted with bottom-mounted slings only, but Model 91/28 carbines that were converted to 7.35mm retained the side mounted sling provisions. (*Author's collection*)

A

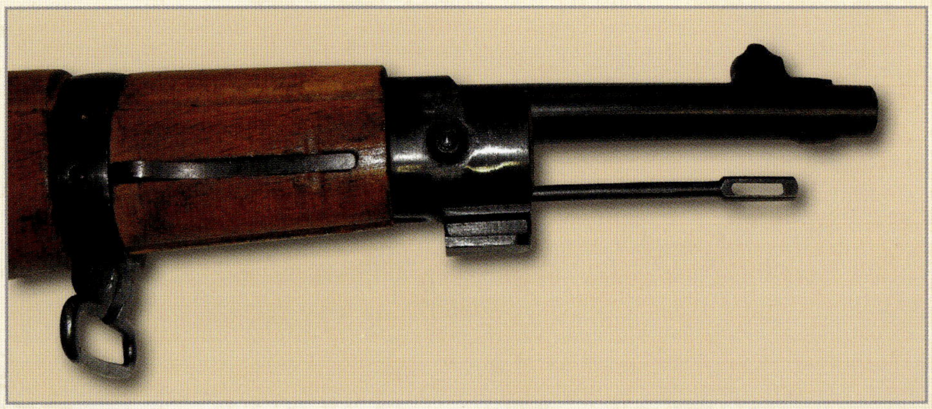

B

REGIA MARINA SMALL ARMS

In addition to the serial number and the CAL 7.35 marking on the stock of this Model 91/38 TS carbine, the small stamp with the shield in the circle indicates Italian Navy issue. (*Author's collection*)

F.N.A. Brescia Model 91/38 TS carbine issued to the Regia Marina. The Navy marking consisting of a shield divided into four quadrants, although incompletely struck, is visible below the serial number. (*Author's collection*)

All ships of the *Regia Marina* carried individual small arms and infantry support weapons, with adequate ammunition, to arm part of the crews and, on larger ships, to arm the "landing company." The *Littorio* class battleships carried the largest small arms inventory. Each battleship was equipped with one or two 13.2mm Breda Model 1931 heavy machine guns on a swivel mount for the boats; six 8mm Breda Model 1937 machine guns that could be mounted either on a standard tripod for use on land or on a simple swivel mount to defend against raiding parties while at anchor; ten to twelve 6.5mm Breda Model 1930 light machine guns; 360 6.5mm Mod. 91 TS carbines and bayonets (with 135,000 rounds of ammunition), and 100 to 150 7.65mm Beretta Model 1915 and 1919 semi-automatic pistols (with 19,800 rounds), as well as more than 2,000 hand grenades. The *Regia Marina* also maintained a naval infantry regiment, the *San Marco*, which was organized, armed and equipped much like a *Regio Esercito* infantry regiment.

» The rear sight is marked 7.35mm on this Model 91/38 TS carbine manufactured by F.N.A. Brescia in 1940. (*Author's collection*)

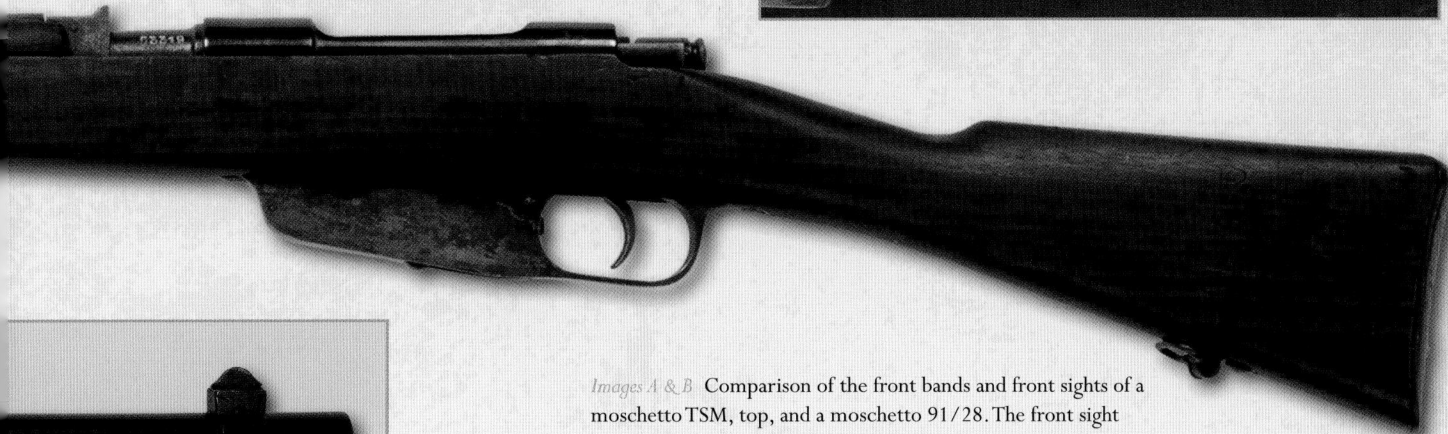

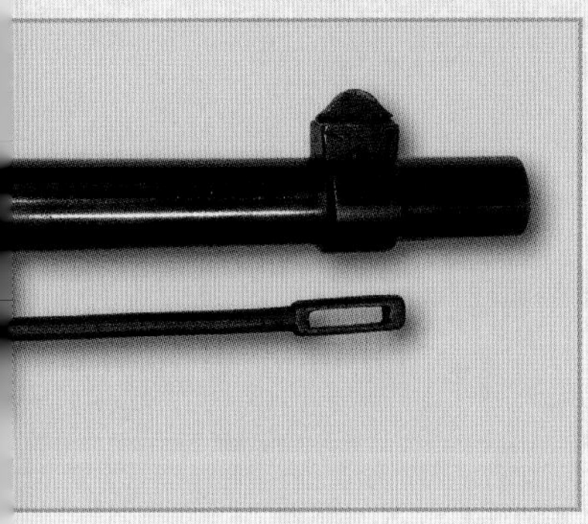

Images A & B Comparison of the front bands and front sights of a moschetto TSM, top, and a moschetto 91/28. The front sight mounted on a sight base on the barrel was replaced by a front sight mounted on a ferrule, and on this particular carbine which was refurbished in 1938 the standard front band was replaced with a recycled front band from a tromboncino mod. 1923 grenade launcher; the tromboncino band has a characteristic rear-facing lip to secure the handguard. (*Author's collection*)

the fixed rear sight) came off the production line with bottom-mounted sling swivels. In 1940, because of the entry into the war, production of the carbine in 7.35mm was suspended and carbines produced between 1940 and 1943 reverted to 6.5mm. The fixed rear sight was retained on the 6.5mm carbines, which had the caliber (cal. 6.5) stamped on the sight, except for late production F.N.A. carbines which had no caliber indicated on the sight. New barrels were constant twist and the fixed notch rear sight was set for 300 meters; production of the *moschetto TS* in 6.5mm was limited to Beretta and F.N.A. Brescia, who between them produced about 198,000 examples.

An interesting sidelight concerning the 91/28 is that after WW II an unknown number, along with 91/24 carbines, were supplied to Bavaria for use by police forces. These carbines may be encountered with markings of BAVARIAN POLICE, BAVARIA POLICE, BAVARIA RURAL POLICE or BAVARIA RURAL POLICE CIV. GUARD (written in English) on either the receiver or on the magazine housing. At least some of the Bavarian carbines were arsenal refinished, to include having their bolts blued. The adjustable rear sight leaf on the Bavarian 91/28 carbines was removed and the rear notch was slightly altered to provide a simple fixed rear sight. Presumably these were supplemented or supplanted by the M1 carbines supplied to the Bavarian border police by the United States.

MODELLO 1891 SPECIALI MODIFICATO 91/28, 91/38, CAL. 7.35, CAL. 6.5

Designer: Modification of Model 1891 rifle designed by Salvatore Carcano
Manufacturers: Fabbrica d'Armi Brescia; F.N.A. Brescia; SFARE Gardone; Metallurgica Bresciana Tempini; Fabbrica d'Armi Terni; Fabbrica d'Armi Pietro Beretta; Pietro Lorenzotti
Caliber: 6.5mm or 7.35mm
Cartridge: 6.5x52mm Mannlicher-Carcano; 7.35x51mm
Overall length: 919mm (36.2") **Barrel length:** 450mm (17.7")
Rifling: RH gain twist, 390mm at breech and 190mm at muzzle (early 6.5mm version); 240mm constant for 7.35mm Model 38 TS; 215mm constant for 6.5mm Model 38 TS
Weight: 326 kg (7.19 lbs)
Front sight: Barleycorn
Rear sight: Quadrant with V notch adjustable to 1500 meters, or fixed notch
Muzzle velocity: 661 m/sec (2169 fps)
Feed system: 6 round integral box using six-round Mannlicher-Carcano clips

Manufacturer's markings on the early versions followed the standard practice consisting of the serial number, manufacturer's name, location of manufacture, and year of manufacture (in both Arabic and Roman numerals after 1923), all on the barrel chamber. F.N.A. 6.5mm 91/38 TS carbines in the RA serial number block (1943) lacked the year designation on the chamber, did not have the customary Cal 6.5 marking on the fixed rear sight, and also lacked a cartouche on the buttstock which was, however, serially numbered. Carbines issued to the Navy bore a cross within a shield stamped on the chamber and on the bottom flat of the bolt handle.

Serial numbers for the Brescia *moschetto per truppe speciali* ran from the A through Z blocks, and from the AA through BI blocks; Beretta serial numbers for the 91/28 TS ran from the A through I blocks – Beretta also produced the 91/28 for the civilian market with serial numbers up to five digits with no letter prefix; F.N.A. Brescia serial numbers for 91/28 military production ran from the A through G blocks, and for the civilian market were up to four digits without a letter prefix; SFARE Gardone numbers ran from the A trough Q blocks; Terni serial numbers ran from the A through I blocks; Pietro Lorenzotti serial numbers were distinguished by the PL prefix only, and Metallurgica Bresciana Tempini serial numbers all bore an MB prefix. The 7.35mm *moschetto 91/38 TS* bore a separate series of numbers: Beretta and F.N.A. numbers were limited to the A through D blocks, Gardone had a small production run and used only part of the A block, and Terni used A through G. The 6.5mm version of the *moschetto 91/38 TS* produced by Beretta used blocks A through G, and F.N.A. used the A through E blocks in 1942 and the RA block in 1943. ■

A group of university volunteers on parade in Padova in 1941 armed with 91/28 TS carbines; this particular group later fought at the battle of Bir el Gobi in November 1941. (*Cronache della Guerra, 1940, Tuminelli Editore, via Andrea and Antonio Tallillo*)

MOSCHETTO MODELLO 91/24

Experience gained in World War I led Italian Army authorities to conclude that the Model 1891 rifle was both too long and too heavy for trench warfare and that although the rifle's long barrel made for an accurate weapon at long ranges this capability was rarely used

A mountain artillery crew emplacing a 75/18 mountain howitzer. The gunner in the right foreground has a 91/24 with a side-mounted sling slung across his back. (*Pignato collection*)

in combat due either to lack of proper marksmanship training or to reduced combat engagement ranges. Accordingly, sometime around 1923, based on the desire to increase the number of carbines in the inventory and reduce the number of long rifles, the decision was made to convert a significant number of Model 1891 rifles to a carbine configuration. The conversion consisted of cutting the rifle barrel down to 450mm in length and shortening the stock and handguard. This arrangement was quite satisfactory, as due to the progressive rifling the barrels of the rifles experienced the greatest wear towards the muzzle. Because the diameter of the shortened barrel at the muzzle was greater than that of the original diameter of the rifle barrel at the muzzle and was greater than the muzzle diameter of the TS cabine, the forward portion of the shortened barrel was turned down to 13mm so that the muzzle would allow fixing the standard Model 1891 bayonet; this also necessitated adopting a modified front band to accommodate the larger barrel diameter. The front sight was mounted on a ferrule, as on the *moschetto modello 91/28*. Although closely resembling the *moschetto per truppe speciali* and the Model 91/28 carbine, the *moschetto 91/24* had a modified 1891 rifle rear sight graduated to 1500 instead of 2000 meters; the rear of the sight leaf had a dovetail cut into it to allow a sight picture when the sight was elevated for long distances. The long rear sight quickly distinguished it from the *moschetto modello 91/28*. The rifle thus modified was officially adopted on 29 January 1925 as the *moschetto modello 91/24*. There were a number of sling attachment combinations similar to those of the TS carbine, i.e., initially bottom-mounted, then side-mounted, and finally, beginning in 1930, both bottom and side mounted.

All of the 91/24 carbines were converted solely by the Terni Arsenal between 1924 and 1929 and have an oval marking on the barrel flat that bears the original date with the letters FARE and TERNI, with the last two digits of the year of conversion positioned between them. The original serial numbers of the rifles were retained during the conversion process. DiGiorgio and Pettinelli estimate that about 263,000 Model 1891 rifles were converted to the *moschetto 91/24* configuration.

Specifications for the *modello 91/24* are essentially identical to those of the *moschetto per truppe speciali*. ■

MANUFACTURING STANDARDS

It is interesting to note that during World War II, in contrast to other nations, most notably Germany, the U.S. and Britain, the Italians generally did little to modify or simplify their issue weapons in order to increase production rates; the exception to this general rule was the continuous evolution and simplification of the Beretta Model 38 submachinegun family. By contrast, the Germans went from beautifully machined and finished Kar98k rifles early in the war to the notably simplified *Kriegsmodell* with stamped parts and phosphate finish; similarly the U.S. significantly simplified the Springfield Model 1903 by introducing the Model 1903A3 with its much simpler sight and stamped parts. Other than installing fixed sights on their 7.35mm and later 6.5mm Model 38 series of rifles and carbines and devoting less attention to the exterior finish of Beretta pistols as the war progressed, there was little attempt by the Italians to simplify production of existing types of weapons. The argument could be made that the Carcano family of weapons (as well as the Beretta Model 1934 and 1935 pistols) were such simple weapons to begin with that there was little room for further simplification. Except for the F.N.A. B 43, Italian submachine guns whose designs did not see the drawing boards until the war years generally embodied trend-setting or state of the art technology using ingeniously designed stampings to minimize material usage, production time and cost. Machine guns presented somewhat of a more mixed picture: the Breda Model 30 standard light machine gun was an overly complicated piece of machinery, but the Italians seem not to have put much if any effort into simplifying, improving or replacing it, while the Breda Model 37 medium machine gun was a well designed and fabricated weapon that did not lend itself to further simplification. ■

Images A & B The moschetto 91/28 and moschetto modello 91/24 were quite similar in appearance, differing chiefly in their rear sight configuration. Shown are a moschetto 91/28, top, and a moschetto 91/24, bottom. (*Author's collection*)

A

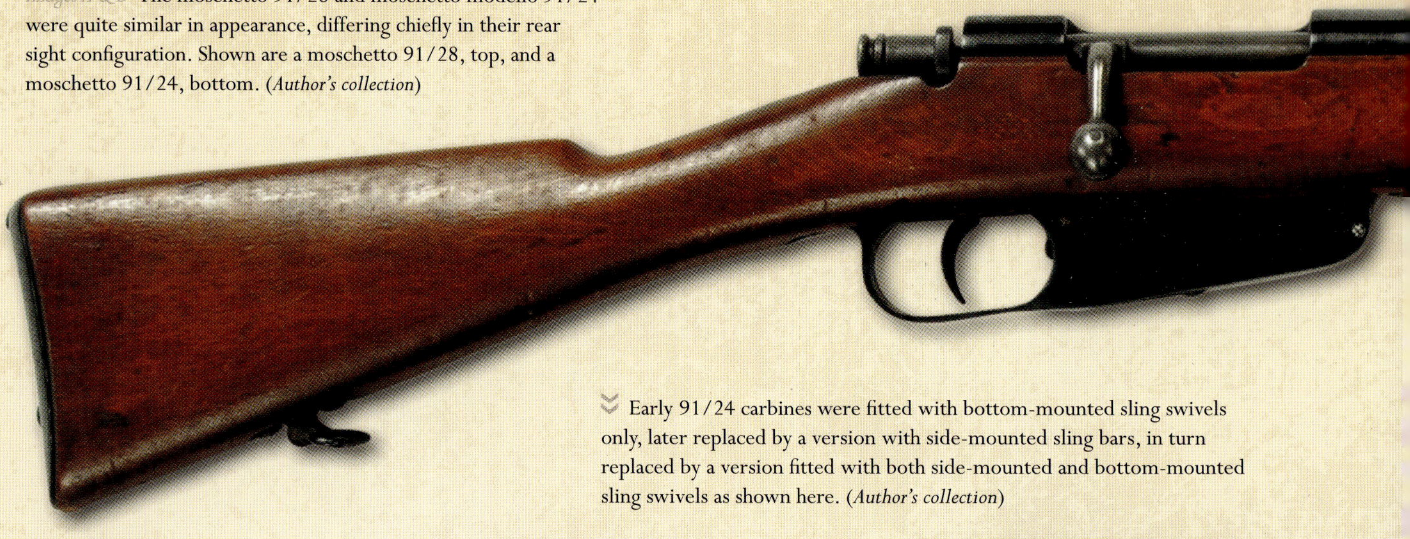

Early 91/24 carbines were fitted with bottom-mounted sling swivels only, later replaced by a version with side-mounted sling bars, in turn replaced by a version fitted with both side-mounted and bottom-mounted sling swivels as shown here. (*Author's collection*)

The front sight of the 91/24 carbine was mounted on a ferrule, which was the prevalent method of mounting front sights on Italian rifles and carbines. (*Author's collection*)

B

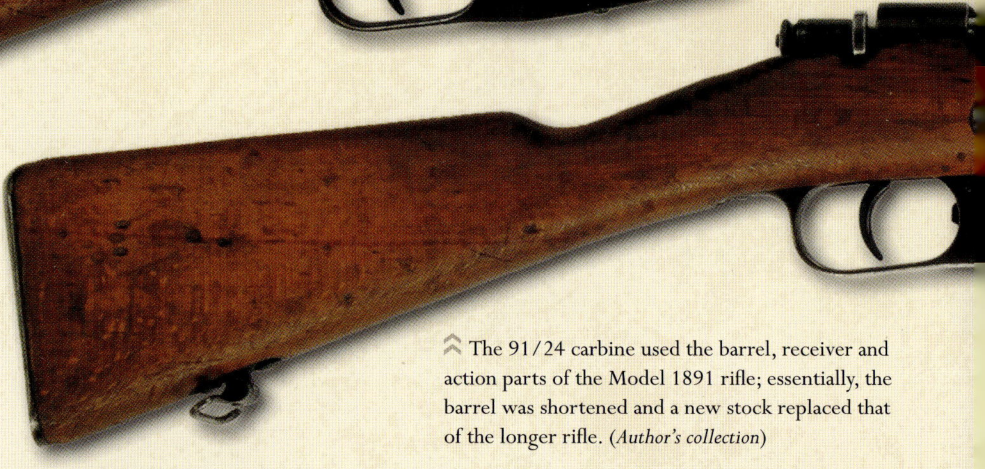

The 91/24 carbine used the barrel, receiver and action parts of the Model 1891 rifle; essentially, the barrel was shortened and a new stock replaced that of the longer rifle. (*Author's collection*)

The marking applied by the Terni Arsenal to Model 1891 rifles that were converted to Model 91/24 carbines; the year of conversion was indicated by the last two digits of the year. (*Author's collection*)

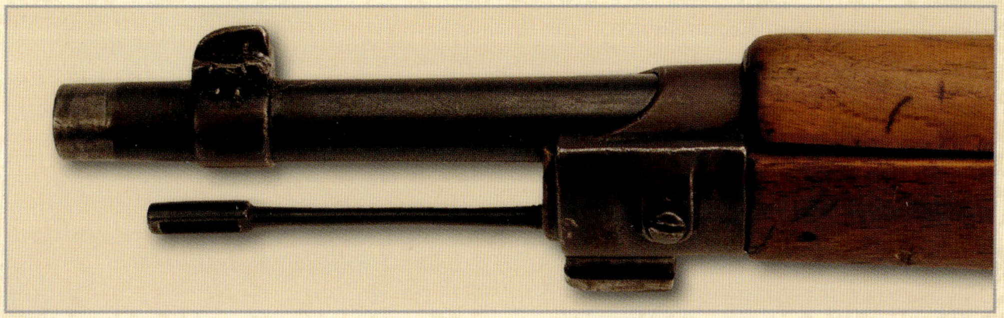

» The front band on the moschetto modello 91/24 accepted the standard bayonet used on the Model 91 rifle and had sights similar to that on the rifle. (*Author's collection*)

» Although rear sight of the 91/24 carbine closely resembled that of the Model 1891 rifle it was graduated only to 1500 meters rather than to 2000 meters as on the rifle. (*Author's collection*)

MOSCHETTO MODELLO 18/30

The Model 1918/30 carbine, based on the Beretta Model 1918 submachine gun, looked somewhat like a Model 1891 cavalry carbine because of its folding bayonet. The cocking ring at the rear of the receiver led to its Italian nickname of "the syringe." (*Beretta*)

The Model 1918/30 with the folding cavalry style bayonet extended. (*Beretta*)

In 1930 Beretta introduced a carbine based on its Model 1918 submachine gun, also chambered for the 9mm Glisenti cartridge. This carbine, designated the *modello 18/30*, is commonly referred to in Italian as *il siringone* (the syringe), as the cocking ring at the rear of the receiver resembles the plunger on a syringe. Although in many respects bearing a marked resemblance to the Model 1918 submachine gun, it nevertheless was a completely different weapon. The magazine was bottom mounted rather than top mounted, offering the most readily apparent difference between the two weapons. Cocking mechanisms were different, as were the rear sights. The weapon fired from a closed bolt. A standard feature of the 18/30 was the folding cavalry-type bayonet. This carbine was standard issue during World War II to some paramilitary units (the Forestry Service, in particular, which still uses it for ceremonial purposes); a number of the carbines were sold to the Argentine police, presumably sometime in the 1930s.

Tenuous information indicates that fifty of these carbines were imported into the United States from Argentina in 1994 and sold to collectors. Markings on the ex-Argentine carbines were PIETRO BERETTA – GARDONE VAL TROMPIA – ITALIA – CAL 9 on the top of the barrel), POLICIA DE LA PROVINCIA DE BUENOS AIRES on the side of the barrel, and BREVETTATO on the rear of the receiver, just forward of the end cap and cocking ring. ■

MOSCHETTO MODELLO 18/30

Designer: Tullio Marengoni
Manufacturer: Fabbrica d'Armi Pietro Beretta
Caliber: 9mm Glisenti
Cartridge: 9x19mm Glisenti
Operating system: Blowback
Overall length: 950mm (37.4") with bayonet folded; 1190mm (46.9") with bayonet extended
Barrel length: 375mm (14.8")
Weight: 3.13 kg (6.9 lbs)
Front sight: Barleycorn
Rear sight: Tangent graduated to 600 meters
Safety: Safety under trigger guard blocks trigger
Muzzle velocity: 381 m/sec (1250 fps)?
Feed system: 25 round magazine

FUCILE MODELLO 91/38, CAL. 7.35; FUCILE MODELLO 91/38, CAL. 6.5

In the 1920s, the Italians began experimenting with a larger caliber round to replace the 6.5x52mm service round, and by 1935 Colonel Giuseppe Mainardi, in conjunction with private Italian ammunition manufacturing firms, had developed the 7.35x51mm round. In 1935, Major Roberto Boragine, an artillery officer at the time most likely assigned to the Direzione Superiore del Servizio Tecnico di Armi e Munizioni (D.S.S.T.A.M. – the army's

An 81mm mortar team equipped with the Model 38 short rifle, likely the 6.5mm version. (*SME via Andrea and Antonio Tallillo*)

Technical Service which oversaw weapons development) was tasked with developing a new rifle using as much as possible of what was already available, i.e., based on the existing Carcano technology. In today's parlance Boragine would be termed the project manager responsible for development of a replacement rifle chambered for the new round. Some initial testing was done simply using a standard Model 1891 rifle that had been rebored and rechambered for the 7.35mm round, but the long barrel did not yield encouraging results. Further testing and experimentation led to adoption of a considerably shorter barrel, resulting in the *fucile modello 91/38*, derived directly from the Model 1891 despite being hailed as a "new rifle" at the time of its introduction in 1938. The rifle is described in Italian as a *fucile corto* (short rifle) rather than as a *moschetto* (carbine); this unique terminology may have been adopted because, although according to Italian classification conventions the weapon would be classified as a *carabina* (a weapon whose overall length was between 951 and 1060mm), in practice this term was rarely if ever used. Italian long arms fell either into the *fucile* (rifle) category (1061mm or longer) or the *moschetto* category (what in English is considered a carbine, and in Italian refers to long arms less than 950mm in length); for whatever the reason, the Italians coined the phrase *fucile corto* to describe the new weapon. Aside from the obvious differences in caliber, length and weight, the chief differences between it and the Model 91 were that its rear sight was an open notch type set for 200 meters, twist was constant, the stock had finger grooves on each side, the sling was side-mounted, and the bolt handle was turned down. Perhaps an easy comparison for English readers would be to compare the *fucile corto modello 91/38* to the German Mauser *Karabiner 98k* (the k standing for *kurz*, or short), which was a modernized version – shortened barrel, turned down bolt handle, new rear sight, and new stock with side-mounted sling – of the World War I *Gewehr 98*. Whether or not Boragine was aware of development of the Kar98k, which made its debut in 1934, has not been reported, and if he was aware of its development, to what extent it may have influenced his own efforts is open to conjecture. However, very much like the Kar98k, the principal components of the Model 38, namely the receiver, bolt, trigger mechanism and magazine, were identical to those of the World War I rifle it was to replace. Either by accident or by design the Italians followed the same path as did the Germans by using dated but proven techology for their follow-on generation rifle, although it should also be noted that the Italians, unlike the Germans who did not begin seriously developing a semi-automatic rifle until 1940, also had planned to introduce a semi-automatic rifle, the Revelli Model 39, to serve along with the Model 38.

Although there has been some oblique reference to the rear sight being fixed for such a short distance as a concession to the lack of marksmanship

FUCILE MODELLO 91/38

Designer: Modification of Model 1891 rifle designed by Salvatore Carcano; the officer charged with and responsible for development was Major Roberto Boragine of the Italian Artillery Corps.
Manufacturers: Fabbrica d'Armi Terni; SFARE Gardone Val Trompia; F.N.A. Brescia; Fabbrica d'Armi Pietro Beretta
Caliber: 6.5mm or 7.35mm
Cartridge: 6.5x52mm Mannlicher-Carcano; 7.35x51mm
Overall length: 1020mm (40.2")
Barrel length: 536mm (21.1")
Rifling: RH constant twist, 240mm (7.35mm); 215mm (6.5mm)
Weight: 3.675 kg (8.1 lbs)
Front sight: Barleycorn
Rear sight: Fixed V notch; 200 meters for 7.35mm, 300 meters for 6.5mm
Muzzle velocity: 760 m/sec (2493 fps) 7.35mm; 680 m/sec (2230 fps) 6.5mm
Feed system: 6 round integral box using six-round Mannlicher-Carcano clips

ability of Italian recruits, in fact, adoption of the fixed sight in lieu of an adjustable sight reflected the Italian Army's assessment, which was groundbreaking at the time and which proved to be remarkably prescient, that average combat distances were in the 200-300 meter range and that under combat conditions, especially at relatively close ranges, most soldiers were not concerned with making range adjustments to the sights.

Early production models of the Model 38 were characterized by a handguard that extended forward as far as the front band that incorporated the front sling swivel. Only about 30,000 of the first type Model 38 were produced, mostly by the Terni Arsenal in 1938, with serial numbers in the A through C blocks; it is believed that beginning with the D block, production of the second, or definitive, version began. At least part of Beretta production in 1939 consisted of the early version. The handguard on the second version was shortened and a new front band was fitted. A lower band was also fitted that incorporated the front sling swivel as well as securing the handguard. Both types of the Model 38 have a recess on the underside of the forestock to the rear of the bayonet lug that served to accommodate the blade of a special short folding bayonet used with the 91/38. The cleaning rod is a three-piece rod that fits into the butt trap when disassembled.

Many of the early production Model 38 rifles of both versions that were manufactured by Terni used Model 1891 rifle barrels that

The early type Model 38 short rifle without the bayonet affixed. The front band retained by a single screw was a weak point of this version. *(Author's collection)*

Marking on the stock of a 7.35mm Model 38 short rifle clearly indicating the caliber. Rifles chambered for 7.35mm were recalled after 1940 and their stock prominently marked with the caliber in order to avoid confusion with similar rifles chambered for the 6.5mm round. This stock is on a Model 38 produced by Gardone in 1939. *(Author's collection)*

A

B

Standard version 7.35mm Model 38 short rifle. The rifle shown is one of about 5,000 produced by Gardone in 1939; the combination of year and manufacturer make this one of the scarcest Model 38 rifles. *(Author's collection)*

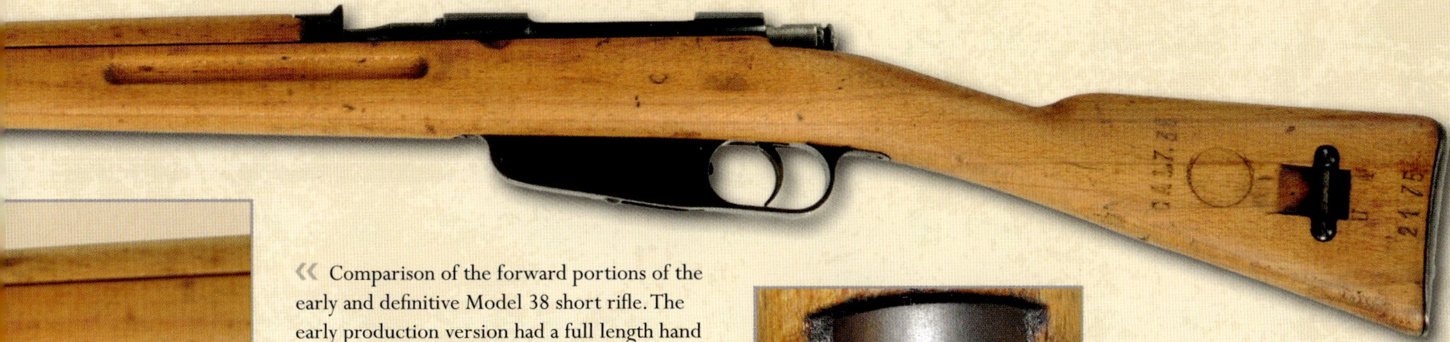

The early version of the Model 38 short rifle accounted for a small fraction of total Model 38 production. Beretta, who produced the rifle shown here, limited its production to 1939, producing only about 10,000 examples. (*Author's collection*)

Comparison of the forward portions of the early and definitive Model 38 short rifle. The early production version had a full length hand guard and the sling swivel mounted well forward on the front band which was retained by only one screw whereas the definitive version had a front band held by two screws, and a second band that held the sling swivel as well as securing the shortened hand guard. (*Author's collection*)

The caliber marking on the rear sight of this 1939 Beretta Model 38 short rifle differs from the normal marking in that the marking uses superscript digits, i.e., 7.35 rather than the normal consistently sized 7.35 digits. (*Author's collection*)

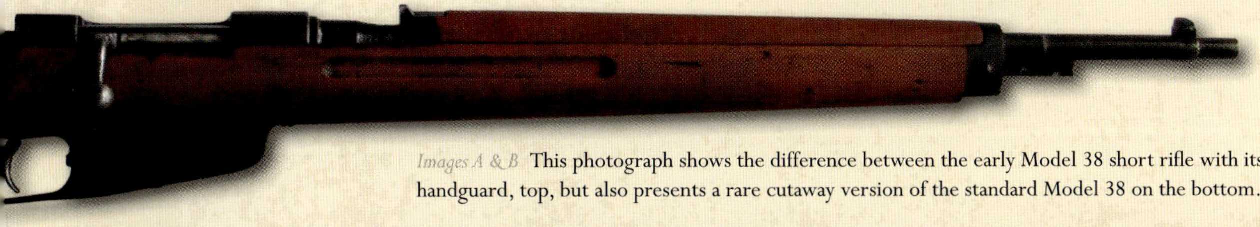

Images A & B This photograph shows the difference between the early Model 38 short rifle with its characteristic long handguard, top, but also presents a rare cutaway version of the standard Model 38 on the bottom. (*Ruggero Pettinelli*)

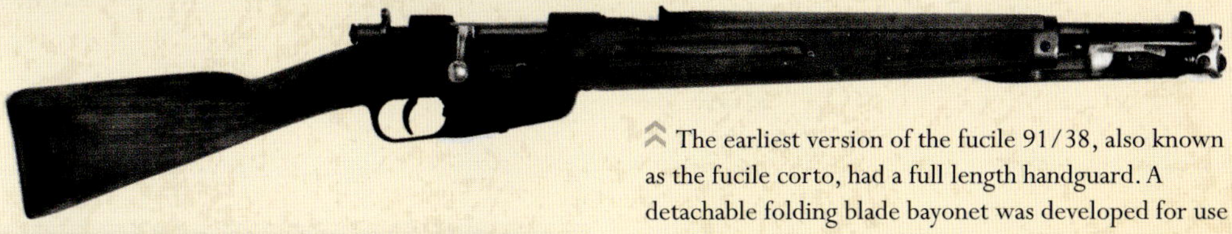

The earliest version of the fucile 91/38, also known as the fucile corto, had a full length handguard. A detachable folding blade bayonet was developed for use with the 91/38; the bayonet shown is the first type, known as the Tipo I. (*Editoriale Olimpia*)

Some early production Model 38 rifles were produced using serviceable barrels and actions taken from Model 1891 rifles. The barrels were shortened and re-bored to 7.35mm and retained the barrel's original date of manufacture in addition to the remanufacture date, as shown on this Model 38. The caliber marking on the rear sight is also prominent. (*Author's collection*)

A 7.35mm Model 38 short rifle furnished to Finland. The Finns replaced the issue front sight with a sight that zeroed the weapon for 150 meters. (*Author's collection*)

Comparison of the standard Italian Model 38 front sight, top, and the modified Finnish front sight that is higher and more angular. (*Author's collection*)

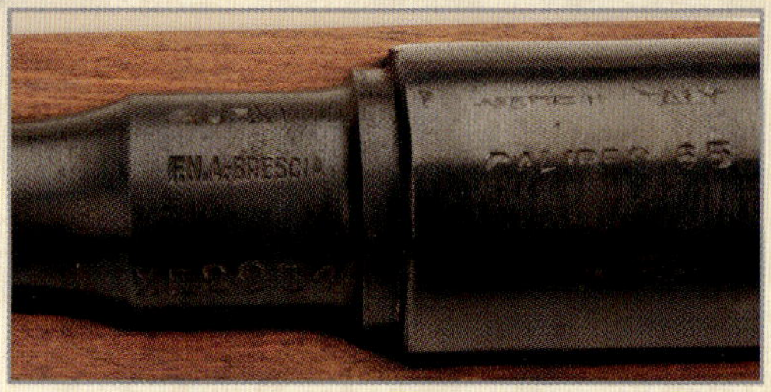

This imported Carcano is stamped MADE IN ITALY on the receiver ring, along with the caliber indication. Strangely, the 6.5mm caliber designation originally stamped on the fixed rear sight was ground off of this rifle, presumably during the refurbishment process. (*Author's collection*)

Model 38 short rifle with the Type II folding bayonet in the extended position. (*Author's collection*)

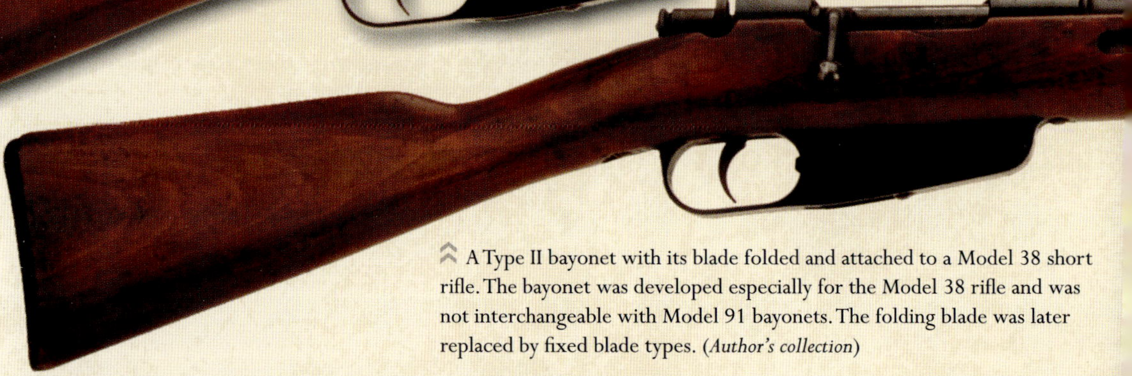

A Type II bayonet with its blade folded and attached to a Model 38 short rifle. The bayonet was developed especially for the Model 38 rifle and was not interchangeable with Model 91 bayonets. The folding blade was later replaced by fixed blade types. (*Author's collection*)

Detail of the folded Type II bayonet mounted on the Model 38 short rifle. (*Author's collection*)

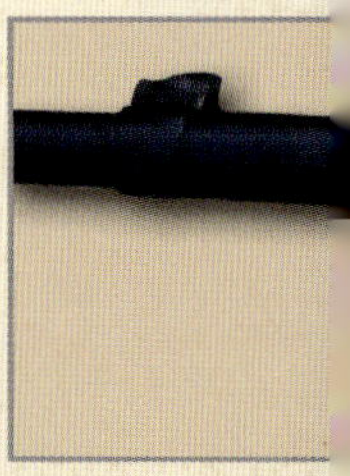

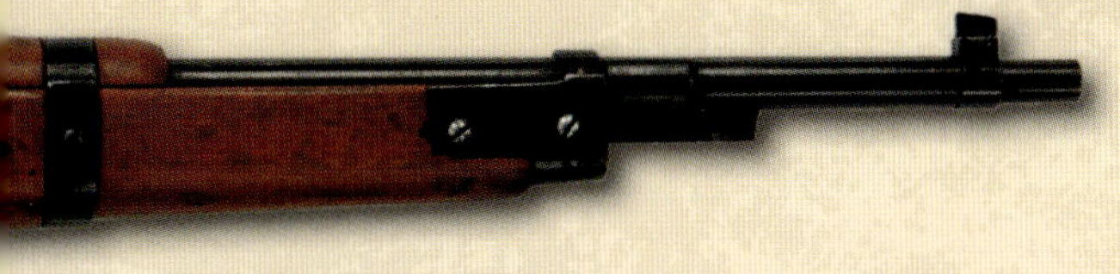

An imported 6.5mm Model 38 short rifle that has been refurbished. During the refurbishment process, the stock was sanded considerably, softening the contours of the finger grooves. (*Author's collection*)

Model 38 short rifles provided to Finland were stamped with the SA mark by the Finns. This marking is frequently encountered on Model 38 rifles in the U.S. collector market. (*Author's collection*)

The Terni stock cartouche on this Finnish issue Model 38 short rifle has been nearly obliterated by sanding. Finnish issue rifles were not stamped with the 7.35mm caliber designation by the Finns. (*Author's collection*)

Bottom-mounted sling swivel on the buttstock of a 1941 Terni Model 38. (*Collection of Mark Decker*)

The stock band on this 1941 Terni Model 38 short rifle has a bottom-mounted sling swivel in addition to the side-mounted swivel. (*Collection of Mark Decker*)

were shortened and re-bored to 7.35mm; these rifles have a new serial number and new year of manufacture on the barrel chamber, but also retain the original date of manufacture on the barrel chamber as well. There is strong reason to believe that some, or possibly all, of the Model 38 rifles that used Model 1891 rifle barrels may also have used the original Model 1891 receiver, trigger and magazine as well. The author has a Model 38 short rifle made with an 1897 Terni barrel that also has a star marking in the tang reflecting an arsenal rebuild, indicating the possibility, if not the likelihood, that barrel, receiver, and action parts were refurbished Model 1891 rifle parts. In essence, such a rifle would be a remanufactured Model 1891 with a shortened and re-bored barrel, turned down bolt handle, new sights, stock and furniture.

Confusion abounds, especially in English language publications, as to how many Model 38 rifles were produced between 1938 and 1941, with many sources claiming a total of only abut 100,000. In fact, nearly 296,000 Model 38 rifles were manufactured in 7.35mm, and an additional 660,000 plus were produced in 6.5mm. Initial issue of the Model 38 was to units of the 6th Army (*Armata del Po*) in northern Italy which included Italy's most capable and best equipped armored and mechanized forces, but between December 1939 and January 1940 the new weapons were removed from service and replaced by earlier Model 91 family weapons. Somewhat ironically, after production of

Italian troops in Greece equipped with the Model 38 short rifle; Italy invaded Greece in October 1940, by which time the 7.35mm Model 38 had been removed from front line service and the 6.5mm version had been issued. (*Cronache della Guerra, 1940, Tuminelli Editore, via Andrea and Antonio Tallillo*)

the 7.35mm version was suspended and production was switched to 6.5mm, many of the 7.35mm rifles were issued to second line territorial mobile coastal defense units, fixed coastal artillery batteries, and anti-parachute defense units. Between April and August 1940, Italy delivered 94,500 7.35mm Model 38 rifles to Finland; these were marked by the Finns on the chamber with the letters SA (for *Suomen Armeija*) in a rectangle with rounded corners. After the war the Finns sold 74,300 Model 38 short rifles to Interarms of Alexandria, Virginia, which in turn sold them to other distributors in the U.S.; a large if not overwhelming percentage of Model 38 rifles found on the collector's market in the U.S. are Finnish marked.

When it was decided to revert to the 6.5mm round for purposes of standardization, production of the Model 38 continued in the old 6.5mm caliber. The 6.5mm version was identical to the 7.35mm version, except that its sights were set for 300 rather than 200 meters to compensate for the different ballistic characteristics of the 6.5mm round; the rear sight was also stamped with the marking Cal. 6.5, whereas the 7.35mm version had been stamped Cal. 7.35. Note should be made of the fact that on rifles exported to Finland, the Finns replaced the original front sight on most rifles with one that zeroed the weapon at 150 meters.

During the early part of Terni's 1940 production run of the 6.5mm Model 38, bottom mounted sling swivels were introduced along with the side-mounted sling attachments. The earliest reported example with this sling attachment arrangement in the 1940 AR serial number block, and the highest observed serial number is in the CA68XX block, which would indicate that possibly as many as about 350,000 Model 38s were produced with this arrangement.

A somewhat debatable or contentious issue arises with respect to the possibility of 6.5mm Model 38 rifles being used to equip Mussolini's *Moschettieri del Duce* honor guard. This author has seen no Italian sources that make any mention the Model 38 being used by the *Moschettieri del Duce*; all Italian sources indicate that the issue weapon for the *Moschettieri* was the Model 91 cavalry carbine with black stocks and nickeled metal parts, as previously described in the section dealing with the Model 91 carbine. However, Hobbs states that the *Moschettieri* were issued the 6.5mm version of the Model 38, but with early type full length stocks dyed black. This seems to present a problem, as the 6.5mm version was not produced until 1940, by which time the availability of early type stocks would be problematic, as well as the fact that in effect the *Moschettieri* were disbanded upon Italy's entry into the war in 1940.

Markings on the chamber consisted of the normal serial number, manufacturer's name, location of manufacture, and date. Serial numbers of 7.35mm rifles produced at Terni ran from the A through X blocks; SFARE Gardone rifles ran from QA through QC; F.N.A. Brescia ran from XA through XB, and Beretta numbers were confined to the UA block. Serial numbers of 6.5mm Model 38 rifles produced by Terni ran from A through Z, and from AA through CB; SFARE Gardone numbers ran from QC through RF; F.N.A. Brescia ran from XB through XF, and Beretta from UB through UE. ■

FUCILE ARMAGUERRA MODELLO 1939

The Armaguerra Model 39, also referred to as the Revelli Model 39, was designed by Gino Revelli, the son of Bethel Abiel Revelli, who designed the Glisenti Model 1910 pistol and the FIAT/Villar Perosa submachine gun. The Model 39 was developed by the Società Anonima Revelli Manifattura Armiguerra (commonly referred to as Armaguerra), which at the time of prototype development had no manufacturing facilities at all, working out of a design office in Mantova.

Selection of a semi-automatic rifle chambered for the 7.36x51mm round began in 1938, when seven prototypes were presented (the Revelli, a Beretta, a Breda, one from the F.A.R.E. Terni, and three different models from Scotti), none of which met the requirements. Another competition was held in September 1939, in which seven different firms participated: Revelli, F.A.R.E. Terni (with two different models), F.N.A. Brescia, Sindacati Studi Armi Firenze, Bardelli, Breda (which submitted the Mod. 35 PG) and Scotti (which submitted the Mod. X). Despite the fact that it did not meet all of the specifications called for, the Model 39 was judged to be the winner. The commission felt that the basic design of the Model 39, as well as its handling characteristics, were such that with a few improvements it would fully meet the requirements of the Italian Army and arrangements were made for troop trials; the trials proved to be highly satisfactory, leading to a contract for 10,000 rifles being awarded to the Armaguerra firm. Due to the fact that it had no production facilities at the time, Armaguerra undertook to build a factory in Cremona for production of the Model 39. However, as a result of the worsening international situation the Italian Army rescinded the order for the rifles which were chambered for the 7.35mm cartridge, and only a limited number were actually produced. Armaguerra undertook development of a 6.5mm version, but conversion of the Model 39 to use the old 6.5mm cartridge was not completely straightforward as the greater chamber pressure developed by the 6.5mm round required a certain amount of redesign; by June 1940 two 6.5mm prototypes had been completed which proved to be satisfactory. The most significant difference between the 7.35mm and 6.5mm versions was that the 6.5mm version had a slightly longer barrel. Limited distribution was planned for the 6.5mm version for "specialized personnel," with later distribution to be extended to three riflemen per squad, officers, NCOs and to parachute units. However, the weapon never reached serial production (a monthly situation report dated 1 July 1942 reflected a total of 100 Model 39 rifles in the army's inventory), and a potentially significant increase in firepower for the average Italian infantryman was never realized. When it was decided to suspend production of the Model 39, the production line at Cremona was converted to the manufacture of the Model 41 bolt-action rifles in 6.5mm.

The Model 39 operated on the short recoil principle with the barrel moving back approximately ½ inch (1.25cm) to lock. Locking was achieved by a dropping block similar to that of the Walther P.38 pistol. The feed system used the standard six-round Mannlicher type clips used by the Model 91 family of rifles. Photographs show two different types of stock and handguard; the first version in 7.35mm has a straight wrist stock with no finger groove and a full length handguard with five ventilating slots per side, while the second version in 6.5mm has a pistol grip, finger grooves, and a short handguard that also has five venitilating slots per side. An unusual feature of the Model 39 was its method of cocking, which was actuated by pulling the sling to the rear, as the forward sling swivel located on the underside of the weapon was actually the cocking handle.

Contrary to normal Italian practice, markings on the Model 1939 were located on the receiver and receiver action cover rather than on the barrel; the serial number was stamped on the left hand side of the receiver below the rear sight, and the caliber was stamped in a groove on the left-hand side receiver rail, behind the rear sight. The action cover behind the receiver bore a profusion of markings, including the inscription FUCILE SEMIAUTOMATICO over an Armaguerra crest, beneath which, on two lines, was the inscription Mod. 39 and BREVETTATO; other markings were GENOVA ARMAGUERRA GENOVA and STABILIMENTO DI CREMONA followed by the four-digit year in Arabic and corresponding Fascist year date in Roman numerals. ■

FUCILE ARMAGUERRA MODELLO 1939

Designer: Gino Revelli
Manufacturer: Armaguerra, Cremona
Caliber: 7.35mm (originally); 6.5mm (conversion)
Cartridge: 7.35x51mm; 6.5x52mm Mannlicher-Carcano
Operating system: Recoil
Overall length: 1170mm (46")
Barrel length: 600mm (23.6")
Weight: Not available
Front sight: Barleycorn
Rear sight: Eccentric, graduated from 100 to 500 meters
Muzzle velocity: 680 m/sec (2230 fps) estimated
Feed system: 6-round Mannlicher-Carcano clips

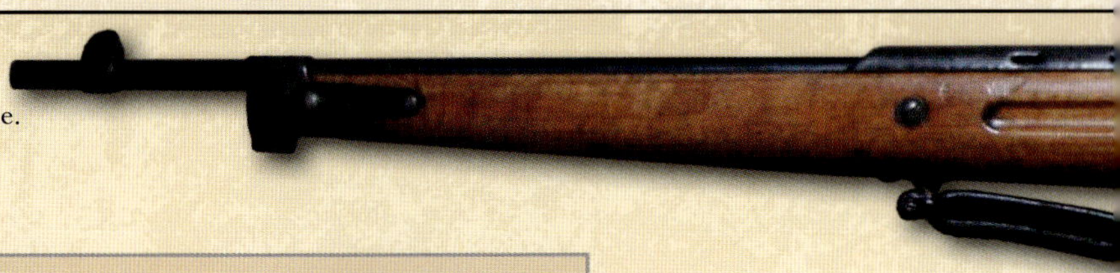

›› Left side view of the Revelli Model 1939 semi-automatic rifle. (*Museo Storico Italiano della Guerra-Rovereto*)

^ Detail view of the receiver, bolt, rear sight and magazine housing of the Revelli Model 1939. Note the absence of a traditional cocking handle on the bolt, as the front sling swivel doubled as the cocking handle. (*Museo Storico Italiano della Guerra-Rovereto*)

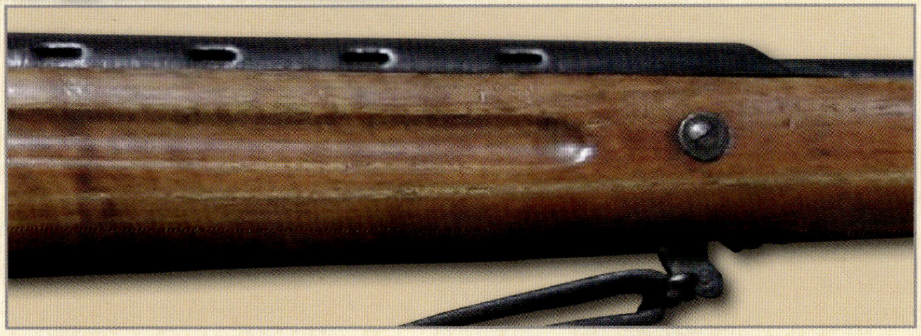

›› Detail of sling and bottom-mounted cocking handle that doubled as the forward sling swivel; pulling the sling to the rear armed the rifle. (*Museo Storico Italiano della Guerra-Rovereto*)

^ Receiver and rear sight of a Revelli Model 1939 rifle; serial number A.9 is visible below the sight, and the Calibro 6.5 marking is stamped in the groove on the side rail. (*Museo Storico Italiano della Guerra-Rovereto*)

›› Magazine opening and follower, and rear sight of a Model 1939 rifle. The cover to the rear of the receiver has the Armaguerra crest stamped on it. (*Museo Storico Italiano della Guerra-Rovereto*)

RIFLES

The Revelli designed Armaguerra Model 1939 was adopted by the Italian Army but never produced in large numbers due to logistics problems associated with changeover from the 6.5mm to 7.35mm cartridge just as the war began. It was a rather sleek looking weapon whose potential never was realized. This may have been a prototype, marked by a straight grip stock, full length upper handguard, and absence of finger grooves in the stock. (*Editoriale Olimpia*)

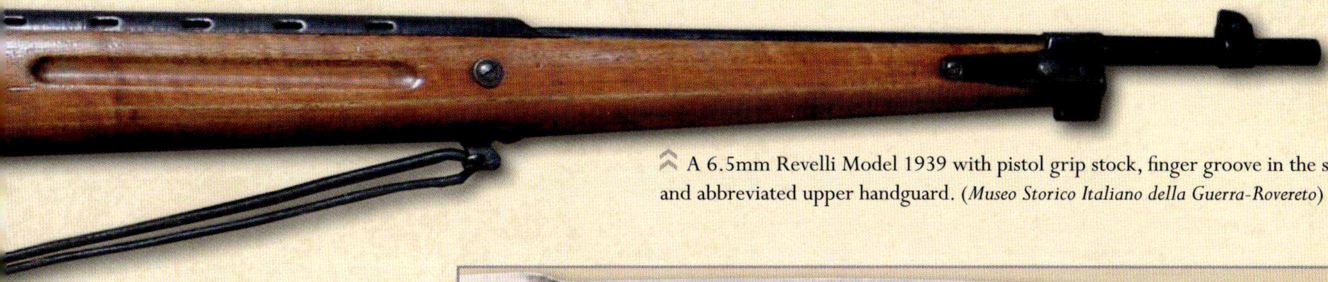

A 6.5mm Revelli Model 1939 with pistol grip stock, finger groove in the stock, and abbreviated upper handguard. (*Museo Storico Italiano della Guerra-Rovereto*)

Receiver housing detail showing Armaguerra crest, company name, and location and date of manufacture. (*Museo Storico Italiano della Guerra-Rovereto*)

Magazine housing and trigger detail, Revelli Model 1939 rifle. (*Museo Storico Italiano della Guerra-Rovereto*)

FUCILE MODELLO 40 & 41

In 1940 the Italian Army officially adopted the *fucile modello 40*, although the weapon was never issued to troop units. The Model 40 was quite similar in appearance to the World War I Model 91; it was in 6.5mm caliber and differed from the Model 91 only in its total length and barrel length, in its constant twist rifling, its rear sight, and in the conical shape of the chamber exterior. The bolt handle was straight as on the Model 91, and the bayonet of the Model 91 was used on the Model 40. The stock was a straight grip type similar to that of the Model 1891 and had no finger grooves; it was fitted with bottom mounted sling swivels as well as side mounted sling bars. The buttplate was solid as on the Model 1891, and a full length cleaning rod was carried under the forearm. The Model 40 was identical to the Model 41, adopted a year later, except that its rear sight was eccentric rather than quadrant as on the Model 41. The eccentric sight was graduated from 100 to 500 meters, in 100 meter increments. Production of the Model 40, which was issued for trial purposes only, likely was limited to the Armaguerra plant in Cremona.

In 1941 the final version of the Model 91 rifle was adopted and issued. This was the *fucile modello 41*, which was identical to the Model 40 except for its more traditional quadrant rear sight. With the sight flipped forward a fixed combat sight set for 200 meters is exposed; with the sight in the normal position the sight is graduated from 300 to 1000 meters. A departure from normal Italian practice was that in 1943 the front sight ferrule of some of the Terni Model 41s had slots milled to accommodate a German type front sight hood; the Kar98k hood will not fit, but the G33/40 sight hood will fit. Earlier, in 1942, apparently inspired by German practice, tests were conducted with a laminated beechwood stock but apparently it was decided to retain the traditional stocks.

Production of the Model 41 was limited to Terni Arsenal and Armaguerra. Terni serial numbers ran from the A through Z blocks, and from AA through BH; Armaguerra number blocks ran from QA through QZ. Terni rifles were marked with RE TERNI and the year in Arabic and Roman numerals, or with a crown over FAT and the last two digits of the year, all enclosed in a rectangle with rounded edges; Armaguerra rifles normally were marked with ARMAGUERRA CREMONA, the date in Arabic and Roman numerals, RE, and 4 UT, although some were marked only with the Savoy crest in an oval, RE, and 4UT.

Only a very small number of the Model 41 – probably less than a thousand – was produced in 1941, but production increased signicantly and by 1944 a total of about 916,000 had been produced by the Terni Arsenal and Armaguerra. Eight Model 1941 rifles were modified to fire the 8x59mm Breda

Left side view of the short lived Model 40 rifle. (*Museo Storico Italiano della Guerra-Rovereto*)

The Model 1940 rifle was a shortened Model 1891 and retained the straight bolt handle. It also incorporated an eccentric rear sight with a prominent adjusting knob graduated to 500 meters. (*Museo Storico Italiano della Guerra-Rovereto*)

FUCILE MODELLO 40; FUCILE MODELLO 41

Designer: Modification of Model 1891 rifle designed by Salvatore Carcano
Manufacturers: Fabbrica d'Armi Terni; Armaguerra Cremona
Caliber: 6.5mm
Cartridge: 6x52mm Mannlicher-Carcano
Overall length: 1173mm (46.2")
Barrel length: 690mm (27.2")
Rifling: RH constant twist, 215mm
Weight: 3.72 kg (8.18 lbs)
Front sight: Barleycorn
Rear sight: Quadrant with V notch, adjustable from 200 to 1000 meters
Muzzle velocity: 680 m/sec (2231 fps)
Feed system: 6 round integral box using six-round Mannlicher-Carcano clips

cartridge for experimental test purposes; these were fitted with heavier barrels devoid of sights, and had modifications to the stock and fittings due to the larger diameter barrel. The receiver was unmodified, without a clearance cut for the longer cartridge that had to be inserted singly by hand.

Specifications for the *fucile modello 40* are the same as those for the *fucile modello 41* entry below, except for the eccentric rear sight as described above.

Soldiers armed with Model 41 rifles on security patrol in Milan in late-1943. (*SME via Tallillo*)

The elevation adjustment knob for the eccentric rear sight of the model 40 rifle. (*Museo Storico Italiano della Guerra-Rovereto*)

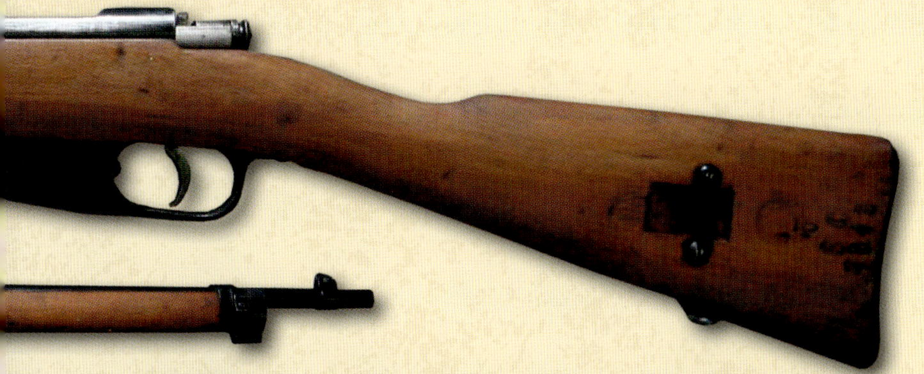

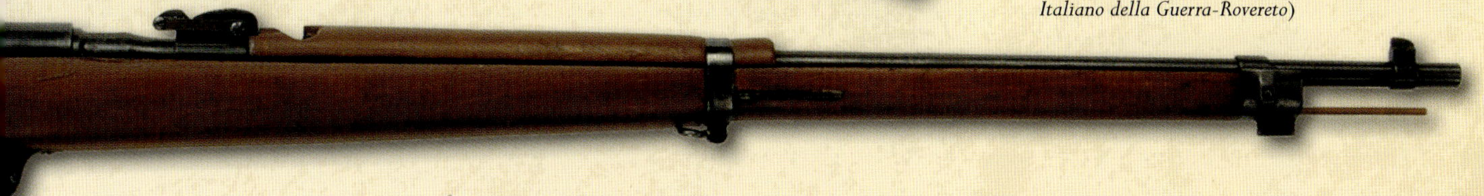

The Model 1941 rifle was the final production version of the Model 91 rifle and equipped Italian forces during World War II. It differed from the Model 1940 rifle in that its rear sight reverted to a tangent sight. (*Author's collection*)

« The front sight ferrule on this 1943 Terni Model 41 grooved for a German style front sight hood; this is an uncommon variation of the Model 41. (*Keith Versaw*)

A

B

Images A & B As shown here, the Model 41 rifle was essentially a slightly shortened version of the Model 1891 rifle above it. The adjustable rear sight on the Model 41 was also simplified. (*Author's collection*)

VETTERLI-VITALI M1870/87/15

Left side view of a Model 41 rifle, showing side-mounted sling points in addition to the bottom mounted swivels. (*Author's collection*)

The cavalry carbine style rear sight of the Model 41 was adjustable to 1000 meters. (*Author's collection*)

A simplified rear band was introduced on late production Model 41 rifles; the band was comparable to the stamped rear band on late-war German Kar98k rifles. (*Keith Versaw*)

Prior to adoption of the Carcano Model 1891, the Vetterli-Vitali rifle was the standard Italian infantry weapon. In 1870 Italy adopted the Swiss Vetterli, modified for Italian use, chambered for the 10.35R cartridge. Production of the Vetterli was undertaken by all four of the government small arms arsenals, namely, Brescia, Roma, Torino and Torre Annunziata. The 1870 was a single shot rifle, and in 1887 the Italians updated their rifles by adding a four-round box magazine designed by Major Giuseppe Vitali, hence the designation Vetterli-Vitali. With large stocks of Vetterli-Vitali rifles still on hand upon the advent of World War I and the need for as many rifles as possible, the Italians resorted to yet another modification of the Vetterli-Vitali by converting about 400,000 of the rifles to fire the 6.5x52mm cartridge that was by now the standard Italian cartridge. The conversions carried out by the government arsenals at Rome and Gardone consisted of fitting a 6.5mm barrel liner and replacing the four-round magazine with a magazine that could accept the six-round Carcano clips. The updated Vetterli-Vitali rifles were designated the M 1870/87/15 and were issued to territorial units, colonial troops, and other second line units during World War I, and in 1937 there were 120,000 Vetterli-Vitali rifles issued to colonial troops in Italian East Africa. ■

Infantrymen of the 104th Infantry Regiment armed with Vetterli-Vitali M1870/87/15 rifles in a 1915 posed photo. (*SME via Andrea and Antonio Tallillo*)

FUCILE VETTERLI-VITALI M 1870/87/15

Designer: Johann-Friedrich Vetterli; modified by Major Giuseppe Vitali
Manufacturers: Reale Fabbrica d'Armi di Torino; Real Fabbrica d'Armi Torre Annunziata; Fabbrica d'Armi di Brescia; Fabbrica d'Armi di Terni
Caliber: 6.5mm
Cartridge: 6.5x52mm Carcano
Overall length: 1349mm (53.11")
Barrel length: 862mm (33.94")
Weight: 4.62 kg (10.19 lbs)
Front sight: Blade
Rear sight: Quadrant, graduated to 2000 meters
Muzzle velocity: 730 m/sec (2395 fps)
Feed system: 6 round integral box using six-round Mannlicher-Carcano clips

The Vetterli was originally a Swiss design that made its debut in 1869 and was adopted by Italy in 1870; it never saw service as a front-line Italian rifle. (*Author's collection*)

During World War I large numbers of obsolete Vetterli-Vitali M 1870/87 rifles were converted to 6.5mm, resulting in the Vetterli-Vitali M1870/87/15 rifle. These rifles were a stop-gap measure and were issued to second-line troops, and later served into World War II. (*Author's collection*)

The quadrant rear sight on the Vetterli-Vitali was similar to that on the Model 1891 Carcano rifle. (*Author's collection*)

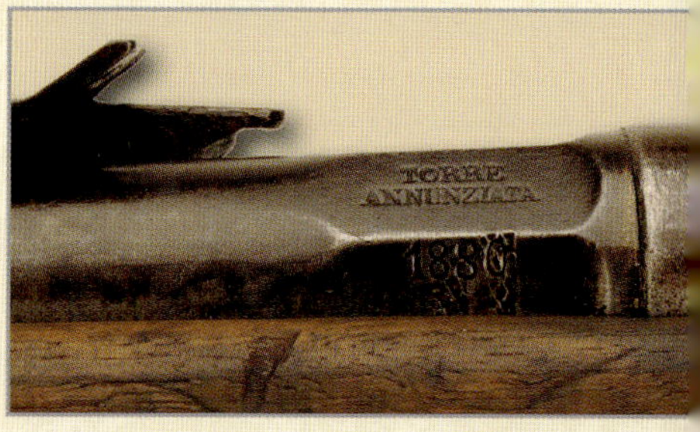

MOSCHETTO REGOLAMENTARE BALILLA MODELLO 1891 RIDOTTO

(moschetto per O.N.B.; moschetto per G.I.L.)

Although this type of weapon was not utilized by the Italian Army per se, it is nevertheless of historical interest. Essentially, these *moschetti*, or carbines, were training rifles used by Fascist paramilitary youth groups and were commonly referred to as the *moschetto Balilla*. The somewhat long designation of the weapon was the *moschetto regolamentare Balilla modello 1891 ridotto* (reduced size Balilla Model 1891 regulation carbine). They were also referred to as the *moschetto per O.N.B*, and later, as the *moschetto per G.I.L.* The initials O.N.B in the designation stand for *Opera Nazionale Balilla*, or National Balilla Organization, which was the Fascist youth organization between 1926 and 1937. "Balilla" was a folk hero, a young boy who allegedly sparked a revolt against Austrian occupation forces in Genoa in December 1746. The initials G.I.L stand for *Gioventù Italiana del Littorio*, or Italian Littorio Youth, which succeeded the O.N.B. in 1937. Members of these

The firm of N&V Castelli produced a Balilla carbine very similar to the Grazian carbine. Shown is a period advertisement for the Castelli Balilla carbine. (*Courtesy Luca Vallebona, Armeria Black Hills*)

The cartouche on the stock of this Vetterli indicates that it was converted from 10.4mm to 6.5mm at the Rome Arsenal in 1916. Vetterli cartouches were applied to the right side of the stock rather than to the left as was the practice for Carcanos. (*Author's collection*)

The Mannlicher-style magazine was the hallmark feature of the Vetterli-Vitali M1870/87/15 rifle; it held the standard six-round Italian clip as used on the Carcano rifles. (*Author's collection*)

This Vetterli-Vitali was originally manufactured at the Torre Annunziata arsenal in 1886. Torre Annunziata, outside of Naples, was the southernmost government arsenal and produced the Carcano Model 1891 rifle from 1894 to 1900. (*Author's collection*)

organizations ranged in age from six to eighteen years, wore uniforms, and were exposed to basic military skills and traditions. The Balilla carbines normally were issued to boys in the 12-14 year old age range; older youths were progressively introduced to regulation carbines and light machine guns.

The Balilla carbines were patterned after either the Model 1891 rifle (or more precisely, after the 6mm Flobert *fucile per allievi tiratori* which itself was patterned after the Model 1891), after the *moschetto per truppe speciali*, or the *moschetto 1891* cavalry carbine and fell into two broad categories: those that could fire live ammunition, and those that could fire only blank ammunition. The earliest carbines were 5-shot repeaters produced by Pietro Lorenzotti in 1928 and fired the 6.35mm (.25 ACP) Browning round. The Lorenzotti carbine was 820mm (32.3 inches) long and externally resembled the Model 1891 rifle, although the turned-down bolt handle was placed much further forward on the bolt than it was on the Model 1891. In 1931 F.N.A. Brescia, successor to Lorenzotti, produced an almost identical version, but in 6mm Flobert, which was single shot only. In 1934 F.N.A. produced a 5-shot 5.5mm (.22 caliber) version.

Beginning in 1931, F.N.A. produced a blank-firing carbine patterned closely after the *moschetto 1891* cavalry carbine, complete with attached folding bayonet; it was 750mm long, and the barrel was a two-piece arrangement consisting of a

MOSCHETTO REGOLAMENTARE BALILLA MODELLO 1891 RIDOTTO

Manufacturers: F.N.A. Brescia; N & V Castelli;Fratelli Grazian
Caliber: 5.5mm carrier round for blank
Overall length: 758mm (29.8")
Barrel length: 362mm (14.25")
Weight: 1.78kg (3.9lbs)

A Fratelli Grazian Balilla carbine; the Grazian carbine was a very faithful reproduction of the Model 91 cavalry carbine. (*Author's collection*)

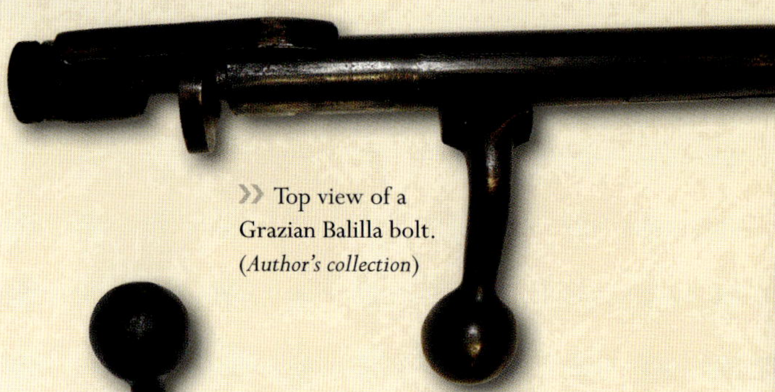

Top view of a Grazian Balilla bolt. (*Author's collection*)

Early style bayonet latch on the Grazian Balilla carbine. (*Author's collection*)

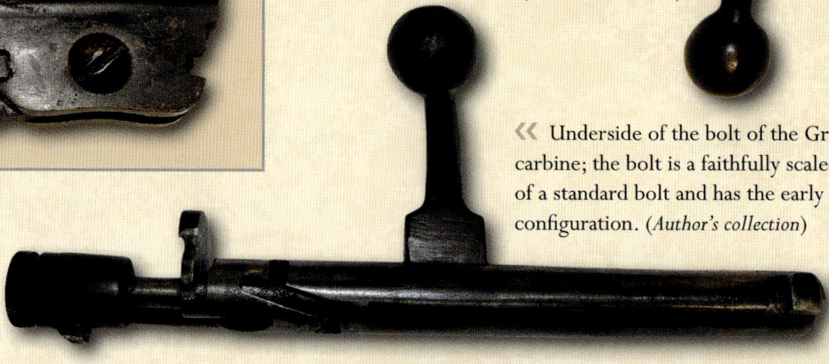

Underside of the bolt of the Grazian Balilla carbine; the bolt is a faithfully scaled reproduction of a standard bolt and has the early style slot configuration. (*Author's collection*)

A

B

Detail of the rear sight on a Grazian Balilla carbine. (*Author's collection*)

The Grazian marking and three digit year of manufacture; the superscript "o" following the Fascist calendar year XIX indicates an ordinal rather than a cardinal number. (*Author's collection*)

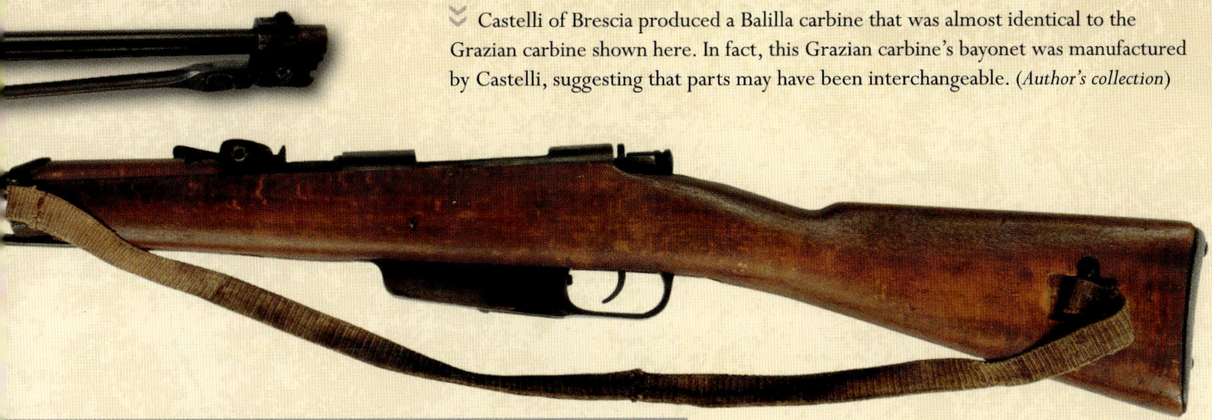

Castelli of Brescia produced a Balilla carbine that was almost identical to the Grazian carbine shown here. In fact, this Grazian carbine's bayonet was manufactured by Castelli, suggesting that parts may have been interchangeable. (*Author's collection*)

A small cartouche on the right side of the stock indicates that this was a G.I.L. issue carbine. (*Author's collection*)

The markings on the underside of the Grazian carbine indicate manufacture by Napoleone and Vittorio Castelli. Castelli also manufactured complete Balilla carbines very similar to the Grazian carbines. (*Author's collection*)

There is some conjecture concerning the F.M.B. marking on Grazian carbines; it may stand for Fucile Modello Brevettato (Patented Model rifle) or more likely for Fucile Modello Balilla (Balilla Model rifle). (*Author's collection*)

Images A & B Aside from their size, the differences between the Model 6.5mm 91/38 cavalry carbine at the top and the Grazian Balilla carbine below are minimal. The Balilla rear sights are patterned after the early model cavalry carbine sights. (*Author's collection*)

The stock cartouche on the Fratelli Grazian Balilla carbine bears the serial number. (*Author's collection*)

A toy clip and 6.5mm dummy cartridges. The small paper caps with fulminate were inserted into the base of the cartridge to act as a powder charge. (*Courtesy Luca Vallebona, Armeria Black Hills*)

The chamber of Balilla rifles normally bore either the O.N.B. or G.I.L. logo; this 1941 Grazian carbine uncharacteristically lacks the logo. (*Author's collection*)

« A group of young Italian boys kitted out in uniform intent on examining their Balilla cavalry-style carbines. The uniforms seem standardized from the waist up, but trousers, socks and shoes vary widely. (*Author's collection*)

firng chamber and a rifled barrel itself; the two pieces joined underneath the rear sight. This type of carbine is conventionally referred to as a 5.5mm carbine, but in fact the bore diameter is 6.5mm and the blank charge is inserted into the base of a dummy carrier cartridge whose dummy "bullet" diameter is 5.5mm. F.N.A. produced an estimated 50,000 of this model between 1931 and 1936, and a very similar carbine was produced or possibly only assembled by Castelli of Brescia; Castelli produced an estimated 3,000, making this the rarest of this type of blank-firing carbine. In 1932 the firm of Fratelli Grazian (Grazian Brothers) of Verona also began producing a copy of the *moschetto 1891*, quite similar to the F.N.A. carbine, but which differed in many details, including a differently configured magazine housing

MOSCHETTO BALILLA GIOCATTOLO

In addition to the reduced caliber blank-firing Balilla carbines, a fairly extensive range of toy (*giocattolo* in Italian) Model 91 carbines were produced during the 1930s and 1940s; these toy carbines are sometimes referred to in Italian as the *balillino* (little Balilla) and varied from very approximate copies of Carcano weapons to models that were quite convincing in appearance. The one described and pictured here in most detail is one of the more accurate reproductions of the *moschetto mod. 1891*, complete with folding bayonet. The manufacturer is unknown, and the only identifying marks are the word *Depositato* (registered) on the buttplate, and the letter G on the bolt stem. The receiver is a soft metal casting and bears a serial number over the chamber; the bolt is functional, cocks on closing, and is made of a piece of sheet metal rolled into a tube with an internal spring but has absolutely no provision for any type of firing pin; it fired paper caps. The barrel is a simple steel tube that force fits into the receiver. The trigger guard and magazine housing are stamped and the magazine housing has an operating follower much like that of the real Carcano. The stock and handguard are one piece, but the configuration mimics that of the real *moschetto mod. 1891*. Length with the bayonet folded is 740mm (29 inches), and with the bayonet extended is

Toy carbine with bayonet extended; the bayonet, whose tip is quite blunt, is made from a piece of sheet metal folded over to achieve thickness. (*Author's collection*)

and the extensive use of bronze parts. Overall Grazian production is estimated at about 57,000.

Markings on both types (firing and blank only) basically replicate those found on standard issue weapons, and consist of the serial number, maker's name, location, and year of manufacture on the chamber facets; Grazian carbines were serially numbered on the buttstock rather than on the barrel. The receiver ring bears either the stylized O.N.B. logo or, after 1937, the G.I.L. logo.

As on regulation carbines, the Balilla carbines also bore stock cartouches. Balilla carbines produced by F.N.A. had a cartouche on the right side of the buttstock consisting of two concentric circles with the inscription FABB NAZ D ARMI BRESCIA in the space between the two circles, and a serial number in the inner circle. Grazian carbines had a similar cartouche on the right side with the inscription FRATELLI GRAZIAN VERONA in the space between the circles and the serial number stamped in the inner circle. Grazian carbines also had a circular cartouche on the left side of the buttstock with the words COLLAUDATO VERONA ("approved" or "tested," Verona) along the inner circumference of the circle, and the initials G.I.L. in the center of the circle (after 1937).

Many Balilla carbines had a brass plate affixed to the right hand side of the stock that commemorated the name of a fallen Italian soldier; the youth to whom such a carbine was issued was expected to honor the name and to consider the fallen soldier as a sort of "spiritual godfather."

Dimensions varied among the variants: The Lorenzotti carbine was 820mm (32.3 inches) long and had a 400mm (15.75 inches) long barrel; the F.N.A. in 6mm Flobert was 825mm (32.5 inches) long with a 397mm (15.6 inch) barrel; in 1934 F.N.A. produced an experimental version of the carbine in 5.5mm that was 840mm (33.1 inches) long with a 460mm (18.1 inch) barrel; the F.N.A. and Castelli 5.5mm blank firing carbines were 750mm (29.5 inches) long with a 360mm (14.2 inch) barrel; the Grazian carbines were 745mm (29.3 inches) long with a 350mm (13.8 inch) barrel. ■

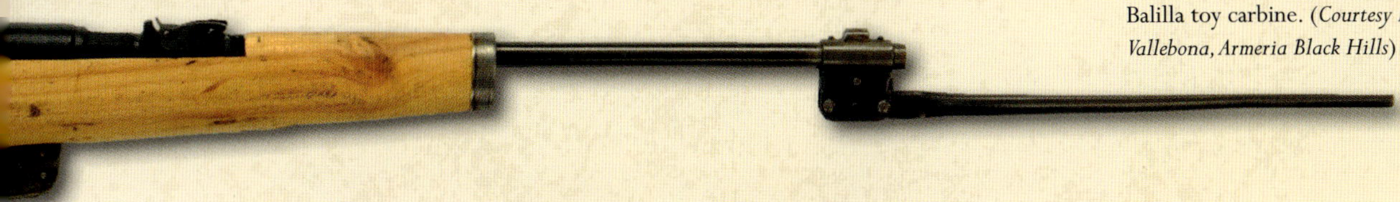

« A toy Model 91 cavalry carbine that quite faithfully replicates the real weapon. There is no indication as to the manufacturer of the replica. (*Author's collection*)

» A blank cartridge used with the Balilla toy carbine. (*Courtesy Luca Vallebona, Armeria Black Hills*)

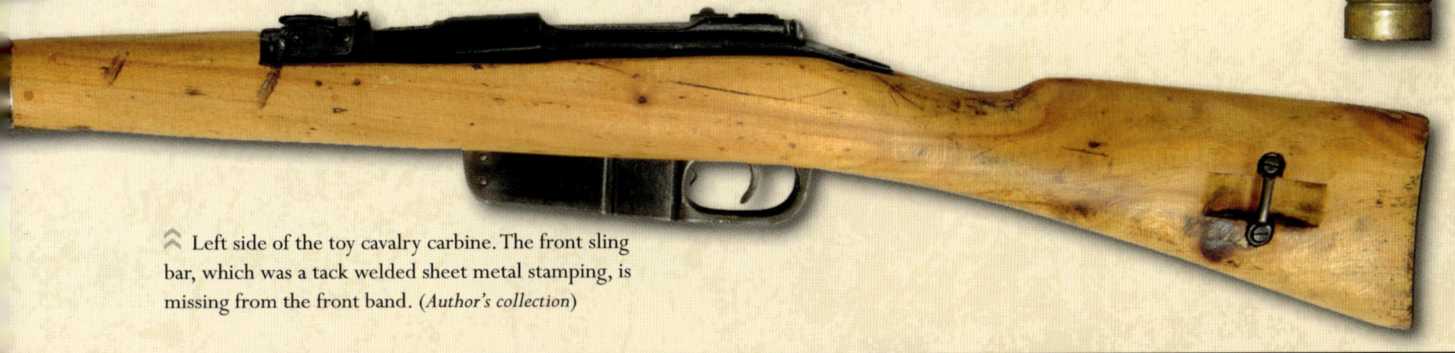

^ Left side of the toy cavalry carbine. The front sling bar, which was a tack welded sheet metal stamping, is missing from the front band. (*Author's collection*)

A

B

Images A & B

Comparison of a regulation 6.5mm Model 91/38 cavalry carbine and a toy carbine. Aside from the smaller size of the toy, visual difference is minimal. (*Author's collection*)

C

D

Images C, D & F

Dimensions of the Balilla and toy carbines are quite close, and both unmistakably are copies of the full size cavalry carbine. (*Author's collection*)

F

» The chamber of this toy carbine bears a serial number; it is believed that all examples of this particular type of toy carbine bore the same serial number as a standard feature. (*Author's collection*)

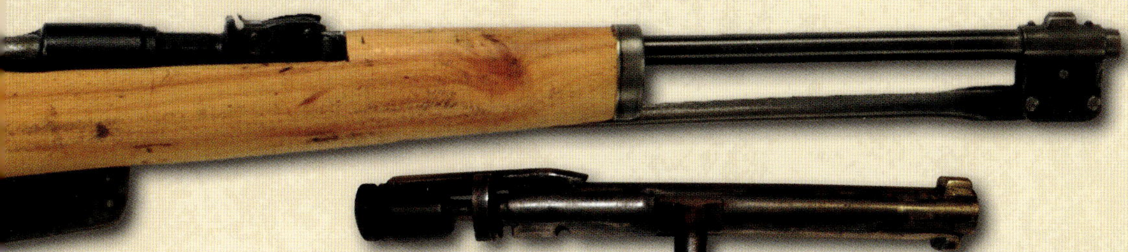

>> The buttplate on the toy cavalry carbine bears the inscription DEPOSITATO (Registered) over the figure of a powderhorn. (*Author's collection*)

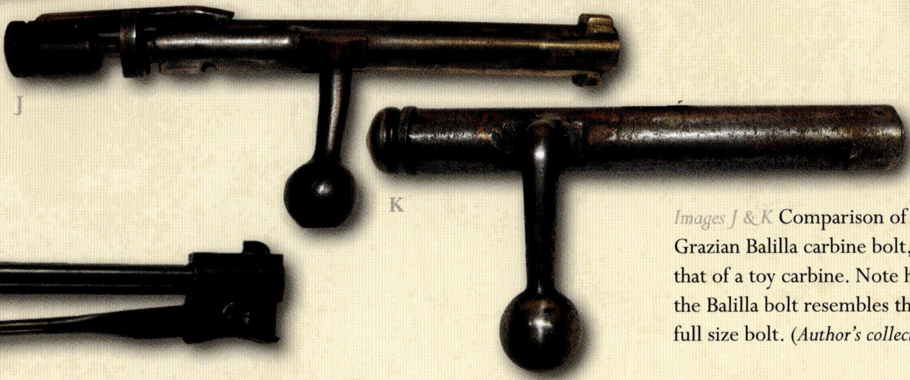

Images J & K Comparison of a Fratelli Grazian Balilla carbine bolt, top, with that of a toy carbine. Note how closely the Balilla bolt resembles the standard full size bolt. (*Author's collection*)

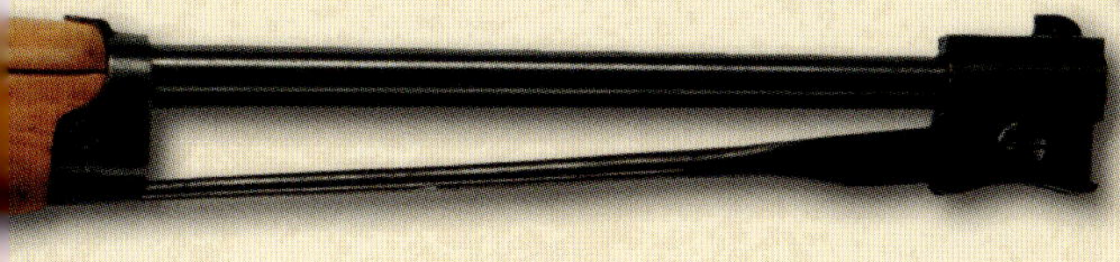

Images G, H & I From top to bottom, a standard Carcano bent handle bolt, a Balilla carbine bolt, and a toy carbine bolt. (*Author's collection*)

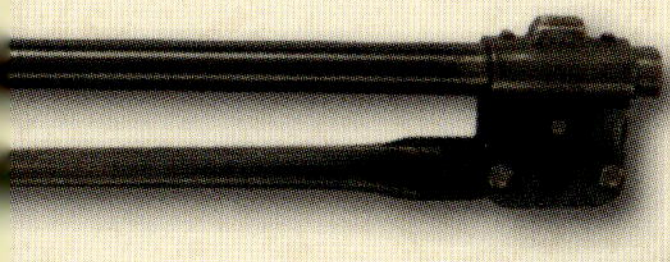

^ The receiver, bolt, trigger mechanism and trigger housing/magazine and follower and rear sight of the toy Model 91 carbine. The entire assembly was quite well made of soft metal castings and stamped parts. (*Author's collection*)

960mm (37¾ inches); these dimensions are quite close to those of the regulation *moschetto Balilla* variants.

Similarly convincing toy cavalry carbines were produced by Meccanica Perfetta (the SX8) and by SMIG; an unidentified firm produced a reasonable copy of the TS carbine. A number of other unidentified firms also produced toy carbines that were somewhat less convincing and true to prototype, especially with respect to shape and position of the bolt, and relative position of the trigger and magazine with respect to the receiver; some utilized stocks that were completely slab-sided. A few of the toy weapons tended, probably by design, to resemble the Revelli Model 1939 semiautomatic rifle than they did the Carcano; these were marketed as the *moschetto automatico Balilla* (Balilla automatic carbine). There seems to be no additional information available concerning the original location, status or fate of any of these companies. ■

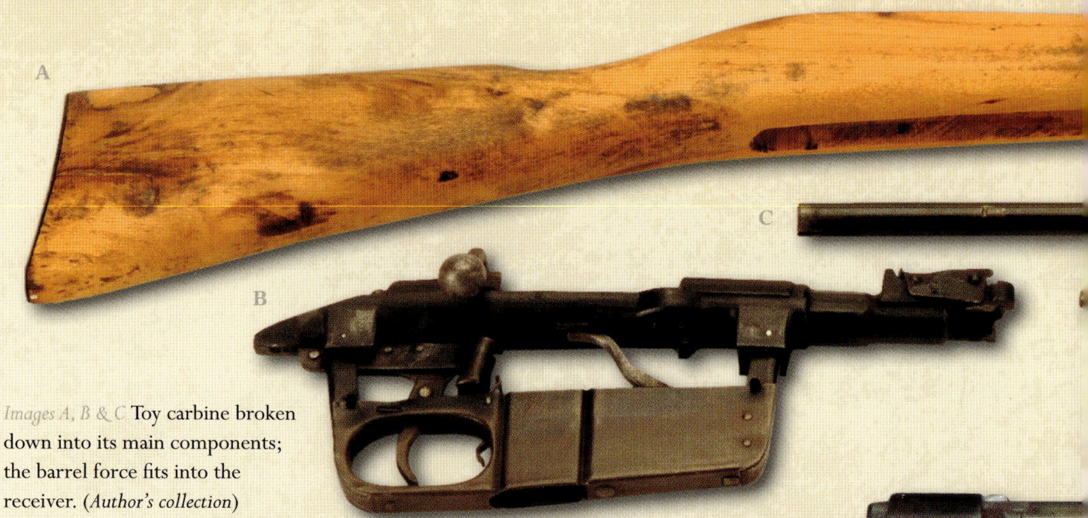

Images A, B & C Toy carbine broken down into its main components; the barrel force fits into the receiver. (*Author's collection*)

« The brass plate on the stock of the toy TS carbine memorialized a fallen Italian soldier named Pasquale Battista. Enclosed in a circle on the left of the plate are a stylized helmet and the letters ANC standing for Associazione Nazionale Combattenti (National Combatants Association); the square on the right has a fasce and the letters ONB for Opera Nazionale Balilla (National Balilla Organization). (*Courtesy Luca Vallebona, Armeria Black Hills*)

« Bolt and chamber detail of the TS toy carbine. (*Courtesy Luca Vallebona, Armeria Black Hills*)

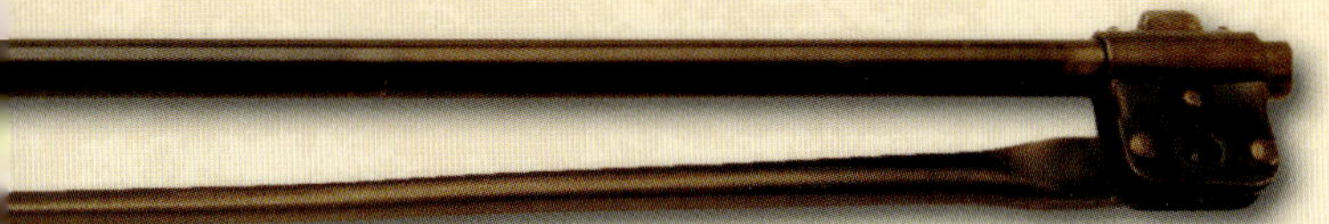

The significance of the letter G on the bolt stem of the toy cavalry carbine is unknown. (*Author's collection*)

Bottom of the bolt of the toy carbine. (*Author's collection*)

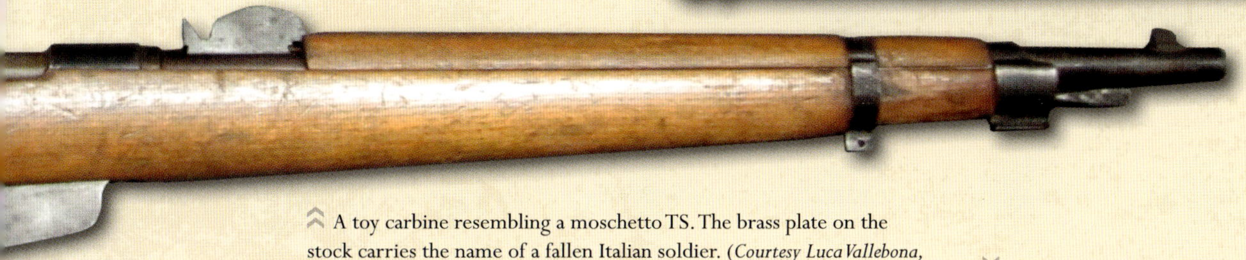

A toy carbine resembling a moschetto TS. The brass plate on the stock carries the name of a fallen Italian soldier. (*Courtesy Luca Vallebona, Armeria Black Hills*)

Left side of the TS carbine look-alike toy, fitted with bottom-mounted sling swivels rather than the side-mounted cavalry style sling bars. (*Courtesy Luca Vallebona, Armeria Black Hills*)

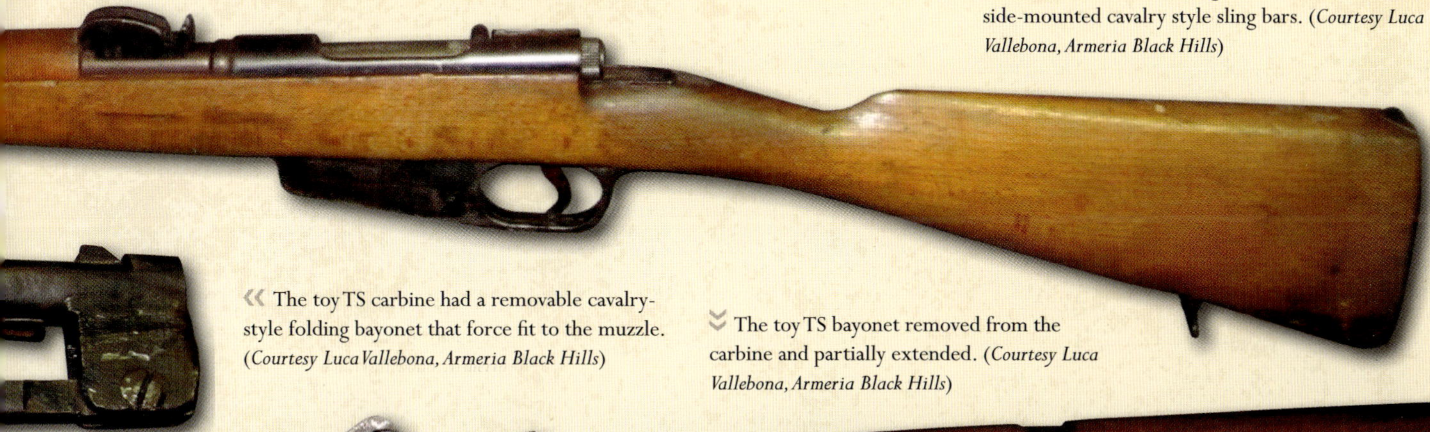

The toy TS carbine had a removable cavalry-style folding bayonet that force fit to the muzzle. (*Courtesy Luca Vallebona, Armeria Black Hills*)

The toy TS bayonet removed from the carbine and partially extended. (*Courtesy Luca Vallebona, Armeria Black Hills*)

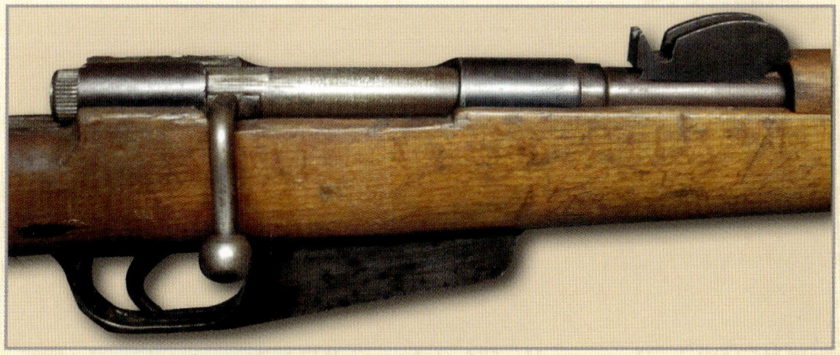

The receiver, rear sight, bolt, trigger housing and magazine of the toy TS carbine were a fairly convincing representation of the real TS carbine. (*Courtesy Luca Vallebona, Armeria Black Hills*)

Images A & B Two variants of toy rifles designated as the moschetto automatico Balilla (Balilla automatic carbine). These were spring-loaded toy weapons whose appearance was somewhat more similar to that of the Revelli model 39 semi-automatic rifle than they were to Carcano bolt-action carbines. Both types seem to have been retailed by a toy store in Torino. (*Courtesy Luca Vallebona, Armeria Black Hills*)

A

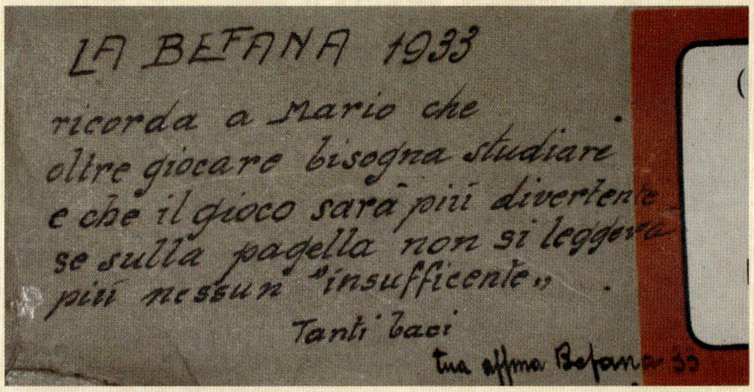

» This toy apparently was a 1933 Christmas present for someone named Mario, with an inscription from "Befana" (the Italian equivalent of Santa Claus). Mario may have been a bit lax in his studies, as the inscription reads "Mario, remember that in addition to playing you must study and that playing will be more fun if there are no more "insufficient" grades shown on your report card. Many kisses, your affectionate Befana 1933." (*Courtesy Luca Vallebona, Armeria Black Hills*)

^ The muzzle end of the "automatic" variant of the toy carbine. (*Courtesy Luca Vallebona, Armeria Black Hills*)

B

» One of the retail outlets that carried the "Universal Patent" toy carbine was a toy store named Saconney in Torino; its label is shown here on the back of the toy's box. (*Courtesy Luca Vallebona, Armeria Black Hills*)

« The butt plate of the "Univesal patent" toy carbine, marked Fabbricazione italiana (Italian manufacture). (*Courtesy Luca Vallebona, Armeria Black Hills*)

The muzzle end of the "Universal Patent Moschetto Automatico Balilla." This toy carbine was spring operated and fired a wooden plug, or a variant of the plug that had a needle tip that made it into a dart. *(Courtesy Luca Vallebona, Armeria Black Hills)*

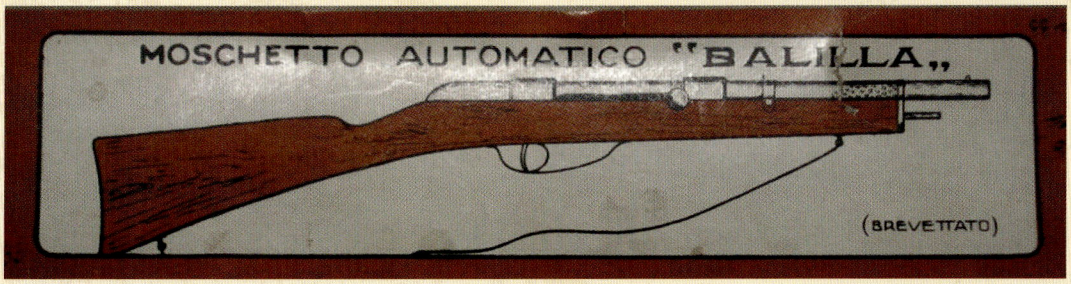

The box in which both versions of the "automatic" rifle were packaged. The drawing on the label is a fairly accurate rendering of the "Universal Patent" version, which bears little actual resemblance to any Carcano or Balilla carbines. *(Courtesy Luca Vallebona, Armeria Black Hills)*

Patent information one the toy "automatic" carbine; the 41 may indicate a 1941 patent. *(Courtesy Luca Vallebona, Armeria Black Hills)*

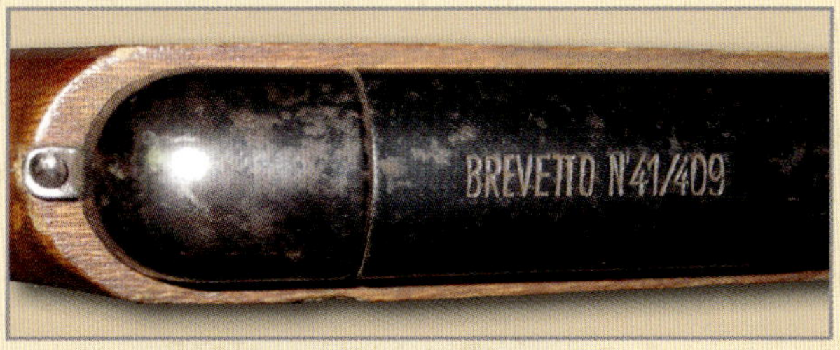

One of the variants of the moschetto automatico Balilla. The stock is slab-sided and is not fitted with a metal buttplate. *(Courtesy Luca Vallebona, Armeria Black Hills)*

Marking on the spring-loaded toy carbine; despite the claim of "Universal Patent" there is no indication of any type of patent number on the toy. *(Courtesy Luca Vallebona, Armeria Black Hills)*

Detail of receiver, bolt, trigger and magazine of a variant of the "Moschetto Automatico Balilla." The general configuration is more like that of a semi-automatic rifle than it is of a bolt-action rifle, reflecting the designation of "automatic." *(Courtesy Luca Vallebona, Armeria Black Hills)*

MOSCHETTO CON TROMBONCINO MODELLO 1928

The tromboncino modello 1928 consisted of a rifle grenade launcher attached to the side of a modified TS carbine. The carbine's bolt did double duty as the bolt for the launcher mechanism. (*Courtesy, Leonardo M. Antaris, MD*)

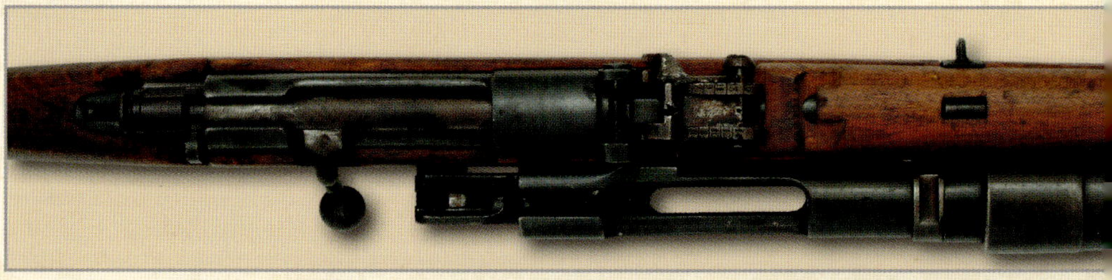

Top view of the tromboncino modello 1928 showing the launcher mounted alongside the carbine. (*Courtesy, Leonardo M. Antaris, MD*)

The Model 1928 grenade launcher was an unorthodox sysem that had a long and complicated history. In 1927 the Italian Army Staff charged the Artillery Technical Branch to develop a grenade launcher that could be used with the Model 91 TS carbine; development of the launcher progressed rapidly, with adoption of the *tromboncino modello 1928* only a year later. The original thought was to equip all members of the rifle squad with the launcher attachment, and each rifleman/grenadier was to be issued 12 rifle grenades. However, trials and experience showed the idea to be impractical and the grenades to be less effective than hoped for. Around 23,000 examples of the *tromboncino* were issued to all infantry, grenadier, *bersaglieri* and alpine regiments as well as to army schools, and in April 1930 directives were given that all infantry regiments would carry out the summer exercises with five *tromboncini mod. 28* in each rifle squad. The *Regia Marina* also issued this carbine and grenade attachment for use by landing troops. By 1932, after having placed an order for 100,000 S.R.C.M. (Società Romana Costruzioni Meccaniche) rifle grenades, the decision was made to use all existing stocks of the grenades for training purposes only. The *tromboncino* eventually was replaced by the 45mm Brixia mortar.

The launcher consisted of a receiver very similar to that of the carbine, a firing chamber, and a launching tube. The launcher mechanism was linked to the trigger of the carbine itself, and the carbine bolt was removed from the carbine and transferred to the launcher receiver for firing. In order to fire the launcher a grenade was put into the launcher tube, a standard ball cartridge was inserted into the receiver chamber, and the bolt was closed. The chamber of the launcher receiver had a slightly increased diameter that

Left side view of the TS carbine modified to accept the tromboncino grenade launcher. (*Courtesy, Leonardo M. Antaris, MD*)

The tromboncino Model 1928 viewed from the bottom. (*Courtesty, Leonardo M. Antaris, MD*)

Detail of the tromboncino launch tube receiver and the modified rear sight installed on the modified carbines. (*Courtesty, Leonardo M. Antaris, MD*)

allowed the neck of the cartridge case to expand and vent the gases past the bullet itself, which was firmly lodged against the base of the firing chamber. When the trigger was pulled and the cartridge fired, the gas pressure that was created escaped through four small vents in the chamber that connected with the launch tube, transmitting the pressure to the base of the grenade and launching it. Upon opening the bolt both the cartridge case and the spent bullet were extracted. By transferring the bolt to the carbine it could be used as a normal weapon.

The launcher was mounted on a TS carbine that was significantly modified to accept the launcher. The right side of the stock had several areas routed out to enable the launcher to be properly fitted, and a special fitting was mounted over the chamber to which the rear portion of the launcher was secured; the front portion of the launcher was secured by a modified second band, and the front band was also modified. The trigger housing was also modified with a transfer bar linked to the trigger mechanism of the launcher. The only parts of the modified carbine that remained interchangeable with those of the standard TS carbine were the bolt, front sight and ferrule, the buttplate, and the rear sling swivel. ■

MOSCHETTO CON TROMBONCINO MODELLO 1928

Launcher tube diameter: 38.5mm (1.5")
Grenade diameter: 38mm (1.5")
Grenade weight: 0.16 kg (0.35 lbs)
Practical range: 200 meters (approximate)
Burst radius: 10-15 meters

TROMBONCINO MODELLO 1943

In 1942 the Italians, having seen the results achieved by the Germans and British, began to look again at the possibility of adopting a rifle grenade. After considering various options it was decided to adopt and copy the German *Gewehrgranatgerät (Schiessebecher) M43*. The Italian launcher differed in the dimensions of the clamp attachment to render it compatible with the muzzle of Italian rifles. It could accept all of the various German rifle grenade types (anti-personnel, anti-tank, etc.), that had been manufactured in Italy with the proper propulsive cartridge. The M43 was issued only in limited numbers and seems to have been manufactured only by F.N.A.; there is some evidence that a very limited number of German Mauser Kar98k carbines were also acquired by the Italians along with the German version of the grenade launcher. ■

TROMBONCINO MODELLO 1943

Launcher tube diameter: 30mm (1.2")
Weight: 0.44 kg (0.97 lbs)
Armor penetration capability: 60mm vertical plate at 100 meters
Practical range: 175-200 meters

PROTOTYPE & EXPERIMENTAL RIFLES

There can be no doubt that the Italians were serious about testing, selecting and adopting a semi-automatic rifle even if the intent may not have been to equip the entire army with such a weapon but rather to issue it, at least initially, to selected elite units and to only a lmited number of riflemen in each infantry squad. As described earlier, in 1938 and 1939 two competitions were held, involving eight different arsenals or companies which submitted a total of fifteen different weapons chambered for the new 7.35mm round for consideration; the rifle selected was the Revelli/Armaguerra Model 1939. Described below are protoypes and limited production semi-auto rifles that were developed either to take part in the 1938 and 1939 competitions, or were developed later as private initiatives in the hope of securing a contract. ■

MOSCHETTO AUTOMATICO BREDA PG & FUCILE SEMIAUTOMATICO BREDA PG

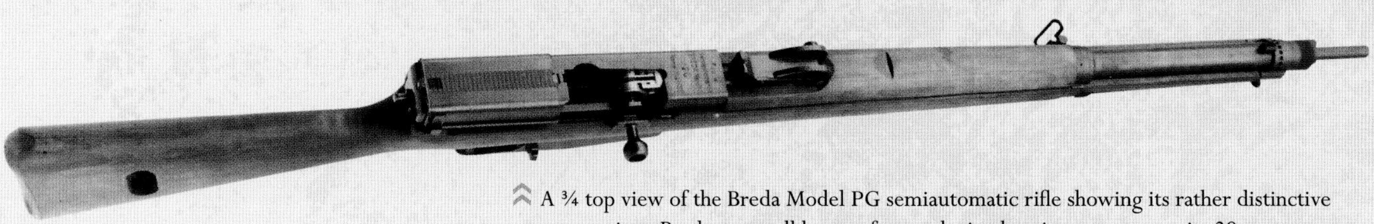

A ¾ top view of the Breda Model PG semiautomatic rifle showing its rather distinctive square receiver. Breda was well known for producing heavier armaments, its 20mm automatic cannon being particularly well known. *(Editoriale Olimpia)*

The Breda Model PG rifle was designed by Sestilio Fiorini and was produced by Breda in its Rome facility between 1931 and 1937. The acronym PG stood for *presa gas*, or "gas operated." A gas piston located close to the muzzle actuated a rod running inside the wooden handguard on the right side of the action, connecting the piston with the bolt carrier. The Breda PG was built in two versions: the first version was known as the *moschetto automatico Breda PG*, and was a relatively short-barrelled carbine; this version enjoyed some commercial success as Costa Rica bought 800 chambered for the 7x57mm Mauser cartridge. The Italian version, developed in 1937, had a longer barrel, was chambered for the 6x52mm Italian service cartridge and was known as the *fucile semiautomatico Breda*

PG. The version built for Costa Rica was fitted with a system that enabled bursts of four shots to be fired with each pull of the trigger, if desired; the Costa Rican PG may have been the first weapon of its type to incorporate a burst limiting feature. The Italian version of the PG fired only in the semiautomatic mode, firing single shots from a closed bolt. Limited numbers – possibly as many as 450 – of the PG were manufactured in 6.5mm for the Italian Army as prototypes.

The PG was a heavy, somewhat complicated rifle that was expensive to manufacture. A magazine feed was used, with feed lips machined on the inside of the receiver, and magazines were available in 20, 30, or 50-round capacities. The barrel was enclosed by a tubular metal jacket much like that of the German *Gewehr 88* for most of its length, with only the forward portion of the barrel exposed on both versions. The rear sights on both the rifle and carbine were typical Italian quadrant sights; the sight on the carbine was calibrated to 1800 meters, and the sight on the rifle may have been calibrated up to 2000 meters, as on the Model 1891 rifle. The stock was a straight wrist type; the carbine version had finger grooves in the stock, but the rifle version did not. There was a sling aperture in the butt; the forward sling swivel was located on the left hand side of the barrel band. The carbine version of the Breda PG sold to Costa Rica had several elements and features that argue that it was an early precursor of the assault rifle; among these were the selective fire capability, a relatively short barrel, and a high capacity magazine.

Markings on both models were located on the top of the rather square receiver, but differed somewhat. The Italian version was marked FUCILE SEMIAUTOMATICO BREDA Mod PG on the top three lines; underneath was a serial number, and the final line was marked Roma, followed by the date in Arabic and Roman numerals. The Costa Rican version was marked GOBIERNO DE COSTA RICA, MOSCHETTO AUTOMATICO BREDA Mod PG with the serial number preceded by the abbreviation No., and the last line as on the Italian model (ROMA, with the two date styles). ■

MOSCHETTO AUTOMATICO BREDA MOD. PG (COSTA RICAN VERSION); FUCILE SEMIAUTOMATICO BREDA MOD. PG (ITALIAN VERSION)

Designer: Sestilio Fiorini
Manufacturer: Società Meccanica Ernesto Breda (Rome facility)
Caliber: 6.5mm (Italian prototypes); 7mm Mauser (Costa Rica)
Cartridge: 6.5x52mm Mannlicher-Carcano; 7x57mm Mauser
Operating system: Gas
Overall length: 1000 mm (39.4") carbine; 1115mm (43.9") rifle
Barrel length: 455mm (17.9") carbine; 500mm (19.7") rifle
Weight: 4.5 kg (9.9 lbs) carbine; 5.25 kg (11.57 lbs) rifle
Front sight: Blade
Rear sight: Quadrant, graduated to 1800 meters (carbine)
Muzzle velocity: 750 m/sec (2460 fps) 6.5mm Carcano; 770 m/sec (2526 fps) 7mm Mauser
Rate of fire: 600 rpm (cyclic rate)
Feed system: Detachable box magazine: 20, 30 and 50 round capacity

The shortened version of the PG 35 as furnished to Costa Rica, shown without its high capacity magazine. (*Courtesy Ian McCollum/Forgotten Weapons*)

The trigger guard was integrated with the magazine housing on the Breda PG. Components of the PG required extensive machining. (*Courtesy Ian McCollum/Forgotten Weapons*)

Knurled muzzle cap, front sight, front band and bayonet lug on a Costa Rican PG; the exposed muzzle portion of the Italian version was considerably longer. (*Courtesy Ian McCollum/Forgotten Weapons*)

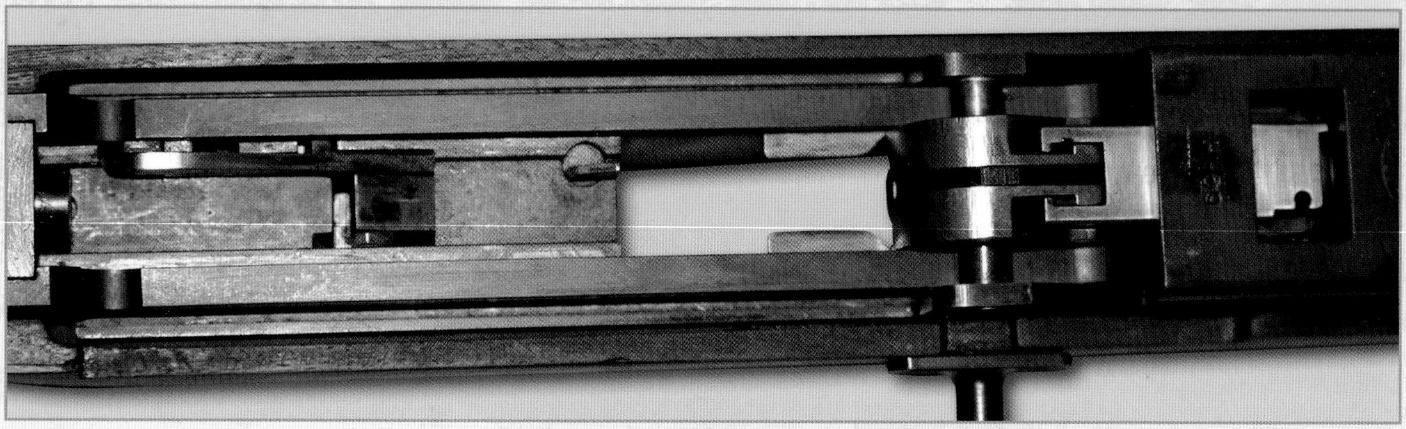

PG 35 bolt in the forward position. The robust construction of the receiver is clearly evident. (*Courtesy Ian McCollum / Forgotten Weapons*)

PG 35 bolt assembly retracted, allowing a clear view of the machined feed lips. (*Courtesy Ian McCollum / Forgotten Weapons*)

FUCILE SCOTTI MODELLO X

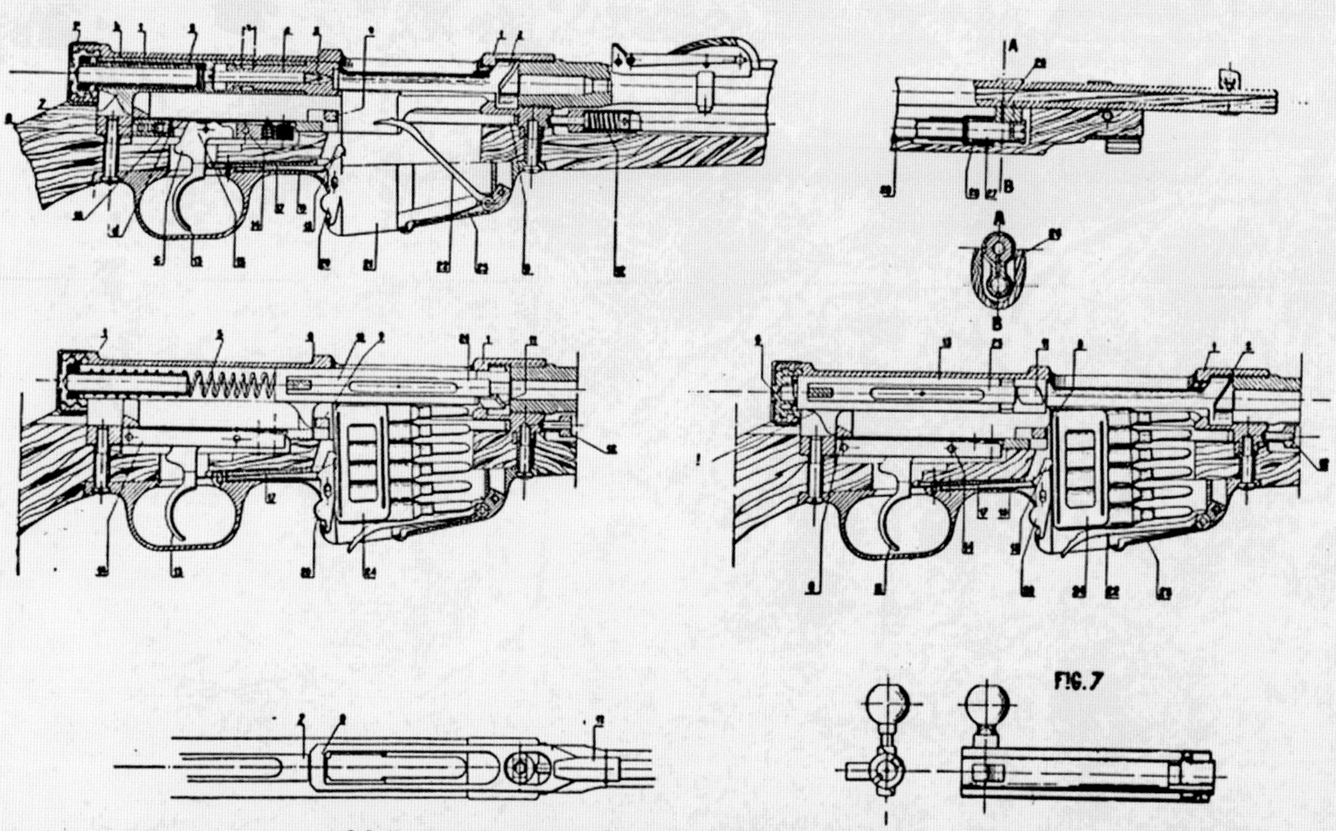

Tab. II - Coupes longitudinales et détails du fusil automatique Scotti, mod. IX.

The Breda PG with magazine attached. The open sides of the magazine were a weak point of the design, allowing dirt or other matter to compromise cartridge feeding. (*Courtesy Ian McCollum / Forgotten Weapons*)

Markings on the Costa Rican version of the Breda Model PG were similar to those on the Italian version. It is interesting to note that the Fascist year designation (XIII) was also included on the export model. (*Courtesy Ian McCollum / Forgotten Weapons*)

The Scotti Model X rifle was designed and developed in response to an Italian Army requirement for a 6.5mm semi-automatic rifle that would use as many parts as possible of the Model 1891 bolt action rifle. Scotti himself is not known to have personally designed the Model X rifle or many of the other weapons that bear his name, but rather orchestrated the efforts of others who designed and produced the weapons. In March 1931 Scotti unveiled the *carabina mod. T.S.* which utilized the barrel, sights, magazine housing and other furnishings of the Carcano, but the receiver, bolt, trigger mechanism and stock were all new. The *mod. T.S.* carbine was quite distinctive in appearance, as it was fitted with a full pistol grip behind the trigger. The carbine likely was a prototype only; in May 1931 it was followed by the *fucile Scotti modello IX* semi-automatic rifle, which mechanically was the same as the carbine. In 1932 the *fucile modello X* (the X denoted the tenth year of the Fascist regime expressed in Roman numerals) was unveiled; aside from its designation, it differed very little from the Model IX rifle of the previous year. In contrast to normal Italian practice, most parts of the Scotti, including the trigger guard, front and rear barrel bands, and magazine release were numbered to the rifle. Scotti rifles bear the markings SCOTTI Mod. X on the receiver ring, and Armi Automatiche Scotti-Brescia on the left side of the receiver. Consistent with the barrel's provenance, the barrel chamber facets bear the markings TERNI on the top facet, the serial number on the left hand facet, and the year of manufacture on the right-hand facet. The left hand side of the receiver ring has an oval with the word GNUTTI inside it; this refers to the Eredi Gnutti company of Lumezzane which produced a range of military

Sectional views of the Scotti Model IX rifle, precursor to the Model X. (*Editoriale Olimpia*)

FUCILE SCOTTI MODELLO X

Designer: Alfredo Scotti
Manufacturer: Serafino e Andrea Eredi Gnutti, Lumezzane (action); Fabbrica d'Armi Terni (barrel)
Caliber: 6.5mm
Cartridge: 6.5x52mm Mannlicher-Carcano
Operating system: Gas, short stroke piston
Safety: Sliding plate which blocked bolt in closed position
Overall length: 1330mm (52.36")
Barrel length: 610mm (24")
Weight: 4.05 kg (8.92 lbs)
Front sight: Barleycorn
Rear sight: Quadrant, graduated to 2000 meters
Muzzle velocity: 700 m/sec
Feed system: 6-round Mannlicher-Carcano clips

« The Scotti stocks did not bear the usual manufacturer's cartouche (which would have been a Gnutti cartouche), but did bear the rifle's serial number. *(Courtesy, Leonardo M. Antaris, MD)*

« Magazine detail of a Scotti Model X. The clip release is a numbered part. *(Courtesy, Leonardo M. Antaris, MD)*

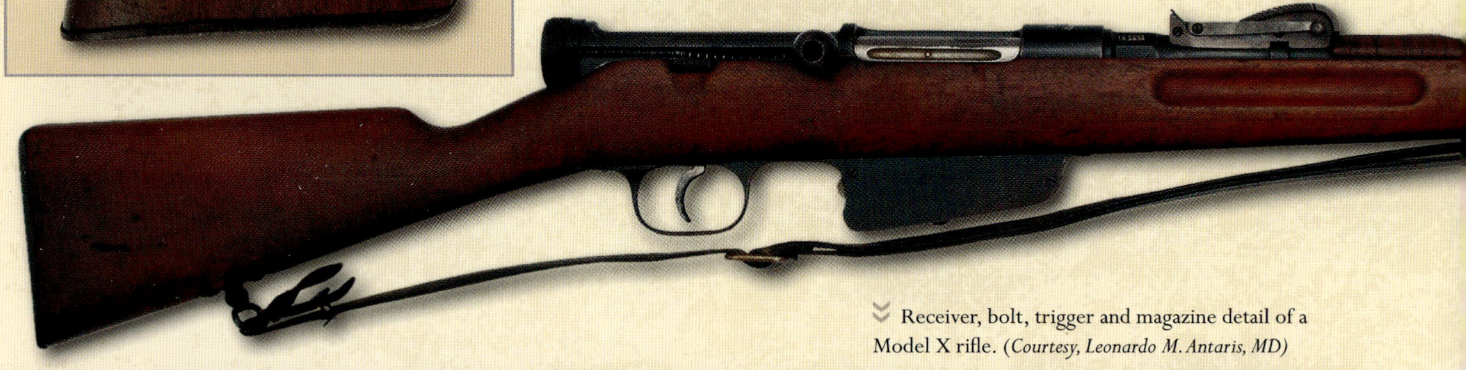

» Receiver, bolt, trigger and magazine detail of a Model X rifle. *(Courtesy, Leonardo M. Antaris, MD)*

« The actual manufacturer of the Scotti model X rifles was Gnutti, as indicated by the name unobtrusively stamped within an oval on the receiver ring. *(Courtesy, Leonardo M. Antaris, MD)*

» The Scotti Model X was produced by Eredi Gnutti, which was well known for making swords and bayonets as well as other military items. Gnutti produced the receiver and action part of the rifle but used barrels supplied by Terni. *(Courtesy, Leonardo M. Antaris, MD)*

« Scotti company proprietary markings on a Scotti Model X rifle. *(Courtesy, Leonardo M. Antaris, MD)*

items and which was the actual manufacturer of the Scotti Model X. Gnutti records reflect a production run of 250 Model X rifles.

The Model X was also made as a prototype in a sporting version which had a "sporter" stock with checkering at the wrist, a rib on the barrel, and rear leaf sights; the rifle was marked with Zurich as the Scotti location, but it is problematic as to whether the rifle was actually produced in Switzerland. At least one military style prototype was also produced in 7.92x57mm, using a Mauser barrel, magazine, sights and front barrel band made in Germany, but it likewise is unlikely that this example was made somewhere other than in Italy or than by someone other than Gnutti. Scotti continued to experiment with semi-automatic rifles until at least 1936 when he developed the Model XIV, for which no details are extant. ■

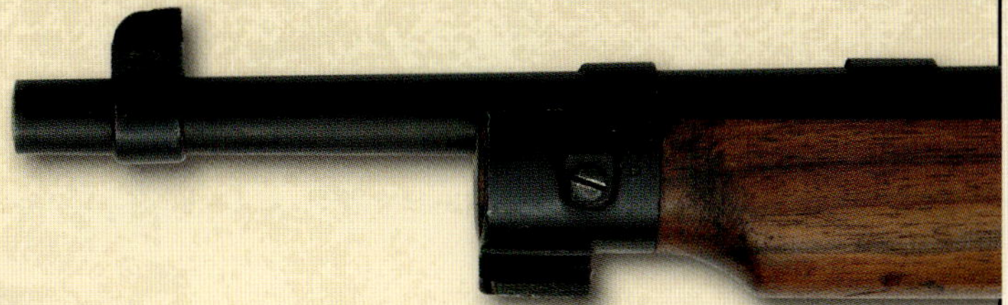

The Model X rifle used many furnishings of the Caracano Model 1891 rifle, such as the front barrel band and bayonet stud. Note that the band, as with many other parts, is numbered to the rifle. *(Courtesy, Leonardo M. Antaris, MD)*

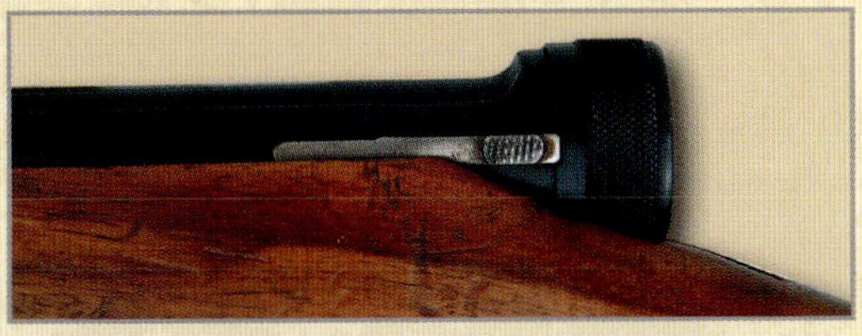

The knurled receiver end cap on the Scotti Model X is similar to that used on Beretta semi-automatic rifles and submachine guns. *(Courtesy, Leonardo M. Antaris, MD)*

The Scotti Model X was designed by Alfredo Scotti, who was also associated with the design of a 20mm cannon produced by Isotta-Fraschini. The Model X was quite similar to the preceding Model IX. Like several other Italian semiautomatic rifle designs the Model X was never produced in large numbers or adopted by the Italian Army and today is a rare collector's item. *(Courtesy, Leonardo M. Antaris, MD)*

Receiver and barrel markings and Model 1891 style rear sight of a low number Scotti Model X rifle. *(Courtesy, Leonardo M. Antaris, MD)*

Detail of barrel and receiver markings on a high number Model X rifle; only 250 Model X rifles were produced. *(Courtesy, Leonardo M. Antaris, MD*

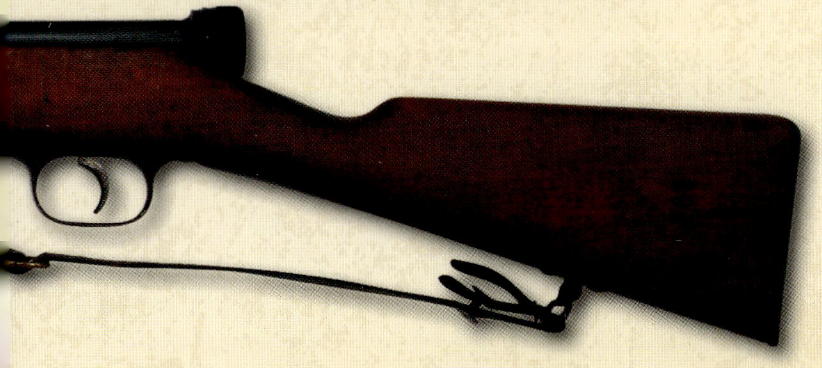

The butt plate on the Scotti Model X was of the type used on the Model 1891 cavalry carbines, with a trap that allowed storage of a sectional cleaning rod. *(Courtesy, Leonardo M. Antaris, MD)*

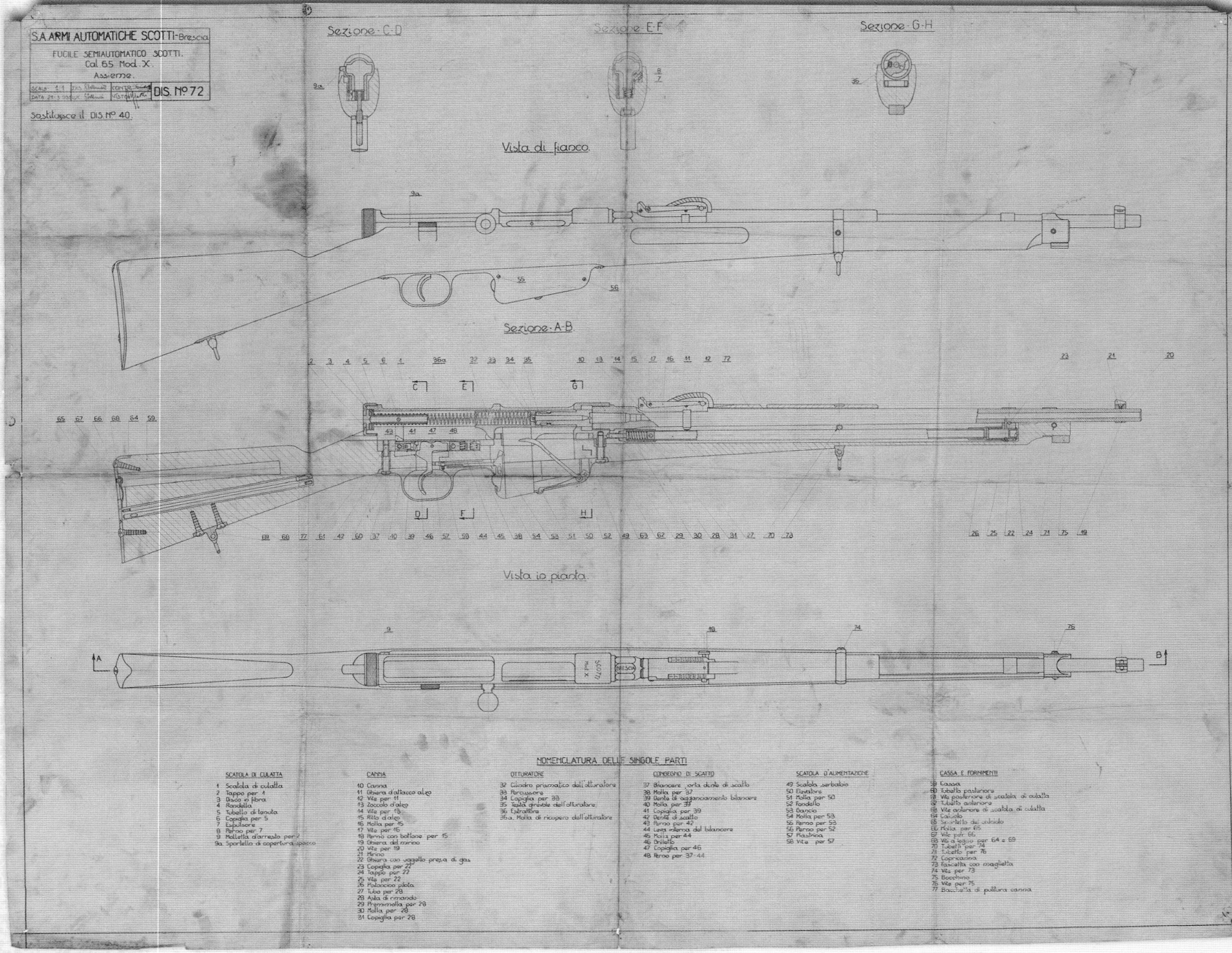

Side, sectional and plan views and nomenclature of the Scotti Model X, from Eredi Gnutti Metalli historical files. (*Courtesy, Eredi Gnutti Metalli*)

FUCILE BERETTA MODELLO 31

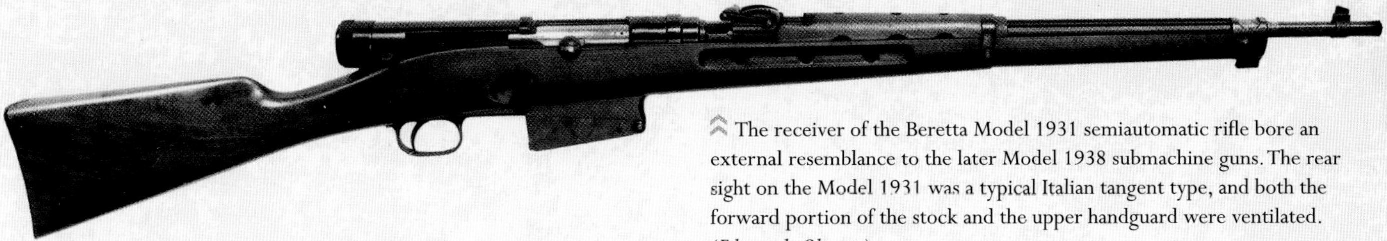

The receiver of the Beretta Model 1931 semiautomatic rifle bore an external resemblance to the later Model 1938 submachine guns. The rear sight on the Model 1931 was a typical Italian tangent type, and both the forward portion of the stock and the upper handguard were ventilated. *(Editoriale Olimpia)*

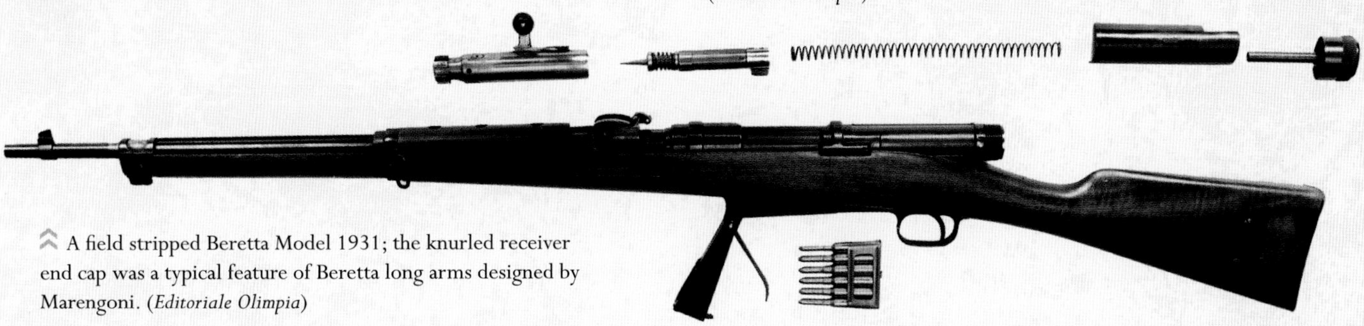

A field stripped Beretta Model 1931; the knurled receiver end cap was a typical feature of Beretta long arms designed by Marengoni. *(Editoriale Olimpia)*

This semi-automatic rifle was designed by Tullio Marengoni, who was later responsible for the design of the Beretta Model 38 family of submachine guns. The general configuration of the receiver housing did in fact bear a strong resemblance to the later submachine gun bolt housings. It functioned on the short recoil system and had a rotating bolt that had six locking lugs in its head. Loading was achieved by inserting a standard six-round Model 91 clip. The bolt was automatically locked in the open position when the last round was fired and could be freed by a release catch. The rear sight was the same as used in the Model 1891 cavalry carbine. The stock was a straight wrist stock with finger grooves; a distinctive feature of the stock was the ventilating holes located in the finger groove channel. The half-length handguard, secured by a single barrel band, was also marked by half moon ventilating holes on the sides and circular holes on the top. ■

FUCILE BERETTA MODELLO 31

Designer: Tullio Marengoni
Manufacturer: Fabbrica d'Armi Pietro Beretta, Gardone Val Trompia
Caliber: 6.5mm
Cartridge: 6.5x52mm Mannlicher-Carcano
Operating system: Short recoil
Safety: Two-position lever on right side
Overall length: 1155mm (45.5")
Barrel length: 630mm (24.8")
Weight: 4.08 kg (9 lbs)
Front sight: Barleycorn
Rear sight: Quadrant, graduated to 1500 meters
Muzzle velocity: 700 m/sec (2295 fps)
Feed system: 6-round Mannlicher-Carcano clip

FUCILE BERETTA MODELLO 37

The Beretta Model 1937 semiautomatic rifle differed externally from the earlier Model 1931 in several respects, including the fixed rear sight, the ventilation holes in the upper hand guard, and the magazine configuration. *(Editoriale Olimpia)*

The Model 37 semi-automatic rifle developed by Beretta for the new 7.35mm cartridge was based on the earlier Beretta Model 31 rifle. In addition to the larger caliber there were a number of other differences. The magazine capacity was increased to nine rounds and loading was effected from above using special stripper clips. After the final round had been fired the follower held the bolt in the open position, and in order to close the bolt it was necessary either to pull back a release catch or to depress the follower. There was a rotating cutoff that could be used to disconnect the semi-automatic feature and make the weapon an ordinary repeater. The rear sight was similar to that used on the later Model 38 submachine guns. The stock was a semi-pistol grip type, and although the finger groove of the previous *modello 31* was retained, it did not have the ventilating holes; however, possibly to compensate for the lack of stock vents, the number of holes in the upper handguard was increased. The forward portion of the stock between the barrel band and the front barrel band was replaced by a metal extension; the front barrel band was the same as on the Model 1931. ■

FUCILE BERETTA MODELLO 37

Designer: Tullio Marengoni
Manufacturer: Fabbrica d'Armi Pietro Beretta, Gardone Val Trompia
Caliber: 7.35mm
Cartridge: 7.35x51mm
Operating system: Short recoil
Safety: Two-position lever on right-hand side
Overall length: 1055mm (41.5")
Barrel length: 533mm (21")
Weight: 4.04 kg (8.9 lbs)
Front sight: Barleycorn
Rear sight: Fixed open notch
Muzzle velocity: 755 m/sec (2480 fps).
Feed system: 9 rounds

FUCILE PAVESI MODELLO 1938

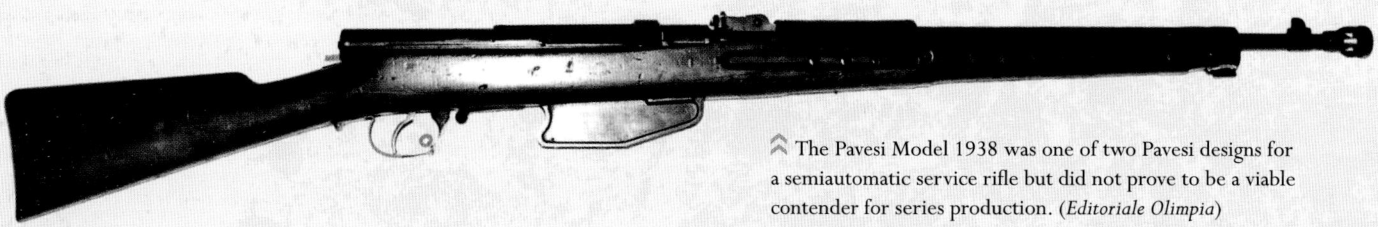

The Pavesi Model 1938 was one of two Pavesi designs for a semiautomatic service rifle but did not prove to be a viable contender for series production. (*Editoriale Olimpia*)

The Pavesi Model 1938 rifle was a gas-operated weapon concerning which very little historical or developmental data is available. Design of the rifle is universally credited to a designer named Pavesi, but it was not until early 2012 that Pavesi's first name and a few personal details were unearthed in the files of the Italian Army's Ufficio Storico (Historical Office). However, it has proven impossible to determine where this rifle was manufactured, but knowledgeable sources in Italy suggest that either F.N.A. Brescia or Meccanica Bresciana Tempini are likely candidates. The Model 1938 was chambered for the 8x59mm Breda Model 35 cartridge – very similar to the German 7.92x57mm round – which had been developed for use in Italian machine guns. The Model 1938 and the later Pavesi model 1942 were the only Italian rifles to be chambered for this round, putting them roughly on a par with semi-automatic rifles such as the U.S. M1 Garand and the later German G-43 semi-auto rifle. The magazine capacity remains open to question, but judging from the one photograph available, a capacity of five or six rounds seems appropriate. Its operating principle was similar to that of the U.S. M-16 rifle, as gas was piped through a tube above the barrel directly to the face of the bolt. The stock was a straight wrist type with finger grooves; the finger grooves had four ventilating holes in the groove channel, and the portion of the stock forward of the retaining band was also marked by a series of ventilating holes. Numbers are unavailable, but the Model 1938 likely was made only as a prototype or in a very limited number of trial models; it is not documented as being issued to Italian troops. Efforts to locate a surviving example have been fruitless. ■

FUCILE PAVESI MODELLO 1938

Designer: Giuseppe Pavesi
Manufacturer: Meccanica Bresciana già Tempini or F.N.A. Brescia (questionable)
Caliber: 8mm
Cartridge: 8x59mm Breda Model 35
Operating system: Gas
Safety: Lever located between trigger guard and magazine housing
Overall length: 1200mm (47.2")
Barrel length: 600mm (23.6")
Weight: 4.26 kg (9.4 lbs)
Front sight: Barleycorn
Rear sight: Quadrant with with V notch, graduated to 1200 meters
Muzzle velocity: 790 m/sec (2600 fps)
Feed system: Uncertain, but likely five or six rounds

FUCILE PAVESI MODELLO 1942

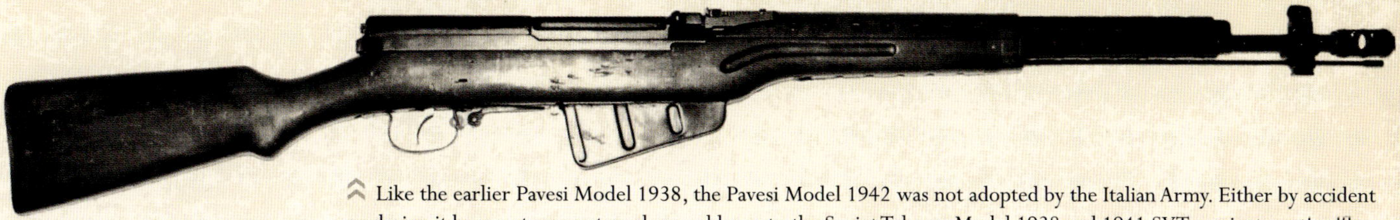

Like the earlier Pavesi Model 1938, the Pavesi Model 1942 was not adopted by the Italian Army. Either by accident or design it bore a strong external resemblance to the Soviet Tokarev Model 1938 and 1941 SVT semiautomatic rifles. Note the ventilation holes on the bottom of the stock and on the handguards. (*Editoriale Olimpia*)

At first glance the Pavesi Model 1942 rifle could be mistaken for a Soviet Tokarev SVT Model 1940 semi-automatic rifle. Like the earlier Pavesi Model 1938, it was chambered for the powerful 8x59mm Breda round. The one available photograph of the rifle suggests that magazine capacity could be ten rounds, but whether the rounds were inserted by stripper clips is not known. It functioned on the short recoil principle and had a rotating bolt with four locking lugs. It had a selector switch for full or semi-automatic fire located between the trigger guard and the magazine housing. The stock had a semi-pistol grip that tapered and narrowed forward of the magazine housing; the finger grooves followed the curve of the taper. The stock had a series of six ventilating holes on the underside forward of the magazine, and the wooden handguard likewise had ventilating holes. A perforated metal jacket reminiscent of the metal piston cover on the Tokarev covered part of the forward portion of the barrel, and the bottom of the front sight assembly incorporated the bayonet lug. The rifle was fitted with a single port muzzle brake. As with the earlier Pavesi Model 1938, the Model 1942 would appear to have been produced either as a prototype only, or in very limited trial production, but was not adopted by the Italian Army. Like that of the earlier Pavesi Model 1938 its place of manufacture is uncertain, nor has any surviving example been found. ■

FUCILE PAVESI MODELLO 1942

Designer: Giuseppe Pavesi
Manufacturer: Meccanica Bresciana già Tempini or F.N.A Brescia (questionable)
Caliber: 8mm
Cartridge: 8x59 Breda Model 35
Operating system: Short recoil
Safety: Lever located between trigger guard and magazine housing
Overall length: 1200mm (47.2")
Barrel length: 600mm (23.6")
Weight: Not available
Front sight: Hooded post
Rear sight: Tangent with V notch, graduated from 300 to 700 meters
Muzzle velocity: 790 m/sec (2600 fps)
Feed system: Integral box magazine, possibly 10-round capacity

FUCILE SEMIAUTOMATICO ZK 391

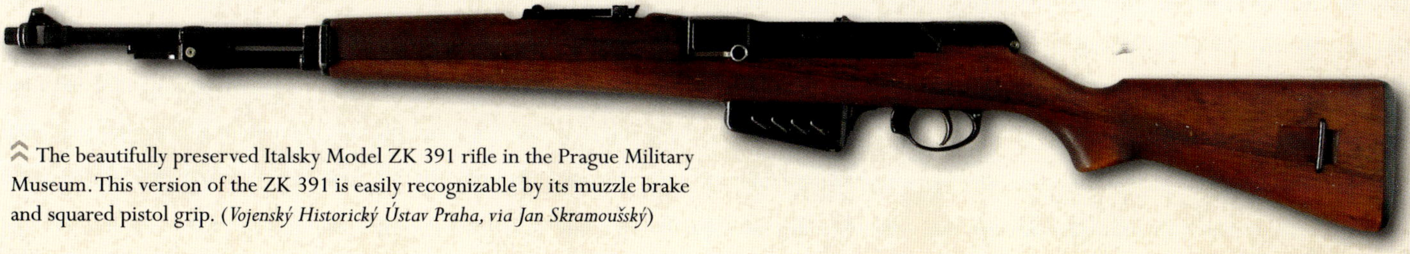

The beautifully preserved Italsky Model ZK 391 rifle in the Prague Military Museum. This version of the ZK 391 is easily recognizable by its muzzle brake and squared pistol grip. (*Vojenský Historický Ústav Praha, via Jan Skramoušský*)

Information on this Czech semi-automatic rifle is sketchy at best, but its World War II Italian connection is intriguing. The rifle was developed by two brothers, Josef and František Koucký (František was later responsible for design of the 9mm CZ 75 pistol) in 1942, and reportedly in 1943 the rifle attracted the interest of Italian technical personnel who carried out tests and evaluation of the rifle and were impressed with its potential. Although details are not clear it seems that one or more prototypes may have been produced at the Armaguerra factory – originally built to produce the Revelli Model 39 semi-automatic rifle in 7.35mm – in Cremona in 1944, but this remains unsubstantiated. There is also some suggestion, likewise unsubstantiated, that the Germans attempted to begin series production of the rifle at the Armaguerra plant after September 1944 but that little progress was made before the war ended. The ZK 391 was a semi-automatic rifle chambered for the 7.92x57mm German service cartridge, and had ten-round integral box magazine fed by stripper clips; it was gas operated and used a piston arrangement similar to that on the U.S. M1 Garand rifle. The so-called Italsky Model was similar to the original Czech model, but had several features similar to the Pavesi and Beretta semi-auto rifles previously described, including a single port muzzle brake, square-base pistol grip, and hinged magazine housing. ■

SAMONABIJECI PUSKA ZK 391 (CZECH DESIGNATION); FUCILE SEMIAUTOMATICO ZK 391 (ITALIAN DESIGNATION)

Designers: Josef and František Koucký
Manufacturer: Armaguerra, Cremona (uncertain; possible prototype only)
Caliber: 7.92mm
Cartridge: 7,92x57mm Mauser
Operating system: Gas operated; piston actuated
Safety: NA
Overall length: 1082mm (42.6")
Barrel length: 548mm (21.57")
Weight: 3.39 kg (7.47 lbs)
Front sight: Blade
Rear sight: Tangent; appears similar to Mauser Kar98k rear sight
Muzzle velocity: Not available
Feed system: Detachable 10-round box magazine,

NON-STANDARD OR MODIFIED RIFLES IN FOREIGN SERVICE

CARCANO TIPO I JAPANESE TYPE I RIFLE

Although not an Italian service rifle, this interesting and unusual weapon deserves mention because it is essentially a variant of the Model 1891 built for export. In the late-1930s the Japanese Army absorbed all Japanese rifle production, and as a consequence the Imperial Japanese Navy was forced to look to foreign sources to arm its Naval Infantry element. This led the Imperial Navy to place an order with Italy for a hybrid rifle that incorporated both Italian and Japanese features, resulting in a rifle that utilized the Model 1891 Carcano action and slightly heavier barrel chambered for the standard Japanese 6x50mm service round, mated to a Mauser type box magazine. The Type I was produced between 1938 and 1939; the rifle's designation as the Type I is a Japanese rather than Italian designation, and the letter I in the rifle's designation likely refers to Italy. In simple terms, the Type I was nothing more than the Model 1891 rifle with a repositioned extractor on the bolt, a heavier barrel chambered for the Japanese 6.5mm cartridge, a Mauser-type magazine, and Japanese-style stock and fittings. The

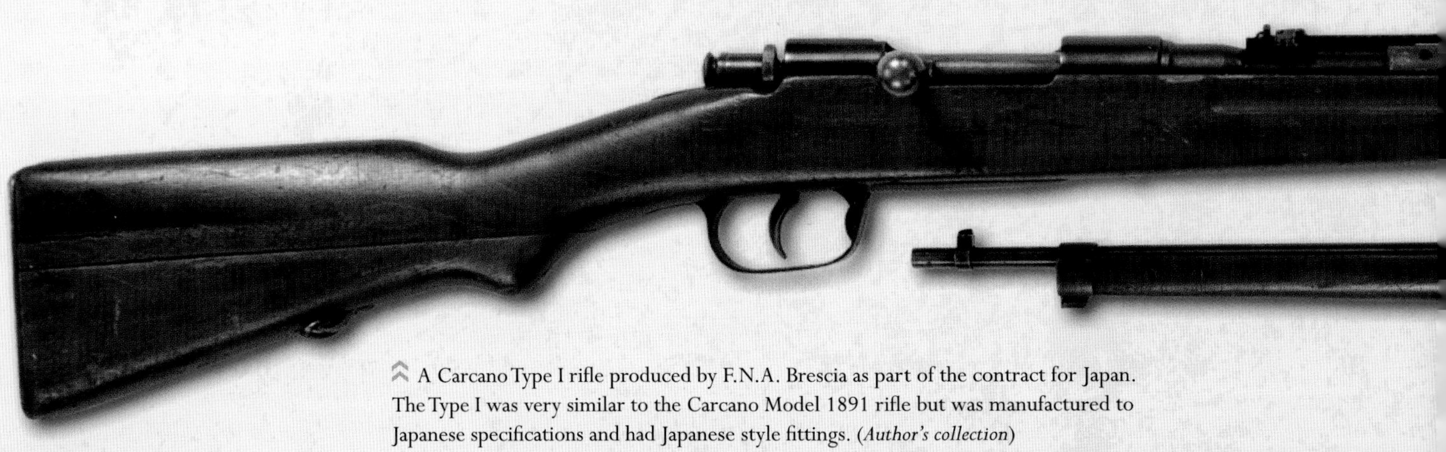

A Carcano Type I rifle produced by F.N.A. Brescia as part of the contract for Japan. The Type I was very similar to the Carcano Model 1891 rifle but was manufactured to Japanese specifications and had Japanese style fittings. (*Author's collection*)

receiver differed slightly as the bridge had milled slots to accommodate the Mauser-style stripper clips and the opening for the ejector was on the centerline rather than off-center. The bolt was a normal Carcano bolt, the only differences being that the extractor on the Type I bolt was centered rather than being on the left, the clearance slot for the ejector was repositioned, and the face of the bolt lacked the groove found on the Italian bolt. The sights were Arisaka pattern, and the furniture and fittings were Japanese style, to include the typical two-piece Japanese style dovetailed buttstock, made of beech; the buttplate had an internal stiffening rib like that of the Model 1891. The Type I was produced with two different stock lengths (1258mm and 1280mm), but how many of each stock variant were produced is open to question. The front band was secured by a Japanese-style retaining spring mounted on the underside of the stock fore end, and the rifle accepted the standard Arisaka Type 30 bayonet; the barrel diameter at the muzzle was 14mm compared to the 13mm on the Model 1891 Carcano. Markings were sparse, consisting of the serial number and small proof marks; some small parts bore the markings PB surmounted by a crown (for Pietro Beretta), F.N.A. (F.N.A. Brescia), FAT (Terni), or FAG (SFARE Gardone). At least on F.N.A. produced rifles the F.N.A. logo and the last two digits of the year of manufacture were stamped on the underside of the receiver ring. Some sights were marked Gnutti. There was no chrysanthemum on the receiver, although some were marked with the naval anchor. Regarding the total number of Type I rifles produced some sources quote a figure as low as 60,000, while others claim that as many as 120,000 were produced The most credible figure comes from Di Giorgio and Pettinelli who cite a total production of 120,000 for certain, and possibly as many as 130,000. Terni Arsenal acted as the point of contact for the order with the Japanese and also seems to have manufactured all of the barrels, which were then mated to the rest of the rifles portioned among three other producers – Beretta, F.N.A. Brescia, and SFARE Gardone. SFARE Gardone produced 60,000, and Beretta and F.N.A. each produced 30,000. A run of 10,000 may have been produced as a pilot lot by Terni. Serial numbers with an A through F prefix were produced by SFARE Gardone; G through I were produced by F.N.A., and J through L by Beretta. It should be noted, however, that these letter blocks appear not to have been strictly adhered to; the Type I in the author's collection bears serial number J 3287, but was manufactured by F.N.A. Brescia rather than by Beretta. SFARE Gardone was the collection point for rifles produced by the other manufacturers, and was responsible for shipping them to Japan. The Type I was used by the Special Naval Landing Force (the Japanese equivalent of the marines) and naval guard troops. Although the Type I was issued to Imperial Navy operational units most are believed to have been little used, as most surviving examples are in excellent condition. ■

FUCILE CARCANO TIPO I

Designer: Modification of Model 1891 rifle designed by Salvatore Carcano
Manufacturer: F.N.A. Brescia; Fabbrica d'Armi Terni; SFARE Gardone Val Trompia; Fabbrica d'Armi Pietro Beretta
Caliber: 6.5mm
Cartridge: 6.5x50mm Arisaka
Overall length: 1258mm (49.53") short stock; 1280mm (50.39") long stock
Barrel length: 780mm (30.7")
Rifling: RH twist, four grooves
Weight: 4.2 kg (9.26 lbs)
Front sight: Fixed blade, without protective wings
Rear sight: Adjustable from 500 to 2400 meters
Muzzle velocity: 765 m/s (2509 fps)
Feed system: Mauser type 5 round integral box

The Carcano Type I was produced with stocks of two different lengths; the example shown has the shorter stock. (*Author's collection*)

Images A & B The Carcano Model 91, top, and the Type I compared. (*Author's collection*)

A

The rear sight on the Type I replicated the rear sight found on Japanese Arisaka rifles. (*Author's collection*

The F.N.A. logo and last two digits of year of manufacture were stamped unobtrusively on the bottom of the receiver ring and were the only indication of the manufacturer and production date of this Type I rifle. (*Author's collection*)

B

The serial number on the barrel chamber was the only clearly visible marking on the Type I rifles. Most Type I rifles with serial numbers in the J block were produced by Beretta, but this rifle was produced by F.N.A Brescia, whose normal block range was G through I. (*Author's collection*)

7.92X57MM CARCANO RIFLES & CARBINES

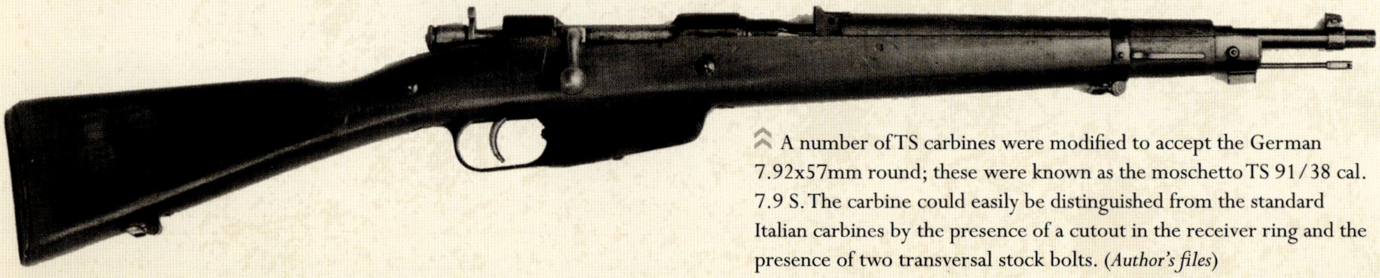

A number of TS carbines were modified to accept the German 7.92x57mm round; these were known as the moschetto TS 91/38 cal. 7.9 S. The carbine could easily be distinguished from the standard Italian carbines by the presence of a cutout in the receiver ring and the presence of two transversal stock bolts. (*Author's files*)

An intriguing sidelight to the Carcano story involves Carcanos that were chambered for the 7.92x57 German service cartridge. It should be noted at the outset that, despite claims by some authors that Carcanos chambered for the 7.92x57mm cartridge were issued to Italian troops on the Russian front, there is no

The Type I stock was a two-piece dovetailed stock; it is not uncommon to encounter examples whose two pieces show signs of separation such as on this rifle. (*Author's collection*)

The Type I rear sight in the raised position. (*Author's collection*)

The front band was retained by a Japanese style undermounted spring rather than being secured by a screw as on Italian rifles. (*Author's collection*)

Although the Type I rear sight was a Japanese pattern sight, the front sight was Italian style and lacked the protective ears typical of Arisaka rifles. (*Author's collection*)

The floorplate on the Type I was a Mauser-style floorplate; the release catch was on the forward portion of the trigger guard. (*Author's collection*)

actual evidence to support such assertions, nor, indeed, were any such weapons ever issued to any Italian troops. Wartime Italian documents that refer to *fucili russi cal. 8* invariably refer to them in the context of captured weapons and are a generic reference to captured 7.62x54mm Mosin-Nagant rifles, but the notion seems to have taken hold that *fucili russi cal. 8* refer to Carcanos chambered for the 7.92x57 cartridge. This ignores the fact that if indeed the Italians had chambered any Carcanos in 7.92mm for use on the Russian front, they would have almost certainly designated them using their normal designation convention that would have resulted in a designation of *moschetto per truppe speciali cal. 7.92*, or something similar for the appropriate weapon. Although there is much fanciful and inaccurate information circulating with respect to these weapons, the truth is that Carcanos chambered for the German 7.92x57mm round fall into two general categories. In the first category were 6.5mm and possibly 7.35mm weapons captured by the Germans, converted to 7.92mm in Germany or northern Italy and issued to German second-line units; Carcanos that remained chambered for the 6.5mm and 7.35mm rounds were instead

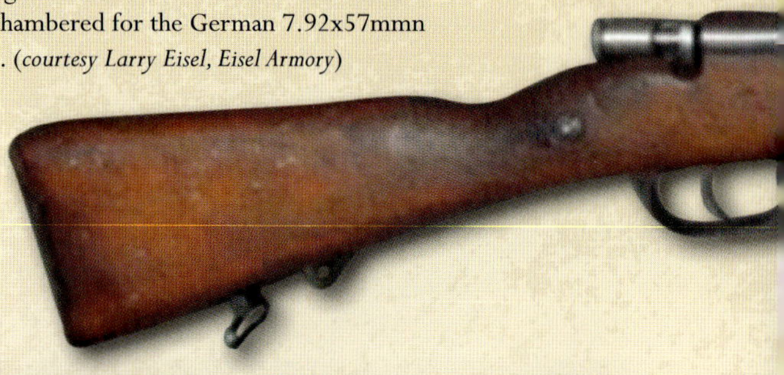

« The rear sight was marked 7.92 to indicate that the weapon was chambered for the German 7.92x57mmn (8mm) round. *(courtesy Larry Eisel, Eisel Armory)*

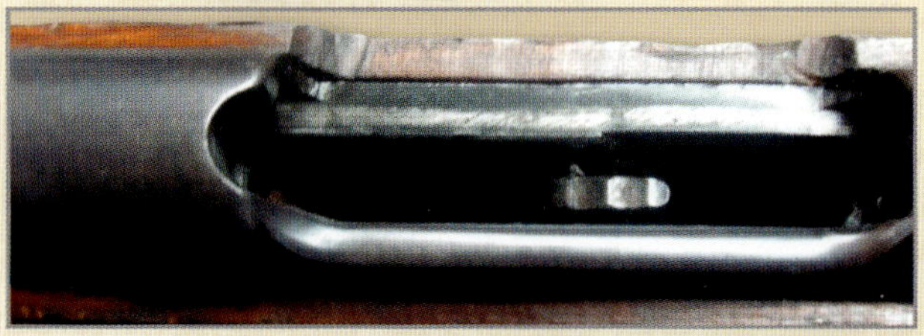

» The clearance cut milled into the receiver ring to accommodate the longer 8mmn round. *(courtesy Larry Eisel, Eisel Armory)*

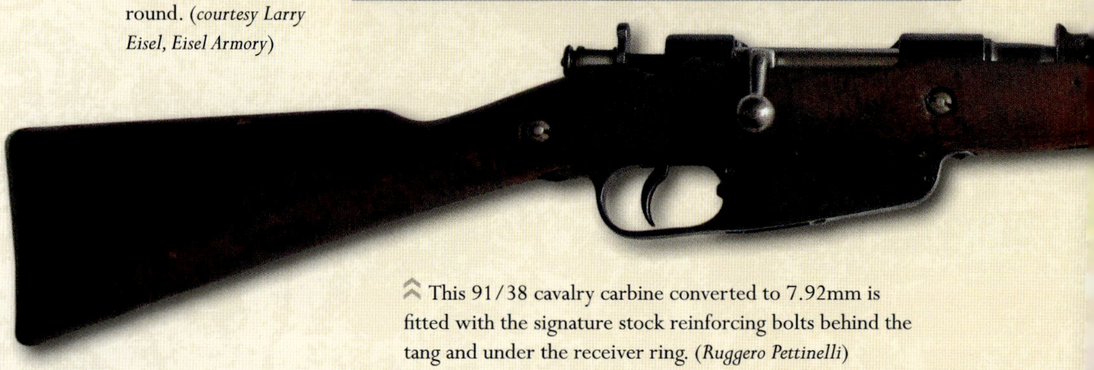

^ This 91/38 cavalry carbine converted to 7.92mm is fitted with the signature stock reinforcing bolts behind the tang and under the receiver ring. *(Ruggero Pettinelli)*

issued to *Volkssturm* units and represented a significant percentage of the *Volkssturm* small arms inventory. The second category consisted of those Carcanos that were altered to 7.92mm in Italy after the war and sold to Egypt.

On 8 September 1943 the Italian government headed by General Badoglio agreed to what is generally referred to as an armistice with the Allies, but which was, in effect, a surrender. A large part of northern Italy was still occupied by the Germans who promptly seized as much Italian military equipment as they could. Among the equipment were close to 400,000 Carcano rifles and carbines chambered for either the 6.5x52mm or 7.35x51mm cartridge; most, if not all, of these weapons were shipped to Germany to be integrated into the *Volkssturm* defense forces which were in dire need of anything that could shoot. Initially, the Carcanos were issued to the *Volkssturm* in their original 6.5mm or 7.35mm configuration, but when it was realized that ammunition was not as readily available as had been assumed measures were taken to rebore and rechamber the rifles for the standard German 7.92x57mm service round. Conversion, which seems to have been limited to the Model 41 rifle, Model 38 short rifle, and Model 91 and Model 91/38 cavalry carbines consisted of reboring the barrel to 7.92mm, adding a stock bolt forward of the trigger housing, removing the follower and inserting a wooden block with a concave groove in the top in the magazine well – effectively rendering the weapon a single-shot weapon – and setting battle sights at 200 meters. Tests were conducted with a Model 38 rifle that had been altered to fire as a repeater, with a milled clearance cut on the chamber to allow the longer 7.92mm round to be used and using a specially modified Carcano magazine. The test results were totally unsatisfactory due largely to excessive recoil forces, which was a problem with all Carcano weapons chambered for the German cartridge.

The conversions began in early-1945 and were carried out in Italy as well as in Germany. Heinrich Krieghoff converted Carcanos in two plants in the Tyrol region, one at Kufstein in Austria, and the other at Sterzing (known as Vipiteno in Italian), in the South Tyrol, where machinery from the Armaguerra plant had been sent; it is estimated that 7,820 Carcanos were converted by Krieghoff. The Italian conversions were carried out in Brescia, and although German references are somewhat generic, it is likely that the facility in question was F.N.A. Brescia, where about 4,500 Carcanos were converted. Markings on the converted rifles and carbines generally consisted of a new serial number stamped on the barrel, receiver and stock, as well as being electro-pencilled on the bolt body. Carcanos pressed into German service may also exhibit German *Heereszeugamt* (army ordnance depot) markings such as HZajt3 on the stock. The Krieghoff logo consisting of the letters HK inside a circle was stamped on top of the receiver ring and a German firing proof might also be stamped on the exterior of the barrel. All of the converted weapons were in the H block (although reportedly some examples may also be found with a K suffix); generally, from the beginning of the H block to the H 4000 or possibly 5000 block were Model 41 rifles, H6000-H7000 were Model 38 short rifles, H7000 block were Model 41 rifles, and H8000-H9000 were cavalry carbines. The German practice of assigning code designators to captured weapons was applied to

The moschetto 91 TS was converted to 7.92x57mm in significant numbers after World War II and exported to the Middle East. *(courtesy Larry Eisel, Eisel Armory)*

The Germans normally electro-pencilled the serial number on the bolt of captured Carcanos; on this cavalry carbine the cocking piece has been numbered as well. *(courtesy Larry Eisel, Eisel Armory)*

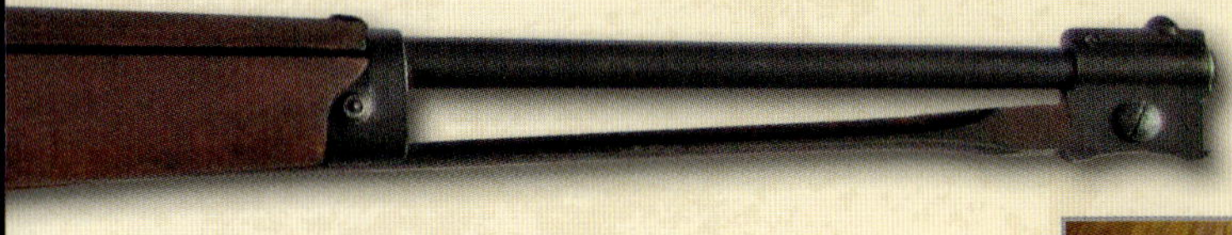

A

B

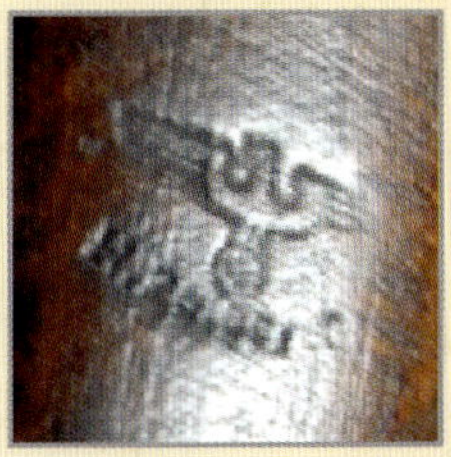

Images A & B Carcanos pressed into German service were marked with a German ordnance depot, or HzA, stamp. Carcanos with this type of marking usually command a premium on the collector market. *(courtesy Larry Eisel, Eisel Armory)*

Carcanos seized by the Germans. The codes were *Gewehr 214(i)* for the *fucile mod. 91*; *Gewehr 231(i)* for the 7.35mm Model 38 short rifle; *Gewehr 209(i)* for the 6.5mm Model 38 short rifle; *Karabiner 408(i)* for the *moschetto 38*; *Karabiner 409(i)* for the *moschetto mod. 91*; *Karabiner 410(i)* for the *moschetto mod. 91 TS*; *Karabiner 416(i)* for the *moschetto mod. 91/24*; *Karabiner 430(i)* for the 7.35mm *moschetto 38 TS*.

The other category of Carcanos chambered for the 7.92mm round were the TS and cavalry carbines converted in Italy for Egypt following the war. On these weapons the receiver ring had a cut milled in it to allow the longer 7.92mm round the clearance it needed to feed into the chamber. A modified Carcano clip holding five rounds was used. Normally, but not always, a large letter S was stamped on the receiver ring and on the flat of the bolt handle. The original caliber markings on the rear sight base were removed and replaced by the numbers 7.9 or 7.92. The stock had two transversal stock bolts, one forward and one behind the trigger housing. The conversions were the work of F.N.A. Brescia and Luigi Franchi, Brescia; the Franchi conversions were stamped with the Franchi name on the underside of the receiver tang. Franchi converted Model 38 cavalry carbines; the serial number range for the Franchi conversion was 1-9999. F.N.A. Brescia converted Model 38 TS carbines; serial numbers were in the 1-9999 block, RA1-9999, RA90001-98999, and RB1-6000. Minor deviations from these numbers may also be encountered; an estimated 10,000 cavalry carbines were converted, as well as 26,400 TS carbines. These carbines were used by Egypt and Syria, mostly for training, and captured examples may also have served in Israel. The Egyptian carbines bore markings in Arabic on the buttstock and on the side of the rear sight base. ■

GERMAN DESIGNATIONS FOR ITALIAN WEAPONS

The Germans made use of many captured Italian weapons and, as they did with all classes of captured weapons, assigned German designations to each type of weapon. Following is a list of German designation for Italian weapons:

- **Pistole 680(i) Pistola a rotazione modello 1889 (Bodeo)**
- **Pistole 671(i) pistola modello 1935, calibro 9 corto**
- **Gewehr 209(i) fucile corto modello 38 (6.5mm)**
- **Gewehr 210(i) fucile modello 41**
- **Gewehr 214(i) fucile modello 1891**
- **Gewehr 231(i) fucile corto modello 38 (7.35mm)**
- **Karabiner 408(i) moschetto modello 38 (6.5mm)**
- **Karabiner 409(i) moschetto modello 1891 (6.5mm)**
- **Karabiner 410(i) moschetto per truppe speciali**
- **Karabiner 416(i) moschetto modello 91/24**
- **Karabiner 430(i) moschetto 38 TS (7.35mm)**
- **MP 43(i) F.N.A. B modello 1943**
- **MP 738(i) Beretta 38/42 SMG**
- **MP 739(i) Beretta 38/44 SMG**
- **LeMG 099(i) Breda modello 30**
- **sMG 200(i) FIAT modello 1914**
- **sMG 255(i) FIAT modello 1935**
- **sMG 259I0 Breda modello 37**
- **KpfwMG 350(i) Breda modello 38**

CHAPTER 3:

SUBMACHINE GUNS

The distinction of having developed and employed the first submachine gun, i.e., a fully automatic carbine length weapon chambered for a pistol cartridge, can be claimed by Italy. This weapon was the Revelli submachine gun designed by Bethel Abiel Revelli, chambered for the 9mm Glisenti cartridge and mounted in pairs. The weapon is often referred to as the Villar Perosa or O.V.P. submachine gun, as it was manufactured by FIAT at their Villar Perosa works (Officine Villar Perosa). The Villar Perosa utilized a number of different mounts ranging from aircraft to ground mounts, as well as a rudimentary stock on which some of the paired sets of Villar Perosas were mounted. In 1918 Beretta manufactured the Model 1918 submachine gun designed by Tullio Marengoni, based on the Villar Perosa. There is some doubt as to whether the Model 1918 was used in combat during the closing phases of World War I or whether it only underwent testing.

Shortly prior to and during World War II the Italians designed and developed a number of submachine guns, some of which were truly innovative and outstanding. Among these were the Beretta series, beginning with the Model 1938 designed by Tullio Marengoni, and the OG 44 designed by Giovanni Oliani. By and large, Italian submachine guns were well designed, well engineered, well built, and reliable. The Beretta 1938 series were highly regarded and were produced in far larger numbers than any other Italian submachine gun and were as good as or better than their German, U.S. and British counterparts. Throughout the war the Beretta was simplified in order to increase production and lower costs, but quality and reliability remained consistently high. Many of the Beretta submachine guns were widely issued in many parts of the world during the post-war period, attesting to the popularity and worth of the design.

Other Italian designers and manufacturers developed much simpler, but equally effective, submachine guns in the 1943-1944 timeframe, which did not however enjoy large-scale production or issue due to the pace of events, but which pioneered and embodied features and production techniques that would later become commonplace in many post-war submachine guns worldwide.

PISTOLA MITRAGLIATRICE FIAT MOD. 1915

Credit for developing the world's first submachine gun, i.e., a long barreled fully automatic weapon firing a pistol round, is universally accorded to the ever inventive and mechanically gifted Italians. This weapon was the Revelli submachine gun designed by Bethel Abiel Revelli in early 1914, chambered for the 9mm Glisenti cartridge and mounted in pairs. The gun was first developed and manufactured by the Società Metallurgica Bresciana; in August 1915 the Italian Army requested 5,000 of the weapons, and subsequently an initial lot of 2,480 was delivered by Società Metallurgica Bresciana, and production was also subcontracted to the FIAT Villar Perosa works. The weapon, whose official Italian designation was the FIAT Mod. 1915, is more commonly referred to as the Villar Perosa submachine gun, as large numbers were manufactured by the Villar Perosa works. As originally conceived the Villar Perosa was mounted as an aircraft weapon, but it was soon adapted for defensive use in the ground role, fitted with a bipod and a small shield to protect the gunner. The shields, which were produced by Ansaldo and Acciaierie di Terni, proved to be too heavy and cumbersome for field use and were not widely used. By the end of 1915 Villar Perosa had produced 350 Mod. 15 weapons, rising to 946 by the end of 1916; large-scale production began in 1917. In

The forefather of all submachine guns, the Villar Perosa in its twin configuration. The official designation of the weapon conceived and designed by Bethel Abiel Revelli was the pistola mitragliatrice FIAT Mod. 1915 (FIAT Model 1915 machine pistol). (*Editorale Olimpia*)

April 1916 the first Mod. 15 guns were distributed to front-line units, and by the end of 1917 there were more than 600 submachinegun sections in the Italian Army, each with two paired guns. In July 1917 the *1o Reparto d'Assalto* (1st Assault Unit), manned by *Arditi* (assault troops) was formed, and was equipped partially with Mod. 15 submachine guns.

The Villar Perosa was a straight blowback weapon and had an extremely high rate of fire of about 1,200 rounds per barrel. The high rate of fire led Italian gunners to nickname it *la pernacchia*, which is the Italian equivalent of the word "raspberry" or the phrase "Bronx cheer." Two identical guns were connected to each other side by side by a cross bar to the rear and by a circular plate further forward. The robust circular plate had three holes through it: the two lateral holes supported the barrels, and the hole in the upper center acted as a sight aperture; the disc was designed to fit into an opening in the protective shield. The guns were fed by two top-mounted 25-round magazines and the gunner had the option of firing each weapon individually, or firing both in tandem. There was some experimentation by the Italians to develop a more mobile version of the Villar Perosa by mounting it on a harness carrier or on the handlebars of bicycles, but these initiatives were found to be impractical. Eventually a rudimentary wooden stock was fitted to some of the

PISTOLA MITRAGLIATRICE FIAT MOD. 1915

Designer: Bethel Abiel Revelli
Manufacturer: Società Metallurgica Bresciana; FIAT, Villar Perosa Works; Canadian General Electric Company Ltd., Toronto
Caliber: 9mm Glisenti
Cartridge: 9x19mm Glisenti
Operating system: Blowback
Overall length: 533mm (20.98")
Barrel length: 318mm (12.52")
Weight: 6.52 kg (14.37 lbs)
Front sight: None
Rear sight: None
Cyclic rate: 1200 rpm per barrel
Muzzle velocity: 365 m/sec (1198 fps)
Feed system: 25- round top-mounted detachable box magazine; unconfirmed if 50-round magazines were available

paired sets, pioneering the way for use of the weapon as a compact automatic weapon for offensive use. The weapon's chief drawback was its astonishingly high rate of fire; a 25-round clip took little more than one second to empty. Gunners tended to fire only one barrel at a time in order to achieve a slightly longer "time on target," but in an attacking role the standard procedure was for the gunner to fire off both clips and then fall to the rear of the advancing troops in order to reload behind cover if possible.

Although there is some lack of clarity as to how many Mod. 1915 guns were produced, serial numbers run as high as 13235, suggesting that at least that many guns were fielded; some sources believe that as many as 15,000 may have been produced. The Villar Perosa was produced and used only during World War I; in addition to being produced in Italy, some sources indicate that some were contracted to the Canadian General Electric Company of Toronto. Interestingly, the Mod. 1915 was also produced by the Austrians who copied captured examples. Some sources indicate that between 2,000 and 3,500 Mod. 1915 weapons were stored in depots in 1940-1941, but that plans to use them in defensive positions along Italy's mountain borders were rejected. Shortly after the end of the war, the O.V.P. submachine gun, which was nothing more than one of the twin Mod. 1915 guns fitted with a stock, was developed (see following entry). ■

Spade grips and twin triggers of the paired Mod. 15 submachine guns. (*Museo della Meccanica e del Cuscinetto-Villar Perosa, via Renzo Turco*)

Rudimentary wooden stock developed to hold the paired Mod. 15; this arrangement proved to be cumbersome and was only moderately successful. (*Museo della Meccanica e del Cuscinetto-Villar Perosa, via Renzo Turco*)

Forward aspect of the Mod. 15 spade grip with the Officine Villar Perosa logo and serial number. (*Museo della Meccanica e del Cuscinetto-Villar Perosa, via Renzo Turco*)

A FIAT Mod. 15 produced by the Villar Perosa Works, with both magazines fitted. The barrels have been cut away for instructional purposes as well as to comply with Italian deactivation laws. (*Museo della Meccanica e del Cuscinetto-Villar Perosa, via Renzo Turco*)

The large spade grips of the Mod. 15 and the twin triggers are evident in this photograph. (*Museo della Meccanica e del Cuscinetto-Villar Perosa, via Renzo Turco*)

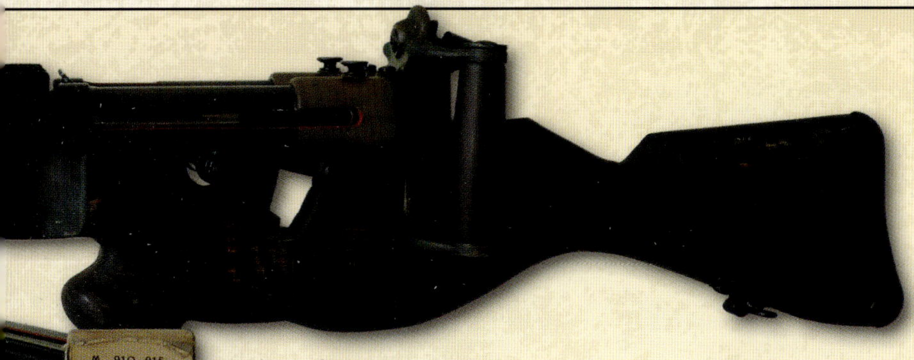

The Mod. 15 guns mounted on the wooden stock. (*Museo della Meccanica e del Cuscinetto-Villar Perosa, via Renzo Turco*)

The circular plate that acted as the forward connecting element between the two guns also served as the sight; the sight disc, resembling a toothed gear, was rotated for range adjustment. The sight selector was numbered from 1 to 5 and corresponded to distances from 100 to 500 meters. (*Museo della Meccanica e del Cuscinetto-Villar Perosa, via Renzo Turco*)

Right-hand view of the Mod. 15 and sample 9mm Glisenti ammunition. (*Museo della Meccanica e del Cuscinetto-Villar Perosa, via Renzo Turco*)

Bottom aspect of the Mod. 15, showing the prominent cocking handles. (*Museo della Meccanica e del Cuscinetto-Villar Perosa, via Renzo Turco*)

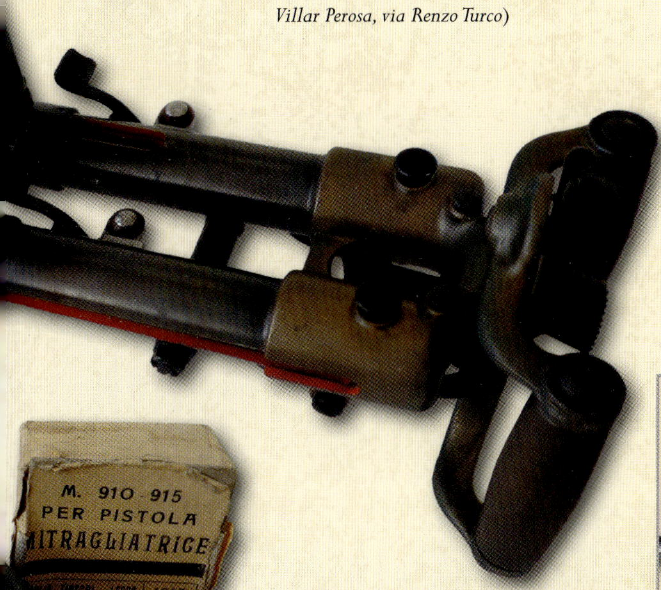

Top and bottom aspects of the 25-round magazines of the Mod. 15; the distinctive conical nose 9mm Glisenti ammunition is visible in the left-hand magazine, and a vintage box of the ammunition is to the right of the second magazine. (*Museo della Meccanica e del Cuscinetto-Villar Perosa, via Renzo Turco*)

Top view of the Mod. 15 showing the magazine slots and detached magazines. (*Museo della Meccanica e del Cuscinetto-Villar Perosa, via Renzo Turco*)

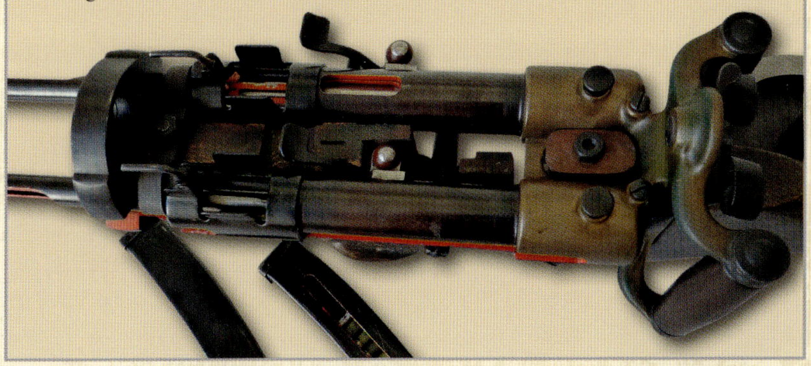

MOSCHETTO AUTOMATICO O.V.P.

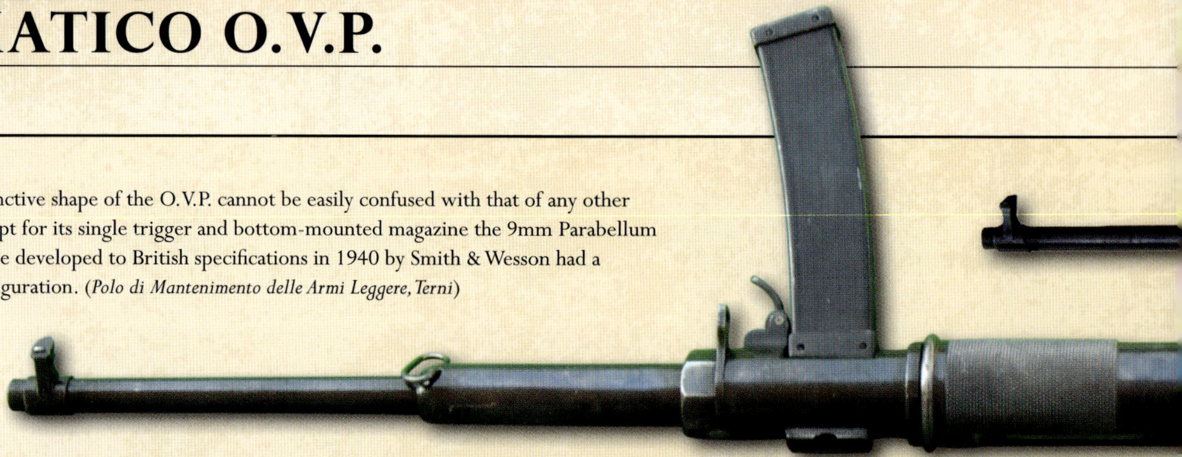

» Although the distinctive shape of the O.V.P. cannot be easily confused with that of any other submachine gun, except for its single trigger and bottom-mounted magazine the 9mm Parabellum Model 1940 Light Rifle developed to British specifications in 1940 by Smith & Wesson had a strikingly similar configuration. (*Polo di Mantenimento delle Armi Leggere, Terni*)

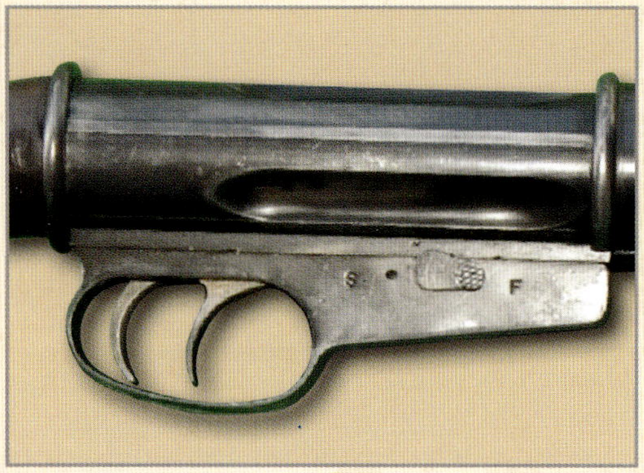

« Detail of the O.V.P. safety; the two triggers provided a selective fire capability. (*Polo di Mantenimento delle Armi Leggere, Terni*)

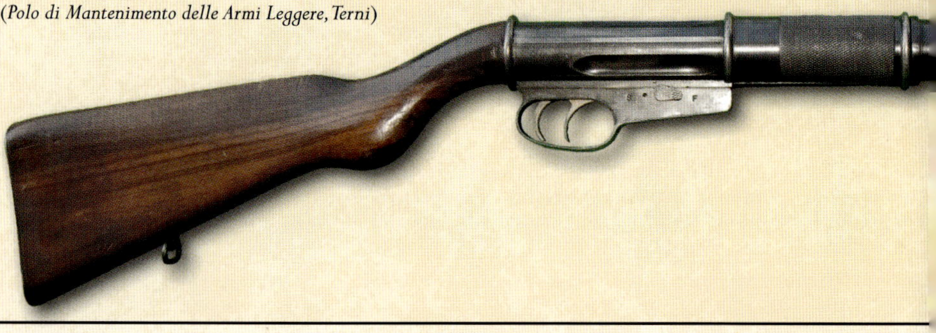

Either shortly before or after the end of World War I the Italians developed a weapon designated the *moschetto automatico O.V.P.* that incorporated all of the basic characteristics ever since associated with a submachine gun: a full auto weapon with a long barrel, chambered for a pistol cartridge, capable of being used by an individual soldier in an offensive role. The O.V.P. was an adaptation of the FIAT Mod. 15 (Villar Perosa) twin guns, and consisted of "half" of a Villar Perosa fitted with a more or less conventional wooden buttstock; the designation O.V.P. reflected the initials of the production facility of the original Villar Perosa gun (Officine Villar Perosa, or Villar Perosa Works). In an attempt to reduce the excessively high rate of fire of the Villar Perosa, the operating system was modified as a delayed blowback, but this did little to remedy the situation, as the cyclic rate was reduced only slightly to 900 rounds per minute. The magazine continued to be top-mounted, and the cocking system consisted of a cylindrical sleeve over the receiver with a slot providing clearance for the trigger mechanism; cocking was achieved by pulling the sleeve back and then returning it forward. The Italians dubbed the O.V.P. the *mezza pernacchia* ("half raspberry"), based on the earlier nickname of *la pernacchia* ("the raspberry") that had been given to the twin-gun Villar Perosa. An estimated 500 O.V.P. submachine guns were produced, in both the selective fire and semi-automatic only versions; the selective fire version had dual triggers, the front trigger for full automatic fire and the rear trigger for semi-automatic fire. The design was not a success due to a number of factors, including its high rate of fire as well as the fact that the Beretta Model 1918 submachine gun designed by Marengoni made its appearance at about the same time as the O.V.P. and proved to be a better design. ■

MOSCHETTO AUTOMATICO O.V.P.

Designer: Bethel Abiel Revelli
Manufacturer: FIAT, Officine Villar Perosa
Caliber: 9mm Glisenti
Cartridge: 9x19mm Glisenti
Operating system: Delayed blowback
Overall length: 902mm (33.5")
Barrel length: 279mm (10.98")
Weight: 3.6 kg (7.94 lbs)
Front sight: Post and blade
Rear sight: Aperture
Cyclic rate: 900 rpm per barrel
Muzzle velocity: 365 m/sec (1198 fps)
Feed system: 25-round top-mounted detachable box

The O.V.P. with its characteristic top-mounted magazine in place. The knurled sleeve on the O.V.P. acted as a cocking handle. (*Polo di Mantenimento delle Armi Leggere, Terni*)

The moschetto automatic O.V.P. was essentially half of a FIAT Mod. 1915, fitted with a wooden stock that configured it as a classic early submachine gun. (*Polo di Mantenimento delle Armi Leggere, Terni*)

MOSCHETTO BERETTA MODELLO 1918

Using the components of the Villar Perosa submachine gun as a point of departure, in 1918 Tullio Marengoni designed the first Beretta submachine gun, the *moschetto modello 1918*, that saw limited action during the closing phases of World War I and which may also have seen very limited use during the early phases of World War II. During the course of development, three different versions of the Model 1918 were produced: one version was full automatic only, a second version was semi-automatic only, and the third version had a selective fire capability. The full auto version used a modified Vetterli-Vitali rifle stock and mounted a cavalry-style folding bayonet; the semi-auto and selective fire versions were fitted with stocks that more closely resembled the *moschetto Mod. 91* stock. The semi-auto version retained the cavalry-style bayonet, while the selective fire version had a shorter barrel and was fitted with a standard bayonet lug; Marengoni introduced his hallmark dual trigger system on the selective fire version, with one trigger for full auto fire and the other for semi-auto fire. An unknown number of the selective fire version were produced by the Manifattura italiana d'Armi (MIDA). About 4,000-5,000 Model 1918 weapons are believed to have been delivered.

MOSCHETTO BERETTA MODELLO 1918

Designer: Tullio Marengoni
Manufacturer: Fabbrica d'Armi Pietro Beretta; MIDA
Caliber: 9mm Glisenti
Cartridge: 9x19mm Glisenti
Operating system: Delayed blowback
Overall length: 880mm (34.7")
Barrel length: 310mm (12.2")
Weight: 3.69 kg (8.12 lbs) without magazine
Front sight: Barleycorn
Rear sight: Fixed V notch
Cyclic rate: 900 rpm
Muzzle velocity: 381 m/sec (1250 fps)
Feed system: 25-round top-mounted detachable box
Note: Above specifications refer to the Beretta-produced Model 1918; MIDA specifications are unavailable. It should also be noted that, as previously stated in the description of the moschetto modello 18/30 (the "siringone"), there is sometimes a tendency to confuse the Model 1918 with the Model 18/30.

The semi-automatic version of the Moschetto Beretta Modello 1918. It had a top-mounted curved box magazine and an ejection chute on the bottom of the weapon. The permanently attached folding spike bayonet and the straight grip stock give the weapon a certain resemblance to the Model 1891 cavalry carbine. (*Beretta*)

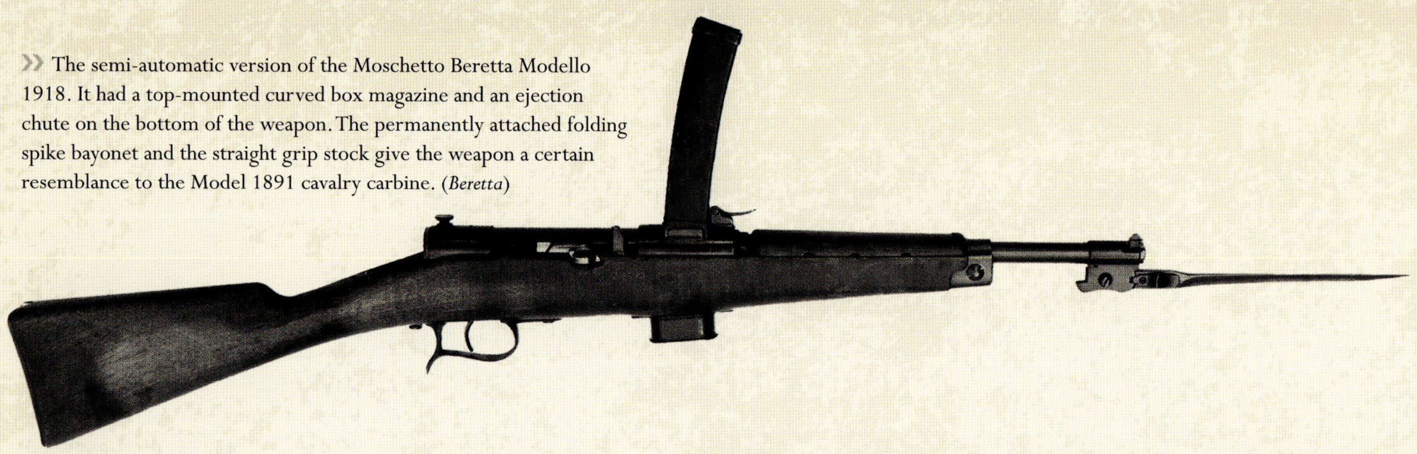

MOSCHETTO AUTOMATICO PAVESI-REVELLI

The Pavesi-Revelli submachine gun was produced in limited numbers; one example observed bears serial number 106, suggesting a very small production run of at least that many weapons. Some sources, however, believe that only about ten weapons were produced around 1920, which leads to speculation that serial numbering may have begun at 100 rather than at 001. The gun was the result of cooperation between Bethel Revelli and Ugo Pavesi, who was an engineer engaged primarily in building tractors. Not surprisingly, the weapon was based on the earlier Villar Perosa Model 1915 submachine gun. Its external configuration was somewhat fururistic; it had a wooden half stock, a front pistol grip, partially finned barrel, and top-mounted magazine. Its outward appearance somewhat resembled that of the later U.S. Hyde Model 35 submachine gun. It is not known to have been adopted by the Italian Army. ■

The finned barrel was not unlike that on early Thompson submachine guns; the forward pistol grip and top-mounted magazine gave it a distinctive look. (*Museo Storico Italiano della Guerra-Rovereto*)

MOSCHETTO AUTOMATICO PAVESI-REVELLI

Designer: Bethel Abiel Revelli
Manufacturer: La Motomeccanica Brevetti Ing. Pavesi (Gomboloita, Milano)
Caliber: 9mm Glisenti
Cartridge: 9x19mm Glisenti
Operating system: Delayed blowback
Overall length: 890mm (35")
Barrel length: 276mm (10.87")
Weight: 3.74 kg (8.25 lbs) with full magazine
Front sight: Blade mounted on ferrule
Rear sight: Fixed V notch, offset to right to compensate for top-mounted magazine
Cyclic rate: 900 rpm
Muzzle velocity: 400 m/sec (1312 fps) approximate
Feed system: 25-round top-mounted detachable box

›› Although very similar to the Beretta Modello 1918 submachine gun, the moschetto MIDA Modello 1918 differed in several respects. It had two triggers, allowing semi-automatic or full automatic fire, its stock had a pistol grip, it had a shorter barrel, and it lacked a bayonet. It shared the same top-mounted magazine and bottom ejection chute with the Beretta version of the Modello 1918. Note the offset front sight. *(Beretta)*

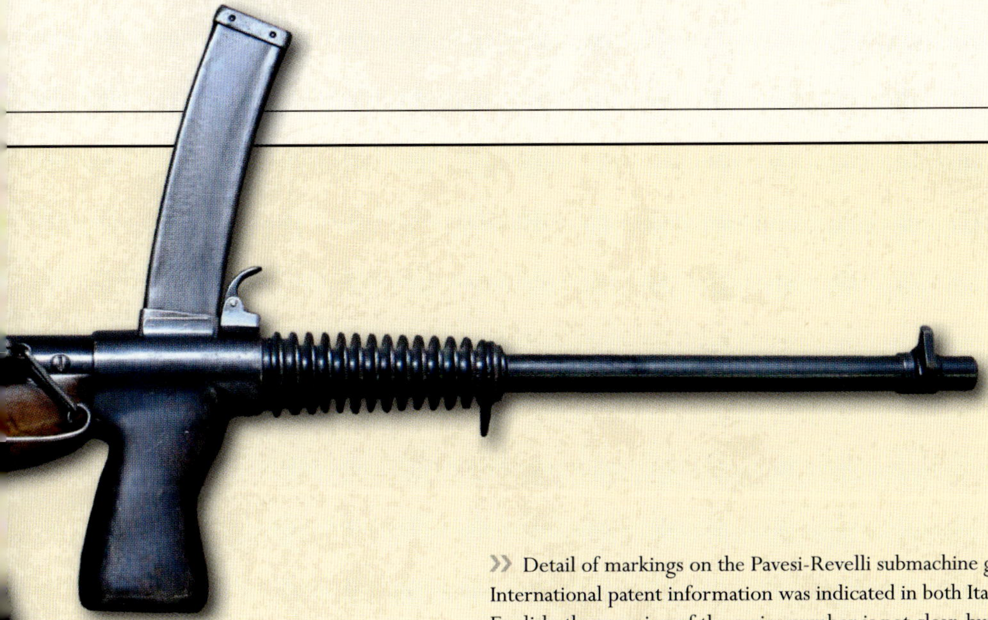

›› Detail of markings on the Pavesi-Revelli submachine gun. International patent information was indicated in both Italian and English; the meaning of the series number is not clear, but the serial number 106 presumably indicates a run of at least that many guns. There are two references to Pavesi-Revelli: the initials are within a circle above the patent information, and the names are spelled out in a diamond behind the rear sight. *(Museo Storico Italiano della Guerra- Rovereto)*

^ The moschetto automatico Pavesi-Revelli designed by the very prolific Bethel Abiel Revelli and produced by the Pavesi company, which normally produced tractors. *(Museo Storico Italiano della Guerra-Rovereto)*

BERETTA MODELLO 38 SERIES

What appear to be two Italian paratroopers in North Africa armed with Beretta 38/A submachine guns. (*Bruno Benvenuti*)

The developmental history of the *moschetto automatico Beretta modello 38* (Beretta Model 38 automatic carbine), or MAB 38, is not easy to trace with any great degree of assurance. Unquestionably the best coverage of the MAB 38's lineage is to be found in Vittorio Balzi's book on Italian submachine guns from 1915 to 1991, but even Balzi admits to uncertainties concerning the sequence of the many early variants of the MAB. The earliest prototype, or precursor, of the MAB 38 descended directly from the Model 18/30 semi-auto carbine which it outwardly resembled to some extent. This prototype, which is believed to have appeared around 1935, had the characteristic cocking ring of the Model 18/30, was known as the *moschetto-mitragliatore extra leggero cal. 9mm*, and was described in the caption of a Beretta photograph as having both semi-automatic and full automatic capability. The weapon had a machined seamless tube steel cooling jacket with large longitudinal cooling slots and a compensator with two large slots on the upper side, and the ejection port was at the top of the receiver. Despite the Beretta photo caption claiming that the weapon had a full automatic capability, there is some reason to believe that it may have been only semi-automatic; it had a single trigger, and photographs do not show any evidence of a selector switch; the prototype has not survived, so it is impossible to assert definitively whether or not there was any type of selective fire capability.

The next step in the evolution of the MAB 38 was what is regarded as the first true prototype of the MAB 38, which made its appearance in 1935 and is sometimes referred to as the *modello 1935* although this designation was never given to the weapon by Beretta which refers to it simply as the prototype of the MAB 38. The prototype was chambered for a new cartridge developed by Fiocchi, known as the Model 38 cartridge, which was a 9mm Parabellum cartridge manufactured to Italian specifications and which could be used interchangeably with the standard German 9mm cartridge, although the Italian cartridge was somewhat more powerful and developed substantially higher muzzle velocities. The MAB prototype had a very unusual and distinctive finned aluminum cooling jacket that gave it a unique appearance. It had two triggers; the forward trigger was for semi-automatic fire, and the rear trigger, which had a knurled surface so that even in the dark the firer could distinguish it from the forward trigger, was for full auto fire. The ejection port was on the top of the receiver and the firing pin was floating rather than fixed. The stock configuration resembled that of the *extra leggero* prototype, with a deep wrist.

In 1935 or 1936 the aluminum jacketed prototype was followed by a version whose cooling jacket was identical, or nearly identical, to that of the *extra leggero*, with the elongated cooling slots and compensator. There followed several other variations, including one with a bayonet lug for a removable Type 38 folding blade bayonet (similar to but not interchangeable with the Type 38 folding bayonet used on the *fucile corto*), and one with the

COMMON CHARACTERISTICS, BERETTA SUBMACHINE GUNS

(Models 38, 38/A, 38/42, 38/43)
Caliber: 9mm Parabellum (Italian 9M38 cartridge)
Operating principle: Straight blowback
Trigger system: Dual triggers; front trigger allows semi-automatic fire only; rear trigger allows full automatic fire
Magazine capacity: 10, 20, or 40-round staggered row box magazines, interchangeable on all models. The magazine was one of the best design features of the weapon.
Front sight: Blade

M.A.B. 38

Year introduced: 1938
Overall length: 947mm (37.3")
Barrel length: 320mm (12.6")
Weight: 3.945 kg (8.71 lbs) with 40-round magazine
Rear sight: Tangent with V notch
Rate of fire: 600 rpm
Muzzle velocity: 430 m/sec (1310 fps)
Rifling: 6 groove RH twist
Safety: Two-position lever on left side
Cooling jacket: Full length, elongated slots or round perforations
Compensator: Dual port
Stock: Wood, with two finger grooves per side
Remarks: Floating firing pin; various models fitted with bayonet stud or with permanently attached bayonet; ejection port on top; recoil spring guide

moschetto 91 type permanently attached triangular folding bayonet. The rear sight was an adjustable sight graduated to 500 meters.

Initial production of the MAB 38 probably began in January 1938, but it was not officially adopted by the *Regio Esercito* until July of that year; it appears that at some point between those two dates the top mounted ejection port was replaced by a side mounted port, and the designation was changed to MAB 38/A. In October 1938 the first order of 500 38/A began to be supplied to the *Polizia dell'Africa Italiana* (Italian Africa Police). This was a transitional period in which several variations appeared, including the previously mentioned versions with the longitudinally slotted jacket and with the bayonet lug or with the permanently attached cavalry-style folding bayonet. The early style cooling jacket was soon replaced by the more characteristic jacket, still made from a seamless tube but with machined small round holes; the stock was also modified with a less pronounced grip at the wrist, and a cutoff lever was added to block the full automatic rear trigger if desired. These changes generally characterize what is referred to as the second version of the MAB 38/A.

Parenthetically, there are different opinions as to what differentiates the Model 38 from the Model 38/A; in addressing this question, Balzi advances the hypothesis that despite many other relatively minor or cosmetic differences such as jacket style and stock configuration between the two versions, the main differentiating factor between the two models is the position of the ejection port. Balzi feels that weapons with the top ejection port were the Model 38, and weapons with the side ejection port were the Model 38/A, regardless of any other features; this seems an entirely logical position. Another interesting observation regards the possible significance of the letter A in the 38/A designation; one of the former curators of the Beretta museum suggested – as a hypothesis only, and not based on Beretta or other official records – that the A may have stood for Africa, as the 38/A was first ordered by the Ministry for Italian Africa, for use by the Italian Africa Police. Although this hypothesis has a certain amount of appeal and plausibility, this author is somewhat skeptical, as Beretta could just as easily have chosen to use the letter C (for *Coloniale*, or colonial), or P (*Polizia*, or police). The letter A could simply have denoted a model change; later versions of the Beretta MAB used the 38 and oblique followed by another two digits denoting the year of introduction of the version (e.g., 38/42), but as the 38/A was introduced in 1938, use of a letter (A) denoting the change would have been more appropriate and certainly less confusing than repeating the year (i.e., 38/38).

The third version of the 38/A, which appeared in late 1938 or early 1939, eliminated the bayonet attachment and replaced the two-port compensator with a compensator consiting of four transversal slots. An unspecified number of 38/A (but surviving specimens have serial numbers between R1 and R20000) were ordered by and delivered to Romania in 1939-1940, which delayed delivery of the first tranche of the MAB 38/A to the Italian Army until 1940 or 1941. Shortly after deliveries to the Italian Army had begun, the fourth and final version of the MAB 38/A appeared; it was identical to the third version in all respects except that the machined seamless steel cooling jacket was replaced by a similarly configured jacket made from a piece of flat steel that had the holes punched in it, and was then formed into a tube and welded along the seam. This version was produced until at least 1944, although sometime in 1941 or possibly 1942 the floating firing pin was replaced by a fixed firing pin. The Model 38/A fires from an open bolt; the cocking handle, located on the right side of the receiver,

M.A.B. 38/A

Year introduced: 1938
Overall length: 947mm (37.3")
Barrel length: 320mm (12.6")
Weight: 4 kg (8.8 lbs)
Rear sight: Tangent with V notch, or L-type flip
Rate of fire: 600 rpm
Muzzle velocity: 430 m/sec (1310 fps)
Rifling: 6 groove RH twist, 252mm
Safety: Two-position lever on left side
Cooling jacket: Full length, perforated
Compensator: Multi-slotted (four slots)
Stock: Wood, with two finger grooves per side
Remarks: Floating firing pin; with or without bayonet lug; ejection port on left side; with or without recoil spring guide

The MAB 38 prototype with the receiver end cap removed and bolt and guide rod assembly disassembled. A 40-round magazine, loading tool, and four 10-round stripper clips are beneath the weapon itself. (*Beretta*)

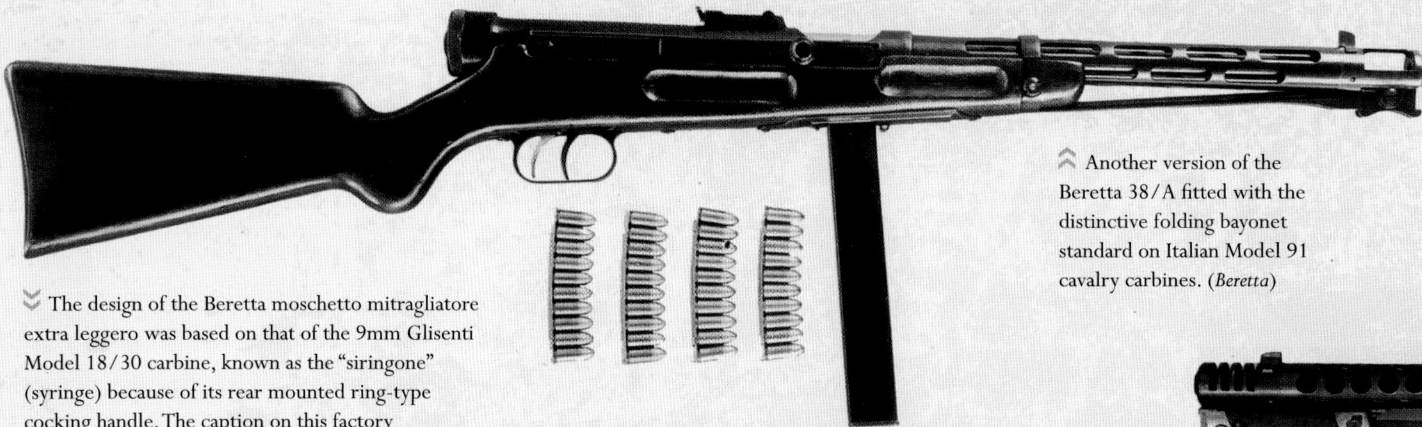

Another version of the Beretta 38/A fitted with the distinctive folding bayonet standard on Italian Model 91 cavalry carbines. (*Beretta*)

The design of the Beretta moschetto mitragliatore extra leggero was based on that of the 9mm Glisenti Model 18/30 carbine, known as the "siringone" (syringe) because of its rear mounted ring-type cocking handle. The caption on this factory photograph indicates that the weapon can fire single shots or in full automatic mode. (*Beretta*)

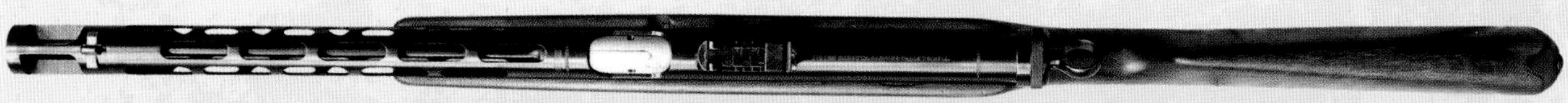

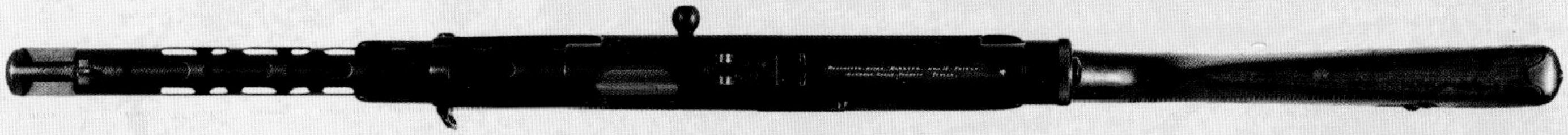

Top view of the 38/A with redesigned side ejection port. (*Beretta*)

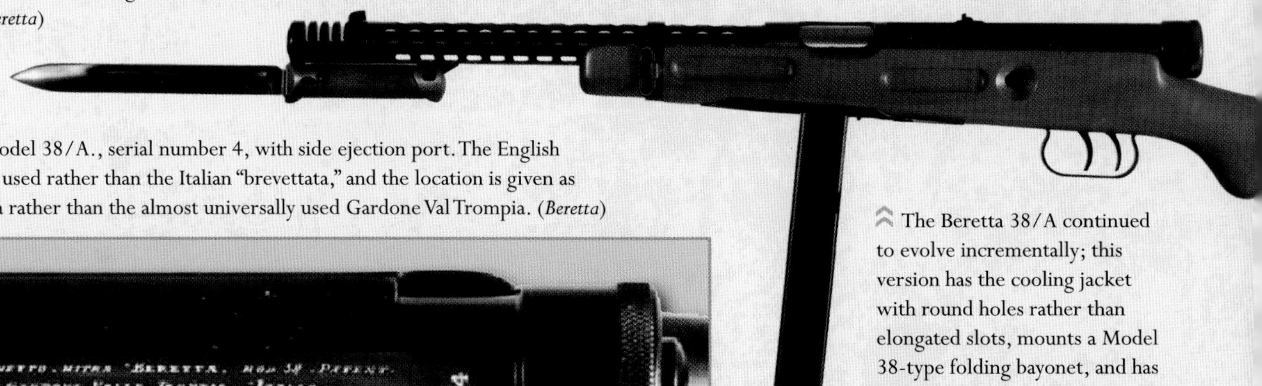

Markings on the Model 38/A., serial number 4, with side ejection port. The English designation "Patent" is used rather than the Italian "brevettata," and the location is given as Gardone Valle Trompia rather than the almost universally used Gardone Val Trompia. (*Beretta*)

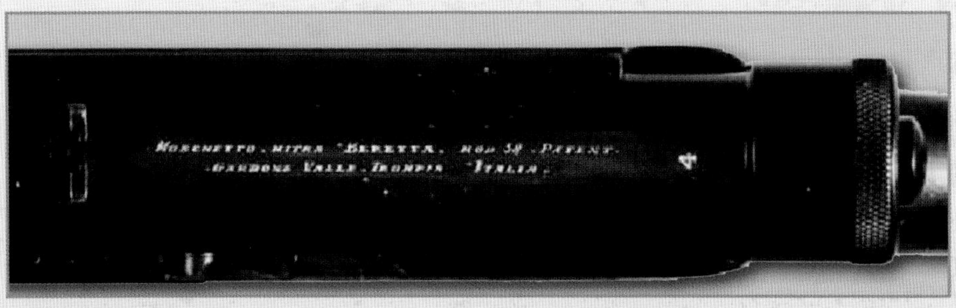

The Beretta 38/A continued to evolve incrementally; this version has the cooling jacket with round holes rather than elongated slots, mounts a Model 38-type folding bayonet, and has a less pronounced pistol grip. (*Beretta*)

Top view of the prototype MAB 38 showing the early top ejection port and the adjustable rear sight. (*Beretta*)

The futuristic looking prototype of the Beretta MAB 38. The distinctive finned cooling jacket was soon dropped in favor of more a more conventional perforated jacket. (*Beretta*)

This version of the Model 38/A retains the elongated slots, has the side ejection port, and has had a bayonet stud added to the jacket. (*Beretta*)

An early Model 38/A with the blade of the folding bayonet in the closed position. (*Beretta*)

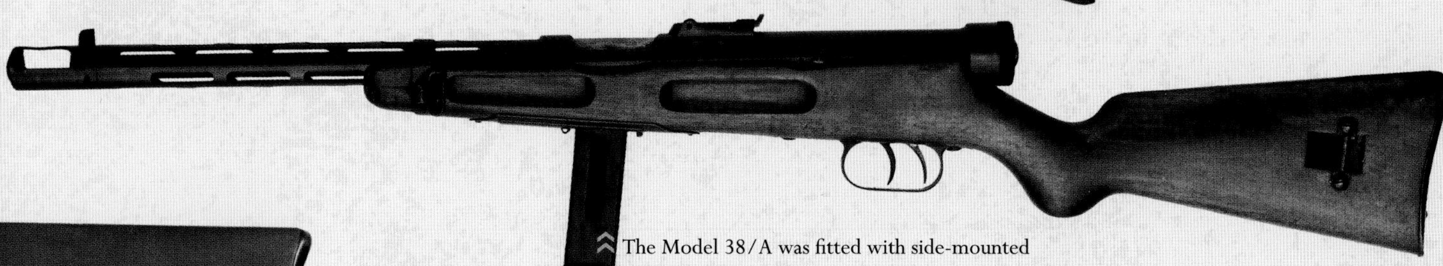

The Model 38/A was fitted with side-mounted sling attachments; the stock had characteristic interrupted finger grooves. (*Beretta*)

An early version of the Beretta 38/A with elongated cooling slots in the barrel jacket, dual triggers, adjustable rear sight, and pronounced pistol grip. (*Beretta*)

Markings on the barrel retaining nut on an MP 38/42. (*Courtesy Dennis Todd*)

An MP 38/42 with a 20-round magazine. The larger capacity magazines were more commonly encountered. (*Courtesy Dennis Todd*)

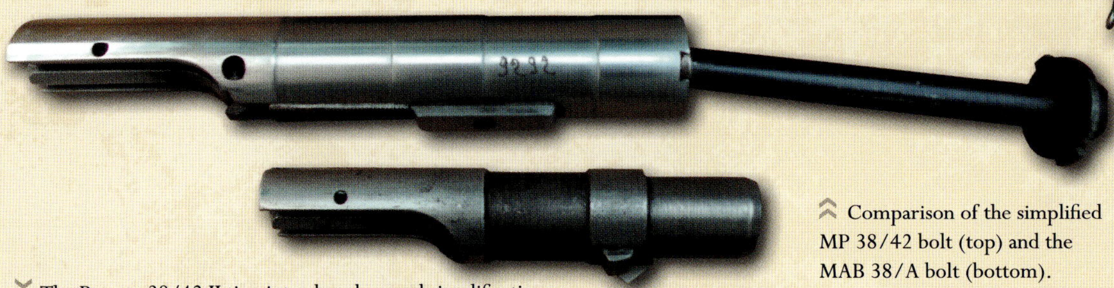

Comparison of the simplified MP 38/42 bolt (top) and the MAB 38/A bolt (bottom). (*Courtesy Dennis Todd*)

The Beretta 38/42 II tipo introduced several simplifications, the most apparent of which were the tapered barrel with its twin slot compensator and the simplified rear sight. (*Beretta*)

Right side view of a Beretta 38/A with extended bayonet mounted. The provision for mounting a bayonet was discarded as production was standardized. (*Beretta*)

The Beretta Arms Museum's MAB 38/A represents the configuration most often associated with this iconic weapon. As the 38/A continued to evolve, the four slot muzzle brake was replaced by a twin port compensator. (*Beretta*)

A Beretta 38/A nearing the definitive configuration; it lacks the bayonet mount on the cooling jacket and has a four slot muzzle brake. (*Beretta*)

An MP 38/42 with a 40-round magazine inserted, and a 20-round magazine detached. Several other Italian submachine guns used Beretta magazines as well. (*Courtesy Dennis Todd*)

The Beretta 38/42 I tipo was characterized by the heavy fluted barrel, lack of barrel jacket, and adjustable rear sight. (*Beretta*)

Top view of a Beretta 38/A, with four slot muzzle brake and the classic Beretta perforated cooling jacket. (*Beretta*)

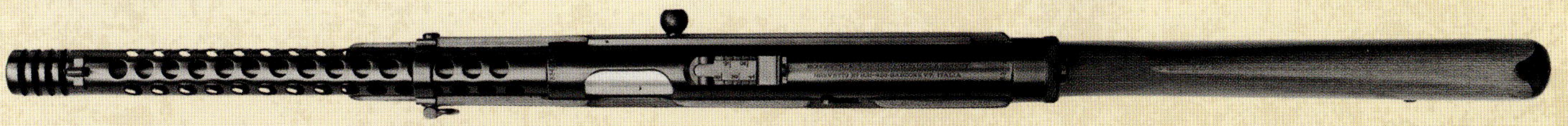

does not reciprocate along with the bolt when firing; a manual safety lever is located on the left side above the trigger guard, marked S in the rear position and F in the forward position.

In 1941 a substantially different version of the MAB was designed by Marengoni. This was the *Modello 1*, likely designed for use by paratroopers. It used the receiver and fixed firing pin bolt of the 38/A, but eliminated the cooling jacket; the barrel was substantially altered, being shortened by 20cm (almost 8 inches), increased in diameter, fluted for strength and increased cooling surface, and with an integral twin slot compensator milled on the muzzle. The rear sight, later used on the 38/42, was a simple flip type set for 100 and 200 meters. Because of its presumed use by paratroopers, its folding stock was copied from and almost identical to that of the German MP 38/40, and it had a pistol grip resembling that of the German weapon as well. The Model 1 – which was a Beretta designation rather than an official Italian Army designation – was not produced in series, as it remained relatively expensive to produce and would have necessitated additional changes to make it suitable for mass production. It did, however, set the stage for the appearance of the MAB 38/42.

Although the earliest production version of the MAB 38/42 was made with the the traditional milled receiver, magazine housing, receiver cap, trigger guard and other parts, significant changes were soon made by replacing the milled components with stamped and welded assemblies; despite this major departure from previous manufacturing techniques, the 38/42 designation was retained. The most readily apparent external differences between the 38/A and 38/42 were the shorter, heavier fluted barrel of the 38/42 (as on the Model 1 prototype) and the forward portion of the stock, which now ended behind the magazine housing; not as readily apparent was a slight shortening of the buttstock as well. As production continued, the bolt group was simplified to ease production time, and as a result the spring guide protruded from the end cap somewhat more visibly than on earlier versions. The heavy fluted barrel version is referred to as the *38/42 I tipo* (38/42 Type I) or, to further confuse the whole designation convention, as the 38/41 at times; this was replaced by a version with a lighter tapered barrel, also fluted, and the two-position flip sight of the Model 1, which is referred to as the *38/42 II tipo* (38/42 Type II). The Type II was supplied to the Germans, who reportedly requested its design, and an unspecified number were furnished to the Romanians as well, who seemed to have had a preference for Beretta weapons. In 1943 the Type II was further simplified by replacing the fluted tapered barrel with a smooth tapered barrel; this version is known alternately as the *38/42 III tipo*, or as the 38/43. Thus, the three versions of the 38/42 are referred to by at least five designations: 38/42 Type I (or 38/41); 38/42 Type II; 38/42 Type III (or 38/43).

The 38/42 was followed in 1944 by the 38/44, whose chief difference was a redesigned and simplified bolt and modified recoil spring and spring guide assembly. Opinions differ as to when production of the 38/44 began and ceased – or if indeed production of the weapon as such did not begin until the post-war period – but it is likely that some production did occur in 1944 and into 1945.

Markings on the MAB series generally reflected the Beretta name and location and the model number. The early Model 38 was marked MOSCHETTO-MITRA BERETTA MOD. 38 PATENT on one line, over GARDONE VALLE TROMPIA ITALIA below it; the use of the extended form of Valle – instead of the usual Val – is unusual. The Model 1938A could be found marked MOSCHETTO AUT – BERETTA – MOD 1938A – PATENT on one line, over BREVETTO No 828-428 – GARDONE V.T. ITALIA, or MOSCH-AUT-P BERETTA-CAL 9-MOD 38A all on a

Benito Mussolini reviewing an honor guard. The soldiers to Mussolini's right are all armed with early model Beretta 38/A submachine guns with bayonets fixed. The soldiers that Mussolini has just walked past are armed with the Mod. 91 cavalry carbine. (*Bruno Benvenuti*)

M.A.B. 38/42

Year introduced: 1942
Overall length: 790mm (31.1")
Barrel length: 228mm (8.97")
Weight: 3.3 kg (7.25 lbs)
Rear sight: L-type flip sight, 100 and 200 meters
Rate of fire: 550 rpm
Muzzle velocity: 410 m/sec (1345 fps)
Rifling: 6 groove RH twist
Safety: Two-position lever on left side
Cooling jacket: None
Compensator: Two slots
Stock: Wood, with one finger groove per side
Remarks: Barrel could be either heavy or tapered; both types of barrel were fluted

single line; presumably there were other variations as well throughout the period of manufacture. On the 38/42, the MOSCHETTO AUT – BERETTA was replaced by M.P. BERETTA; the letters M.P. – for *Maschinenpistole* – reflected the fact that the 38/42 had been produced for German use even prior to the 8 September 1943 armistice. The serial number was stamped on the receiver, perpendicular to the axis.

There are no precise production totals for the MAB series; Balzi speculates that as many as 360,000-384,000 per year may have been produced beginning in mid-1943 which, if applied to the years from 1942 through the end of 1944 would result in a total of well over a million weapons of the type. Balzi further notes that, even if the figures are exaggerated and production was only half that figure, it would still be a remarkable achievement considering not only the labor intensive methods needed to produce the earlier models – before adoption of stamping and welding – but also of the disruption caused by bombing and civil chaos at the time. Pignato and Cappellano provide somewhat more precise figures, citing various sources, including German sources: an October 1944 German document quotes a figure of 95,234 Beretta submachine guns produced between 1 October 1943 and 30 September 1944, while another German source indicates production figures of 234,311 for 1943, 228,582 for 1944, and 57,100 for 1945. An April 1945 German document indicates that in March 1945 32,000 submachine guns and 132,000 magazines had been produced. Pignato and Cappellano also refer to an American intelligence document, not further identified, that indicated that other companies also were engaged in production of Beretta submachine guns, specifically, the Società Parma Antonio e Figli of Saronno (which supposedly produced the 38/42) and S.A. Sebino of Pilone (Beretta 38/A); the same document credited Agrati & Figli of Ponticello Brianza, F.N.A. Brescia, and F.lli Inuggi of Amegna (sic) with producing "accessories." This author could find no trace of S.A. Sebino or of Agrati & Figli, but as of 2013 Parma Antonio e Figli S.p.A., which produces safes, keys, locks and metal goods was located at Via Garibaldi 43 in Saronno, and the Fonderia Fratelli Inuggi, which produces metal goods, was located at Via Oddino Pietra 18/20 in Omegna; Inuggi produced magazines. Pignato and Cappellano maintain, with some degree of logic, that it is believable that for production levels to reach those quoted, it is entirely possible that other firms were engaged in production of either complete weapons or of significant parts or subassemblies.

During the war Beretta submachine guns were issued primarily to assault troops and to elite units such as the paratroopers, but issue was extended to regular units as well, subject to availability. The Germans were quite happy to have Beretta continue production of the MAB family following the September 1943 armistice between Italy and the Allies; reportedly, in April 1944 6,500 Model 38/A and 1,000 Model 38/42 were delivered to the Germans. German designations were MP 739 (i) for the Model 38/a, and MP 738 (i) for the 38/42.

The 38/44 marked the end of wartime production of the MAB 38 family of submachine guns, but it did not take long for Beretta to begin to receive export orders for modified versions of the MAB. As early as 1949 Egypt placed an order for what was designated the 38/49. It is beyond the scope of this book to address all of the post-war variants of the MAB, but suffice it to say that Beretta enjoyed considerable commercial success with foreign sales, exporting MAB variants to countries in Europe, Latin America, the Middle East, Asia and Africa. Some collectors confuse the Egyptian MAB, fitted with a bayonet, with the PAI MAB; the Egyptian bayonets have bronze furnishings.

The MAB 38 family of submachine guns reflected the quality standards universally attributed to Beretta products. They were well designed, well built, superbly finished – especially considering the wartime conditions – robust, reliable, and capable of being modified for more rapid production without sacrificing any of their essential qualities. The MAB 38 family ranks as one of the most popular, successful and widely produced submachine guns in the world. ■

M.A.B. 38/43

Year introduced: 1943
Overall length: 800mm (31.5")
Barrel length: 210mm (8.3")
Weight: 3.2 kg (7 lbs)
Rear sight: Fixed notch (100 meters)
Rate of fire: 550 rpm
Muzzle velocity: 400 m/sec (1220 fps)
Rifling: 6 groove RH twist
Safety: Two-position lever on left side
Cooling jacket: None
Compensator: Two slots
Stock: Wood, with one finger groove per side.
Remarks: Barrel could be either smooth or fluted; both types were tapered

PISTOLA MITRAGLIATRICE TZ 45

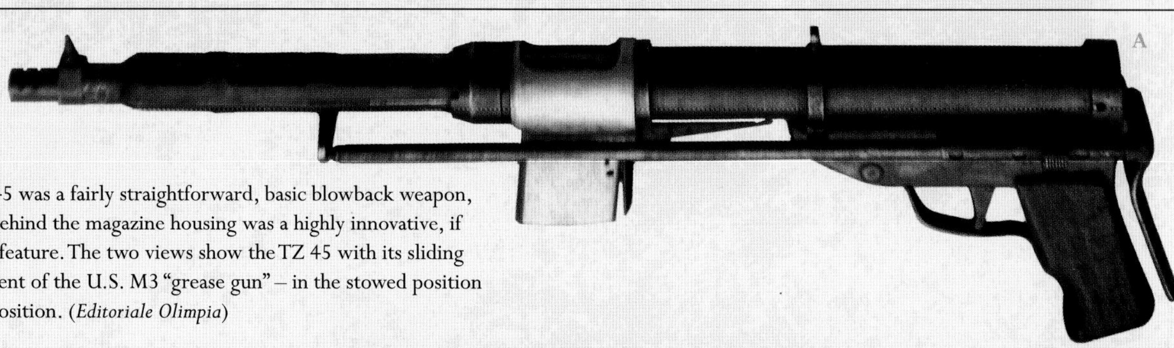

Images A & B The TZ 45 was a fairly straightforward, basic blowback weapon, although it its safety behind the magazine housing was a highly innovative, if somewhat imperfect, feature. The two views show the TZ 45 with its sliding wire stock – reminiscent of the U.S. M3 "grease gun" – in the stowed position and in the extended position. (*Editoriale Olimpia*)

There is much confusion and misinformation concerning who designed and who manufactured the TZ 45. The idea seems to have become firmly entrenched and accepted as fact by many sources that the TZ 45 was designed by two brothers, Tonon and Zorzoli Giandoso. This bit of misinformation seems to have gained more credence by having been repeated, almost verbatim, by a significant number of Internet sites that obviously have borrowed from each other. However, the truth is that the weapon was in fact designed by two individuals unrelated to each other and that the Giandosos were not brothers, but father and son. The TZ 45 was designed by Aldo Zorzoli and a lieutenant colonel whose surname was Tonon who was the director of the SFARE in Gardone Val Trompia but whose first name remains unknown. The prototypes were tested at Piossasco, near Torino in August 1943, and series production was entrusted to the firm of Ermenegildo Giandoso and Son, located in Gardone. There is some indication that the receiver may have been manufactured by Luigi Franchi and the bolt by a company named Peverelli, leading to the suspicion that the TZ 45 was assembled by Giandoso (or possibly by SAMT – see following) from subcontracted parts rather than from in-house capabilities. A detailed line drawing exists of the *Pistola mitra – Zorzoli*, dated 26.6.43, indicating the Soc. Man. Meccanica Torinese (Società Manifattura Meccanica Torinese) as the manufacturer, with a manufacturing location at Piassasco (sic) and an office location in Torino; this adds a bit to some of the uncertainties concerning the weapon, as following the war the TZ 45 was marketed as the AZ 50 (AZ standing for Aldo Zorzoli) by the Società Anonima Meccanica Torinese (SAMT), with a manufacturing facility in or near Torino (likely Piossasco) and corporate or representational offices in Rome rather than Torino.

The TZ 45 was a rather simple weapon, whose trigger, trigger housing, magazine well and barrel shroud were made from welded stampings, and whose receiver was simply a tube in which the bolt rode; despite its relatively short barrel with its twin slot compensator, overall the weapon was a bit long for a submachine gun. It was a blowback weapon and had a sliding wire stock quite reminiscent of the stock of the U.S. M3 submachine gun; a very small number were fitted with a wood stock. In common with all other Italian submachine guns it had a selective fire capability; a three-position lever on the right side of the receiver, forward of and above the trigger, when in the fully forward position was on safe; when in the vertical position it was in the semi-automatic mode, and when fully to the rear was in full automatic mode. It accepted 10, 20 or 40-round Beretta magazines. In addition to the normal safety/selector it also had a grip safety located behind the magazine housing that apparently was not a very satisfactory arrangement, as reportedly it caused a great deal of inconvenience as well as some accidents; this is somewhat ironic in view of the fact that it was specifically designed to avoid the fault common to many submachine guns to accidentally discharge. The magazine housing on some exmples was made of aluminum. Despite the poor ergonomics of the safety, which required pressure from the shooter's left hand, it did mark an innovative breakthrough that was copied on many later submachine guns, beginning with the Danish Madsen M50 that had a similar arrangement. The grip safety as incorporated on the TZ 45 has been described as an excellent idea that was badly executed on the weapon itself. About 6,000 copies of the TZ 45 were produced and issued to R.S.I. (*Repubblica Sociale Italiana* – Italian Social Republic) forces in northern Italy and to some German *Wehrmacht* units in northern Italy as well. Although the TZ 45 was cheaper and easier to manufacture than other Italian submachine guns such as the Beretta M38 series, it had a poor reputation for reliability and was not judged favorably when evaluated by British and American technical personnel.

During the early-1950s, the manufacturing rights and production machinery for the TZ 45 were sold to the Burmese Army, which manufactured a small number as the BA-52. ■

PISTOLA MITRAGLIATRICE TZ 45

Designer: Lt Col Tonon; Aldo Zorzoli
Manufacturer: Società Manifattura Meccanica Torinese
Caliber: 9mm
Cartridge: 9x19mm Parabellum
Operating system: Straight blowback
Length, stock extended: 851mm (33.5")
Length, stock retracted: 546mm (21.5")
Barrel length: 230mm (9")
Weight: 3.27 kg (7.2 lbs)
Front sight: Spherical post
Rear sight: Aperture
Muzzle velocity: 380 m/sec (1160 fps)
Rate of fire: 550-600 rpm
Feed system: 20 or 40 round detachable box magazine

PISTOLA MITRAGLIATRICE F.N.A. B MODELLO 1943

A

B

Images A & B Two views of the F.N.A. B Model 43, shown with stock folded and stock extended. Markings on the left hand side of the receiver read "Pist.Mitr.FNA.Brescia Mod.43" on the top line, and "Brevetto Scalori" underneath, which translates as "Machine pistol FNA Brescia Model 43, Scalori Patent." The F.N.A. B 43 relied on traditional production methods, resulting in an expensive and somewhat heavy weapon. (*Editoriale Olimpia*)

The only Italian submachine gun produced during the war that did not operate on the straight blowback principle but which was a delayed blowback instead was the F.N.A. B Model 43, manufactured by the Fabbrica Nazionale d'Armi plant in Brescia. Virtually nothing is known about its designer other than his last name, Scalori, which appears on the receiver of at least one surviving example of the weapon. The F.N.A. B 43 was also known as the "Zerbino," which was the name of the Minister of the Interior of the R.S.I. Rather than relying on stamped parts as was the developing trend in 1943, production of the F.N.A. B 43 relied on traditional gunmaking methods and was machined out of steel forgings which made it slow and very expensive to produce. Despite its superlative finish, aesthetically it was rather crude looking, especially for an Italian weapon of this type. Its combination three port muzzle brake and compensator was very much like that of the Soviet PPSh 41 submachine gun, although its cooling jacket had round holes very much like that of the Beretta MAB 38A. The F.N.A. B 43 had a selective fire capability; the selector was located on the left hand side of the receiver behind the trigger and was marked *raffica* (automatic) in the upper position, and *colpo* (single shot) in the lower position. There was also a two-position safety on the left-hand side forward of and above the trigger guard, marked S in the vertical position and F in the horizontal position; the letters S and F stood for *Sicura* (safe) and *Fuoco* (fire). Its stock was a single steel strut type that folded to the right-hand side of the weapon. An interesting innovation was the magazine housing that could be folded forward, making a very compact weapon; this feature was also adopted on a few other Italian wartime submachine guns. A variant has also come to light whose cooling jacket and magazine housing differ from those of the production model weapons; the holes on the barrel jacket of the variant have been replaced by a series of elongated slots not unlike those of the Soviet PPSh 41, and the magazine housing is a fixed stamping rather than a hinged assembly. The selector lever also differs from the production model, as do the safety catch and magazine rlease. Given what appear to be simplifications to the production version and the model number indicated as 48 rather than 43 (see following description of markings), it would appear that this was a post-war prototype. The F.N.A. B 43 utilized Beretta 10, 20 and 40-round staggered row box magazines. The F.N.A. B 43 itself was an extremely well built and finished weapon, fired from a closed bolt, and was sturdy, reliable and accurate, and was well controlled in the full automatic mode. Reportedly, 7,000 of these weapons were manufactured in 1943-1944 and were used by R.S.I. forces in northern Italy, although there is also speculation that as few as only 1,000 (and possibly many less) were produced, based on observed serial numbers no lower than 5000 and no higher than 5999. Despite the relatively small number produced it is likely that some were used by the Germans, as they assigned the code of MP 43(i) to the weapon.

Markings were not consistent on the F.N.A. B 43, despite the relatively small number produced. Surviving examples of the series version show at least two different styles on the left-hand side of the receiver, above the trigger: one style of markings reads Pist. Mitr. FNA Brescia Mod. 43 on one line, with Brevetto Scalori on a line below. A second style reads F.N. A-B-Mod. 1943. Mat. 5093 on one line, with the word Brevettata on a line below; the abbreviation Mat. stands for *Matricola*, or "serial number." Markings on the variant described above read *Pist. Mitr. Scalori Mod. 48* on one line, and the word *Brevettata* on a line below, all in italic letters. ■

PISTOLA MITRAGLIATRICE F.N.A. B MODELLO 1943

Designer: Scalori, first name unknown
Manufacturer: Fabbrica Nazionale d'Armi, Brescia
Caliber: 9mm
Cartridge: 9x19mm Parabellum
Operating system: Delayed blowback
Length, stock extended: 790mm (31.1")
Length, stock folded: 530mm (20.9")
Barrel length: 250mm (9.8")
Weight: 3.2 kg (7 lbs)
Front sight: Blade
Rear sight: Fixed V notch
Muzzle velocity: 341 m/sec (1120 fps)
Rate of fire: 400 rpm
Feed system: 10, 20 or 40 round detachable box magazine

PISTOLA MITRAGLIATRICE ISOTTA-FRASCHINI CALIBRO 9 PARABELLUM, MODELLO ALBERTINI

In late 1944 the Isotta-Fraschini automotive firm, which had considerable experience in the field of automatic weapons, began to manufacture a submachine gun that had been designed by Giuseppe Albertini in 1943. The weapon was very simply made utilizing stamped and riveted construction, in part influenced by Isotta-Fraschini's experience and familiarity with aeronautical construction techniques. Aside from its characteristic cooling jacket with very large cutouts its appearance is similar to that of the later Danish Madsen submachine gun, as well as a certain similarity to its Russian contemporary, the Sudaev PPS 43. Design and construction of the Albertini weapon were ingeniuously simple and reflected an excellent grasp and understanding of stamping technology of the times. The only parts of the weapon that required any machining were the barrel, bolt, and barrel support brackets; all other parts were stamped and riveted, and no welding was involved. The receiver walls and cooling jacket consisted of two pieces of stamped sheet steel with stamped stiffening ribs in the receiver area; internally, the bolt moved on two U-shaped guide channels riveted to the inside face of the receiver wall. The forward portion of the sheet had a

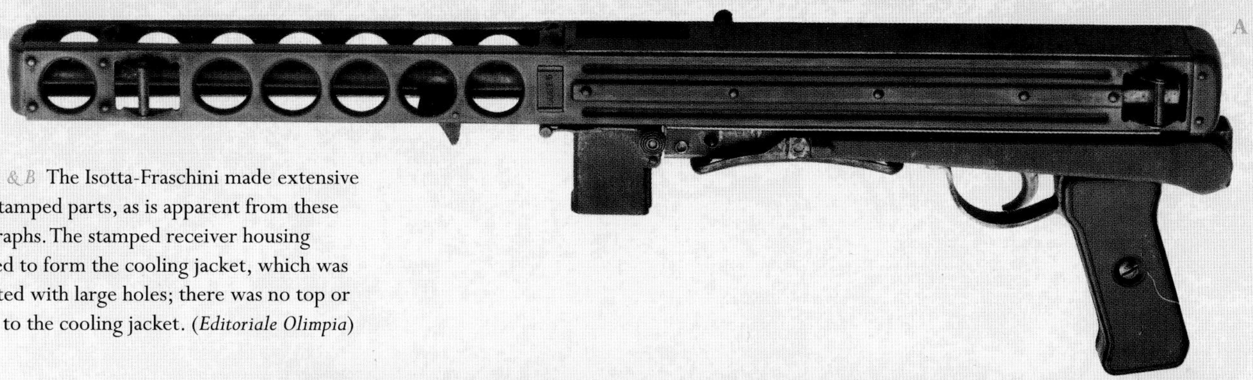

Images A & B The Isotta-Fraschini made extensive use of stamped parts, as is apparent from these photographs. The stamped receiver housing extended to form the cooling jacket, which was perforated with large holes; there was no top or bottom to the cooling jacket. (*Editoriale Olimpia*)

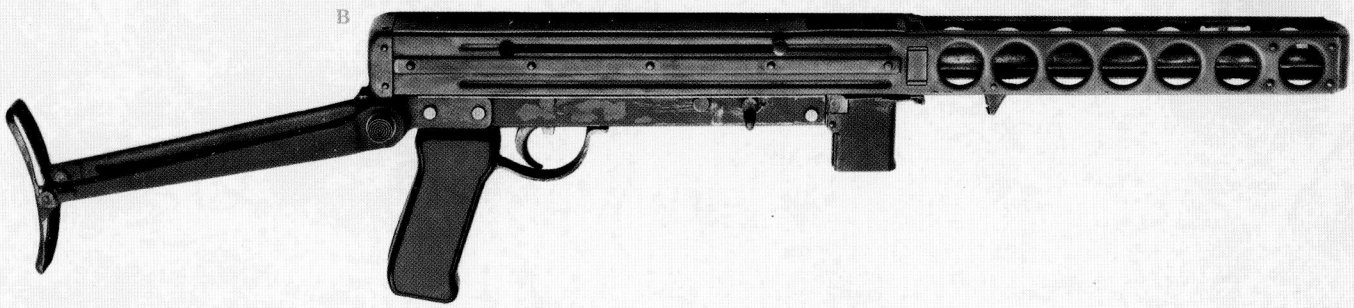

series of seven large vent holes on each side, all of which were round except for the second opening on the left-hand side which instead was square, but which was stamped so as to leave two triangular tabs which were then bent outward and joined by a post and ferrule that acted as the front sling bar. The rear sling bar was also a U-shaped stamping with triangular tabs and post and ferrule similar to those of the front sling attachment point. The two sheets were joined together at the front and back by stamped U-shaped brackets riveted to the sides, forming a sort of box; the front bracket had a hole in it that provided clearance for the barrel muzzle, and the rear bracket had a receiver plug that allowed removal of the bolt and recoil spring. A stamped sheet metal cover secured by rivets formed the top of the receiver. Two guide brackets held the barrel: the forward bracket, riveted between the first and second forward ventilating holes also served as the front sight base, while the rear bracket, which was machined from a block of steel and was located behind the last vent hole, secured the barrel at the chamber end and also incorporated the fixed V-notch rear sight. The trigger group, which included the pistol grip and the folding metal stock, attached to the receiver by means of stamped tabs. Two versions of the Isotta-Fraschini were made, one utilizing staggered row Beretta magazines and one utilizing straight row MP40 magazines. They were both fitted with a magazine housing that could be folded forward, although the housings themselves differed. Another difference lay in the type of selector mechanism: on the Beretta magazine version, a three-position selector lever was located on the right-hand side of the receiver, to the rear of the magazine housing; in the horizontal position it was on "Safe"; the intermediate position was for full automatic fire, and the rearmost position was for semi-automatic fire. On the MP 40 magazine version, the safety lever was on the left-hand side of the weapon and acted only as a safety; the selector consisted of a small lever incorporated in the trigger guard, directly forward and above the trigger which when in the forward position allowed only semi-automatic fire, and in the rear position allowed full automatic fire. There is some controversy as to the number of weapons actually produced, some sources quoting a figure of 250 while others quote an initial contract figure of 500. Surviving records indicate that a number of the Isotta-Fraschinis were delivered to R.S.I. "Nembo" paratroopers based near Tradate, and to a Decima Flottiglia MAS (commonly referred to as X MAS, a commando unit) garrison in Sesto Calende. Only a very limited number of these weapons have ever actually been accounted for (probably less than ten).

PISTOLA MITRAGLIATRICE ISOTTA-FRASCHINI, MODELLO ALBERTINI

Designer: Giuseppe Albertini
Manufacturer: Isotta-Fraschini, Cavaria small arms plant
Caliber: 9mm
Cartridge: 9x19mm Parabellum
Operating system: Straight blowback
Length, stock extended: 815mm (32")
Length, stock folded: 620mm (24.4")
Barrel length: 280mm (11")
Weight: 3.5 kg (7.7 lbs) with empty magazine
Front sight: Blade
Rear sight: Fixed notch
Muzzle velocity: 400 m/sec (1312 fps) approximate
Rate of fire: 450 rpm
Feed system: Different versions used Beretta magazines or German MP 40 magazines

PISTOLA MITRAGLIATRICE ARMAGUERRA OG 42

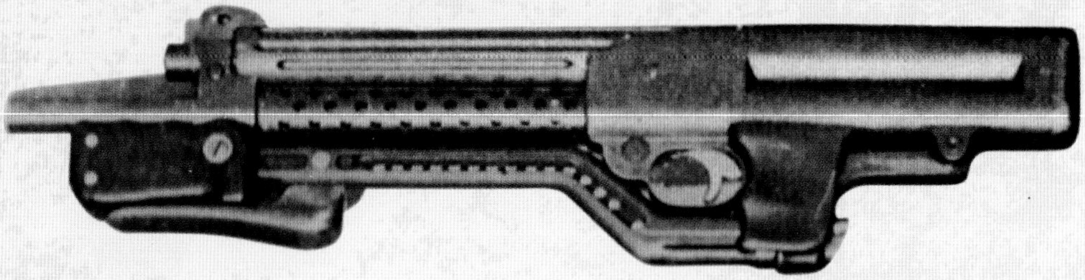

Prototype of the OG 42, with stock in folded position, resulting in a very compact weapon. The pistol grip on the OG 42 served as the magazine housing. (*Editoriale Olimpia*)

The OG 42 submachine gun was designed by Giovanni Oliani (the letters OG in the weapon's designation are the initials for Oliani Giovanni) and produced by Armaguerra in Cremona, probably only as a single prototype, in early 1942. The OG 42 presented some unusual features, the most revolutionary of which was the use of a bolt whose mass was over the barrel. It also had the magazine housing incorporated in the rear grip and had a new type of folding metal stock. At any rate, this promising design languished until 1944, at which time consideration was given to series production of the weapon; the weapon that did finally see very limited production, however, was not the OG 42 but its radically modified successor, the OG 44 (see following entry).

Credit is given to the Czech CZ Model 23 as being the first submachine gun to use a bolt whose center of mass was well forward of the chamber, and although the CZ 23 design likely predated that of the OG 42, the OG 42 was actually produced before the CZ 23, albeit only as a prototype. Another feature of the OG 42 was the magazine housing incorporated into the pistol grip which was also a feature of the CZ 23, but again, the OG 42 was the first submachine gun to be actually produced with both the revolutionary bolt and the pistol grip magazine. The overhung bolt, which results in less muzzle climb and allows a much shorter overall weapon length, has since been adopted on many other submachine guns, including the Israeli UZI and the Beretta PM 12. All considered, the OG 42 was a groundbreaking weapon whose existence is often overlooked in English-language publications, and whose influence on succeeding generations of submachine guns is largely unknown and thus unappreciated. The prototype is not known to still exist. ■

PISTOLA MITRAGLIATRICE ARMAGUERRA OG 42

Designer: Giovanni Oliani
Manufacturer: Armaguerra, Cremona
Caliber: 9mm
Cartridge: 9x19mm Parabellum
Operating system: Straight blowback weapon. Bolt had fixed firing pin.
Length, stock extended: NA
Length, stock folded: NA
Barrel length: NA
Weight: NA
Front sight: Blade
Rear sight: L-type flip
Muzzle velocity: 430 m/sec (1310 fps)
Rate of fire: 500-550 rpm
Feed system: 10, 20 and 40 round Beretta magazines

PISTOLA MITRAGLIATRICE ARMAGUERRA OG 44

This extremely interesting submachine gun was produced in very limited numbers – only 14 as far as can be determined. The OG 44 was a radical redesign of Oliani's earlier OG 42, and unlike the OG 42 which used traditional gunmaking materials and methods, the OG 44 was redesigned to be able to utilize as many stampings and new techniques as possible to facilitate mass production. In addition to the new technologies involved, major differences between the OG 44 and earlier OG 42 were that the magazine housing of the OG 44 was moved from the pistol grip to a more conventional position forward of the trigger housing, and the folding stock was completely redesigned. The overhung bolt, the hallmark feature of the OG 42, was retained. Due to the turn of events, however, series production never was in fact initiated.

Although the OG 44 was designed to be produced cheaply and quickly, simplicity did not impair the excellent technical characteristics of this weapon. The body of the weapon (bolt carrier/receiver/barrel jacket) was stamped from a single sheet of metal 1.5mm thick, which was welded along the underside. The stock struts, buttplate and trigger mechanism were also

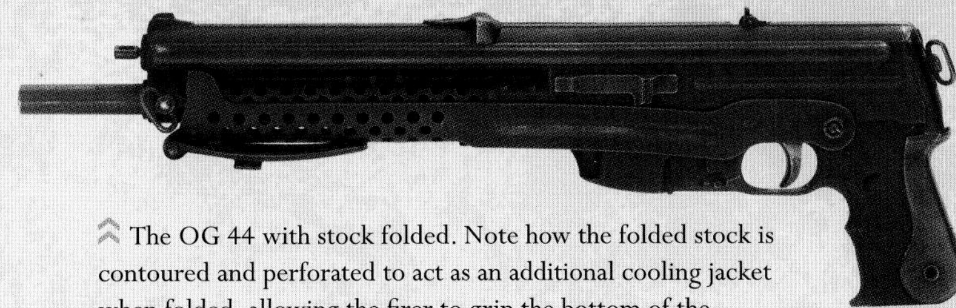

The OG 44 with stock folded. Note how the folded stock is contoured and perforated to act as an additional cooling jacket when folded, allowing the firer to grip the bottom of the weapon without risk of burning the hand. (*Editoriale Olimpia*)

Detail of the OG 44 displaying markings indicating the manufacturer (ARMAGUERRA), gun designation, and caliber. (*Editoriale Olimpia*)

The OG 44 with its stock extended. The OG 44 was also produced with a wooden buttstock in lieu of the folding stock. This example is devoid of all markings. (*Editoriale Olimpia*)

A wartime image of the proper method of firing the OG 44 with the sling attached. (*Editoriale Olimpia*)

stampings. What appears to be a grip safety was in fact only a detent to ensure that the stock remained in the open position. The manual safety that blocked the bolt was located on the left-hand side of the weapon; the selector lever was located on the right side of the weapon. The cocking lever was another stamping, mounted on top of the weapon. The recoil spring was housed inside the bolt, and the cleaning rod, which screwed into the upper portion of the body, doubled as the recoil spring guide. The original design of the OG 44 called for a 25-round staggered box magazine, but a modification was made to accept the Beretta 10, 20 and 40-round magazines; the original design also incorporated a hold-open feature which worked in conjunction with the 25-round magazine, but which would not work with the Beretta magazines. The stock was designed so that it could be swung into the open or closed position without first removing the magazine.

The right-hand side of the receiver, above the trigger, bore the markings ARMAGUERRA- Cremona on one line, with Pist.Mitr. O.G. 44 – Cal.9 on a line below.

It could be convincingly argued that the OG 44 was the precursor of a number of post-war submachine guns in its design concept. The bolt arrangement of submachine guns such as the Beretta Model 12 and the Israeli UZI probably can be traced back to the OG 44 bolt. Certainly, in all of their essential characteristics, the Walther MPL and MPK submachine guns developed in the 1960s are almost identical to the OG 44, and the Franchi LF 57 is likewise strikingly similar. ■

PISTOLA MITRAGLIATRICE ARMAGUERRA OG 44

Designer: Giovanni Oliani
Manufacturer: Armaguerra, Cremona
Caliber: 9mm
Cartridge: 9x19mm Parabellum
Operating system: Straight blowback weapon. Bolt had fixed firing pin.
Length, stock extended: 770mm (30.3"); 787mm (31") with wooden stock
Length, stock folded: 500mm (19.7")
Barrel length: 295mm (11.6")
Weight: 3.11 kg (6.8 lbs); 3.5 kg (7.7 lbs) with wooden stock
Front sight: Blade
Rear sight: L-type flip
Muzzle velocity: 430 m/sec (1310 fps)
Rate of fire: 500-550 rpm
Feed system: 10, 20 and 40 round Beretta magazines

PISTOLA MITRAGLIATRICE VARIARA

The Variara was a successful amalgam of features borrowed from Italian, British and German submachine guns of the period. (*Editoriale Olimpia*)

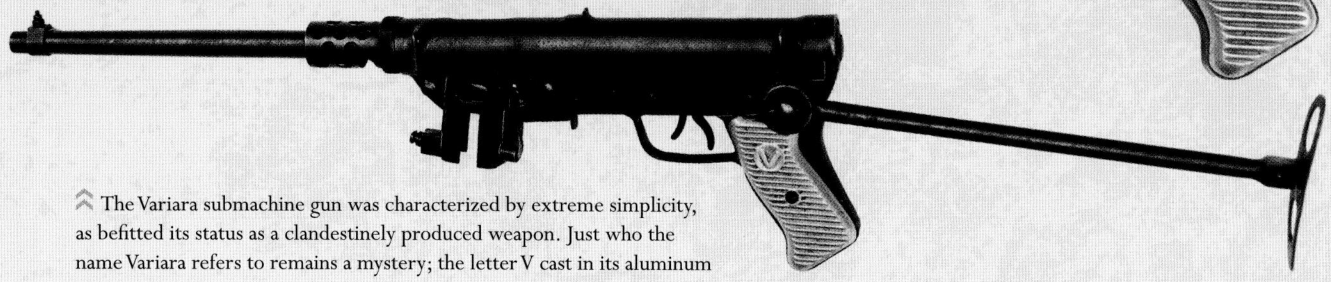

The Variara submachine gun was characterized by extreme simplicity, as befitted its status as a clandestinely produced weapon. Just who the name Variara refers to remains a mystery; the letter V cast in its aluminum grips is the only concession to the identity of the presumed designer. (*Editoriale Olimpia*)

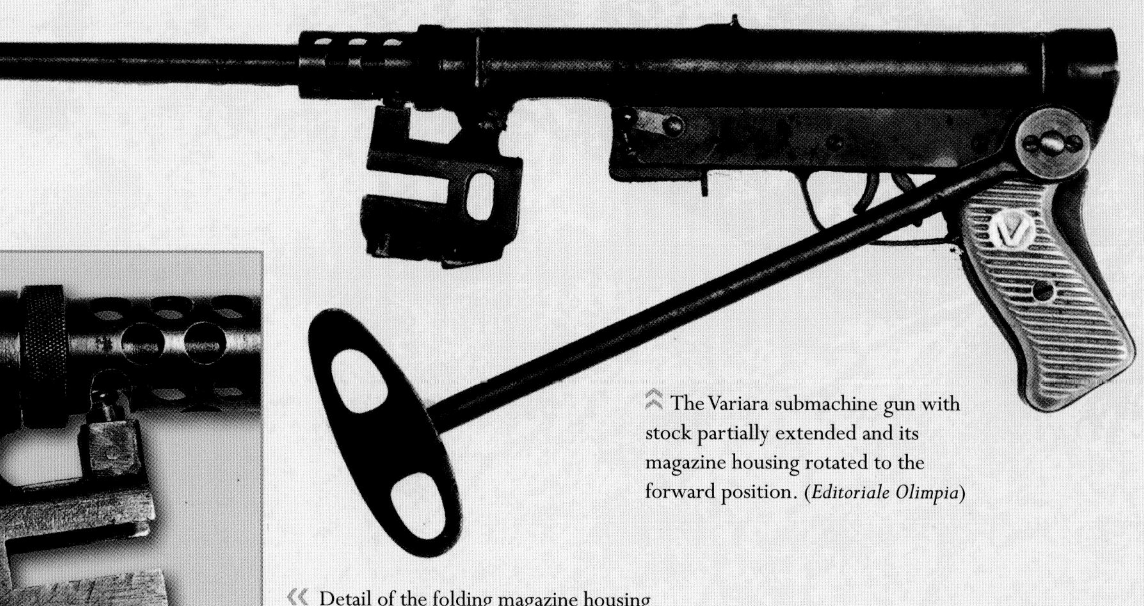

The Variara submachine gun with stock partially extended and its magazine housing rotated to the forward position. (*Editoriale Olimpia*)

Detail of the folding magazine housing of the Variara and of the knurled barrel retaining collar. (*Editoriale Olimpia*)

The Variara submachine gun, or machine pistol, was the most successful clandestinely made Italian submachine gun of the war. Even though this weapon could not be said to have presented any original or unusual features, it was in fact a unique weapon as it merged many of the best features of contemporary Italian and foreign submachine guns. Manufacture of the Variara probably began around mid-1944; the barrel and bolt were almost certainly made utilizing machine tools from one of the FIAT plants that had been dispersed in northern Italy, while most other parts were made in rudimentary workshops at other locations and assembled somewhere other than at the FIAT facility. Precisely who was responsible for the design of the Variara remains, and probably will forever remain, a mystery. There is some suggestion that the designer may have been a FIAT technician who was a member of the resistance movement. Although the name Variara normally would indicate the designer of the weapon, considering the circumstances in Italy at the time anyone named Variara who claimed paternity of the weapon, or who might be suspected by the Germans or Fascists of having designed it, likely would have been shot as soon as he was caught. Several alternative hypotheses have been offered, among them that the weapon was named after a fallen partisan, or that Variara was a pseudonym or *nom de guerre*, which was much in vogue at the time. The Variara was a straight blowback weapon, and fired from an open bolt. The bolt, and the method of mating the barrel to the receiver and the receiver to the trigger housing resemble those of the British STEN MK II; the trigger group, consisting of dual triggers allowing single shot or full automatic fire, was essentially the same as that on the Marengoni designed Beretta weapons, and the standard Beretta staggered box magazines could be used. The hinged magazine housing that could be folded forward under the barrel was copied from the F.N.A. B 43 submachine gun; grip design was reminiscent of the German Schmeisser MP38, whereas the Bergmann MP 18 inspired the cocking lever safety. The Variara also incorporated a grip safety.

As is obvious from the date and circumstances of its manufacture the Variara was not issued to Italian Army units, but rather, was used exclusively by partisan forces in northern Italy during the last year of the war. It is believed that production amounted to about 150 copies. Nine examples of the Variara are known to have survived in museums or private collections. Markings, including serial numbers, were virtually nonexistent on the Variara; the only concession to an identifying mark was the letter V cast into the aluminum pistol grips. ■

PISTOLA MITRAGLIATRICE (OR MITRA) VARIARA

Designer: Unknown
Manufacturer: Clandestine partisan workshops, northern Italy (possibly near Biella)
Caliber: 9mm
Cartridge: 9 x 19mm Parabellum
Operating system: Straight blowback
Length, stock extended: 820mm (32.3")
Length, stock folded: 560mm (22")
Barrel length: 300mm (11.8")
Weight: 2.8 kg (6.2 lbs)
Front sight: Post, mounted on ferrule support
Rear sight: Fixed V notch
Rate of fire: 550 rpm cyclic; 100-200 rpm practical
Muzzle velocity: 410 m/sec (1250 fps)
Rifling: 6 groove RH twist
Feed system: Beretta staggered box magazines, varying capacities

MOSCHETTO MITRAGLIATORE MM 745

There is little information concerning the MM 745 submachine gun, and what little is subject to much question and uncertainty. Available information indicates that it incorporated many of the characteristics of the TZ 45 – not surprising, as it was designed by Aldo Zorzoli, one of the designers of the TZ 45 – and reportedly was issued in very limited numbers to the RSI in the waning days of the war, although this cannot be confirmed and is one of the many doubts surrounding the origin and background of this weapon. The few known photographs purporting to show this weapon in use during the waning days of World War II are highly suspect, as due to photo angle and light conditions and overall image quality, may actually be of the Beretta MAB 38A. The MM 745 (MM stood for *moschetto militare*, or military carbine) was 745mm long (as reflected in the weapon's designation) and was fitted with a wooden stock. A novel feature and distinguishing characteristic of the weapon was a very substantial coil spring wrapped around the barrel that served as a cooling jacket. Balzi indicates that the weapon was produced by a firm named Genar, whose main office was in Rome, but that it may have been the successor of the Società Anonima Meccanica Tirrena (SAMT); however, other sources indicate that the producer of the TZ 45, whose acronym also was SAMT, was the Società Anonima Meccanica Torinese, leading to the possibility that SAMT (Torinese), either during the very last days of the was reorganized as Genar or that more likely, Genar was founded in the immediate post-war period as a successor to SAMT, and that the MM 745 was in actuality a post-war weapon. ■

CHAPTER 4: MACHINE GUNS

At the outset of World War I the Italian Army had a total of 600 machine guns; by the end the war the number had risen to about 10,000 automatic weapons, including a very small number of submachine guns whose design and development Italy had pioneered. The standard heavy machine gun at the end of the war was the FIAT Model 14, supplemented by large numbers of Austrian 8mm Schwarzlose war booty machine guns; the newly developed S.I.A. was the candidate to fill the light machine gun role. During the interwar years the Italians were well aware of the fact that the rifle caliber (6.5mm) ammunition of the FIAT Model 1914 was inadequate for a machine gun, and consequently they experimented with and developed a number of machine guns whose caliber ranged between 6.5mm and 8mm. The list of designers and manufacturers who provided prototypes for consideration was quite large, and included FIAT, Brixia (MBT), Scotti, Isotta-Fraschini, Breda, Ottico Meccanica Italiana, SAFAT and SISTAR. By the time World War II began, the *Regio Esercito* had adopted the FIAT Model 1935, which was a fairly successful upgrade of the FIAT Model 1914, as its standard machine gun, and which in turn was replaced during the course of the war by the excellent Breda Model 37 (both chambered for the Breda 8x59mm round); the disappointing Breda Model 30 in 6.5mm was adopted as the standard light machine gun. The Breda Model 30, along with other Italian light machine guns, was reclassified as a *fucile mitragliatore* (automatic rifle, comparable to the Browning Automatic Rifle) when in the 1926-1927 timeframe it became apparent that the Italian light machine guns then available did not fully satisfy military requirements. Apparently the military authorities believed it was simpler to reclassify the type of weapons on hand rather than to develop more capable weapons that would meet the requirements. During World War II, the Army also used a number of foreign weapons, some of World War I vintage, generally in second line duties, usually in Italian territorial defense units but also in overseas territories; these included the venerable Austrian Schwarzlose Model 1912, the French St. Etienne Mle 1907, Hotchkiss Mle1914, Model 1924/29, and Chauchat C.S.R.G. Mle 1915, and the Czech ZB 30 captured from the Yugoslavs.

MITRAGLIATRICE S.I.A. MODELLO 18

The S.I.A. Model 1918 machine gun was developed in World War I for aircraft use but was never used as originally intended as a number of shortcomings due to the haste in which it was developed soon showed up. The Italian Army, faced with a pressing need for a light machine gun that could compete against the Austrian Schwarzlose and MG-08, turned to the 6.5mm S.I.A. as the answer. However, use in the field soon showed that it was not reliable and therefore inspired little faith in the troops and it was accordingly viewed as only a stopgap weapon until something better could be developed and issued. Nonetheless, in 1926 the S.I.A. was issued on the scale of four guns to each alpine battalion's machine gun company, along with two FIAT mod. 14 machine guns. The S.I.A. was subsequently withdrawn from service, but in the spring of 1941 they were taken from storage and assigned to second-line units, namely the *Guardia alla Frontiera* (G.a.F. – border guards) and territorial defense units in place of the Breda 30 light machine gun. However, after only about a month, distribution of the S.I.A. was suspended except for 168 that had already been issued to G.a.F. units, as there were plans to convert the guns to the heavier 7.35mm cartridge. This initiative was soon cancelled, and in September deliveries of the S.I.A. resumed to G.a.F, coastal and territorial defense units, and to the *Gioventù Italiana del Littorio* units.

The gun was a delayed blowback type and was rather simple in design but did not turn out to be a particularly reliable weapon. In order to ensure proper functioning, cartridges as well as the weapon itself had to be lightly oiled. The chief differences between the aircraft and infantry versions of the S.I.A. were their barrels and mountings. The barrel of the aircraft version had longitudinal grooves cut into it for cooling, whereas the infantry version had a series of large circular aluminum fins that aided heat dissipation to a large degree, and was fitted with a flash hider. The barrel was attached to the receiver by a sleeve with a bayonet thread. Up to 600 rounds could be fired consecutively without overheating and without affecting accuracy, although the barrel had to be replaced about every 5,000 rounds. The bolt was cylindrical and housed the firing pin and spring. The extractor was fixed. Grips were of the spade type, with a thumb trigger. Feed was from a top-mounted curved box magazine. The sights were offset to the left-hand side of the weapon to compensate for the top-mounted magazine.

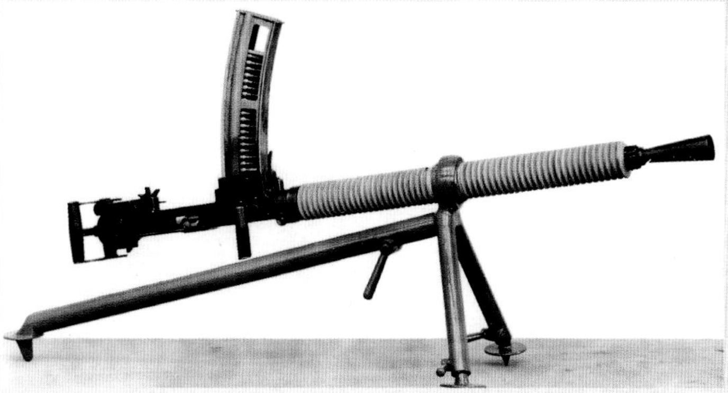

The SIA Model 1918 light machine gun. Its finned barrel, flash hider, and top-mounted magazine were hallmark features. The open sided magazine, as with all such similar magazines, increased the possibility of feeding malfunctions due to dirt or debris on the cartridges. (*Fiat*)

The S.I.A. infantry version was mounted on either a very simple tripod or on a frame in lieu of the tripod. The frame had folding front legs and a rear leg that rotated towards the spade grip for carrying and had a shoulder harness that enabled the gun and frame to be back-packed by one man. ■

MITRAGLIATRICE S.I.A.

Designer: Bethel Abiel Revelli
Manufacturer: Società Italiana Aviazione (S.I.A.)
Caliber: 6.5mm
Cartridge: 6.5x52mm Mannlicher-Carcano
Operating system: Delayed blowback
Overall length: 1160mm (45.7")
Barrel length: 450mm (17.7") with flash hider; 400mm (15.7") without flash hider
Weight: Gun: 11 kg (24.2 lbs); tripod: 5.6 kg (12.3 lbs)
Feed system: 50-round staggered row curved box magazine
Front sight: Barleycorn, offset on left-hand side of receiver
Rear sight: Adjustable knob mounted on left-hand side of receiver, graduated for 300, 700, and 1000 meters
Rate of fire: Approximately 750 rpm cyclic; 150 rpm practical
Safety: Lever on right-hand side of receiver
Muzzle velocity: 630 m/sec (2067 fps)
Feed system: 50-round curved box magazine, top mounted

MITRAGLIATRICE LEGGERA FIAT MODELLO 1926

The FIAT Mod. 24 was the precursor of the Model 25 and Model 26 light machine guns. Its finned barrel resembled that of the S.I.A. Model 1918 light machine gun, but was replaced by a fluted barrel on the Model 1925 version. (*Fiat*)

An early version of the FIAT Model 1926 light machine gun, also referred to as the FIAT Model 1925. The barrel of this version had full-length longitudinal cooling slots. (*Fiat*)

Information pertaining to the FIAT Model 1926 light machine gun is quite scarce, even in Italian publications. In 1924 FIAT had offered the Army the FIAT Model 1924 light machine gun, but only a limited number were acquired for test and evaluation purposes. The barrel on the Model 1924 had aluminum cooling fins similar to those on the S.I.A. light machine gun, giving it a quite distinctive appearance. The Model 1924 was soon followed by an improved version, the Model 1926, sometimes referred to as the *fucile mitragliatore modello 1925*, as it was developed in 1925 but was not acquired by the Army for evaluation until 1926. It is also referred to as the SAFAT because it was manufactured by a FIAT subsidiary, the Società Anonima Fabbrica Armi Torino, abbreviated SAFAT. At least two different versions existed which differed in their external appearance primarily with regard to the barrel and sights. The earlier version had a barrel jacket that had wide cooling slots cut into it for almost its entire length, whereas the later version had a barrel and barrel jacket arrangement quite similar to that used on the later FIAT Model 35 machine gun. The sights on the early type consisted of a leaf rear sight mounted well to the rear of the receiver and a Barleycorn front sight mounted on the forward portion of the receiver. The later version had sights laid out basically as on the Model 35, with a leaf type rear sight mounted about midway along the receiver and a Barleycorn front sight mounted on the forward portion of the barrel jacket. A distinctive feature of the later version was the skeleton shoulder stock that could be attached to the left-hand side of the spade grip.

The weapon was short recoil operated, with a rotating cam that joined together the barrel and the bolt for a short travel,

« Italian bersaglieri with their collapsible bicycles on maneuvers in the Irpinia district of southern Italy in 1936. The standard issue weapon of the bersaglieri was the Model 91 cavalry carbine, amply in evidence in this photograph. The bersagliere in the center of the photo is carrying the squad's automatic weapon, a Fiat Model 1926 light machine gun complete with tripod, but without the skeleton shoulder stock. (*Author's files*)

FIAT produced about two thousand Model 1926 guns at its own expense in hopes of securing an Italian Army contract, but the Army adopted the Breda Model 30 light machinegun, a decision it came to regret. (*Fiat*)

The definitive version of the FIAT Model 1926 light machine gun with a skeleton stock. (*Fiat*)

The FIAT Model 1925 and its ammunition chest containing 20 6.5mm chargers. (*Fiat*)

as in the FIAT 14 and the Glisenti 1910 pistol. As with most other Italian machine guns the Model 1926 had an oil reservoir and oil pump for lubrication. The cartridge feed system was another of the many systems that the Italians adopted for their machine guns. It consisted of a box magazine mounted on the left-hand side of the gun and was loaded with 20-round chargers that were also used on the later Model 28 machine gun as well as on the Breda Model 30 light machine gun. The tripod associated with the Model 1926 was a very light affair with adjustable legs and with a harness that allowed it to be backpacked.

The weapon was never officially adopted by the Italian Army. The 2,000 copies that were produced were at FIAT expense, in the hopes of being awarded a contract for series production, but the Army opted for the Breda 5C – later designated the Breda 30 – light machine gun. ■

MITRAGLIATRICE LEGGERA FIAT MODELLO 1926

Designer: Bethel Abiel Revelli
Manufacturer: Società Anonima Fabbrica Armi Torino (SAFAT)
Caliber: 6.5mm
Cartridge: 6.5x52mm Mannlicher-Carcano
Operating system: Gas operated blowback
Overall length: 1040mm (41") without skeleton stock; 1335mm (52.5") with skeleton stock
Barrel length: 535mm (21")
Weight: Gun: 11 kg (24.2 lbs); tripod: 2 kg (4.4 lbs); skeleton shoulder stock: .45 kg (1 lb)
Front sight: Barleycorn
Rear sight: Leaf type, graduated from 100 to 1500 meters
Safety: Lever on right-hand side of receiver
Muzzle velocity: 680 m/sec (2230 fps) estimated
Feed system: 20-round staggered row box magazine

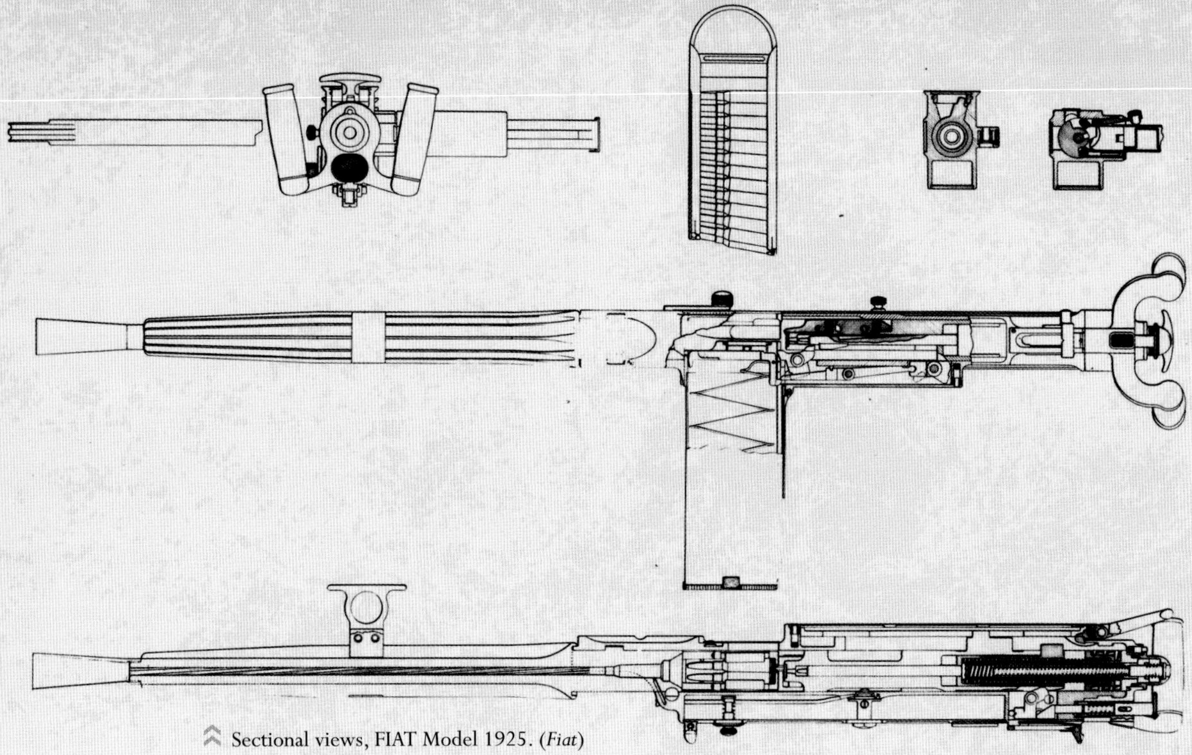

Sectional views, FIAT Model 1925. (*Fiat*)

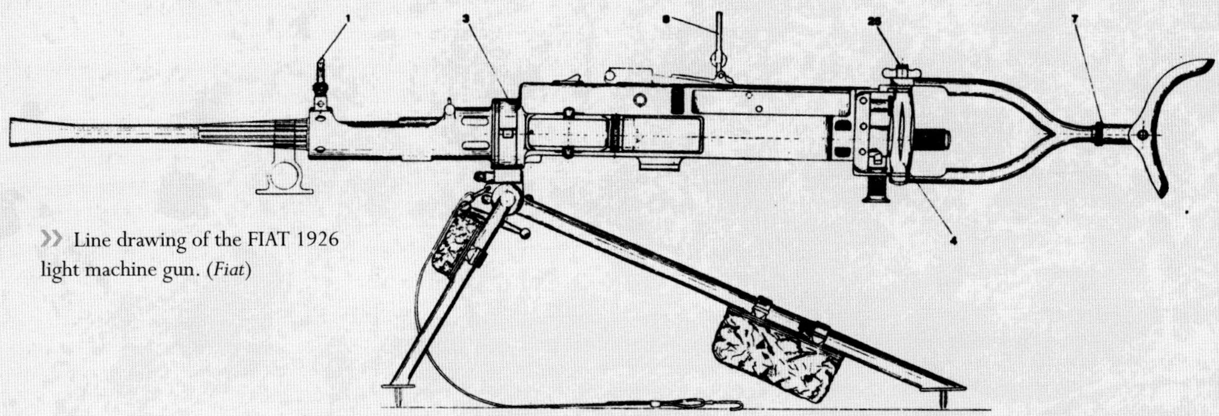

Line drawing of the FIAT 1926 light machine gun. (*Fiat*)

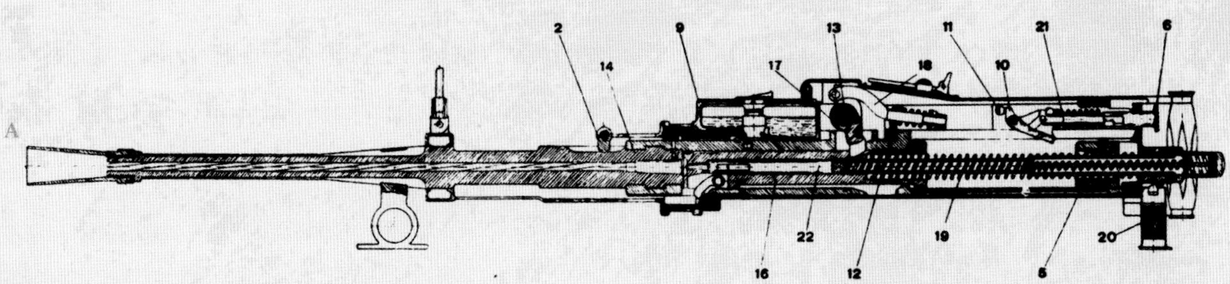

Images A & B Sectional drawings of the Mod. 1926. (*Fiat*)

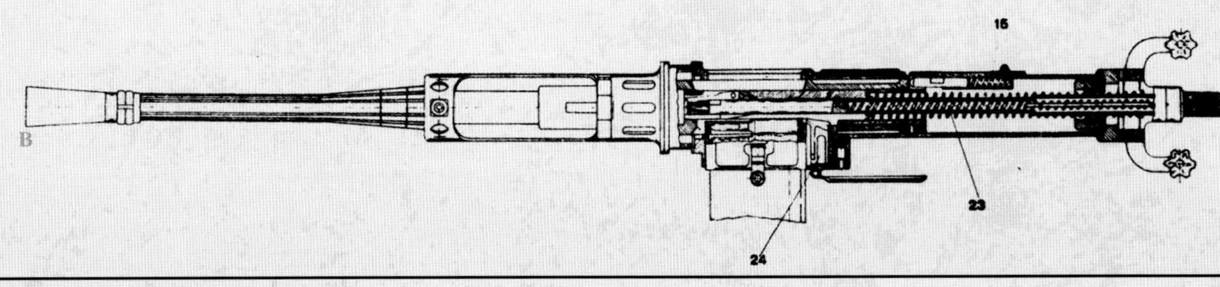

MITRAGLIATRICE LEGGERA FIAT MODELLO 1928

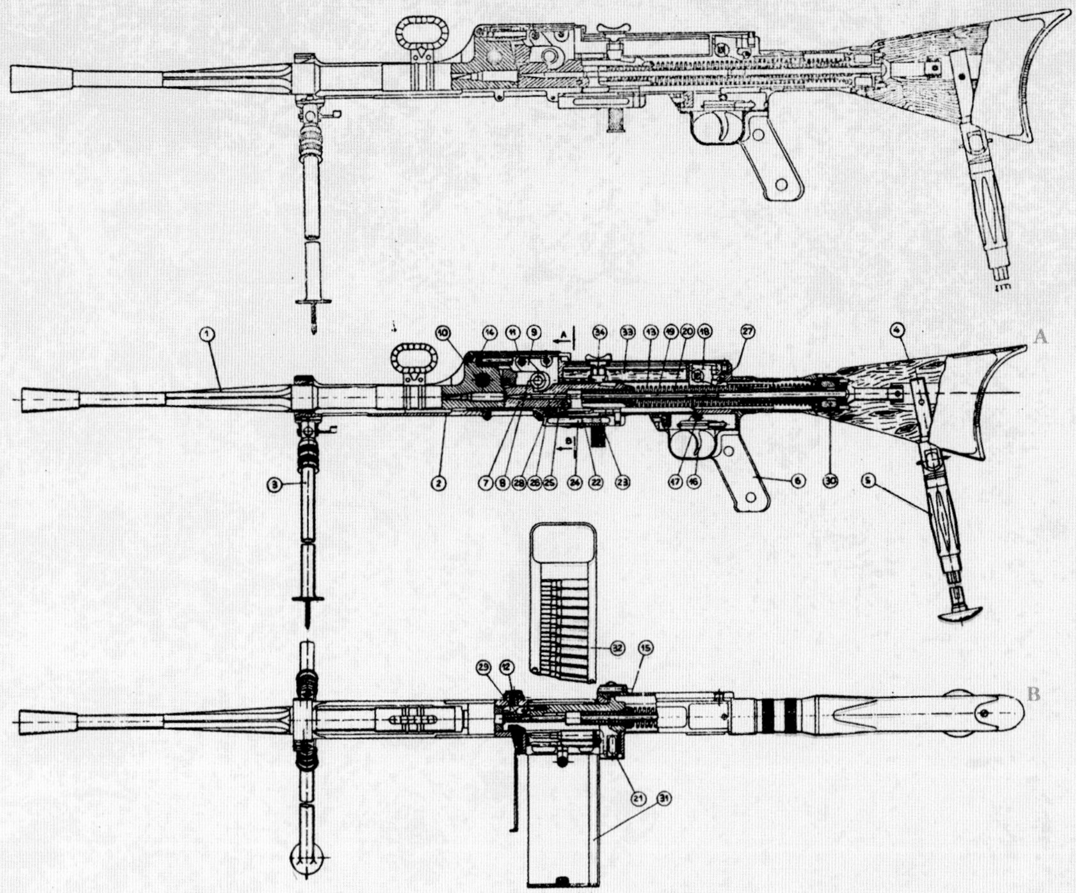

« The FIAT Model 1928 light machine gun with shoulder stock. (*Fiat*)

Images A & B Sectional drawing of the FIAT Mod. 1928 light machine gun. Only 700 examples of this weapon were ordered by the Italian Army for trial purposes, but the gun was not adopted. (Fiat)

The FIAT Model 1928 light machine gun shares a certain lack of notoriety along with the earlier Model 1926 weapon. Mention of this weapon is not common in English-language publications and is almost non-existent in Italian publications. The Model 1928 was a locked breech weapon, with a locking system designed by Giuseppe Mascarucci; the locking system was the biggest change from the earlier Model 1926 light machine gun. Externally it bore a strong resemblance to the Breda Model 30 light machine gun, having been developed for the same specification. It was mounted on a bipod but also had a third leg located towards the rear of the buttstock (a feature later incorporated on the Breda Model 30). The Model 1928 featured a quick-change barrel, and the cocking handle folded down during firing. Features it shared with the earlier Model 1926 were the oil pump for cartridge lubrication and the left-mounted box magazine that was loaded by the same chargers used on the Model 1926. The front sight was mounted on the forward portion of the barrel jacket, and the rear sight on the receiver.

The Model 1928 was tested along with the Breda 30 which ultimately was selected to be the Italian Army's standard light machine gun. Only 700 copies of the Model 1928 were acquired by the Army for trial purposes and were distributed to infantry, alpine, *bersaglieri* and cavalry units for field trials. Testing was also carried out in the Italian colony of Libya, and in 1940 there were still 38 FIAT Model 1926 and 14 FIAT Model 1928 machine guns in Italian depots in Libya. ■

MITRAGLIATRICE LEGGERA FIAT MODELLO 1928

Designer: Giuseppe Mascarucci
Manufacturer: FIAT (most likely by its SAFAT subsidiary)
Caliber: 6.5mm
Cartridge: 6.5x52mm Mannlicher-Carcano
Overall length: Not available
Barrel length: Not available
Weight: Not available
Front sight: Barleycorn
Rear sight: Leaf type, graduated from 0 to 1500 meters, with 200 and 300 meters omitted
Rate of fire: Not available
Safety: Lever on left-hand side of receiver
Muzzle velocity: 680 m/sec (2230 fps) estimated
Feed system: 20-round staggered row box magazine

FUCILE MITRAGLIATORE BREDA MODELLO 30

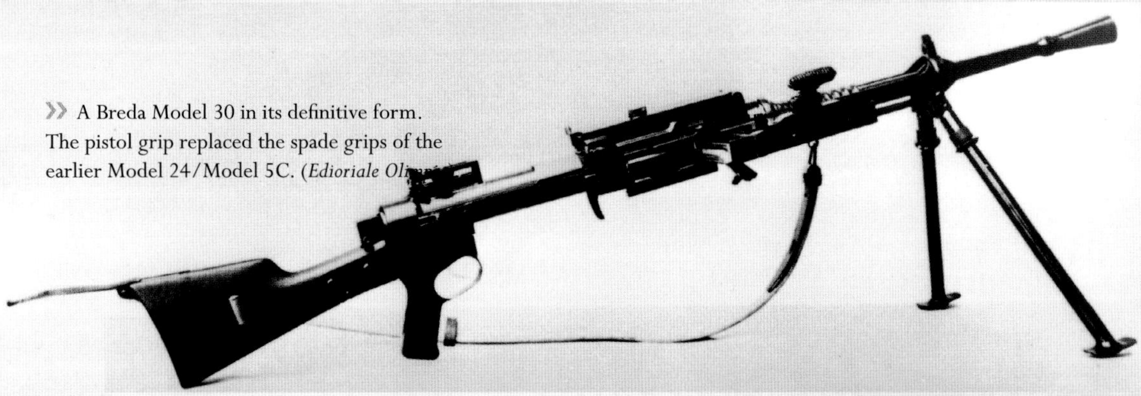

›› A Breda Model 30 in its definitive form. The pistol grip replaced the spade grips of the earlier Model 24/Model 5C. (*Edioriale Olimpia*)

›› The Breda Mod. 24/Model 5C was characterized by its spade grips and shoulder stock. (*Breda*)

⌃ A Breda Model 30 gunner and team chief, possibly in Albania. The stencil on the helmet is believed to belong to the 1st Bersaglieri Regiment which was operationally active in Albania in 1940 and 1941. (*Bruno Benvenuti*)

For all practical purposes the only light machine guns employed by the Italians in World War II were the Breda series based on the 6.5mm Breda Model 5C, also known as the Model 1924. The weapons in this series were the Breda Model 29, Model 30 and the Model 30/38 (used by the Navy), all in 6.5mm, and the Model 38 in 7.35mm. All of these weapons were essentially identical mechanically, differing only in details of their configuration. The Model 24 was mounted on a tripod, had spade grips and a thumb-operated trigger; the Model 29 and subsequent models had a bipod and a pistol grip instead. The chief difference between the Model 29 and the Model 30 was that the pistol grip of the Model 30 was made of steel (with wood grips) and angled to the rear, whereas that of the Model 29 had been vertical and made of wood. Another feature of the Model 30 was a telescoping leg mounted towards the rear of the buttstock, although this feature did not appear until 1934. All versions featured a quick-change barrel that was supposed to be changed every 250-300 rounds during sustained fire and every 1000 rounds during normal firing to compensate for excessive overheating inherent in the weapon. Two spare barrels were provided with each gun and had a quick-change capability; barrel life was between 8,000 and 12,000 rounds.

By 1 September 1939 the army had taken delivery of 28,462 Model 30 weapons. Scale of issue seems to have varied; in 1930 the Model 30 equipped the weapons squad (the fourth squad) of the rifle platoon, but later may have been issued on the scale of one or two per infantry rifle squad. The Breda machine gun team consisted of a team chief (who carried the accessories chest with two spare barrels, to be changed every 250-300 rounds), the gunner, and the ammunition bearer.

Perhaps the biggest fault of these weapons was that they were far too sophisticated for use under combat conditions. Cartridges were lubricated by an oil pump prior to chambering, and under dusty or sandy conditions the gun was prone to jamming as the oil attracted and retained foreign matter in the

» A bersaglieri machine gun team manning a Breda Model 30. Two of the bersaglieri are wearing distinctively plumed tropical helmets, while the third sports a fez, also unique to the bersaglieri in the Italian Army. The soldier in the foreground is armed with the widely issued Model 91 cavalry carbine, with its bayonet extended. *(Bruno Benvenuti)*

» A Breda Model 30 in action. The assistant gunner on the right is grasping a 20-round charger, ready for reloading. *(Bruno Benvenuti)*

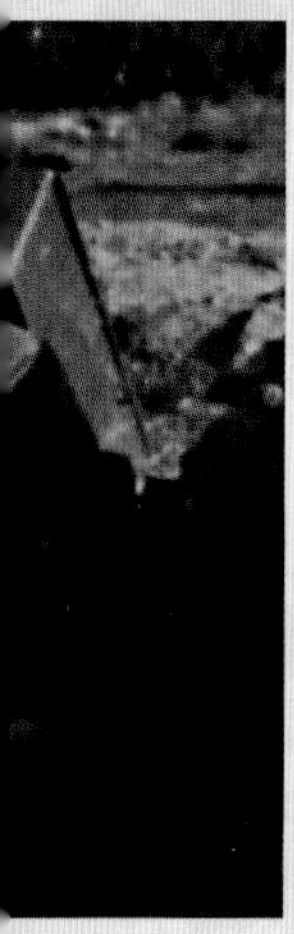

^ A Breda Model 30 light machine gun team in action. The gunner is flanked by the team chief on his left, who has the wooden spare parts chest with its two spare barrels on his back, and by the ammunition bearer to his right. The ammunition chest, which could be made either of metal or of cloth, carried fifteen 20-round magazines for the Breda. *(Bruno Benvenuti)*

mechanism. The oil itself had to be a special Breda type of a specific viscosity. The hinged magazine was another weak point, as if either it or the chargers that were used to load it were bent or damaged the gun would not feed. The problems often experienced with the magazines contributed to the rather slow rate of fire. During the war, reports submitted by using units uniformly complained of frequent jams, especially in adverse weather, lubrication problems, problems due to sand easily entering the mechanism, and the general delicate nature of the gun. Several reports suggested replacing the Breda Model 30 with submachine guns which were more reliable, and at least one report alluded to a preference for use of captured British Bren guns when available. In addition to all of the practical difficulties encountered in the field that were engendered by over-complicated and sophisticated mechanisms, the gun was also very expensive to produce due to the same factors. Stated differently, the Breda Model 30 was in many ways the antithesis of other Italian small arms used during World War II: it had none of the simplicity, and robustness of the Carcano rifles, and it lacked the reliability of the sophisticated Beretta submachine guns. ■

FUCILE MITRAGLIATORE BREDA MODELLO 30

Designer: Unknown; as head of the Breda Technical Department, Sestilio Fiorini is likely to have been involved in its design
Manufacturer: Società Italiana Ernesto Breda
Caliber: 6.5mm or 7.35mm
Cartridge: 6.5x52mm Mannlicher-Carcano
Operating system: Blowback
Overall length: 1230mm (48.4")
Barrel length: 390mm (15.4")
Weight: 10.6 kg (23.3 lbs)
Front sight: Barleycorn
Rear sight: Leaf type
Rate of fire: 400-500 rpm cyclic; 120-150 rpm practical
Muzzle velocity: 630 m/sec (2067 fps)
Feed system: 20-round box magazine

MITRAGLIATRICE FIAT MODELLO 1914

« The water-cooled FIAT Mod. 1914 machine gun was the prevalent Italian machine gun during World War I. It served well during the war and proved to be very suitable for improvement, resulting in the Model 1935 that served in World War II. (*Fiat*)

The FIAT *modello 1914*, or FIAT 14 as it is also known, derives from the Revelli designed FIAT *modello 1910* machine gun. There is some contention as to whether or not the *modello 1910* was ever adopted by the Italian Army, but at any rate in 1914 a modified version of the *modello 1910*, with the official designation of *modello 1914*, was adopted. The Model 1914 was accepted largely because of the pressure of circumstances – the Italian Army actually had selected the Maxim machine gun for its forces, but due to the deteriorating political situation in Europe only a small number of Maxim guns had been delivered to Italy before shipments were stopped. As a result the FIAT 14 was prepared in haste and thrown into World War I as was, with no time available to remedy its inherent deficiencies. Notwithstanding these difficulties, the FIAT 14 was built under license by Metallurgica Bresciana giá Tempini in some 37-40,000 examples and performed well during the war. The FIAT 14 was later reworked into the 8mm FIAT *modello 1935* machine gun. Subsequent to World War I the FIAT 14 was employed by the Italians in Ethiopia in 1935, in Spain in 1937, and to some extent in Italian East Africa during World War II itself.

The weapon was a water-cooled, short recoil delayed blowback type chambered for the standard 6.5mm rifle cartridge. It was produced in a version with a corrugated jacket as well as the more common version with a smooth water jacket and it could be fitted with an optional flash hider. An air-cooled version was also produced for aircraft use. The barrel was of chrome nickel steel through which about 1,000 rounds could be fired before exhibiting any adverse effects; after about 6,000 rounds the barrel had to be

MITRAGLIATRICE FIAT MODELLO 1914

Designer: Bethel Abiel Revelli
Manufacturer: Metallurgica Bresciana giá Tempini, under license from FIAT
Caliber: 6.5mm
Cartridge: 6.5x52mm Mannlicher-Carcano
Operating system: Delayed blowback
Overall length:1410mm (55.5") with flash hider; 1250mm (49.2") without flash hider
Barrel length: 650mm (25.6")
Rifling: Constant twist, 162mm
Weight: Gun: 17 kg (37.4 lbs); 22 kg (48.4 lbs) with water for cooling; tripod: 21.5 kg (47.3 lbs)
Front sight: Barleycorn
Rear sight: Leaf, graduated from 200 to 2200 meters, in 100-meter increments
Rate of fire: 450-500 rpm
Muzzle velocity: 680 m/sec (2080 fps)
Feed system: 50-round compartmented magazine
Note: Water tank issued carried 11.5 liters (3 gallons) of water. The gun could be used with or without the tank

The FIAT Model 1914 was still widely issued prior to Italy's entry into World War II, as show in in the 1939 photograph of a Model 1914 issued to a Granatieri (Grenadier) unit. (*SME via Andrea and Antonio Tallillo*)

A FIAT Model 1914 in action in 1918; the ammunition tray has fed partly through the gun. There is no evidence of the water tank. (*SME via Andrea and Antonio Tallillo*)

Alternate view of the FIAT air-cooled version of the Mod. 1914 (*Fiat*)

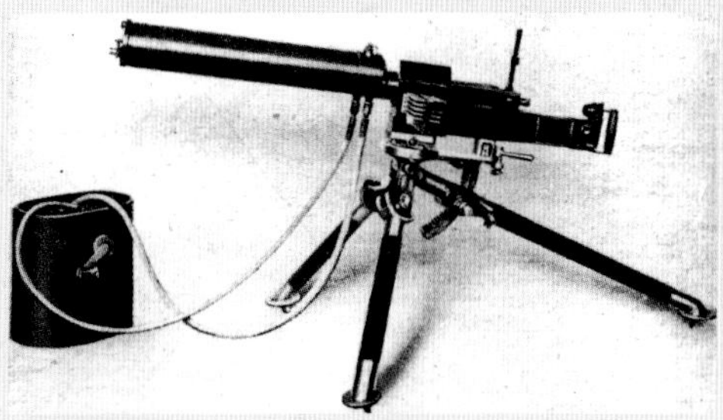

A factory photograph of a FIAT Mod. 1914 complete with its water tank and supply hoses. (*Fiat*)

The air-cooled version of the FIAT Mod. 1914. Shown here mounted on a tripod, its primary use was as aircraft armament. (*Fiat*)

A well dug-in FIAT Mod. 1914 with flash hider in 1916; the rear sight is not raised and the gun crew are wearing gas masks, both suggesting a training exercise. (*SME via Andrea and Antonio Tallillo*)

changed as accuracy decreased and too much gas escaped to allow proper functioning of the weapon. A selector lever above the thumb trigger allowed for slow or rapid fire to be chosen, as well as acting as a safety lever. Feeding was accomplished by a magazine divided into ten compartments, each holding five cartridges; as each row of five cartridges, feeding from bottom to top, was exhausted the entire magazine shifted from left to right to align another row of cartridges with the feed mechanism. This system was one of the chief drawbacks of the weapon, and it is estimated that about 50% of the malfunctions experienced by the FIAT 14 were attributable to the feed system. The tripod for the weapon had a bronze body, steel legs, and incorporated the elevating and traverse mechanism. Finally, a water tank was also issued with the gun, incorporating a manually operated pump for water circulation. ■

MITRAGLIATRICE FIAT MODELLO 1935, CALIBRO 8

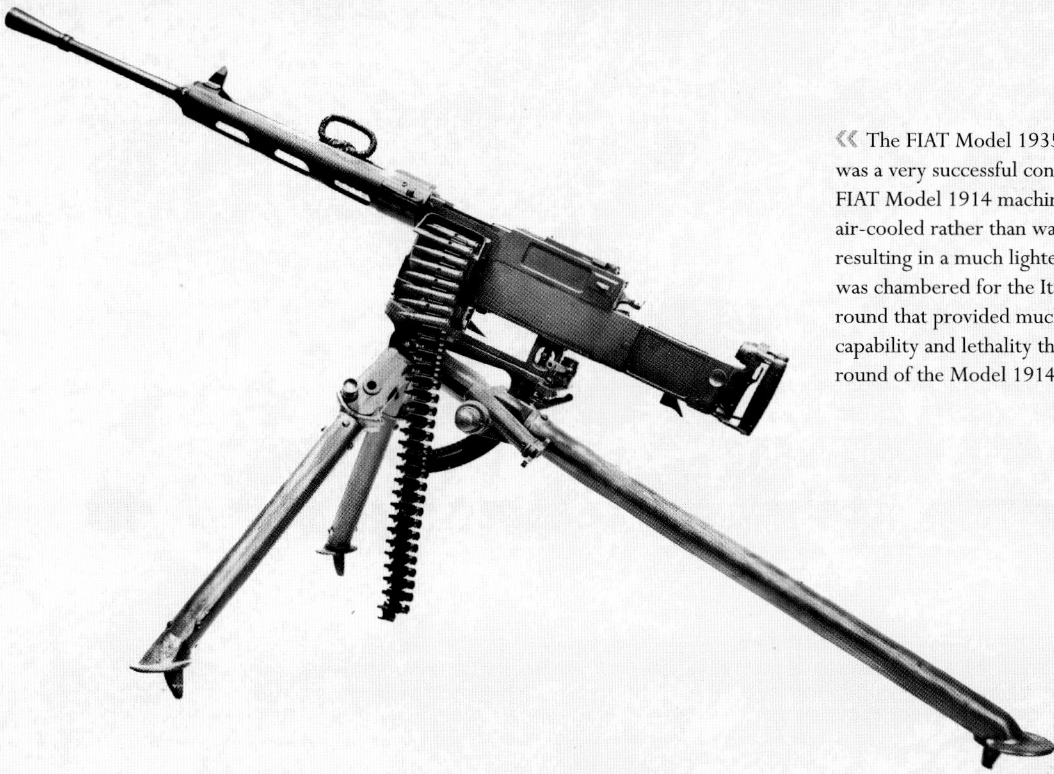

« The FIAT Model 1935 machine gun was a very successful conversion of the FIAT Model 1914 machine gun. It was air-cooled rather than water-cooled, resulting in a much lighter system, and was chambered for the Italian 8x59mm round that provided much more capability and lethality than the 6.5mm round of the Model 1914. *(Fiat)*

The FIAT *modello 35* was an improved version of the FIAT 14 machine gun in which the principal shortcomings of the Model 1914, namely its feed system and its cooling system, were rectified. Most FIAT 35s were actually reworked Model 1914s, although some were of new manufacture.

In the period between the two World Wars, the Italian Army undertook studies to determine the feasibility of adopting a new machine gun that incorporated the latest technological developments in the field or of modifying the Model 1914 so that it could be brought up to contemporary standards. Following research by Italian military authorities and by private firms the latter course was chosen and a number of changes were made, including increase of caliber from 6.5mm to 8mm, changing the cooling system from water cooled to air cooled, and changing the feed system from magazine to belt feed.

Caliber was increased in order to provide greater muzzle velocity, range, penetration, and to furnish better ballistic characteristics than those of the FIAT 14. The basic 1914 gun was sufficiently well built to accept the larger caliber with no fear of structural inadequacy manifesting itself. The 8x59mm cartridge that was developed was assessed to be at least as good ballistically as similar cartridges then being used by other armies. The increase in caliber naturally meant an attendant barrel change, which led to the decision to adopt an air-cooled system rather than retaining the water-cooled system. This resulted in the positive benefits that accrued from eliminating the bulk and weight of the water tank, as well as eliminating one of the major disadvantages of the FIAT 14 deriving from the need to provide water in hot climates and to guard against water freezing in the cooling jacket in cold climates. A tapered cooling jacket that also served as a barrel guide and support

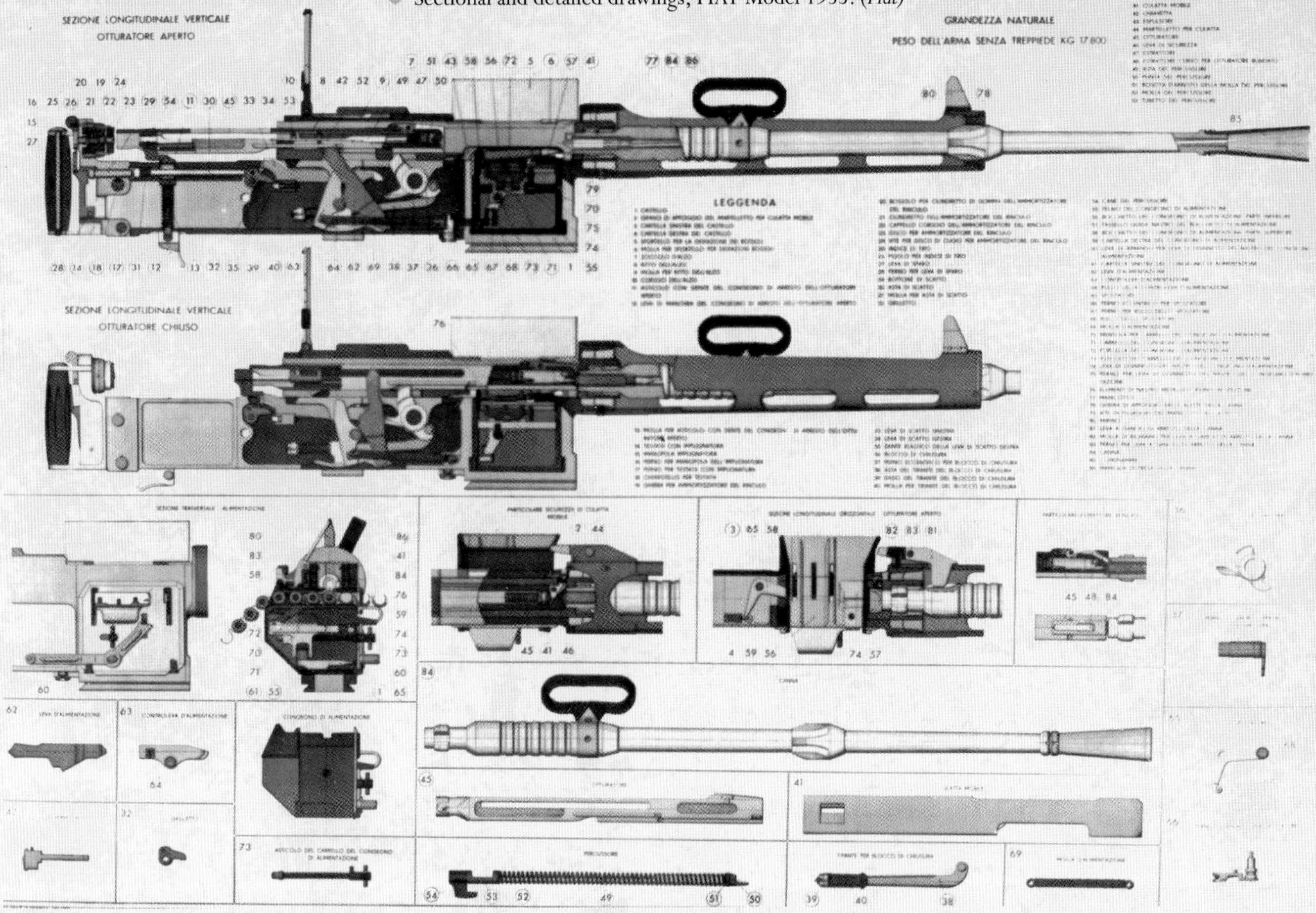

Sectional and detailed drawings, FIAT Model 1935. (*Fiat*)

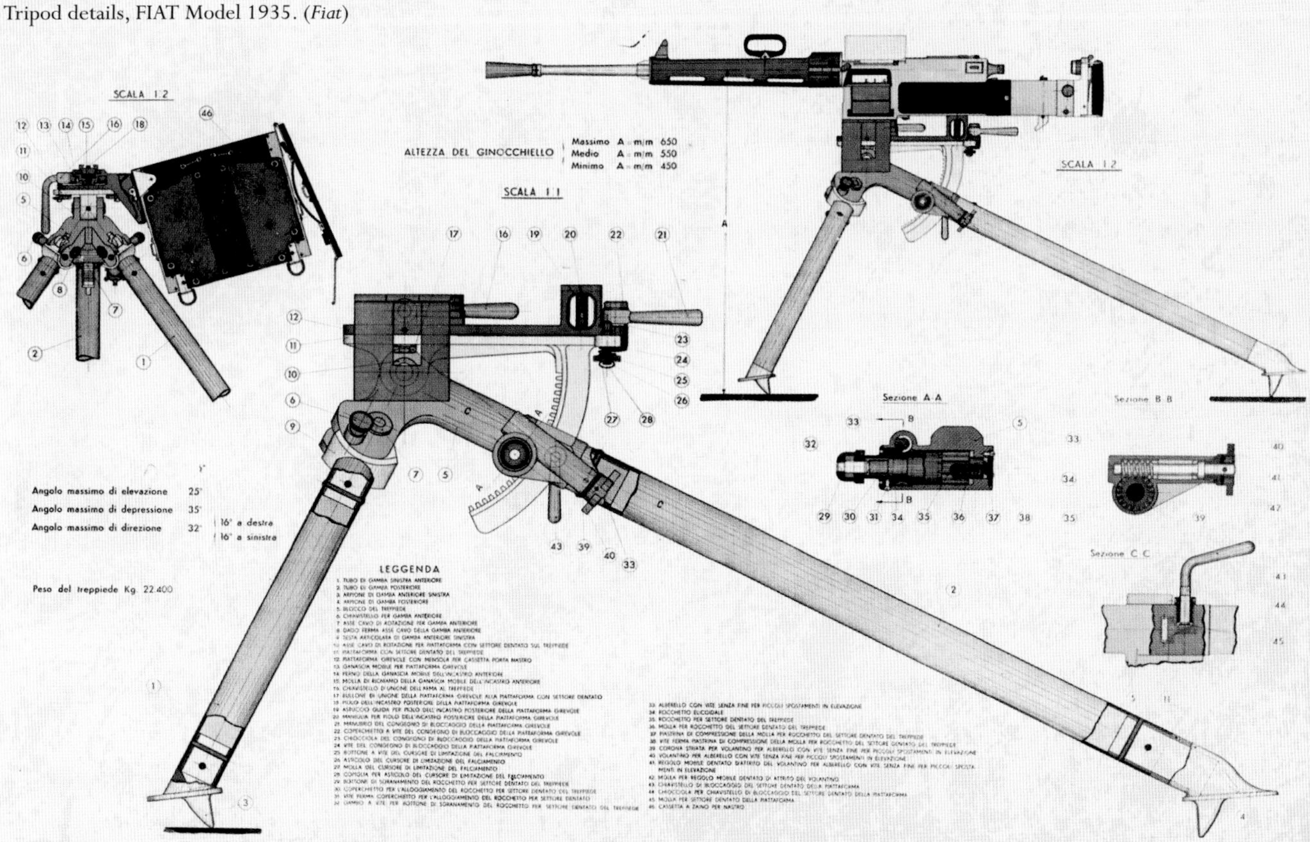

Tripod details, FIAT Model 1935. (*Fiat*)

ANTI-AIRCRAFT MOUNTS FOR MACHINE GUNS

The Italians developed anti-aircraft mounts for most or all of their light, medium and heavy machine guns. Possibly as many as fifty different types were produced or tested, among them models by Donnini, Soriani, Chiappi-Soriani and Valente. These mounts usually consisted of either a very simple single leg extension for use with automatic rifles, which could be adjustable for height, or of somewhat more substantial arrangements with some sort of tripod base and an extension; these latter types were used with heavier machine guns such as the FIAT 14, FIAT 35, Breda 37, Schwarzlose and Saint Etienne. The Chiappi-Soriani mount used with the Breda Model 30 light machine gun consisted of a bipod leg and a long extension staff to which the Model 30 was attached for anti-aircraft fire; this arrangement supported and raised the gun high enough so that the gunner, who assumed a kneeling position, could elevate the gun at high angles and traverse the weapon quickly. The mount for the heavier Breda Model 37 was issued in a wooden box that contained an anti-aircraft bipod, an extension mount, front and rear anti-aircraft sights, and a detachable shoulder stock. ■

A FIAT Model 1935, probably during an exercise in Italy; the officer seems to be inspecting the belted ammunition. (*Bruno Benvenuti*)

A FIAT Model 1935 and gunner somewhere in North Africa, date unknown. The fez worn by the gunner indicates that he is a bersagliere (light infantryman); despite largely inferior armament, the bersaglieri often distinguished themselves in the fighting in the North African theater. (*Bruno Benvenuti*)

A FIAT Model 1935 on an anti-aircraft tripod mount in North Africa. The truck in the background is a Lancia 3 Ro, extensively used as a troop transport and supply vehicle in the desert, as well as serving as a platform for a 90mm gun. (*Bruno Benvenuti*)

was affixed to the receiver, replacing the water cooling jacket of the Model 1914. The barrel itself had four wings at the breech end for mounting as well as a slot for the barrel locking lug. A series of cooling rings were located slightly forward of the locking slot. A handle wrapped in asbestos was also attached to the cooling ring bulge to facilitate barrel changing. The rest of the barrel proper was smooth, except for an expanded section with four wings slightly more than midway along the barrel that acted as the forward barrel support surface in the cooling jacket. A flared flash hider was affixed to the muzzle of the barrel. The chamber was fluted to assist cartridge extraction. Under normal operating conditions the barrel had to be changed every 250 rounds to allow for cooling, although for rapid barrel cooling it could also be removed, immersed in cold water, and replaced in the gun without causing any damage to the barrel. Average barrel life was from 13,000 to 15,000 rounds, which was a marked improvement over the 6,000 round life of the Model 1914 barrel.

The feed system underwent a substantial modification and was a significant improvement over that of the FIAT 14. A non-disintegrating linked belt was adopted, feeding from left to right. The adoption of belted ammunition considerably increased the reliability of the FIAT 35 as the inconveniences inherent in the compartmented magazines of the FIAT 14 were eliminated. A number of modifications to the rest of the gun also were made such as a provision for a bolt stop, replacing the Model 14 extractor with a stronger one, and changing the sight graduations on the rear leaf by eliminating all of the odd-numbered hectometer graduations. The tripod remained the same as that of the FIAT 14 except for the provision of a positive locking handle for the elevating mechanism and the addition of a support on the left-hand side for the ammunition box.

The Model 35 normally was issued at the battalion level, but could be attached to company level units. A limited number of Model 35s were mounted in pairs on light vehicles for use in the anti-aircraft role in North Africa. The Model 35 also was used as main armament on the L.3 tankette. It was gradually replaced in front line units by the more modern Breda Model 37. ■

MITRAGLIATRICE FIAT MODELLO 1935

Designer: Bethel Abiel Revelli
Manufacturer: FIAT (Fabbrica Italiana Automobili Torino), Torino; most were conversions of existing Model 1914 guns built by Società Metallurgica Bresciana (MBT)
Caliber: 8mm
Cartridge: 8x59mm Breda
Operating system: Delayed blowback
Overall length: 1350mm (53.2") with flash hider; 1250mm (49.2") without flash hider
Barrel length: 650mm (25.6")
Rifling: 4 groove RH constant twist, 245mm
Weight: Gun:17.2 kg (37.8 lbs); tripod: 23 kg (50.6 lbs)
Front sight: Barleycorn
Rear sight: Leaf, graduated from 200 to 2200 meters, in 200 meterincrements
Rate of fire: 600 rpm cyclic; 450 rpm practical
Muzzle velocity: 760 m/sec (2320 fps)
Feed system: 250-round non-disintegrating linked belt

MITRAGLIATRICE BREDA MODELLO 37

The Breda Model 37 (originally designated the Model 1936) undoubtedly was the best Italian machine gun used in World War II. Although developed as early as 1933, it was not adopted by the Italian Army until 1936 as a replacement for the FIAT Model 1935. The initial order of 2,000 Model 37s was delivered between 10 December 1936 and 11 September 1937. The onset of the war led to an increased production rate and by mid-1942 monthly production had risen to 1,000 weapons a month, further increasing to 4,000 for the first quarter of 1943. However, demand was so heavy that in 1943 some consideration was given to production of the Model 37 by Beretta as well, although this never came to fruition and Breda remained the sole producer. As was the case with many other weapons, the changeover to the Breda 37 had not been completed prior to the beginning of the war but the inconvenience was somewhat attenuated by the fact that both the FIAT 35 and the Breda 37 were chambered

MITRAGLIATRICE BREDA MODELLO 37

Designer: Unknown; as head of the Breda Technical Department, Sestilio Fiorini is likely to have been involved in its design
Manufacturer: Società Italiana Ernesto Breda
Caliber: 8mm
Cartridge: 8x59mm Breda
Operating system: Gas operated
Overall length: 1270mm (50")
Barrel length: 880mm (34.6") with flash hider; 780mm (30.7") without flash hider
Rifling: 4 groove RH twist, 240mm
Weight: Gun: 19.4 kg (42.7 lbs); tripod: 18.8 kg (41.4 lbs)
Front sight: Barleycorn, adjustable
Rear sight: Leaf, graduated from 300 to 3000 meters, in 100 meter increments
Safety: NA
Rate of fire: 450 rpm cyclic; 200 rpm practical
Muzzle velocity: 800 m/sec (2440 fps)
Feed system: 20-round tray

The Breda Model 37 was a robust, reliable general purpose machine gun chambered for the Breda 8x59mm round. It functioned well under varied climatic conditions, and captured examples were willingly pressed into service by the Allies. (*Editoriale Olimpia*)

Italian colonial troops manning a Breda Model 37 mounted on what appears to be the roof of a truck cab. (*Bruno Benvenuti*)

An R.S.I. officer, decorated with a German Iron Cross, addressing a detachment of troops somewhere in Northern Italy. This is likely a heavy weapons detachment, as five Breda Model 37 machine guns are visible. (*Bruno Benvenuti*)

for the same 8mm Breda cartridge, thus obviating ammunition compatibility problems. The Breda 37 was quite heavy for its caliber, but was very reliable and accurate as a result.

The weapon, which was rather massive in appearance, normally was mounted on a tripod and used in a ground role although a special mount and sights were available for use in an anti-aircraft role. The tripod was patterned after that of the Austrian Schwarzlose machine gun, with telescoping legs; the front legs could be folded back. It was also mounted on reconnaissance vehicles, using a gooseneck mount, during the latter part of the war. The barrel was smooth and not tapered and had a ferrule about two-thirds forward on which the front sight was mounted. A cylindrical flash hider was affixed to the barrel. The barrel itself was changed every 400-500 rounds for cooling, and had a life of some 20,000 rounds. Rate of fire could be adjusted by means of a gas cylinder adjustment and a selector permitted semi-automatic or full automatic fire. Feeding was by a 20-round tray that also retained the empty cartridge cases. Overall, this weapon was much simpler and more rugged than the FIAT 35 and as a consequence was much more reliable. Tactically it was organic to corps and division level machine gun detachments, and was also

A bersaglieri machine gun team dug in with their Breda Model 37. An ammunition chest is to the side of the gun, and a pair of SRCM hand grenades can be seen next to the ammunition. (*Bruno Benvenuti*)

A Breda Model 37 in action on the Russian front. The assistant gunner has a tray of ammunition ready to feed into the gun. (*Bruno Benvenuti*)

Italian alpine trooper standing guard by a Breda Model 37 fitted with anti-aircraft sights and shoulder brace, mounted on an extended anti-aircraft mount. (*Bruno Benvenuti*)

issued down to company and battalion level; a battalion machine gun squad was issued with two of these weapons. The three-man gun team consisted of the gunner, who carried the gun itself, a tripod bearer, and a soldier who carried the 9 kg (19.8 lb) backpack chest that held spares and accessories. The machine gun team was supported by an ammunition team consisting of a team chief and six ammunition bearers who carried a total of 2,100 rounds of ammunition; each box of fifteen 20-round ammunition trays weighed 16.1 kg (35.5 lbs). There was also a smaller chest with carrying handles that held twelve 20-round ammunition trays.

Following the Italian armistice of September 1943, the Breda Model 37 continued to be manufactured for German forces, to whom some 1,300 were supplied; in German service it was designated the *8mm sMG 259(i)*. During the war the Model 37 was very popular with Italian troops but was also well respected by Allied troops who happily pressed them into service when captured. The Model 37 was issued to the post-war Italian Army and served until at least the 1950s. The Model 37 was also adopted by the Portuguese Army as the *Metralhadora Pesada 7.92mm m/938*. ■

MITRAGLIATRICE BREDA MODELLO 38 PER CARRO ARMATO

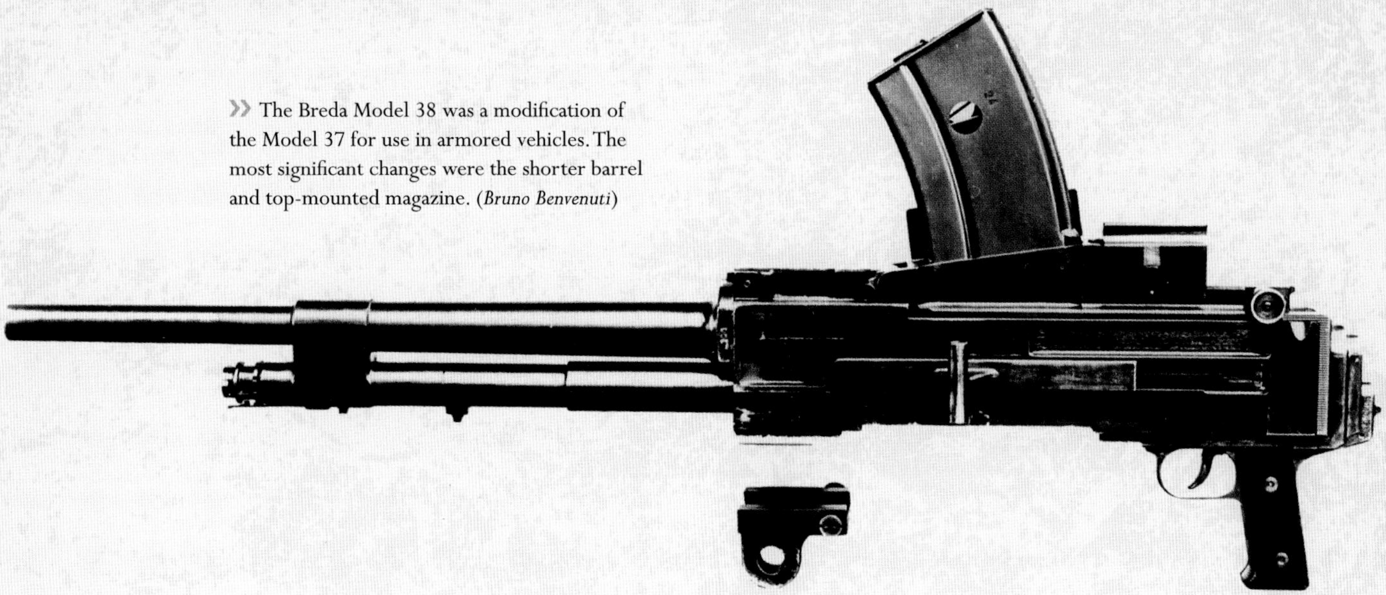

The Breda Model 38 was a modification of the Model 37 for use in armored vehicles. The most significant changes were the shorter barrel and top-mounted magazine. (*Bruno Benvenuti*)

The Breda Model 38 tank machine gun was derived from the Breda Model 37; it was specially designed to mount in tandem in tanks and other armored vehicles. Although basically the same weapon as the Model 37, the Model 38 did have a number of features that differed both externally and internally. Overall length and barrel length were reduced; the spade grips were replaced by a pistol grip and finger operated trigger, and the sights were discarded. The feed system was changed considerably, consisting of a top-mounted 24-round curved box magazine, and the expended cartridge cases were ejected from the bottom of the gun where they were caught by a canvas bag. When the last cartridge was fired the magazine was automatically ejected and the bolt remained open. Internally, the bolt differed and the firing pin was of the fixed type. The Model 38 was designed so that when mounted in tandem the cocking handle could be mounted on either side of the gun. Although normally mounted in vehicles, the Model 38 could also be mounted on the FIAT 35's tripod for ground use in emergencies.

Except as noted below, specifications for the Breda Model 38 are the same as for the Model 37.

MITRAGLIATRICE BREDA MODELLO 38 PER CARRO ARMATO

Overall length: 897.5mm (35.3")
Barrel length: 600mm (23.6")
Weight: 16.3 kg (35.9 lbs)
Rate of fire: 600 rpm cyclic; 350 rpm practical
Muzzle velocity: 770 m/sec (2350 fps)
Feed system: 24-round curved box magazine

APPENDICES

APPENDIX 1: FOREIGN WEAPONS USED BY THE ITALIAN ARMY IN WORLD WAR I AND WORLD WAR II

During the campaign in Russia the Italians made use of captured Soviet weapons such as the PPsh-41 submachine gun and, as shown here, the Degtyarev DP 28 light machine gun. The Degtyarev was much more reliable than the Breda Model 30. (*SME via Andrea and Antonio Tallillo*)

During World War I, except for a few types of handguns produced in Spain and a large infusion of arms provided by France to replace losses suffered by the Italian Army during the disastrous battle of Caporetto in October-November 1917, virtually all of the small arms used by Italian forces were of Italian design and manufacture. After World War I, the French weapons were maintained in depots and were used to a limited extent by territorial and second line units; the end of World War I also brought huge stocks of small arms from the former Austro-Hungarian Empire as war booty. Axis victories early in World War II led to another influx of foreign weapons captured by the Italians in France, Greece and Yugoslavia; a limited number of weapons were also supplied by the Germans from stocks they captured elsewhere in Europe. In August 1942, Italy had appropriated 6,668 machine guns, 12,000 light machine guns, and 224,338 rifles from France. Finally, after the 8 September 1943 armistice between Italy and the Allies, with Italy divided between the German controlled north and the Allied controlled south, remaining and newly constituted Italian forces fought alongside both the Germans and the Allies. Italian units of the R.S.I. allied with the Germans were armed with a mix of Italian and German weapons, while the Italian Co-Belligerent Forces fighting alongside the Allies were instead armed with a mix of Italian, British and U.S. small arms.

Italian alpine troops manning a captured Austro-Hungarian Schwarzlose machine gun at Passo Lares in the Alps in 1916. The Schwarzlose was pressed into Italian service whenever available. (*SME via Andrea and Antonio Tallillo*)

Following is a brief summary, by nation, of foreign weapons used by Italy during both World Wars. The list is not all-inclusive, as World War II statistical reports indicate the presence of very small numbers of various other types of weapons that had been captured in Yugoslavia, Greece, and possibly Ethiopia. ■

AUSTRIA-HUNGARY

RAST-GASSER M1898: The Rast & Gasser Model 1898 was a double-action revolver used by Austria-Hungary during World War I. Chambered for the 8x27R Gasser round, it had an 8-round cylinder. About 200,000 were built, numbers of which were obtained by Italy following World War I as reparations, and may have seen limited Italian use during World War II.

ROTH-STEYR M1907: The Roth-Steyr, also known as the Roth-Krnka M.7, was designed by Karel Krnka, a Czech working for the George Roth ammunition company, and was produced by Steyr in Austria and Fegyver és Gépgyár (FEG) in Budapest. It has the distinction of being the first semi-automatic pistol to be adopted by a major army, being issued to the Austro-Hungarian cavalry during World War I. It is a locked breech pistol chambered for the 8x18.5mm Roth-Steyr cartridge and is loaded from the top with stripper clips. About 90,000 were made, and a sizeable number were acquired by Italy from Austria-Hungary as war reparations after World War I and used up to and through World War II.

STEYR M1912: Commonly known as the Steyr-Hahn, this pistol, chambered for the 9x23mm Steyr cartridge, was based on the Roth-Steyr M1907 and was developed for the Austro-Hungarian Army which adopted it in 1912. As many as 300,000 were built, many of which found their way into the Italian Army inventory following World War I; they saw limited use in Italian Army and R.S.I. service during World War II.

REPETIERGEWEHR M1895: The Steyr-Mannlicher Repetiergewehr M1895 was a straight-pull bolt action rifle designed by Ferdinand Ritter von Mannlicher produced in huge numbers by the Österrechische Waffenfabrik-Gesellschaft Steyr, Austria, and was the standard Austro-Hungarian infantry weapon in World War I. Following the war, large numbers of the rifle, and its carbine variant, the Repetierkarabiner 1895, were obtained by Italy as war booty. During World War II many of these rifles were issued to colonial units and to second line units in Italy; in 1937 225,000 Mannlichers were on hand in Italian East Africa.

MASCHINENGEWEHR PATENT SCHWARZLOSE M.07/12: Commonly referred to simply as the Schwarzlose, the Model 07/12 was the standard medium machine gun of the Austro-Hungarian Army during World War I. Ultimately the Schwarzlose – some rechambered for other calibers – was used by over a dozen nations; a significant number (at least 900) were acquired by Italy after World War I as war booty and during World War II, along with the Repetiergewehr M1895 rifle, were issued to colonial troops. At least some of the captured Schwarzlose machine guns were converted from the original 8x50R caliber to the smaller Italian 6.5x52mm caliber. There is some indication that an unspecified number of the Schwarzlose were issued to Italian 1st and 4th Army and to D.I.C.A.T. (*Difesa Contro Aerea Territoriale* – Territorial Anti-aircraft Defense) units. ■

CZECHOSLOVAKIA

KULOMET ZB VZ/30: The ZB vz/30 (ZB are the initials of the Zbrojovka Brno arms factory, and vz is the Czech abbreviation for Model) was very similar to the iconic British Bren gun, itself basically a license-built copy in .303 caliber of the Czech ZB v/26, the precursor of the vz/30. The ZB vz/30, chambered for the 7.92mm Mauser cartridge, was adopted by Yugoslavia as the Puska-Mitralez 7.9mm M37, and by Ethiopia as the ZB 30. An unspecified number were captured in Ethiopia between 1935 and 1938 and in Yugoslavia in 1941 and were issued to second-line Italian territorial units; a July 1942 report reflected 936 of the Yugoslav M37 in the Italian Army inventory. In February 1943 experiments were conducted at the Fabbrica d'Armi di Terni to study the feasibility of converting the ZB 30/M37 to the 8x59mm Breda cartridge, but this initiative is not known to have been pursued. In March 1943 the ZB 30/M37 was issued to territorial defense units in Lazio, Toscana and Liguria. ■

FRANCE

FUSIL MLE 1886 M93: More commonly known as the Lebel 1886/93, at the time of its introduction it was a revolutionary weapon as it was the world's first successful small bore smokeless powder rifle. The rifle was a bolt action and was fed by an eight-round tubular magazine. It was supplied to several French allies during World War I, and after the battle of Caporetto in late 1917 was supplied in large numbers to Italy which was in desperate need of weapons to make good losses sustained during the defeat. Although the Italian Army had almost 9,000 Lebels on hand in 1942 and apparently issued them to second line units, there are no indications as to what specific units may have been issued with the rifle; Lebels were issued by the Italians to anti-Communist volunteer militia units in Yugoslavia in 1943. Two Italian firms produced ammunition for the Lebel in the 1930s and early-1940s ensuring a ready supply as needed.

FUSIL MLE 1907/15: Better known as the Berthier 1907/15, this rifle was developed from the Berthier Mousqueton (carbine) Mle 1890 and Mle 1892, and was chambered for the 8mm Lebel cartridge and fed by a 3-round clip. During World War I, 435,000 Mle 1907/15s were manufactured by French state arsenals and private contractors. After Caporetto, along with the Lebel 1886/93, France supplied large quantities of the Berthier to Italy. None of the Berthiers appear to have been issued to any type of Italian or Italian colonial units during World War II.

FUSIL MITRAILLEUR MLE 1915 CSRG: Development of the Fusil Mitrailleur Mle 1915 CSRG – commonly referred to as the Chauchat – began in 1903; the resulting weapon, which functioned on the long recoil principle with gas assist, was simple, inexpensive and easy to manufacture and became the standard French light machine gun during World War I. The CSRG had a straight-line stock, a pistol grip, a curved box magazine, and a bipod. France supplied the Chauchat to a number of other nations, including Italy. In July 1942 the Italian Army had 2,540 CSRG on hand chambered for the 8x50Rmm Lebel cartridge and another 456 chambered for the 7.92x57mm German service cartridge; the latter weapons may have been captured Polish weapons furnished by the Germans. During World War II the Chauchats were distributed to second line and territorial defense units in lieu of the Breda Model 30 light machine gun; some were also used by the *Regia Aeronautica* for airport defense.

MITRAILLEUSE MLE 1907: Commonly known as the St. Etienne, the Mitrailleuse Mle 1907 was the prevalent French machine gun during the early part of World War I, but was replaced by the Hotchkiss Mle 1914 beginning in 1917. The Model 1907 was a gas-operated weapon chambered for the 8x50mmR Lebel cartridge. As the Mle 1907 was withdrawn from French service a number were ceded to Italy; a report dated 1 July 1942 reflects 319 St. Etienne guns in the Italian Army inventory, and also notes an additional 4,286 assigned to the M.A.C.A. *(Milizia Artiglieria Contro Aerei* – Anti-Aircraft Artillery Militia). Unspecified numbers of the St. Etienne were issued to *Guardia alla Frontiera* and *Milizia per la difesa antiaerea territoriale* (Territorial Anti-aircraft Defense Militia) units.

MITRAILLEUSE MLE 1914 HOTCHKISS: The Hotchkiss Model 1914 was the standard French Army machine gun during World War I, chambered for the 8mm Lebel service round. It was a simple, sturdy and reliable weapon consisting of only thirty-two parts, with no screws or pins. It was easy to maintain and was capable of long periods of sustained fire; when overheated, its air-cooled barrel could be changed fairly quickly. It was exported widely and was copied by Japan as the Type 3 heavy machine gun. Italy received an unspecified number of Model 1914 machine guns during World War I, and additional numbers likely were captured from France and possibly Greece in 1940-1941; a 1 July 1942 report listed 1,098 in the army inventory, and in March 1943 an undetermined number of the Model 1914 were assigned to Italian units on the islands of Pantelleria and Lampedusa. At least one Italian source also refers to an unspecified "heavy" Hotchkiss machine gun in 7.92mm, but offers no details as to their origin or use.

FUSIL MITRAILLEUR MLE 1922: The Hotchkiss M1922 light machine gun was a commercial venture and was offered in a variety of calibers; it was adopted by Greece as the M1926, chambered for the Greek 6.5x54mm Mannlicher-Schönauer round. It was a gas-operated, air-cooled fully automatic weapon that fired from an open bolt; there were two feed versions, either from a top-mounted magazine or from a strip. In 1941 the Italians captured about 2,500 of these weapons from the Greeks; a July 1942 report indicates that there were 1,929 6.5mm Hotchkiss light machine guns on hand. In March 1943 an unspecified number were issued to *Guardia alla Frontiera* and *Milizia Confinaria* (Border Militia) units in Italy.

FUSIL MITRAILLEUR MLE 1924 M29: The Chatellerault Model 1924/29 light machine gun was developed in 1924, based on the Browning Automatic Rifle. It was chambered for the French 7.5x54mm cartridge developed specifically for the M29, and was fed by a 25-round box magazine. Following the Italian attack on France in June 1940, which met with only limited territorial gains, at least 1,000 Model 1924/29 were seized by the C.I.A.F. (*Commissione Italiana d'Armistizio con la Francia* – Italian Armistice Commission with France) and later were assigned to the Italian V and IX Corps and coast defense units. A report dated 24 December 1941 reflected 2,259 Model 24/29 light machine guns operationally available for Italian coastal defense battalions. Because of the numbers available and popularity of this weapon the Italians themselves manufactured magazines and spare parts for it.

PISTOLET MITRAILLEUR MAS MODÈLE 1938: The MAS Model 38 submachine gun stemmed from the earlier MAS-35 design, was chambered for the French 7.65mm Longue cartridge and was first produced in 1938. Less than 2,000 were produced before France fell to German forces in 1940 and the Saint-Ètienne arms plant was captured by the Germans; an unknown number of the MAS Model 38 were produced under German supervision. The gun was issued to some German forces and French police units. An unknown number were taken as war booty by the Italians, but to what extent they may have been issued to Italian forces is not known. A MAS 38 may have been the weapon used by partisans to kill Benito Mussolini on 28 April 1945. ■

GERMANY

PISTOLE PARABELLUM 1908: The P.08, universally referred to as the Luger, is one of the world's classic firearms. The Luger was the standard German service pistol during World War I and the early part of World War II. It was a 9mm Parabellum pistol with an 8-round capacity. Unspecified numbers of the P.08 were supplied to Italian R.S.I. forces that fought alongside the Germans in northern Italy after September 1943.

WALTHER P.38: The Walther P.38 9mm Parabellum pistol replaced the P.08 Luger in German service beginning in 1941. Like the P.08, it had an 8-round magazine, but was simpler to manufacture and was somewhat more reliable. One source indicates that the P.38 was acquired by the *Regia Marina* for use by the San Marco Naval Infantry battalion. Unspecified numbers of the P.38 were supplied to Italian R.S.I. forces that fought alongside the Germans in northern Italy after September 1943.

MAUSER KAR 98K: The Mauser Kar 98k, a modified version of the World War I Mauser Gewehr 98, was the standard German service rifle during World War II. It was a bolt-action rifle chambered for the 7.92x57mm cartridge; magazine capacity was five rounds. The Kar 98k is generally considered to be the finest military bolt action rifle ever to have been produced; over 14 million were produced between 1934 and 1945. Following the September 1943 armistice between Italy and the Allies some reconstituted Italian units (of the R.S.I.) were issued with the Kar 98k.

MASCHINENGEWEHR 08 (MG 08): The MG 08 was a close copy of the British Maxim machine gun and is often referred to as the Spandau. It was a water-cooled, tripod mounted gun chambered for the 7.92x57mm Mauser cartridge and was the German Army's standard machine gun in World War I. It is not entirely clear how many MG 08 – and the lighter MG 08/15 – were in the Italian inventory, or when and how they were acquired; there is some suggestion that some were acquired following World War I and that others may have been captured from the Yugoslavs. The MG 08, generically referred to in some Italian publications as the "Maxim," was used in Italian coastal defense installations during World War II.

MASCHINENGEWEHR MODELL 34 (MG 34): The MG 34 was Germany's most widely used general purpose machine gun during World War II. Chambered for the 7.92x57mm German service cartridge, it was produced from 1936 to 1945. It was an extremely well built weapon and was popular with the troops. The MG 34 was issued to some R.S.I. units after September 1943.

MASCHINENGEWEHR MODELL 42 (MG42): The MG42 was one of the Wehrmacht's two standard general purpose machine guns during World War II; over 750,000 were produced. It was chambered for the standard 7.92mm German service cartridge, was belt fed, and had a high rate of fire (1200 rounds per minute). It made extensive use of stamped parts, and as a testament to its design, was adopted by the post-war German army as the MG1 or MG 42/59, chambered for the 7.62mm NATO round. Photographic evidence indicates that the MG42 was issued to R.S.I. units, but the scale of issue or units to which issued have not been determined. ■

GREAT BRITAIN

PISTOL, REVOLVER, NO. 2 (ENFIELD): Commonly known simply as the Enfield, this top-break double-action revolver was chambered for the .380 British Service cartridge; it was adopted in 1931 and was widely issued to Commonwealth forces. After September 1943, it was issued to Italian co-belligerent forces that were equipped by the British.

SHORT MAGAZINE LEE-ENFIELD NO. 1 MK. III: Commonly referred to as the S.M.L.E. No. 1 Mk III, or simply as the Enfield, this rifle was the standard British and Commonwealth service rifle during World War I and most of World War II. It was a bolt action rifle chambered for the British .303 cartridge and had a ten-round removable box magazine. Some Italian units of the *Corpo Italiano di Liberazione* (C.I.L.) formed after the 8 September 1943 armistice between Italy and the Allies were equipped with the Enfield. The Enfield served with the Italian Army into the immediate post-war period but was soon replaced with weapons of U.S. origin, although it was retained in service somewhat longer by the Italian Navy.

CARBINE, MACHINE, 9MM STEN: The Sten gun was the iconic British submachine gun during World War II; it was a very simple, basic design conceived so that it could be assembled from components supplied by a number of subcontractors. Between 1941 and 1945 some four million Stens of various versions, chambered for the 9mm Parabellum cartridge, were produced. Small numbers of captured Stens are known to have been used by Italian forces during the war, and after the September 1943 armistice, Italian units in southern Italy that fought alongside the Allies were equipped with the Sten. There is also some evidence that the Germans furnished R.S.I. units with Stens but whether these were captured Stens or Sten clones manufactured by the Germans themselves is not known.

GUN, MACHINE, BREN: The British Bren gun was a modified version of the Czech ZB v/26 light machine gun, the principal differences consisting of being chambered for the British .303 round and being fed by a top-mounted magazine. The Bren, adopted by Britain in 1938, was a hugely successful light machine gun. In North Africa captured Bren guns were often pressed into service by the Italians; along with the Enfiled rifle and the Sten submachine gun, the Bren was furnished to Italian co-belligerent units after September 1943.

GUN, MACHINE, VICKERS, .303IN MARK 1: The Vickers machine gun was adopted by Britain in 1912 and remained the standard support fire machine gun throughout World War I and World War II. It was a large, somewhat heavy water-cooled weapon with a relatively low rate of fire – about 450 rounds per minute – but was reliable and well liked. The Vickers was supplied to Italian co-belligerent forces after September 1943. ■

GREECE

MANNLICHER-SCHÖNAUER MODEL 1903 AND MODEL 1903/14: In 1903 Greece contracted with Steyr of Austria for about 130,000 bolt action, rotary feed rifles chambered for the 6.5x54mm Mannlicher-Schönauer round. The 1903/14 was a slightly modified version; in 1927 Greece, unable to obtain additional rifles from Austria which was prohibited from producing weapons after World War I, obtained about 150,000 of the Model 1903/14 rifle and carbine from Breda in Italy, although whether Breda manufactured the rifles on Steyr machinery or merely assembled them from parts furnished by Steyr is open to question. After 1930 another small batch of the rifles was supplied by Steyr. At least one source indicates about 10,000 of the 1903/14 rifles and carbines on hand in the Italian Army inventory in June 1942 – presumably captured from the Greeks in 1940-1941 – although it is unclear if any were actually issued to Italian second line or territorial units. The Greek 6.5mm cartridge was not interchangeable with the Italian 6.5mm Carcano cartridge. ■

HUNGARY

GEWEHR 98/40: The Gewehr 98/40 was a modification of the Hungarian 35M rifle; it was produced in Hungary under German supervision and was modified to accept the 7.92x57mm Mauser service cartridge, as well as adopting the Mauser 5-round charger system. Information on use of this weapon by Italian forces is scant; only one source indicates possible use, probably by R.S.I. forces. ■

POLAND

KARABIN PRZECIWPANCERNY WZÓR 35: The wz 35 Maroszek was a bolt action anti-tank rifle developed in Poland in 1935. It was based on the Mauser bolt action, and was chambered for the Maroszek 8x107mm cartridge developed specifically for the wz 35. The wz 35 was a reasonably effective anti-tank rifle in its day; with the fall of Poland to the Germans in 1939, most of the wz 35 rifles were captured by the Germans and German sources indicate that by June 1943 588 had been furnished to Italy. The wz 35 was issued to Italian infantry and parachute units, but although a 1942 army circular specified that some rifle squads should be issued with one of the anti-tank rifles precise scale of issue is unclear. ■

SPAIN

REVOLVER TETTONI MOD. 1916: With World War I in full swing, Italy sought other sources of weapons to supplement its own capabilities. In 1916 an individual, company or agency identified only as F. Tettoni of Brescia contracted with the firm of Orbea Hermanos of Eibar for an undetermined number of their Model 1914 revolvers which appear to have been inspired by, if not outright copies of, the Smith & Wesson Model 1889 top-break revolver. The revolvers ordered by Tettoni were chambered for the 10.35mm Italian Ordnance round and were designated Revolver Mod. 1916 cal. 10-35. These revolvers are commonly referred to in Italy as the Tettoni because they bore that name rather than the manufacturer's name on the gun. The top strap is marked REVOLVER MOD1916 CAL 10-35, and the left-hand side of the frame is marked F TETTONI – BRESCIA. The grips and left-hand side of the frame bear a highly ornate Orbea Hermanos logo, which is the only concession to the manufacturer's identity. Curiously, it appears that the revolvers were not serially numbered. The revolver was never officially adopted by the Italian Army but was fairly widely distributed to officers during World War I, and is not known to have been used during World War II.

PISTOLA AUTOMATICA RUBY: The designation Ruby is a generic term for a large variety of essentially similar semi-auto pistols manufactured in Spain during World War I. The first Ruby was developed by Gabilondo y Urresti of Eibar, based on the Browning M1903 pistol, chambered for the 7.65x17mm (.32 ACP) round. Gabilondo offered the Ruby to France, which was in dire need of foreign sourced weapons to supplement its own production capabilities; ultimately, French demand was so high that about 50 Spanish firms, most based in the traditional gun-making city of Eibar, manufactured and furnished Ruby-type pistols to France. Although these pistols were essentially similar, depending on the manufacturer there were differences in overall length and barrel length; some 750,000 Rubys were supplied to the French. Italy suffered similarly from a lack of sidearms, and followed France's lead with respect to the Ruby, and it is estimated that about 230,000 Spanish Rubys were supplied to Italy during World War I. ■

UNITED STATES

U.S. SUBMACHINEGUN, CALIBER .45 M1: The classic "Tommygun," the Thompson M1 was a simplified version of the original Thompson M1928A1 and was the U.S. Army's standard submachine gun during World War II. It was a somewhat heavy but well made weapon chambered for the Colt .45 ACP round, fed by 20- or 30-round detachable box magazines. Small numbers of the Thompson, most likely from British stocks, were supplied to Italian co-belligerent forces after September 1943. ■

YUGOSLAVIA

MODEL 1924 MAUSER: Also known as the Serbian Model 1924 Mauser; in 1925 Yugoslavia initially purchased a lot of 100,000 of the Model 1924 Mauser rifle from FN in Belgium, but shortly thereafter a duplicate set of machinery to produce the rifle was transferred to Kragujevac. Production began in Yugoslavia in 1927 and continued until World War II, by which time nearly a million had been produced. The Model 1924 was chambered for the 7.92x57mm Mauser cartridge and was quite similar to the German Mauser Kar 98k. The Italians captured a significant number of these rifles from the Yugoslavs; about 42,000 are reflected in as being available in a 1942 Italian Army report, although there is no indication as to whether or not they were issued to any type of Italian territorial or other units. An unspecified number were ceded by the Italians to the Croatian government.

MODEL 1924 VARIANTS: Precise data are unavailable, but it is believed that small numbers of Mauser Model 1924 variants were captured by the Italians in Yugoslavia. One source that lists weapons on hand in the Italian inventory in July 1942 reflects "Turkish rifles cal. 6.5, various types," "Mauser short rifles cal. 7.92 Czechoslovak," and "Mauser Mod. 24 carbines," all in relatively small numbers; these types of weapons were all in the Yugoslav inventory during the 1920s and 1930s, so it is likely that these, and possibly other Mauser variants such as the Model 1888, as well as some Austrian Mannlicher M1895 rifles and carbines, were part of the Yugoslav war booty. ■

APPENDIX 2: CARCANO BARREL, BOLT, RECEIVER & SMALL PARTS MARKINGS

BARREL

Rather than applying the serial number to the receiver, as is the practice on most other military long arms, the Italians identified the Carcano (and the earlier Vetterli rifles) by placing the serial number, as well as other identifying data, on the barrel; the barrel chamber on Carcano rifles contains a wealth of information about the weapon. Early Carcano rifles and carbines (until about 1935) had a chamber with five facets visble: the topmost facet bore the name of the producer; the upper left facet carried the serial number; the upper right facet was stamped with the year of manufacture using Arabic numerals, and after 1929 also bore the corresponding Fascist era year in Roman numerals; the bottom left facet bears the inspectors mark or initials in a small oval, and the Savoy crest; the bottom right facet bore one or two upper case letters that indicated the supplier of the facility suppying the steel for the barrel. Any one of the facets could be stamped with a five-pointed star signifying that the barrel had been repaired or gone through an arsenal rebuild, and about ten percent rifles also had a marking consisting of crossed rifles surmounted by two concentric circles and a dot representing a target. Navy rifles bore a shield with a cross inside, the shield being surrounded by a circle. Model 38 short rifles furnished to Finland are marked with the letters SA in a rectangle with rounded corners on the chamber (or exceptionally on the receiver ring). Weapons produced by Gardone in 1943, and possibly later as well, did not indicate either the maker's name or year of manufacture, and are identifiable as Gardone guns by their serial number range. Beginning in 1935 or 1936 the faceted chamber began to be replaced on newly manufactured carbines by a conical profile chamber, but the chamber markings continued to be applied in more or less the same relative positions; by 1938 all new production weapons had the conical chamber exterior. The bottom of the chamber, hidden by the stock, had a number of marks, either alpha or numeric, that were applied during various phases of assembly; there seems to be no general rule as to the number, type or placement of these marks, as some rifles have only a few marks while others bear an abundance of marks. ■

This Model 1891 rifle bears a serial number identifying it as having been produced by the Arsenale di Roma in 1918, despite the 1897 Terni barrel markings. The rifle went through an arsenal rebuild at Terni in 1931 when a serviceable Terni barrel replaced the original Roma barrel whose serial number was used on the replacement barrel. (*Author's collection*)

A nicely struck Savoy crest on the barrel facet of a Terni 1929 Model 91/28 carbine. Also visible is the PL inspector's mark. (*Author's collection*)

Detail of the rebuild mark on a 91/24 carbine. Originally a Model 1891 rifle produced by Terni in 1917, the markings in the circle indicate conversion by Terni (FARE TERNI) in 1925. (*Author's collection*)

The year on this Gardone Model 38 short rifle is indicated by the last three digits, rather than the full four digits. (*Author's collection*)

Model 41 rifles produced by Armaguerra were particularly rich in markings. Visible on the side of the barrel chamber are part of the maker's name, the location of the manufacturing plant in Cremona, an RE surmounted by a crown, the letter R on its side which may be an acceptance mark, the 4 UT stamp in a circle in which the 4 is essentially illegible, and the serial number. (*Author's collection*)

The markings on this Model 38 short rifle indicate that the barrel used was a serviceable Model 1891 rifle barrel, made in 1897, shortened and rebored to 7.35mm. Many early Model 38 rifles had such barrels; the serial number and other markings on this rifle reflect a Model 38 produced by Terni in 1939. (*Author's collection*)

To the left of the maker's name and location on this Model 41 rifle are the initials FAG and the digits 46, indicating a rebuild at Gardone in 1946. The rifle was marked for export, and MADE ITALY is struck over the original date and part of the FAG rebuild date as well. (*Author's collection*)

Markings on the barrel chamber of a Model 38 short rifle produced by F.N.A. Brescia include the last two digits of the Christian year date, the Fascist date in Roman numerals, and the serial number. This rifle was imported into the United States as indicated by the MADE IN ITALY marking and the caliber marking on the receiver ring. (*Author's collection*)

Model 91 cavalry carbines produced by Gardone sometimes bore only the serial number and were bereft of the normal date and manufacturer's markings on the chamber. (*Author's collection*)

An F.N.A Brescia 91/38 TS carbine in 6.5mm. Presumably this was a Navy issue carbine as the Navy anchor is struck twice on the underside of the receiver ring. This particular carbine has no other discernible Navy markings on the barrel, bolt or stock. (*Author's collection*)

A moschetto TSM manufactured at the Brescia Arsenal in 1918. (*Author's collection*)

The underside of the barrel on this Gardone Model 1891 cavalry carbine bears a profusion of assembly, inspection and alignment markings. (*Author's collection*)

Matching numbers on the underside of the barrel and receiver ring on a 1915 Brescia early model moschetto TS; these numbers bear no relation to the carbine's serial number. (*Author's collection*)

Markings on the underside of the barrel of a 1929 Terni Model 91/28 carbine. (*Author's collection*)

The number 17 on the rear sight of this 1942 Armaguerra Model 41 rifle is likely an assembly or identification number added during a post-war refurbishment. (*Author's collection*)

The Finnish Army SA marking on a Terni Model 38 short rifle. Finnish marked Model 38 rifles are commonly encountered in the U.S. collector market. (*Author's collection*)

The PF marking on the barrel of this 1915 Brescia TS carbine is a code indicating the steel supplier. (*Author's collection*)

BOLT ASSEMBLY

Carcano bolts can be encountered with markings on both the upper and lower and side bolt handle flats and on the bolt knob. Until 1919 the upper flat bore the serial number of the rifle or carbine, but this practice was discontinued after 1919. In theory, rifles that were converted to the Model 91/24 carbine should have a bolt with the serial number, but in practice this probably is the exception rather than the rule. Inspector marks, usually consisting of two letters, are commonly encountered on both upper and lower flats, and some side flats may also be marked; the lower handle flat on Navy rifles was stamped with a shield with a cross in it, surrounded by a circle. The bolt knob was stamped with a small crown, indicating that the bolt had been proof tested. Many of the smaller bolt components such as the cocking piece and safety were subcontracted to small firms, usually in the Brescia area, and often, but not always, bore the maker's mark or an inspector's mark. Beretta pieces were marked with PB; other fairly common markings were FNA and Rocca. Although not falling within the category of markings, the checkering on the ear of the safety catch varied noticeably depending on manufacturer, subcontractor, and possibly timeframe of manufacture. The checkering could be quite coarse or relatively fine, with many variations between the extremes. ■

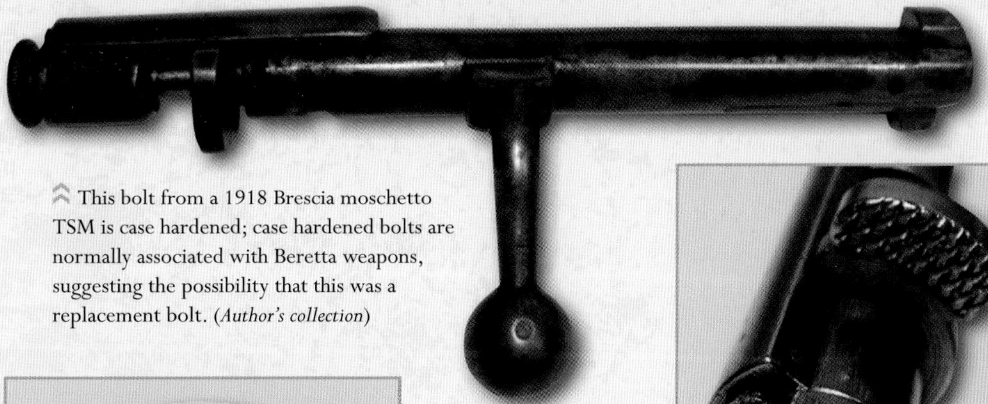

This bolt from a 1918 Brescia moschetto TSM is case hardened; case hardened bolts are normally associated with Beretta weapons, suggesting the possibility that this was a replacement bolt. (*Author's collection*)

Examples of improperly assembled bolt, left, and a properly assembled bolt, right. If the firing pin and safety catch are not properly aligned before the cocking piece is slipped over the firing pin, the threaded portion of the firing pin will not protrude far enough for the cocking nut to fully seat. The end of the firing pin will protrude slightly from the end of a properly installed cocking nut, as shown on the right, but will remain recessed if improperly installed, as shown on the left. (*Author's collection*)

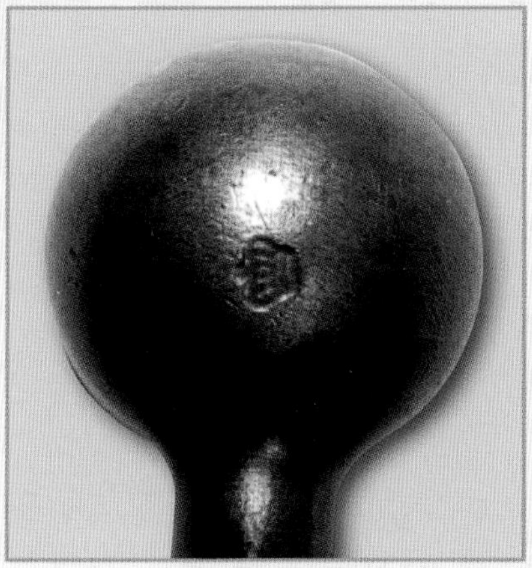

Crown marking on the Carcano bolt knob attesting to the fact that the bolt has been proofed. (*Author's collection*)

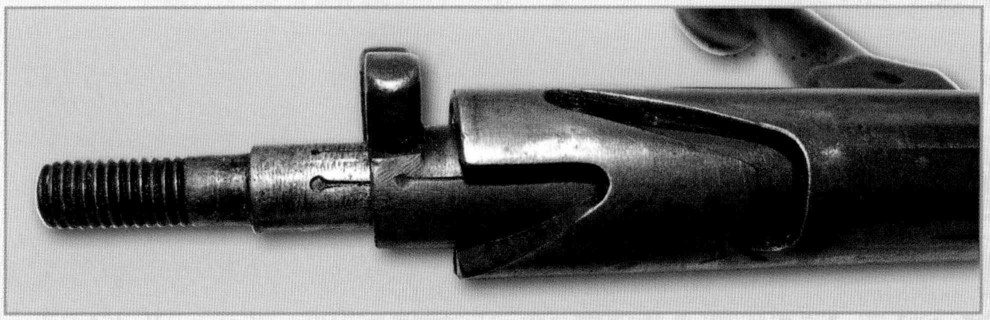

The witness marks are standard on the firing pin and the safety catch of all Carcanos. Failure to line these up properly before attaching the cocking piece when reassembling the bolt makes it difficult if not impossible to assemble the bolt correctly. (*Author's collection*)

A

B

C

D

E

F

G

H

I

J

K

L

M

Images A through M Markings on the top flat of the bolt root on Carcano bolts. (*Author's collection*)

» Marking on the shank of a firing pin. The firing pin assembly usually is devoid of markings. (*Author's collection*)

N
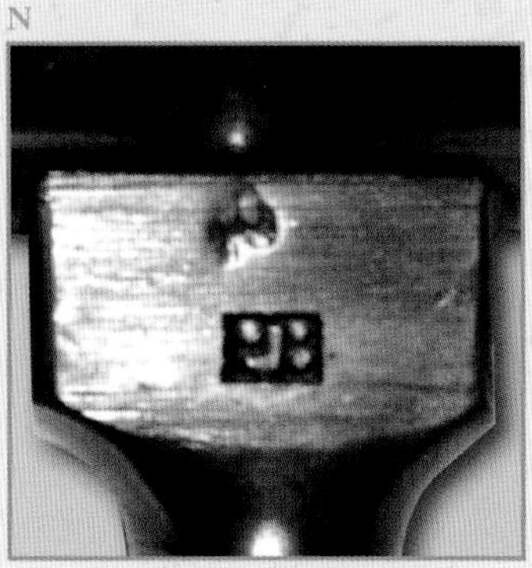
O

P

Q
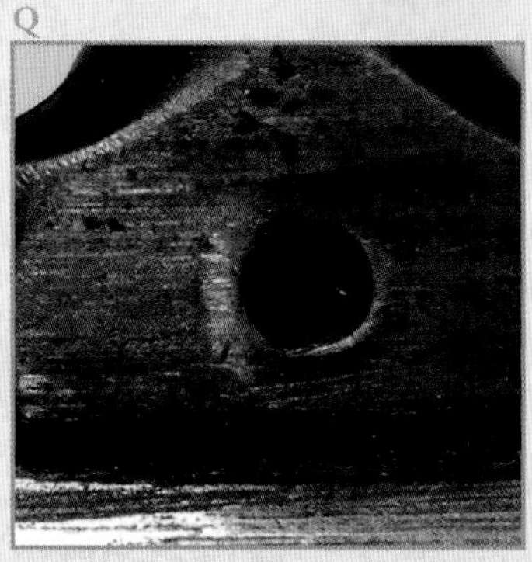

Images N through Q Markings on the bottom flat of the bolt root on Carcano bolts. (*Author's collection*)

S

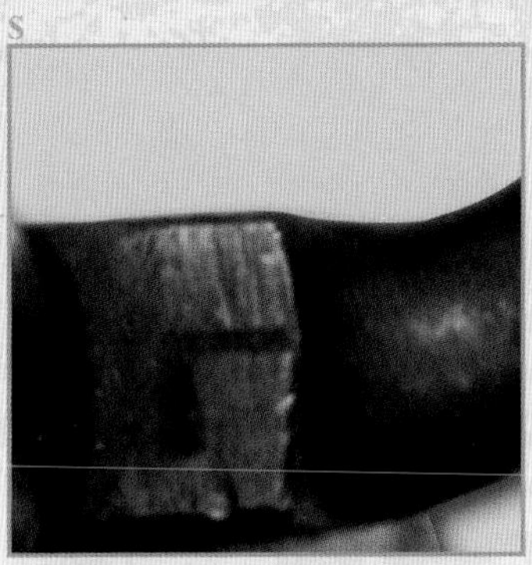

T

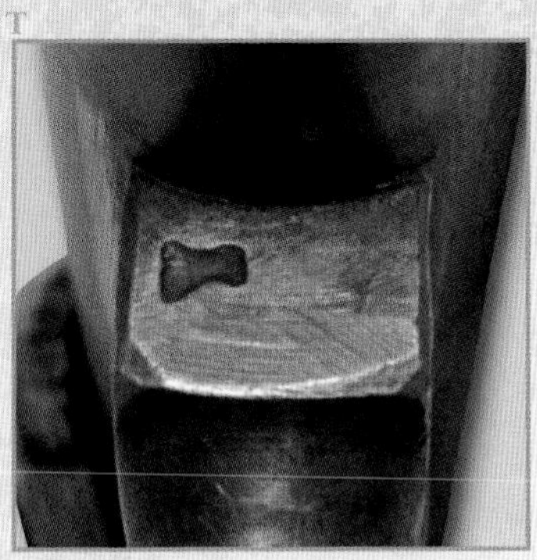

U

V

W

Images S through W Markings on the sides of the bolt root on Carcano bolts. (Author's collection)

» Galesi marking on the underside of a cocking piece arm. Very few cocking pieces were marked with a full name; the norm was for the top of the cocking piece to be marked with only two or three initials. (*Author's collection*)

« Markings on the obverse side of safety catches. From left to right: unmarked; what appear to be the letters M and S intertwined; VG; RV. The cross-hatch pattern varies considerably. (*Author's collection*)

︽ The reverse side of the safety catches shown in the previous photo. The first three on the left are unmarked, while the far right piece has an indistinct mark to the lower left and a cross inset in a circle to the upper right. The milling and finishing marks show large variations. (*Author's collection*)

︾ Markings on cocking pieces are quite small and often indistinct; the piece on the far right is unmarked. (*Author's collection*)

« Markings on cocking piece nuts. From left to right: unmarked; OCR; indistinct; BL; PG. Note the difference in surface finish, especially the very rough finish of the middle nut. (*Author's collection*)

CARCANO BUTTPLATE TYPES

« Carcano butt plate types, from left to right: Model 1891 rifle; Model 1891 carbine (with butt trap); Model 1891 Truppe Speciali and Model 91/24 carbines; Model 41 rifle. The butt plate with the trap used on the model 1891 carbine was also used on the Model 38 short rifle. (*Author's collection*)

» Inner side of a Model 1891 rifle butt plate, showing the stiffening rib; the butt plate on the Japanese Type I rifle also had the same stiffening rib arrangement. (*Author's collection*)

^ Likely assembly number marking on inside of the butt plate of an Armaguerra Model 41 rifle. The letter/number combination is consistent with a similar marking on the rifle's rear sight, and with the penciled number 17 on internal stock locations and on the handguard. (*Author's collection*)

^ A clearly struck rampant lion marking on the heel of a 6.5mm F.N.A. TS carbine buttplate produced in 1943. The rampant lion was the logo of the subcontractor who produced the buttplate for F.N.A. (*Courtesy Larry Eisel, Eisel Armory*)

^ Probable assembly number on the inside of a Terni Model 91/28 carbine butt plate manufactured in 1929 and refurbished at Gardone in 1938. (*Author's collection*)

Carcano rifles and carbines used four distinct types of buttplates. The buttplate of the Model 1891 rifle was a solid casting that was secured to the stock with two screws; the exterior was machined to a smooth finish, and the inside side of the plate had a stiffening rib that ran the entire length of the buttplate, from top to bottom. The buttplate used on all versions of the Model 1891 cavalry carbine, as well as on the Model 38 short rifle, was also a casting secured with two screws; it had a small trap door that could be opened to allow access to the trap that contained the cleaning rod segments. The buttplate for the TS and 91/24 carbines was similar to that of the cavalry carbine, except that it did not have an opening, as the TS and 91/24 carbines had a one-piece cleaning rod that fit into the front band and under the stock forearm. The most noticeably different buttplate was that of the Model 41 rifle which was slightly larger than the other buttplates, had a flatter cross-section and had a very pronounced tongue that fit into the heel of the stock. Buttplate markings are normally on the inside of the buttplate and consist of numbers, but 6.5mm F.N.A. TS carbines produced in the 1943-1944 timeframe also may have a rampant lion on the heel of the buttplate; some sources suggest that the rampant lion was used on buttplates of carbines converted to 7.92mm for export to Egypt in the post-war period, but unaltered 1943 carbines in the RA serial number block commonly have the rampant lion on the heel of the buttplate. These buttplates were subcontracted items produced by the tool and cutlery firm of Ausonia Nanutti Beltrame of Maniago, whose logo is the very same rampant lion that appears on the buttplates. The same logo may be found on cavalry bayonets produced by Ausonia. ■

RECEIVER

Because of the Italian practice of applying most identifying marks to the barrel chamber, there are not a great many markings to be found on Carcano receivers. Some manufacturers applied no marking at all on the receiver, while others applied either the inspector's initials, a crown, or the manufacturer's initials, often surmounted by a crown and/or in a circle or oval. These markings usually were on the receiver ring, but could also be found on the underside of the receiver. Some rifles and carbines that did not have their date stamped on the barrel had the date stamped on the underside of the receiver ring instead. A five-pointed star in the mortise on the receiver tang indicates arsenal reconditioning. On carbines converted to 7.92x57 by Franchi, "L. Franchi Brescia" is stamped on the underside of the receiver tang; the Franchi marking can also be found on the tang of at least some 6.5mm Model 91/38 cavalry carbines produced by F.N.A. ■

« Star marking in the mortise of the tang of a Model 38 short rifle indicating arsenal reconditioning. This rifle is an early Model 38 and also bears a reconditioned Model 1891 rifle barrel; it is likely that, in addition to the barrel, the receiver itself was a recycled Model 1891 receiver, thus accounting for the star marking indicating a "reconditioned" weapon. (*Author's collection*)

« Markings on the underside of a 7.35mm F.N.A. Model 91/38 TS carbine include a partially visible F.N.A. logo. (*Author's collection*)

« Letter and number markings on the underside of the tang of a Terni Model 38 short rifle produced in 1939 using the barrel and receiver of an 1897 Terni Model 1891 rifle. (*Author's collection*)

Marking on the underside of the tang of a 1942 Armaguerra Model 41 rifle. (*Author's collection*)

The date on this Gardone cavalry carbine is stamped on the underside of the receiver ring. (*Author's collection*)

Franchi marking on the underside of the tang on a 6.5mm Model 91/38 carbine manufactured by F.N.A. in 1943. This marking is anomalous, as Franchi markings usually consist of the inscription L. Franchi on one line and Brescia on a line beneath. (*Author's collection*)

Markings on the underside of the receiver ring of an F.N.A. Model 91/38 carbine; the numbers and letter bear no apparent correlation to the year of manufacture (1943) or serial number. The letter L may stand for lotto, or lot. (*Author's collection*)

In addition to the Finnish SA marking normally stamped on the barrel, this Model 38 short rifle also has a separate, somewhat larger SA marking stamped on the receiver ring. This is a rarely seen duplication of such markings. Note also that the serial number has been applied over the original Terni 1897 barrel marking. (*Author's collection*)

Markings on the underside of the receiver of a Terni Model 91/28 carbine include what appears to be part of the crossed rifle symbol; this particular carbine does have the crossed rifles stamped on any of the barrel facets. (*Author's collection*)

SMALL PARTS

Many of the small parts on Carcanos can be encountered with subcontractor markings or inspector's marks, but there is absolutely no consistency to which parts on a given rifle may be marked. Parts that may be marked include, but are not necessarily limited to, the trigger guard/magazine, trigger, sear, cocking piece, cocking piece knob, safety catch, front band, rear sling swivel, the bayonet mount and bayonet itself on the cavalry carbine, and buttplate. The markings range from quite visible, such as the Rocca marking frequently encountered on the cocking piece, to very small markings on interior surfaces that can be seen only if the weapon is disassembled and closely scrutinized, such as markings on the underside of the rear sling swivel assembly. ■

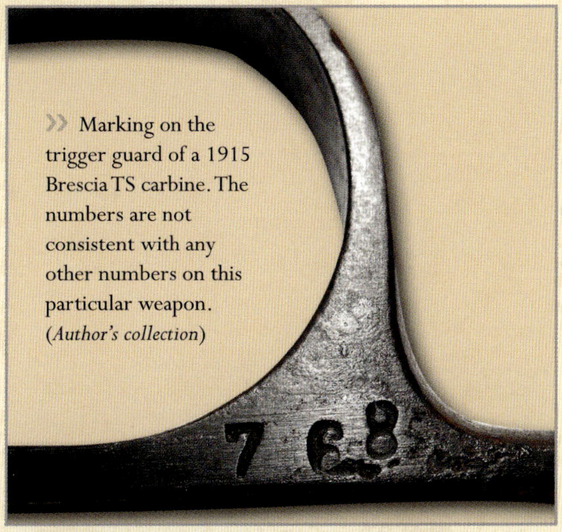

» Marking on the trigger guard of a 1915 Brescia TS carbine. The numbers are not consistent with any other numbers on this particular weapon. (*Author's collection*)

« Marking on the sear of a Terni-produced Model 91/28 carbine. (*Author's collection*)

» Probable subcontractor marking on the sling swivel assembly of a 1915 Brescia TS carbine. (*Author's collection*)

« The letters PS marking on the sear of this Armaguerra Model 41 rifle may indicate that the sear was a subcontracted part produced by Polotti Scherma. (*Author's collection*)

» Model 91/28 carbines supplied to Bavaria after World War II were marked in English as belonging to the Bavaria Rural Police. Several variants of the marking can be encountered; this carbine is also marked Civ. Guard. (*Author's collection*)

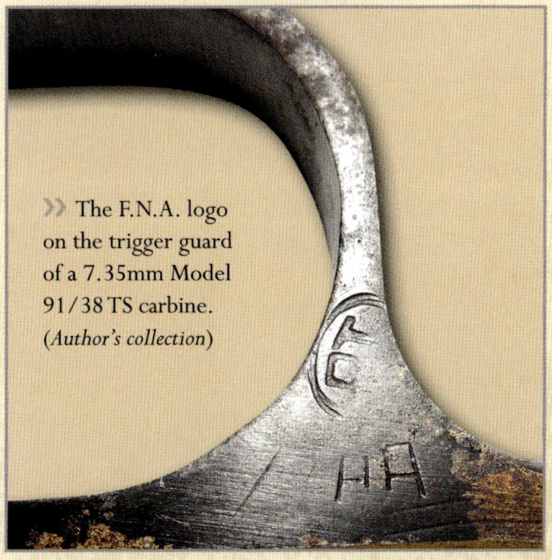

» The F.N.A. logo on the trigger guard of a 7.35mm Model 91/38 TS carbine. (*Author's collection*)

FOREIGN MARKINGS

Markings on the Carcano Type I rifles, rifles in German service, rifles supplied to Finland and rifles converted post-war for export to the Middle East have been covered previously in the text. However, Carcanos were used by a number of other counties, often to a limited extent. Not all countries added their own specific or distinctive markings, but among that did were Austria-Hungary which marked the receivers of Carcanos captured during World War I with the acronym AZF (for *Artilleriezugfabriken*); China, which applied a series of Chinese *hanzi* ideograms and the number 25 on the receiver, and Greece, which stamped an upper case letter E on the receiver ring. Also as previously mentioned a number of Model 91/24 and 91/28 carbines were supplied to Bavaria after World War II for police use and were marked in English indicating that they were issued to the Bavarian Rural Police. ■

APPENDIX 3: CARCANO STOCK MARKINGS

The Italians embellished their rifle stocks with markings to a much greater degree than did any other nation. In addition to reflecting the rifle's serial number, Carcano stocks exhibit an astounding variety of cartouches depending on manufacturer and date of manufacture or repair or rebuild. Cartouches were often quite ornate and indicated the manufacturer or rebuild facility and the date. The following is a synopsis and provides only an introduction to the basic elements that could be encountered, but does not pretend to address or describe all of the many variants that have been identified. Each manufacturer or repair facility had its own style of stock cartouche and it was not uncommon for cartouche styles to be changed from time to time. Almost all Carcano stocks bore cartouches, but late war production rifles, in particular those produced by F.N.A. in 1943, often had only the serial number on the buttstock.

Stock cartouches were applied to the left side of the buttstock, perpendicular to the axis of the stock, and above the serial number which was stamped into the stock just above the buttplate. The basic elements of the cartouche were a circle, oval, hexagon or rectangle with rounded corners that contained the manufacturer's name and the date of manufacture or arsenal reconditioning, although not all cartouches had the date stamped. Many variations in the name of some manufacturers could be encountered; for instance, rifles or carbines produced by Terni could be marked "Artiglieria fabbrica d'armi Terni," "Fabbrica d'armi Terni," "Fabbrica d'armi R. Esercito Terni," or "Fabbrica d'armi R.E. Terni," among others. Some manufacturers at times used abbreviations, such as TO for Torino or FAT for Terni, and other manufacturers such as Lorenzotti and MBT used only the serial number and a small Savoy logo. Stocks could also be replaced at artillery repair shops; until about 1910 the artillery markings were rather complete, and indicated the date and place of repair, the word *riparazione,* and a royal crown. Model 1891 rifles that had been converted to Model 91/24 carbines could have a cartouche with the word *trasformazione* (transformation) added beneath it. During the post-World War II years, the artillery markings were greatly simplified and consisted of a rectangle enclosing the abbreviation of the repair facility (DABo for Bologna, DAVe possibly for Venezia, and DAV possibly for Verona).

Letter styles varied considerably, with or without serifs, and the method of indicating dates also varied from the full four digit year, to only the last three digits, or only the last two digits.

After 1940, stocks on the 7.35mm rifles and carbines that remained in Italian service were prominently marked with CAL 7.35 above the cartouche; this was done to clearly differentiate the weapons from the 6.5mm versions that were produced from 1940 onward. Buttstocks of the 7.35mm Model 38 rifles furnished to Finland were not similarly marked, presumably because there were no 6.5mm versions in Finland and thus no confusion could arise.

Despite the wide variety of sizes and styles, the stock cartouches and serial numbers adhered to a standard pattern in terms of placement of the items. However, an astonishing number of other markings can be found on Carcano stocks, but these supplemental markings exhibit no discernible or coherent pattern as to placement, size, or style. Various types of markings, usually consisting of small numbers or letters, can be found on the exterior of the stock, or internally in the barrel channel or recever channel, or in the magazine recess. These markings are often enclosed within some sort of geometric figure, and could be either manufacturer's codes or inspector codes. The forward end of some stocks exhibit one or more letters or numbers; these may be assembly numbers or may be related to stock blank or

« Stock cartouche on a Model 1891 rifle that was repaired in 1931 at the Terni Arsenal; the oval encloses the name of the arsenal, a Cross of Savoy, an Italian Army crest, and the date in both Roman and Arabic numerals. The repair is clearly indicated by the word "Riparazione" in the banner beneath the oval. The rifle's serial number is also stamped on the butt; it appears that the first digit 2 is struck over a 1. (Author's collection)

» Serial number and very faint cartouche on a 1933 Terni Model 1891 rifle. (*Author's collection*)

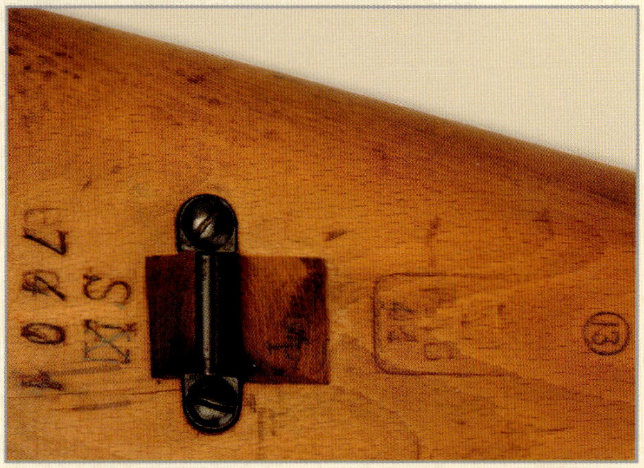

« Serial number and Gardone cartouche on a 6.5mm Model 91/38 cavalry carbine. The barrel of this weapon has a 1943 manufacture date, but the date on the cartouche appears to be 44. The stock is a recycled stock, as the serial number clearly has been struck over a previous number. (*Author's collection*)

» The stock of a 1929 Terni moschetto 91/28 refurbished by Gardone in 1938, as shown by the stock cartouche. (*Author's collection*)

^ The Navy shield has been stamped on the butt of this Navy issue 7.35mm Model 91/38 TS carbine. (Author's collection)

^ Stock marking consisting of the letters LP within a circle. This is believed to be a subcontractor marking, normally found on rifles produced from the 1930s up until the 1950s; this marking is on the stock of a Model 1891 rifle that was repaired in 1931. Whether the order of the initials is LP or PL is open to question. (*Author's collection*)

seasoning lots. Likewise, at the heel end of the stock, letters, numbers or other markings can be found underneath the buttplate on some rifles and carbines. There seems to be absolutely no consistency to any of these minor stock markings, as some stocks exhibit none at all, some have only a single marking, and others have a veritable profusion of marks, ranging from a single number or letter standing alone, to combinations of numbers and letters and markings such as the arsenal rebuild star, the crossed rifle mark, the royal crown, the Navy shield, or the manufacturer's logo.

The sling wells on rifles or carbines with side-mounted slings often have one or more letters stamped in the well, but this is not a universal practice. The letter usually stands alone, but may also be enclosed by a small diamond, as well as possibly by other shaped enclosures.

The markings on Vetterli-Vitali stocks generally followed the same conventions as those on the Carcano stocks, but the markings were applied to the right-hand side of the buttstock rather than to the left-hand side. ■

The barely legible cartouche on this moschetto 91/24 reflects the conversion of a Model 1891 rifle by Gardone in 1939. The serial number on the stock, RH 1676, identifies the original rifle as produced by Terni in 1917. (*Author's collection*)

Markings on a 7.35mm Model 38 short rifle, which consist of the caliber marking, CAL 7.35, the manufacturer's logo – FAG, for Fabbica d'Armi Gardone – surmounted by a royal crown, and the last two digits of the year of manufacture – 1939. The rifle's serial number is stamped between the butt plate and the sling attachment. The 7.35mm caliber marking was added to the rifles to clearly distinguish them from the 6.5mm version produced beginning in 1940. (*Author's collection*)

Two letters in the sling well of a 6.5mm Gardone Model 91/38 cavalry carbine; the P is quite distinct, and the other letter appears to be an M. (*Author's collection*)

This seldom encountered style of stock marking indicates that this Model 41 rifle was refurbished by Gardone in 1946 and is limited to the letters FAG and the last two digits of the date, 46. The number 1 under the date may indicate the month of refurbishment. (*Author's collection*)

Close inspection of the butt of this Model 1891 rifle repaired by Terni in 1931 reveals at least four markings. Two are identical, one struck over the other, and a third faint mark in a circle has been struck over them; finally, a clearly visible letter C has been struck along the edge of the bottom mark. (*Author's collection*)

What appears to be a partially struck letter R on the butt of an Armaguerra Model 41 rifle. (*Author's collection*)

Small cartouche on the left side of the stock of a 1918 Brescia TSM carbine, above the trigger. (*Author's collection*)

Marking consisting of a letter O in the sling well of a Model 91/24 carbine. This same marking has been observed in the sling well of a 1943 Gardone cavalry carbine. (*Author's collection*)

The sling well of a 6.5mm F.N.A. Model 91/38 cavalry carbine marked with a letter M enclosed by a diamond. (*Author's collection*)

Probable inspector's initials on the stock of a 1918 Brescia moschetto TSM. (Author's collection)

Mark on the butt of a 1918 Brescia TSM carbine. (*Author's collection*)

Markings on the butt of a 1915 Brescia TS carbine. (*Author's collection*)

Some late war stocks, such as on this 1943 6.5mm F.N.A. 91/38 TS carbine, were not stamped with a cartouche although the serial number was present. (*Author's collection*)

« The Navy shield marking on the stock of a 7.35mm Navy issue F.N.A. Model 91/38 TS rifle. (*Author's collection*)

Penciled assembly number in the magazine assembly mortise on an Armaguerra Model 1941 rifle. (*Author's collection*)

Assembly number 17 penciled in the handguard of the Armaguerra Model 1941 rifle. (*Author's collection*)

« The forward edge of stocks on Italian rifles and carbines often contain one or more numbers or letters, such as on this Model 91/38 cavalry carbine. The meaning of the marks is not known; they may reflect assembly numbers or information relating to seasoning of the wood or stock blank lot. (*Author's collection*)

» Assembly number 17 marked in pencil in the receiver channel of an Armaguerra Model 41 rifle refurbished in 1946; this number matches a number stamped on the rear sight base and butt plate of this rifle. (*Author's collection*)

APPENDIX 4: BAYONETS

Of the "eight million bayonets" so famously referred to by Mussolini, most were the *sciabola-baionetta mod. 91* (Model 91 sword-bayonet) developed for use with the Model 1891 rifle which was used in World War II as well as in World War I. Between 1898 and about 1920, a similar bayonet, but with a transversal cut to allow attachment to the *moschetto modello 1891 per truppe speciali*, was also in use. Also, during World War I a number of expedient or emergency type bayonets were produced: these consisted of several different modifications of Vetterli bayonets. Interestingly, during the course of World War I the Austrians produced what was called the Model 1917 *ersatz* bayonet, which was an ingenious, rudimentary bayonet for use on captured Model 1891 rifles; it consisted of a blade whose rear portion was bent lengthwise at a 90o angle to the blade itself to form the hilt, and had an extremely simple L-shaped crossguard with muzzle ring riveted to the hilt. In 1938, with the adoption of the new Model 38 short rifle, a new folding type bayonet was introduced as well; the first type Model 38 folding bayonet was followed by an improved type, and as the war progressed, the folding blade bayonet was replaced by two types of fixed blade bayonets. The Model 1891 and Model 38 bayonets were not interchangeable.

From 1892 to 1938, Model 91 bayonets were produced by the government arsenals at Brescia, Terni, Torino and Torre Annunziata, and by the private firms of Gnutti and MIDA. From 1938 until the end of the war, the only government arsenal still involved in producing bayonets was Terni; most bayonets during the post-1938 period were produced by private concerns and included Castelli (code CR), Franchi, Gnutti (code CG), Polotti Scherma (code PS), and Rocca. The full extension of the SBF code remains unknown. ■

SCIABOLA-BAIONETTA MOD. 91 (MODEL 91 SWORD-BAYONET)

Typical crossguard marking on a Model 1891 bayonet. (*Author's collection*)

Manufacturer's marking, Eredi Gnutti Lumezzane, on a Model 1891 bayonet. (*Courtesy Eredi Gnutti Metalli*)

An 1891 bayonet and leather scabbard with brass fittings. (*Author's collection*)

1891 bayonet and ribbed steel scabbard. (*Author's collection*)

This was the bayonet originally issued with the Model 1891 rifle. It had a straight blade with a rectangular profile fuller or blood groove; the fullers on blades marked with the CR manufacturer's code may be encountered with a shallow semicircular profile. Early bayonet blades were in the white, but beginning in World War I were blued. The upper part of the crossguard had a 13mm diameter muzzle ring, and the lower part tapered and had a small ball at the end. The pommel, which had a push-button press stud, was steel, and the wood grips, were held by pins peened over countersunk washers. The grips were made from wood that was left over from the stock making process; the earliest grips were made of sorb-apple, but during World War I walnut, beech and ash were used. During World War II a variant was produced with a brass handle and crossguard. A wide variety of markings can be encountered on Model 91 bayonets, including the manufacturer's name or code on the ricasso or on the crossguard, the rifle's serial number on the crossguard, or a code consisting of Roman and Arabic numerals on the tang of the blade. Other marking variations include bayonets with no markings other than an inspection mark consisting of the letters OCR and a small crown on the ricasso or crossguard. A final type of marking that can be encountered on bayonets produced during World War II are markings related to the *4o Ufficio Tecnico* (4th Technical Office), and could consist of the letters IVU in an oval, or the marking 4oUT. Early maker's marks had letters with serifs, while later marks were without serifs.

The early scabbard for the Model 91 bayonet was made of leather dyed black, with brass, metal or – rarely – aluminum fittings; there is also some reference to a rare version made of rubber with metal fittings. Later versions of the scabbard were made of steel, with either a smooth or ribbed exterior. The leather scabbards had the name of manufacturer and the date stamped along one of the edges. ■

SCIABOLA-BAIONETTA MOD. 91 (MODEL 91 SWORD-BAYONET)

Blade length: 300mm (11.8")
Overall length: 414mm (16.3")
Blade width: 25mm (0.98")
Grip type: Wood or brass
Weight (bayonet): 340 grams (0.75 lb)
Weight (Scabbard): 136 grams (0.3 lb)

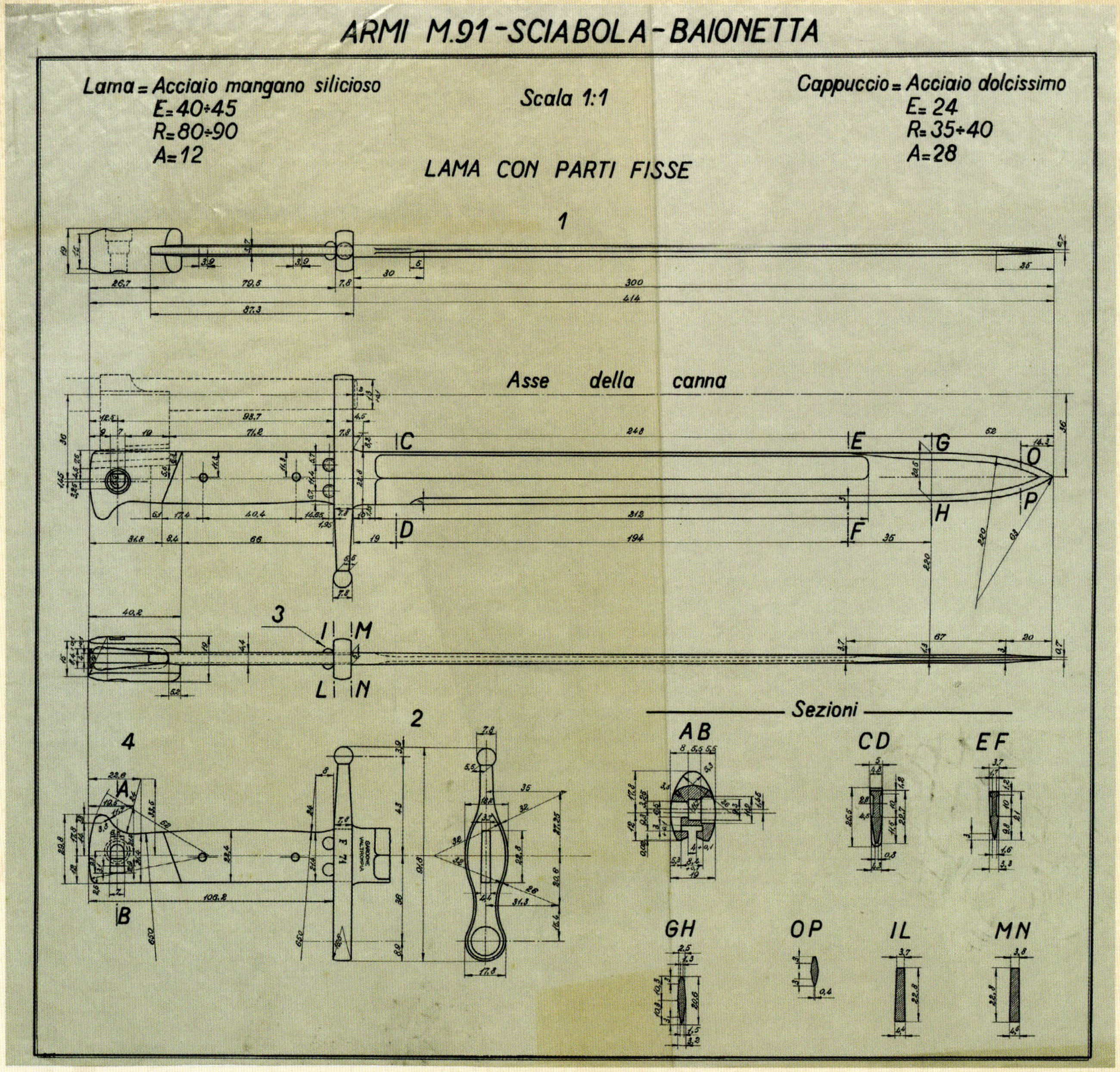

Gnutti engineering drawings, Model 1891 bayonet. (*Courtesy Eredi Gnutti Metalli*)

SCIABOLA-BAIONETTA
(Model 91 T.S. sword-bayonet)

This bayonet was issued with the *moschetto modello 1891 per truppe speciali*, whose front band incorporated a bayonet lug different than that used on the Model 1891 rifle. Accordingly, the bayonet for the TS carbine had a transversal mortise slot and catch rather than the normal long axis slot and catch of the Model 91 bayonet; otherwise, the bayonet was the same as the standard Model 91. The push-button press stud was located on the rear of the pommel rather than on the side, as on the standard bayonet. When the front band on the *moschetto TS* was changed to the same type as on the Model 1891 rifle, with a longitudinal lug, the transversal catch bayonets were converted to standard bayonet configuration by welding the old slot and milling a new longitudinal mortise slot. Markings on these bayonets followed the same conventions as for the standard bayonet, and scabbards likewise were the same as those used with the standard Model 91 bayonet. Dimensions and weights were as noted above for the standard Model 91 bayonet. ■

BAIONETTA PER MOSCHETTO
(bayonet for Model 91 & Model 91/38 carbines)

The bayonet for the Model 91 carbine (commonly referred to as the cavalry carbine) consisted of a triangular section blade attached to a support bracket at the muzzle end of the barrel. The bayonet folded back under the barrel; when folded back, most of its length was exposed but the tip fit into a groove in the stock forearm. There were three different locking systems: the earliest system was a spring-loaded release; the second transitional type, adopted before 1916, used a latch on the support bracket; the third definitive type, beginning on carbines produced in 1916, used a spring-loaded button on the support bracket. There was no provision for any type of scabbard or protective sheath for the blade. ■

BAIONETTA PER MOSCHETTO BAYONET FOR MODEL 91 & MODEL 91/38 CARBINES

Blade length: 347mm (13.66")
Total length: 480mm (18.89")
Weight: 145 grams (0.32 lb)

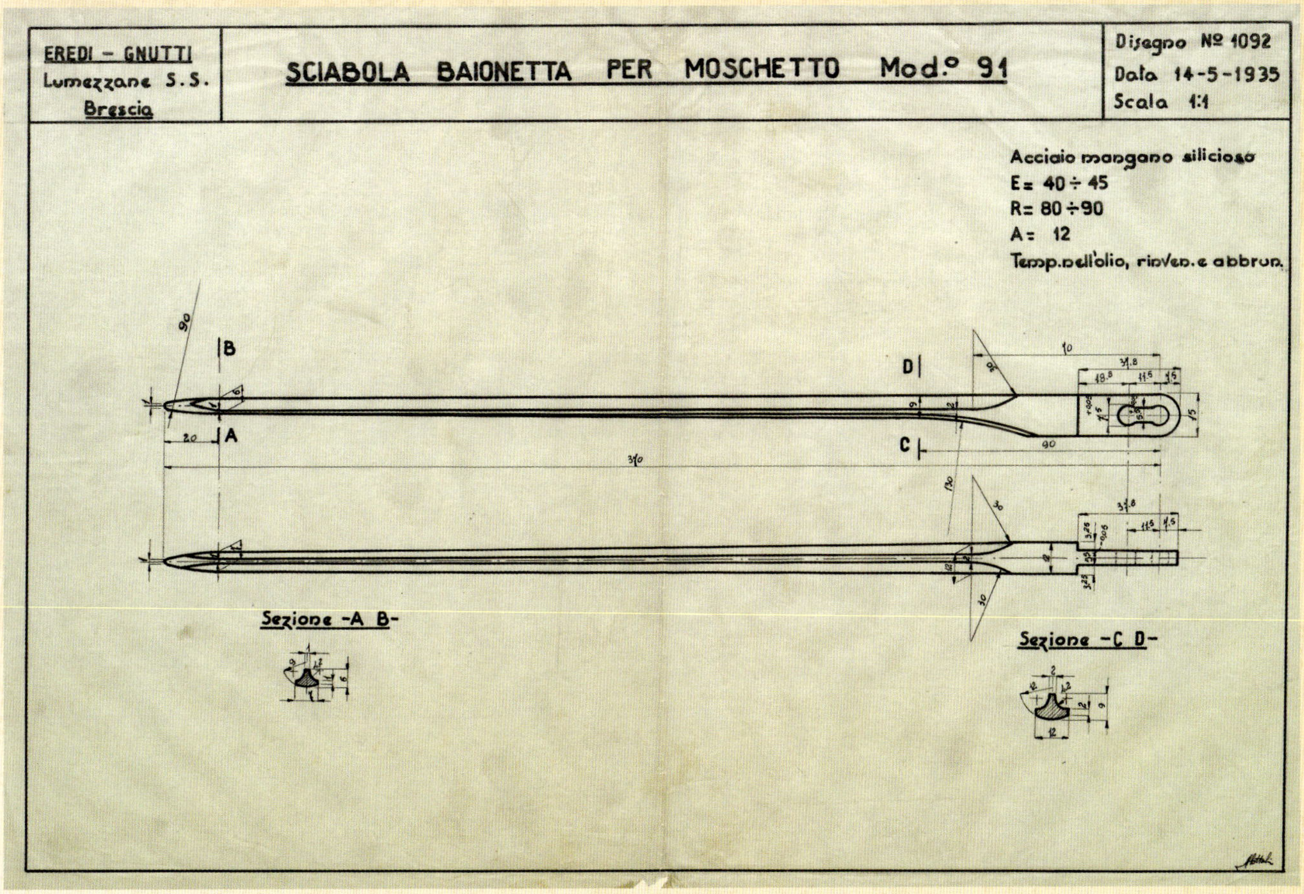

Gnutti engineering drawings, moschetto Mod. 91 cavalry bayonet. (*Courtesy Eredi Gnutti Metalli*)

PUGNALE-BAIONETTA A LAMA RIPIEGABILE
(Model 38 folding blade dagger-bayonet)

This folding blade bayonet was developed especially for the Model 1938 short rifle and was produced in two versions, the *tipo I* (Type I), and the *tipo II* (Type II). The Type I had a latch lock that proved totally unsatisfactory in service, as when the rifle was fired with the bayonet attached the recoil forces often caused the bayonet to disengage from the bayonet lug and fall from the rifle. The *tipo I* is the scarcest of the bayonets used on the Model 38 rifles, with slightly less than 29,000 produced, all by one manufacturer, Polotti Scherma (PS). The *tipo I* was replaced by the *tipo II*, which had a redesigned catch consisting of a more traditional and reliable push-button press stud. The blade had a fuller, and on both types the crossguard attached to the handle had a muzzle ring, the pommel was steel, and the wood grips were secured by screws. A spring-loaded push button acted as a pivot for the blade to rotate around so that it could assume the open or closed position. The folding blade measured 210mm (8.27") overall, of which 175mm (6.89") was exposed when the bayonet was in the fixed position in the handle. When fitted to the rifle in the folded position, the sharp edge of the blade rested in a slot cut into the underside of the forearm. About 350,000 *tipo II* bayonets were produced.

It is believed that initially scabbards were not issued with the folding blade bayonets as the bayonets were supposed to be attached to the rifle as a matter of practice. However, at some point a sheet metal scabbard with a smooth exterior was developed and issued to accompany the bayonet. The scabbard for the Type I and Type II bayonets was made of steel with a smooth exterior; it did not have a frog stud, but instead was fitted with a steel loop slightly angled below the throat to enable a belt to be passed through. ■

PUGNALE-BAIONETTA A LAMA RIPIEGABILE MODEL 38 FOLDING BLADE DAGGER-BAYONET

Blade length: 175mm (6.89") when in extended position; overall blade length 210mm (8.27")
Overall length: 290mm (11.4")
Blade width: 20mm (0.79")
Grip type: Wood
Weight: 280 grams (0.62 lbs)

« Latch of a Type I bayonet as seen from above; the serial number is also visible. (*Keith Versaw*)

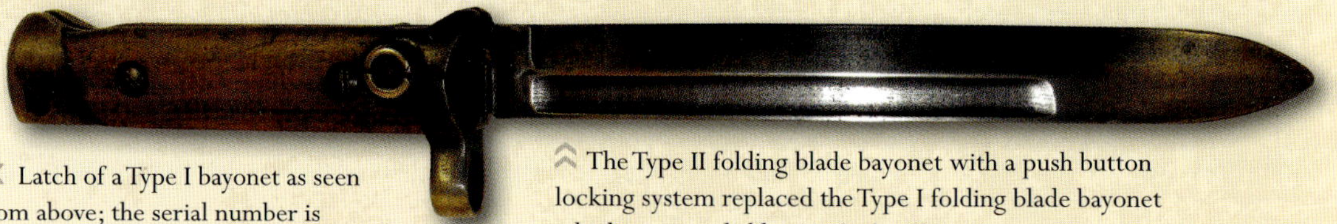

^ The Type II folding blade bayonet with a push button locking system replaced the Type I folding blade bayonet which was unreliable. (*Author's collection*)

^ The Model 1938 Type I folding bayonet with the early latch style catch. The Type I bayonet is the rarest of the Model 1938 bayonets. (*Keith Versaw*)

A

B

« Latch detail of a Type I folding blade bayonet. (*Keith Versaw*)

Images A & B Model 1938 Type II folding bayonet, top, and Model 1938 Type IIM fixed blade bayonet, bottom. The scabbard for the Type II bayonet has a wide belt loop, whereas the scabbard for the Type IIM bayonet had the standard frog stud as used on Model 1891 scabbards. (*Author's collection*)

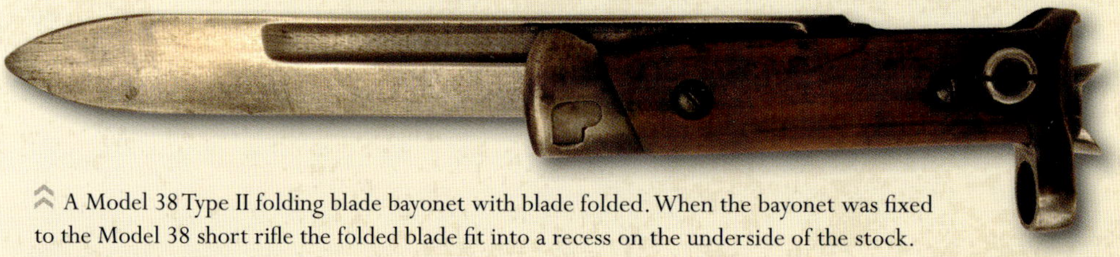

^ A Model 38 Type II folding blade bayonet with blade folded. When the bayonet was fixed to the Model 38 short rifle the folded blade fit into a recess on the underside of the stock. (*Author's collection*)

PUGNALE-BAIONETTA MOD. 38, TIPO IIM E TIPO III

(Model 38 dagger-bayonets, Type IIM and Type III)

Around 1940, when the 7.35mm rifles were phased out of production and the Model 38 rifles began again to be chambered in 6.5mm, production of the folding blade bayonet was discontinued and two types of fixed blade bayonet were adopted. The first type was known as the *tipo IIM* (Type IIM) and used the blades and handles from Type II folding blade bayonets that had not yet been assembled; none of the Type I or Type II were converted to Type IIM bayonets. The Type IIM was fitted with a short crossguard that replaced the crossguard and pivot of the Type II, and was welded so that the blade could not fold; the wood handle of the Type IIM was retained with screws as used on the Type I and Type II. The final variant was the *tipo III* (Type III), which was manufactured from new parts and had a differently configured crossguard, and whose wood handle was secured by pins peened over countersunk washers as on the Model 1891 bayonets. The scabbard for the Type IIM and Type III fixed blade bayonets was a smooth steel scabbard whose body and throat were identical to those of the scabbard for the Type I and Type II, but instead of the belt loop had a frog stud as found on the Model 1891 rifle scabbards. ■

PUGNALE-BAIONETTA MOD. 38, TIPO IIM E TIPO III (MODEL 38 DAGGER-BAYONETS, TYPE IIM AND TYPE III)

Blade length: 175mm (6.9")
Overall length: 290mm (11.4")
Blade width: 20mm (0.79")
Grip type: Wood
Weight (bayonet): 285 grams (0.63 lbs)

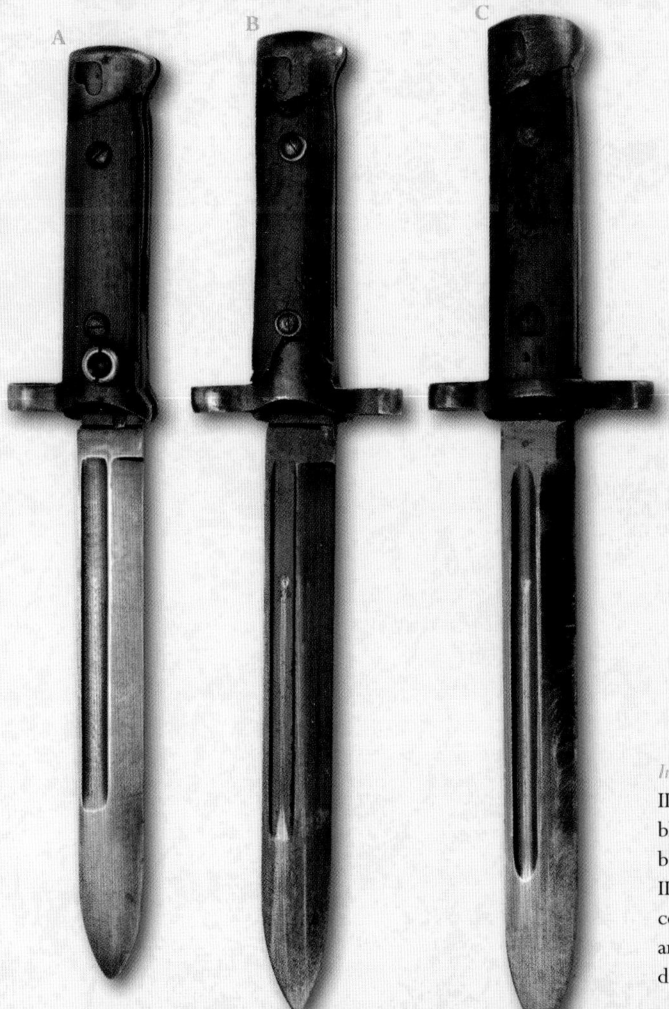

« A brown holster for the Model 1889 Bodeo revolver. The hanger strap was quite prominent. (*Aleš Kratochvil*)

Images A, B & C Top, a Model 1938 Type II folding blade bayonet; middle, a fixed blade Model 1938 Type IIM bayonet; bottom, a fixed blade Model 1938 Type III bayonet. The Type IIM used Type II components modified as a fixed blade, and the Type III was an entirely different design. (*Author's collection*)

VETTERLI MODIFIED "EMERGENCY" BAYONETS

(World War I)

In order to meet demand for bayonets during World War I some use was made of Vetterli bayonets modified so that they could be used on the Model 1891 rifle. There were several variations of these modified bayonets: one type had the original Vetterli bayonet blade that was shortened from the original 520mm (20.47") to 315mm (12.4"), a new crossguard was fitted that was compatible with the muzzle diameter of the Model 1891, and the mortise slot likewise was modified as appropriate; another type had a shortened blade but retained the original crossguard whose muzzle ring was resized from 17mm to 13mm diameter; yet another type used the forward portion of the Vetterli blade that had been cut off to shorten the original bayonet, attaching it to a very rudimentary hollow steel tube that served as a handle. Although not inconceivable, it is unlikely that any of the modified Vetterli bayonets were issued during World War II. ■

APPENDIX 5: ACCESSORIES & ACCOUTREMENTS

HOLSTERS

There were several varieties of holsters used during both World Wars that accommodated sideams from the Model 1884 revolver through the Model 1934 and Model 1935 Beretta pistols. The color of the holsters varied according to the time period, arm of service, or rank of the bearer and could be black, grey-green, or brown. Canvas holsters can be encountered with a belt loop or with metal belt hangers in varying shades of green or drab; those with the metal hangers are post-World War II manufacture. ■

« A postwar canvas holster for the Beretta Model 1934 and Model 1935 pistols. This type of holster was used with the British 1937 pattern web belt used by Italy after the war. In 1975 the tan holster, whose production began in the 1947-1948 timeframe, was replaced by an identical holster made of olive drab canvas. (*Author's collection*)

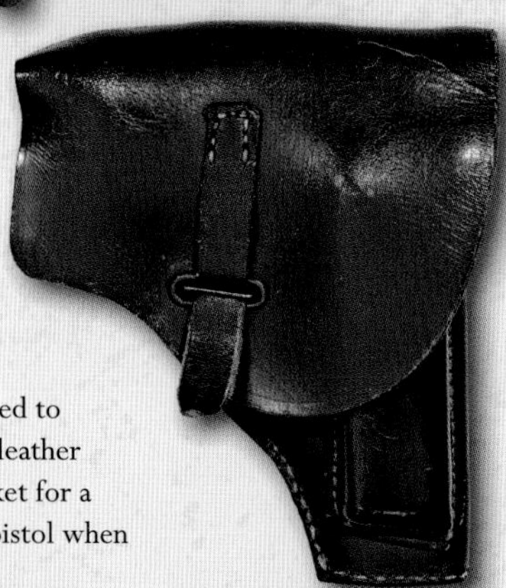

» Each Beretta Model 1934 pistol issued to officers was supplied with a brown soft leather holster as shown. The holster had a pocket for a spare magazine, also supplied with the pistol when issued. (*John Moss collection*)

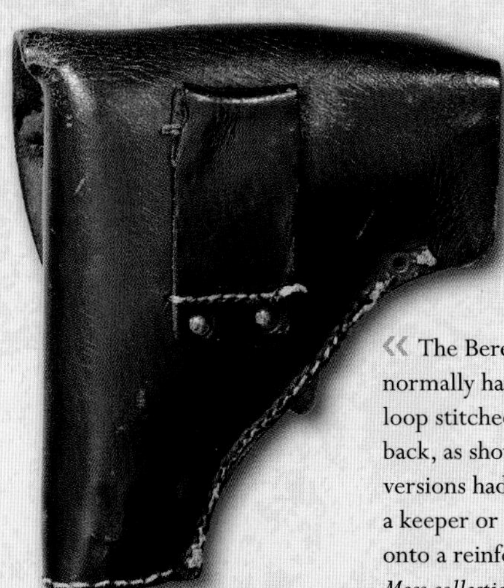

« The Beretta holster normally had a large single belt loop stitched and riveted on the back, as shown here, but other versions had a larger loop with a keeper or a metal clip sewn onto a reinforcing gusset. (*John Moss collection*)

SLINGS

Most Italian slings were unmarked; this grey-green sling is marked with the crown, the Terni FAT initials, and the last two digits of the year, 1939. (*Author's collection*)

A new old stock (NOS) sling as part of a lot of parts and accessories that was purchased by a French dealer in the 1980s. The sling is about 1250mm (49 inches) long (*Author's collection*)

A short (1055mm/41½ inches) sling with sliding brass buckle. (*Author's collection*)

Slings supplied to Finland by Italy along with the Model 38 rifles were marked with the Finnish Army SA logo by the Finns. (*Author's collection*)

An 1180mm (46½ inches) long grey-green sling with buckle and prong and 42 adjustment holes. The stud for this particular type of sling was larger than the standard stud used on other slings and was a two-piece assembly that made it much easier to pass through the slits. (*Author's collection*)

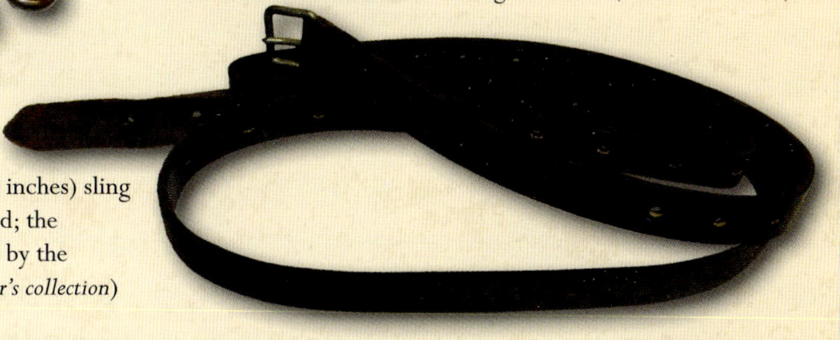

A long (1675mm/70 inches) sling without the fastening stud; the looped sling was secured by the buckle and prong. (*Author's collection*)

Slings varied considerably in length, method of fastening, buckle types and other details. The right sling, which measures about 1675mm (66 inches) long and 20mm (.75 inches) wide, has 53 adjustment holes, a wire buckle, and is fastened to the front band using the buckle. The left sling measures about 1260mm (49.5 inches) long, is also 20mm wide, has 43 adjustment holes, a stamped buckle, and fastens to the front band with a loop and stud. (*Author's collection*)

A number of different slings were used for the Carcano rifle family. The standard sling for the model 1891 rifle, which was also used on the Model 41 rifle and the *moschetto per truppe speciali*, was a brown leather sling that measured 1150mm (45.3 inches) long by 30mm (1.2 inches) wide by 3mm (0.12 inches) thick; some slings were Italian Army grey-green. The sling was fastened by means of brass or steel collar studs passing through slits cut into the leather that allowed adjustment only to the end that passed through the front sling swivel; length could be adjusted by about only 50mm (2 inches). Many other types of slings could be encountered, ranging from about 1180mm (46.5 inches) long to as long as 1675mm (66 inches) long. These could be secured to the sling swivels by a collar stud securing the looped sling or by a buckle and prong arrangement. The number of adjustment holes also varied, from as few as 42 to as many as 53, depending on sling length. Another type of sling 1055mm (41½ inches) long had the stud and slot arrangement for the rear attachment point but had a simple brass H-buckle that allowed for adjustment. A model adopted during World War II had the stud arrangement for the rear attachment point but used a sliding sling buckle similar to that used on World War II U.S. web slings. The Italian Navy used cloth webbing slings on their TS carbines. ■

AMMUNITION POUCHES

There were a number of types of ammunition pouches in use. Most were made of leather and differed in their carrying capacity. Early Mod. 1907 (World War I) pouches had two cartridge pockets, each of which could carry one six-round clip; there were also pouches with three pockets, also each with a one clip capacity. Another type of pouch, in black or grey-green leather, had two pockets, but each pocket could carry a cardboard box that contained three six-round clips. Artillery troops wore a bandolier that had two sets of two pockets, with each pocket carrying a six-round clip. Alpine troops had a white web bandolier with four pockets, each of which held three six-round clips. There was also a single pocket pouch that had a three clip capacity that normally was issued to the police. The Navy used a pair of web suspenders with two single pouches, also of web material, each carrying one six-round clip.

In addition to the regulation pouches, scaled down versions of the pouches and belt were made for use with the Balilla carbines and were made of either leather or of a fairly strong cardboard type material. Another Balilla pouch, belt and suspender combination was made of white canvas webbing and reportedly was worn only by children whose fathers had fallen while serving with the Italian Legion in the Spanish Civil War. ■

A pair of downsized leather ammunition pouches for use with the Balilla carbine. (*Courtesy Luca Vallebona, Armeria Black Hills*)

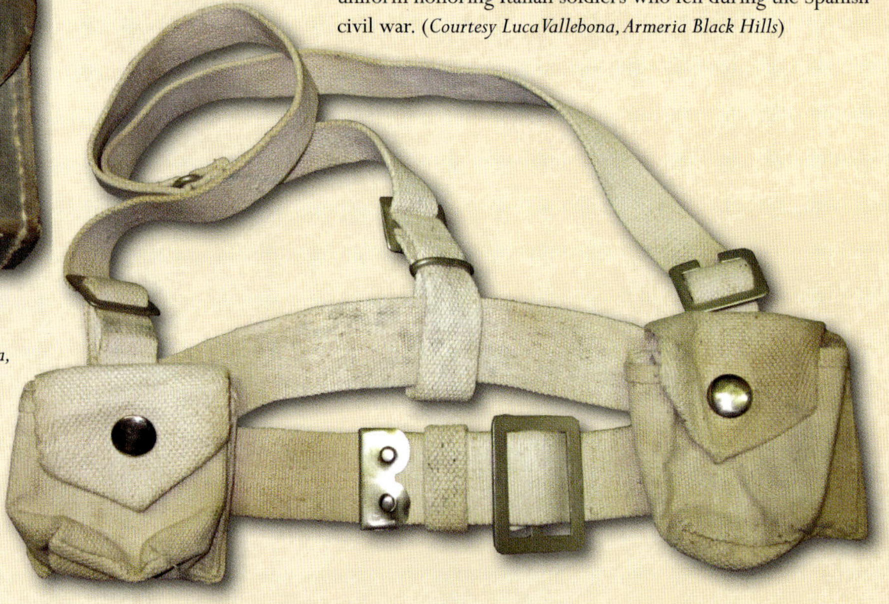

The white canvas web ensemble used with the Balilla special uniform honoring Italian soldiers who fell during the Spanish civil war. (*Courtesy Luca Vallebona, Armeria Black Hills*)

Belt and single ammunition pouch used with the Balilla uniform. Both were made of a cardboard material; surviving examples of this type of accessory are difficult to find in good condition. (*Courtesy Luca Vallebona, Armeria Black Hills*)

A

B

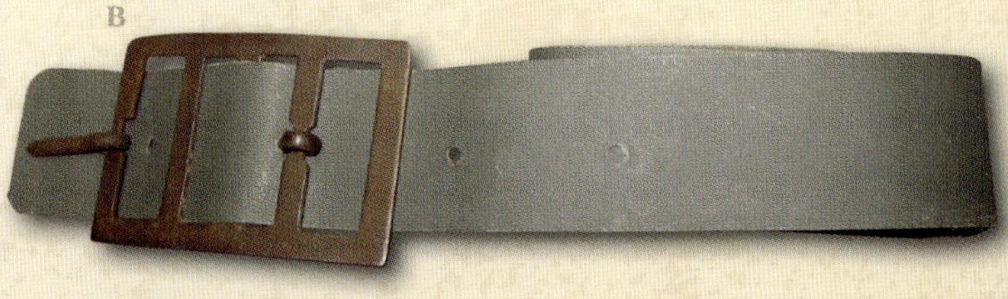

Images A & B A pair of grey-green cardboard ammunition pouches and accompanying belt for use with the Balilla carbine. (*Courtesy Luca Vallebona, Armeria Black Hills*)

BAYONET FROGS

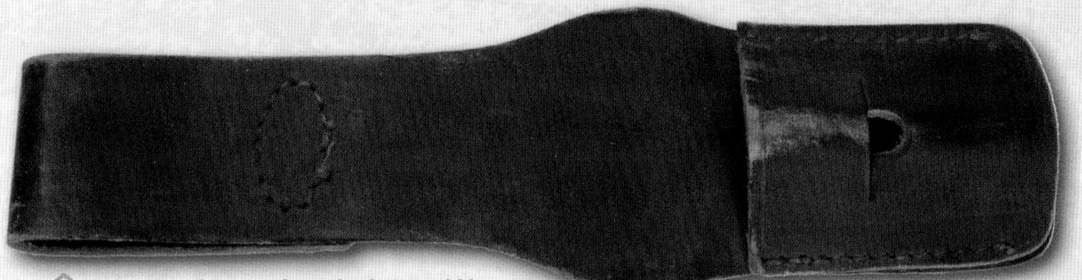

Grey-green bayonet frog; the frog could be used for Model 1891 or Model 1938 bayonets. (*Author's collection*)

Frogs for the Model 1891 bayonets were made of brown leather until World War I; World War II frogs were grey-green. The frogs could also be used with the scabbards of Model 1938 bayonets that had the frog stud; these were the scabbards issued with the Type IIM and Type III fixed blade bayonets. ■

C

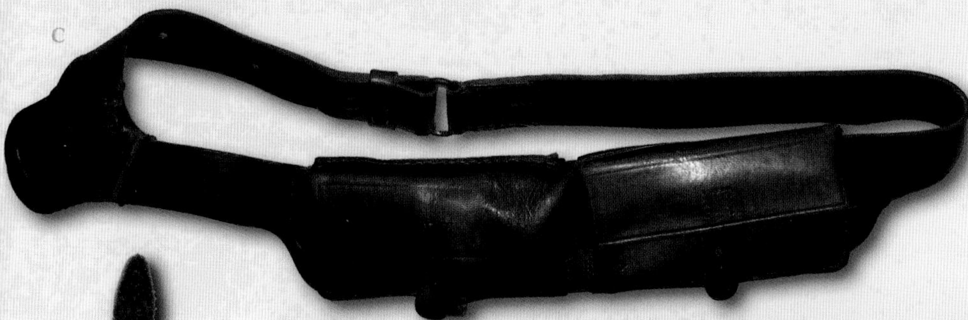

D

E

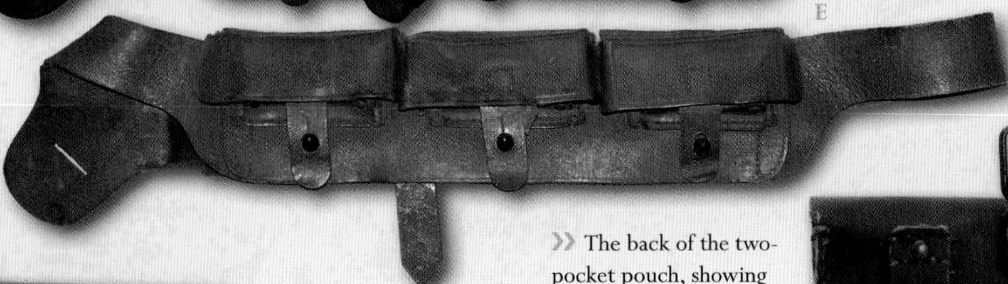

Images C, D & E Black two-pocket pouch and brown and grey-green three-pocket ammunition pouches. A wide variety of styles and colors of ammunition pouches were produced and issued. (*Aleš Kratochvil*)

A two-pocket pouch in grigio verde (grey-green). Each pocket could carry a full box of three clips. (*Author's collection*)

The back of the two-pocket pouch, showing belt loops and harness attachment ring. (*Author's collection*)

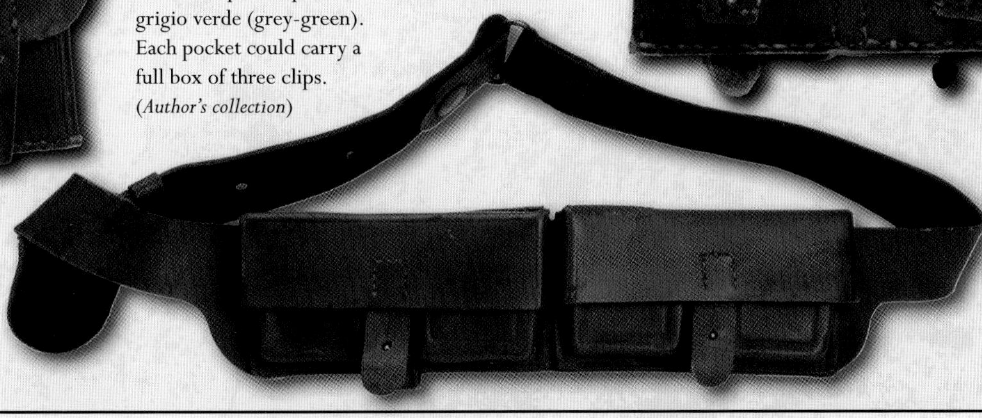

A four-pocket ammunition pouch in grey-green. (*Author's collection*)

CLEANING AND MAINTENANCE TOOLS

MAINTENANCE KIT

Each rifle or carbine was issued with a small maintenance kit consisting of a tin box measuring 113x21x45mm (about 4½x¾x1¾ inches) that included an oiler, a bore brush, and a screwdriver. There were three basic types of oiler: the earliest type was a blued steel cylinder with a bottleneck and a threaded female cap. This was replaced in 1907 by a conical oiler made of an 80% lead alloy; it had a threaded male cap; the inside of the cap had an integral steel rod or needle used to apply the oil. Both types of oiler were about 77mm in length. During World War II these oilers were supplanted or replaced by cylindrical oilers made of black or brown Bakelite, about 68mm long, with a threaded female cap. The Bakelite oilers originally were designed for use with the Beretta Model 38 submachine gun but were also issued with rifles and carbines as available. The screwdriver consisted of a handle and a reversible blade with two different blade widths – 7mm and 4mm. The handle was made of boxwood, walnut or beech and had a brass or steel ferrule. Early handles bore inspector's marks, and early blades were deep blue and had few machine marks; later blades were in the white and showed machine marks. ■

CLEANING RODS

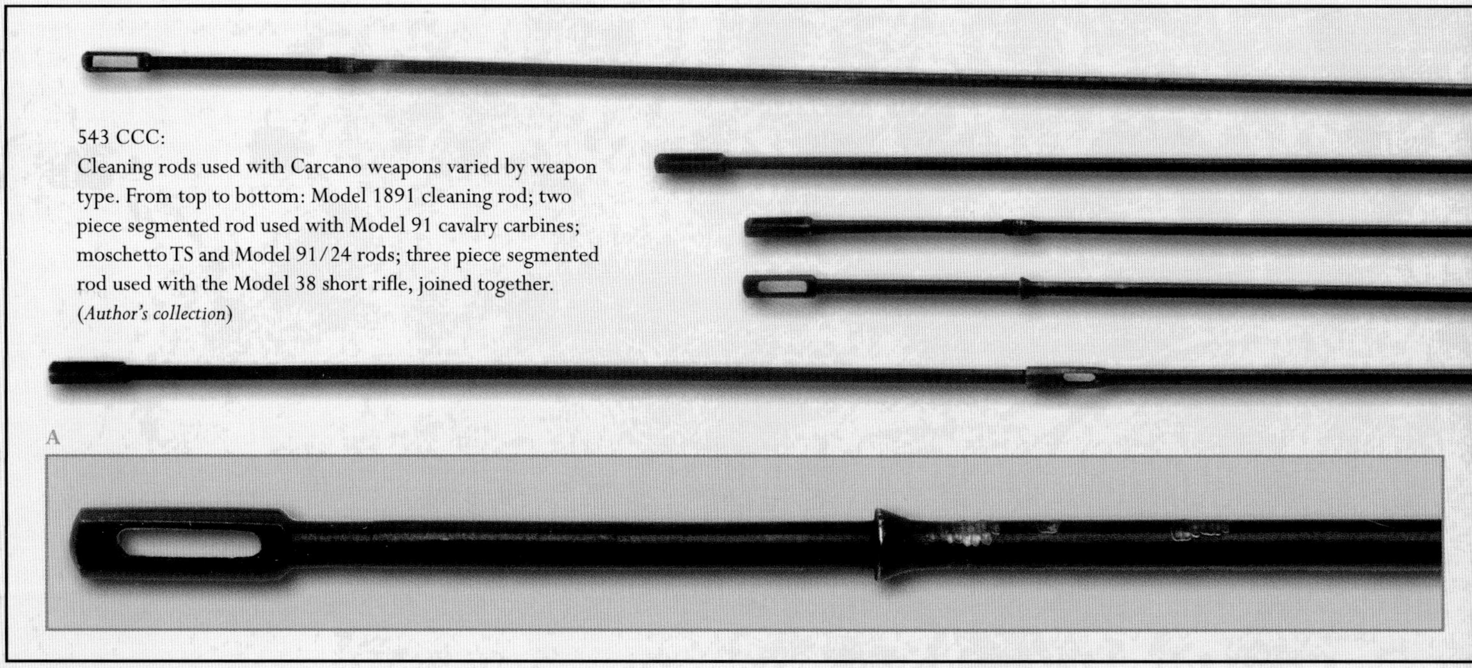

543 CCC:
Cleaning rods used with Carcano weapons varied by weapon type. From top to bottom: Model 1891 cleaning rod; two piece segmented rod used with Model 91 cavalry carbines; moschetto TS and Model 91/24 rods; three piece segmented rod used with the Model 38 short rife, joined together.
(*Author's collection*)

A

There were two basic categories or types of cleaning rods for the Carcano rifle family: one-piece rods and segmented rods. The one-piece rods were used on the Model 1891 rifle, the Model 1941 rifle, and on the TS and 91/24 carbines; the cleaning rod for the Model 1891 rifle was 750mm (29.5 inches) long, that for the Model 41 rifle was 665mm (26.2 inches) long, and that for the TS carbine was 420mm(16.5 inches) long. The rod for the TS and 91/24 carbines had a male thread at one end and a slotted tip at the other end, as well as having a male thread about 65mm (2.5") from the slotted tip that threaded into the front band; a rare variant of this rod was fitted on carbines made by F.N.A. Brescia which instead of the forward threaded portion had a cone-shaped bulge that fit into the front band. Segmented rods were used with the 1891 carbine and the Model 38 rifle; the 1891 carbine had a two-piece rod that measured 475mm (18.7 inches) long when joined together; one segment had a slotted tip at one end and

>> The reversible blade screwdriver issued with Model 1891 weapons. (*Author's collection*)

<< A variety of oilers were used with the Model 1891 rifles and carbines. From left to right: early type blued steel cylinder with a bottle neck and a threaded female cap; two 80% lead alloy conical oilers with threaded male cap; two cylindrical and one semi-conical oilers made of brown and black Bakelite, with threaded female caps. The Bakelite oilers were originally designed for use with the Beretta Model 38 submachine gun, but use was later extended to rifles and carbines as available. (*Courtesy Ruggero Pettinelli*)

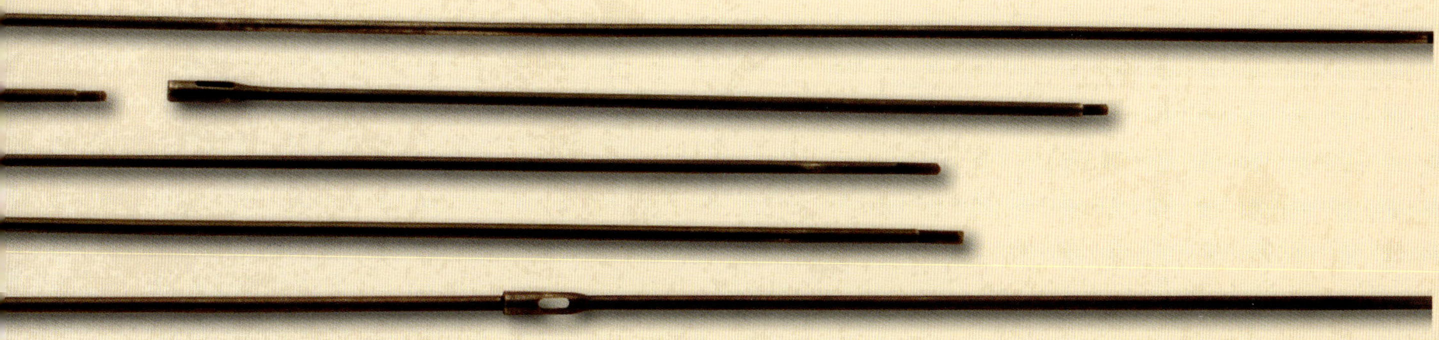

B

Images A & B Comparison of carbine cleaning rods. The right rod is a standard rod with male threads that mated with the front band; the left rod is a rare variant produced by F.N.A. Brescia which replaced the threaded portion with a smooth conical section. (*Author's collection*)

female threads at the other end, and the other segment had male threads at one end and female threads at the other end. The carbine and Model 38 rifle used the same rod segments; the only difference was that the Model 38 had a three-piece rod consisting of the slotted rod and two male/female threaded segments that measured 710mm (30 inches) long when joined together with the slotted segment. Except for the Model 38 rod combination, all other rods were not as long as the barrels they were meant to clean, but the cleaning brush attachment added another 123mm (4.8 inches) to the length of the rods. The brush fit on the female threaded end of the rod; the slotted end of the rod was not meant to be used to hold a cleaning patch, but rather was to allow the blade of a screwdriver to be inserted to enable the rod to be turned in case it became stuck in the barrel. Cleaning patches were held by a brass rod attached in lieu of the brush. ■

MUZZLE PLUG

All rifles and carbines were issued with a muzzle plug made of wood. The plug consisted of a dowel and a larger diameter head; the configuration of the head varied. The muzzle plug was designed to keep foreign matter out of the bore and although it fit snugly, the rifle could be fired with the plug in the bore without causing any damage due to pressure buildup – in an emergency the plug was simply shot out of the bore. ■

SQUAD LEVEL MAINTENANCE ITEMS

Each squad leader carried a small maintenance or armorer's kit consisting of a firing pin spring, firing pin, extractor, ejector spring, and cocking piece nut. All parts except the extractor could be changed by the individual soldier; the extractor could only be replaced by the squad leader or by an armorer. ■

APPENDIX 6: AMMUNITION

Although the preponderance of Italian small arms were chambered for the 6.5x52mm Mannlicher-Carcano round, the Italian supply system had to stock and provide a bewildering variety of ammunition for the broad range of rifles, pistols, submachine guns and machine guns in the inventory. In addition to the ammunition for Italian weapons the supply system also had to stock ammunition for various captured foreign weapons that were included in the Italian inventory and often issued to second-line or colonial units. This appendix briefly profiles the ammunition types used by the weapons covered in this book, but does not address all variations of each individual type. A point to bear in mind is that all muzzle velocities quoted are approximate, as in practice the velocity would vary with cartridge loadings, barrel wear, ambient temperature, and other variables.

AMMUNITION TYPES
PISTOL

Italian 7.65mm ACP pistol cartridge variations; brass case and experimental aluminum case. (*Jon Cohen collection*)

Italian 9mm Corto pistol cartridges. (*Jon Cohen collection*)

9mm Glisenti pistol cartridges; 2 ball variations and a dummy/drill loading. (*Jon Cohen collection*)

Italian 10.4mm revolver cartridge. (*Jon Cohen collection*)

7.65X22 GLISENTI: Information concerning production and use of the 7.65x22 Glisenti round is elusive at best; the round was developed by Glisenti specifically for the Glisenti Model 1906 pistol and adopted on a very limited scale. Dimensionally, the 7.65 Glisenti round was very similar to the German 7.65x21 Parabellum round; the 7.65 Glisenti differed from the Parabellum in that it had a slightly longer shoulder and correspondingly shorter neck, and was about 10% less powerful than the Parabellum. The 102 grain bullet was jacketed in cupro nickel/clad steel (referred to in Italian as maillechort), and the cartridge was Berdan primed. As aptly stated by John L. Moss in a 2009 article in the *Journal of the International Ammunition Association*, there is much confusion and contradiction concerning the 7.65x22 Glisenti round. Indeed, the 2011 book by Marcianó and Simoni devotes considerable space to coverage of the 9mm Glisenti round but virtually none to the 7.65mm round, and although in a specifications table it indicates the caliber of the Glisenti Model 1906 as 7.65 Glisenti, the text states that the Model 1905 was chambered for the 7.65 Parabellum cartridge. This seems to confirm Moss's contention that the 7.65 Glisenti round may have in fact been used only in experimental prototypes, and that production models of the Glisenti pistol were chambered for the 7.65mm Parabellum round. What little evidence exists points to very limited production, possibly by Deutsche Waffen – und Munitionsfabriken in Germany, of a round very similar to the DWM 7.65 Parabellum round.

7.65X25MM BROWNING (.32 ACP): Popularly known as the .32 Automatic Colt Pistol (ACP), the Browning 7.65 mm round was developed by John Moses Browning for use in the FN M1900 semi-auto pistol and was first produced by Fabrique Nationale in 1899. The round was produced in Italy by Fiocchi, SMI, Lèon Beaux, Martignoni, and the Pirotecnico di Bologna. Cases normally were brass with Berdan primers, but wartime examples with aluminum cases were produced on an experimental basis. It is a straight-walled semi-rimmed cartridge with a rounded nose jacketed bullet; the bullet weighs 74 grains and muzzle velocity is in the range of 250-290 m/sec (820 – 950 fps). The 7.65 Browning round was used by a number of Beretta semi-auto pistols.

9X17MM BROWNING SHORT (.380 AUTO): The .380 Auto was developed by John Moses Browning for early blowback pistols and was introduced in 1908 by Colt. It is known by several other names, including the 9mm *corto* (9mm short), in Italian. This type of cartridge was first produced in Italy by Fiocchi in 1918, probably for use in pistols captured from the Austrians, as it was not until 1934 that the Italians adopted a pistol chambered for that round; in Italian service the round was designated the 9M34. During World War II the round was produced by Fiocchi, Lèon Beaux, and the Pirotecnico di Bologna; during the post-war period it was produced by the Pirotecnico di Capua and Martignoni. Cases are brass and are Berdan primed. It is a rimless, straight-walled cartridge with a rounded nose jacketed bullet; bullet weight is 93 grains and muzzle velocity is 300 m/sec (985 fps). The 9mm *corto* was used by Beretta in the Model 1934 pistol.

9X19MM GLISENTI: The 9x19mm Glisenti cartridge was developed to replace the earlier bottlenecked 7.65x22 Glisenti round (quite similar to the 7.65x21.5mm Parabellum round), which was judged to be too weak for Italian military requirements. The 9mm Glisenti round was itself dimensionally identical to the 9x19mm Parabellum cartridge, however, due to the construction of the Glisenti Model 1910 pistol, the Glisenti round was produced as a less powerful round compatible with the stresses that the Glisenti pistol could withstand. The 9mm Glisenti round became the standard Italian military pistol round for a period, and was also used in Italy's earliest submachine guns; although the loadings for the pistol and submachine gun cartridge were different, there is no apparent external distinction or any identifying marks or features between the rounds. With the exception of a lot produced in aluminum in 1930 (or 1935, depending on the source consulted) by the Pirotecnico di Bologna, cartridge cases were brass, with Berdan primers. The bullet, which has a conical rather than a rounded nose, weighs 123 grains and has a muzzle velocity of 295 m/sec (970 fps); it was cupro-nickel jacketed until 1917-1918, when the shortage of materials caused the change to a brass jacket. In addition to the ordinary ball cartridge, several different types of dummy rounds were also produced. The cartridge was produced by Pirotecnico di Bologna, Giulio Fiocchi (Lecco), Pirotecnico di Capua, SMI Campo Tizzoro, Lèon Beaux (Milano), as well as by Western Cartridge Company and Maxim Munitions Corp., USA.

9X19MM PARABELLUM/FIOCCHI 9M38: See entry under Ammunition types (submachine gun)

10.35X22MM ITALIAN ORDNANCE: The 10.35x22 (commonly called the 10.4 Bodeo, but also referred to as the 10.35x20mm) cartridge was developed by Siderurgica Glisenti for the Italian Model 1874 service revolver and was also used in the Model 1889 revolver. The original cartridge, officially designated as the Model 1874 cartridge, was 23mm long, had a slight bottle neck, was made of brass and had a flat base with a rounded edge, and was boxer primed. The propellant was black powder; the lead bullet had a rounded nose and weighed 180 grains. Adoption of the Bodeo revolver in 1889 led to modification of the cartridge, known as the Model 1890. The caliber remained unaltered, as did the brass cartridge case, which however was shortened to 21mm to accommodate the new smokeless powder propellant, and was Berdan primed. The bullet itself was brass jacketed and weighed 175 grains and developed a muzzle velocity of 252 m/sec (825 fps). In 1899 another version appeared, with slight changes to the base. Around 1906-1908 the bullet was crimped at three places. Blank and dummy versions were produced. Because the Model 1889 rovolver was used by the *Carabinieri* until the 1950s, the round continued to be manufactured until that time. The round was manufactured by Pirotecnico di Torino, Pirotecnico di Bologna, Pirotecnico di Capua, Lèon Beaux, and Giulio Fiocchi. ■

AMMUNITION TYPES RIFLE

6MM FLOBERT (.22 BB CAP): This cartridge was not used by the Italian military per se, but was used for target shooting with a variety of military-style rifles. It was a rimmed cartridge with a case similar to that of a .22 short, but only half the length. There was no powder charge, the sole propellant being the primer itself. The bullet weighed only 19 grains and had a range of only about 20 meters. Although production data are imprecise, it is known to have been produced by the Pirotecnico di Bologna and Fiocchi, and production is believed to have continued until the end of World War II.

6.5X52MM MANNLICHER-CARCANO: The Italian 6.5x52mm cartridge, designated the M91/95, is a rimless, necked cartridge developed by Luigi Scotti, the chief technician at the Pirotecnico di Bologna (Bologna Ammunition Plant) and officially adopted for use in the new service rifle in April 1890. The M91/95 served in both World Wars as the standard Italian military cartridge for rifles and machine guns. The original cartridge was a bottle necked rimless brass case 52.5mm long with an 11.45mm base. The bullet had a rounded ogive, was 6.5mm in diameter, and consisted of a lead core with a cupro-nickel jacket. The cartridge was Berdan primed, and the propellant charge was balistite granules. In 1895 a groove was added to the base of the rim and the markings, which previously had been stamped in negative, were now in relief; the modified cartridge was designated the *modello 91-95*. In 1896 the balistite propellant was replaced by a new double base nitro-cellulose propellant called solenite, developed by the Fontana Liri military ammunition plant. Balistite consisted of equal parts of cotton colloid and nitroglycerin, while solenite consisted of one third nitroglycerin and a two-thirds mixture of trinitrocellulose and dinitrocellulose. Until 1915 cartridges loaded with solenite were marked with an X on the base of the rim in addition to the year of manufacture; after 1915 the practice of using the X was discontinued as all ammunition was by then being manufactured using solenite. The case was normally made of brass, but during World War II – probably from late-1941 – the Bologna and Capua government ammunition plants, SMI, BPD and Lèon Beaux all produced lacquered steel cases. The standard ball load was a 162 grain round nose full metal jacket bullet, with a muzzle velocity of 700 m/sec (2297 fps).

In addition to standard ball ammunition, other ammunition types included special loading for accuracy testing, proof, blank, blank for machine gun, riot control, propulsive round for rifle grenades, reduced range, frangible, Magistri frangible, reduced charge, dummy, armor piercing, experimental spitzer, tracer, tracer-incendiary, armor piercing incendiary, semi-armor piercing incendiary, explosive piercing, time delay and Bts incendiary.

The 6.5mm round was produced by the Pirotecnico di Bologna (1890-1944), Pirotecnico di Capua (1893-1945), Società Metallurgica Italiana (1912-1945), Bombrini Parodi Delfino (1931-1945), and by Lèon Beaux (1935-1945).

7.35X51MM: The 7.35x51mm round was developed by Colonel Giuseppe Mainardi in 1935 in collaboration with SMI CampoTizzoro and BPD; the round entered service in 1938 for use with the new M38 short rifle variant of the Carcano. Due to its caliber and case dimensions, the round is sometimes cited as a precursor of the modern assault rifle intermediate round. The cartridge is a rimless, necked cartridge, and the bullet is a semi-spitzer type, more pointed than the 6.5x52mm Carcano, but not as pointed as a conventional spitzer. In addition to standard ball ammunition, other types included special loadings for accuracy testing, proof, blank, riot control, reduced range, dummy and frangible.

Essentially, the 7.35mm round was a reworked 6.5mm round; the case was the same case whose shoulder profile was slightly altered to accommodate the neck for the larger 7.35mm bullet. The bullet itself weighed 128 grains and had a semi-spitzer shape, with a somewhat flattened tip. The bullet was part lead and part aluminum; the bottom half was lead and the top half was aluminum, which resulted in increased terminal effectiveness as the round tumbled once it hit flesh. Until mid-1939 the bullet was jacketed in cupro-nickel, after which it was jacketed in gilding metal (referred to in Italian as tombac). Muzzle velocity varied depending on the weapon type; muzzle velocity for the *fucile 38* was 760 m/s (1494 fps), and for the carbines was about 740 m/s (2428 fps).

The 7.35mm cartridge was produced by SMI, BPD, and by the government ammunition factories at Bologna and Capua. Fullscale production of the round was halted in 1940, although limited production continued until at least 1944. ■

Some uncommon 6.5mm Carcano cartridge variations; 2 different multi-ball guard loads, 4 different frangible gallery loads, and 2 reloadable gallery cartridges. (*Jon Cohen collection*)

6.5mm Carcano blank cartridge variations; Magistri type in a steel case, Magistri with a brass case, orange wood bullet, red wood bullet, plain wood bullet, roll crimp, rosette crimp. (*Jon Cohen collection*)

Some uncommon 7.35mm Carcano cartridge variations; dummy/drill, frangible-practice, multi-ball guard. (*Jon Cohen collection*)

7.35mm Carcano cartridge variations; gilding-metal ball, cupro-nickel ball, roll crimp blank, plain wood bullet blank, orange wood bullet blank. (*Jon Cohen collection*)

A Finnish 7.35mm Carcano short-range practice cartridge. (*Jon Cohen collection*)

Four variations of 6.5mm Carcano ball cartridges. (*Jon Cohen collection*)

Three variations of 6.5mm Carcano dummy/drill cartridges. (*Jon Cohen collection*)

6.5mm Carcano loading variations; fluted-bullet dummy/drill in a steel case, non-fluted dummy/drill in a brass case, fluted-bullet dummy/drill in a brass case, gallery-practice, tracer, armor-piercing. (*Jon Cohen collection*)

AMMUNITION TYPES SUBMACHINE GUN

« Italian 9mm Parabellum pistol and sub-machine gun cartridge variations. (*Jon Cohen collection*)

9X19MM FIOCCHI M38:

The Fiocchi 9x19mm M38 cartridge, also known as the 9mm SuperFiocchi and 9M38, was developed specifically for the Beretta MAB submachine gun. Dimensionally identical to the 9mm Parabellum, it had a hotter powder charge, resulting in a considerably higher muzzle velocity (450 m/sec) than the Parabellum (400 m/sec) with a 115 grain bullet. Depending on a number of variables, chief among them barrel length, muzzle velocities developed by the Fiocchi M38 round ranged from 20 to 70 m/sec (66 fps to 230 fps) higher than the corresponding Parabellum round; the lower value applied to barrels about 200-220mm long, while the higher value was registered with barrels about 320mm long.

In addition to being produced by Fiocchi, the 9M38 was produced by the Pirotecnico di Bologna, Pirotecnico di Capua, Lèon Beaux, SMI, BPD and Martignoni. ■

AMMUNITION TYPES MACHINE GUN

« 8mm Breda cartridge loading variations; dummy/drill, Magistri blank in a steel case, Magistri blank in a brass case, tracer, armor-piercing in steel and brass cases, and a white-phosphorous observation cartridge. (*Jon Cohen collection*)

» 8mm Breda ball cartridge variations. (*Jon Cohen collection*)

8X59MM BREDA

The 8x59mm Breda cartridge was developed for Italian machine guns being developed in the mid-1930s in order to replace the 6.5x52mm rifle cartridge used by Italian machine guns then in service. The cartridge was introduced in 1935 for use in the FIAT Model 1935 and Breda Model 37 machine guns. Dimensionally it is quite similar to the German 8mm Mauser (7.92x57mm) cartridge, but has a rebated rim. The bullet itself is a 210 grain spitzer type, and can be either copper clad or nickel clad steel. Muzzle velocity for ball ammunition is 790 m/sec (2,600 fps). Cases were brass, but beginning in 1941 could be either brass or lacquered steel. The cartridge was available in ball, armor piercing (white tip), observation/incendiary (blue or black tip), tracer (red or green tip), blank (some with black tip) and dummy. The cartridge was manufactured by the Pirotecnico di Capua, Lèon Beaux, SMI, and BPD. ■

AMMUNITION SPECIAL USE

8MM BRIXIA MORTAR PROPULSUION CARTRIDGE

An 8mm Brixia mortar propulsion cartridge. (*Jon Cohen collection*)

The 8mm Brixia mortar propulsuion cartridge was specially designed as an ignition cartridge for use with the 45mm Brixia Model 35 light mortar. The round was hand fed into the breech of the mortar and was fired by a trigger.

6.5X54MM MANNLICHER-SCHÖNAUER (6.5 GREEK)

6.5mm Mannlicher-Schönauer cartridge. (*Jon Cohen collection*)

This Greek military cartridge was designed in 1900 and was used in the Greek 1903 Mannlicher bolt action rifle and Hotchkiss M1926 light machine gun. It had a 156 grain bullet with a muzzle velocity of 750 m/sec (2460 fps). The cartridge was not manufactured in Italy, but significant stocks of this ammunition appear to have been captured from the Greeks by both the Italians and Germans.

FOREIGN CALIBERS

8X27R RAST & GASSER

8mm Austrian Gasser revolver cartridge, made in Italy. (*Jon Cohen collection*)

The straight brass case had a 3.7 grain load and was Berdan primed; the 120 grain flat nose bullet was jacketed in gilding metal; muzzle velocity was about 240 m/sec (790 fps). In 1918 the cartridge was produced in Italy by Fiocchi for use in weapons captured from Austria-Hungary.

7.5X54 MAS

French 7.5mm Model 1929 cartridge. (*Jon Cohen collection*)

This cartridge was the round used with the captured French Chatellerault Mle 24/29 light machine gun, as well as in the wing-mounted machine guns of the Dewoitine D.520 fighter aircraft used to a limited extent by the Italian *Regia Aeronautica*. The 138 grain bullet achieved a muzzle velocity of 823 m/sec (2700 fps). This round was not manufactured in Italy; only French origin captured stocks were used.

Typical German 7.92mm ball and Austrian dummy/drill cartridges, similar to what would have been used in Italian service. (*John Cohen collection*)

7.92X57MM MAUSER

Also known or referred to as the 8x57mm or 8x57 IS, this cartridge adopted in 1905 was the standard German rifle and machine gun service round during both World Wars I and II. The case, of either brass or steel, is a rimless bottleneck type; the spitzer bullet weighed 197 grains and developed a muzzle velocity of 760 m/sec (2493 fps). Under German occupation after September 1943 the cartridge was manufactured by SMI with both brass and steel cases. ■

8mm Maroszek armor-piercing cartridge, used by Italy in captured Polish anti-tank rifles. (*Jon Cohen collection*)

8X107MM MAROSZEK

This unusual and powerful 8mm cartridge was used in the Polish Maroszek anti-tank rifle that was issued on a limited scale to Italian forces during World War II. The large cartridge case was loaded with 172 grains of powder and enabled the bullet to reach a muzzle velocity of 1275 m/sec (4183 fps). The bullet itself had a tungsten core and was able to penetrate 22-25mm of special steel at 100 meters. Most, if not all, of this type of ammunition used by the Italians was of Polish or German manufacture and although SMI is known to have developed the machinery necessary to produce this round, actual production by SMI has not been confirmed. ■

9x23 Austrian Steyr cartridges. (*Jon Cohen collection*)

9X23MM STEYR

Italy received a significant number of 9mm Steyr-Hahn pistols as war reparations from Austria-Hungary following World War I; the number of pistols in the Italian inventory was large enough to prompt production of the 9mm Steyr cartridge in Italy by at least three manufacturers: the Pirotecnico di Bologna, Fiochhi, and Lèon Beaux. The straight brass case was Berdan primed and had a 6.2 grain load; the 115 grain bullet was jacketed with copper washed brass or cupro-nickel. Muzzle velocity was 320 m/sec (1050 fps). ■

7.63X25MM MAUSER

In 1889 the Italian Navy adopted the Mauser C96 semi-automatic pistol, chambered for the 7.63mm Mauser Parabellum (.30 Mauser Automatic) round. The cartridge was based on the 1893 Borchardt 7.65x25mm cartridge; in turn, the 7.63 Mauser was the basis for the Soviet 7.62x25mm Tokarev cartridge. Likely due to the onset of World War I and the impracticality, if not impossibility, of obtaining ammunition from Germany, Fiocchi began to manufacture this round in 1916, or possibly earlier. The Fiocchi cartridge was a bottle necked cartridge

7.63mm Mauser pistol cartridge, made in Italy. (*Jon Cohen collection*)

with a Berdan primed brass case with a 6.63 grain load; the 85 grain bullet was round nosed and jacketed in cupro-nickel clad steel. Muzzle velocity was 440 m/sec (1444 fps). ■

French 7.65mm pistol cartridges. (*Jon Cohen collection*)

7.65X20MM LONGUE

The 7.65mm Longue cartridge was based on the U.S. .30 caliber Pedersen cartridge and was used in the French Model 1935 pistol and the MAT submachine gun. It was a straight rimless cartridge with an 85 grain bullet; muzzle velocity was 360 m/sec (1181 fps). The Italians used this ammunition with their captured MAT submachine guns, but did not manufacture the cartridge themselves. ■

8mm Austrian Roth-Steyr pistol cartridge, made in Italy. (*Jon Cohen collection*)

8X18.5MM ROTH-STEYR M7

Only one weapon, the Roth-Steyr M1907 pistol, was ever chambered for this cartridge. The case is a straight brass case loaded with 4 grains; the 113 grain jacketed bullet has a muzzle velocity of 335 m/sec (1100 fps). To supply the ammunition necessary for the M1907 pistol in Italian service Fiocchi began production of the round in Italy as early as 1918; Lèon Beaux production followed at a later, undetermined, date. ■

8mm Mannlicher ball cartridges, made in Italy. Ball cartridge on the left, orange wood bullet blank on the right. (*Jon Cohen collection*)

8X50MMR MANNLICHER

The Italians received huge quantities of Mannlicher Model 1895 rifles and Schwarzlose Model 07/12 machine guns chambered for the 8x50mmR Mannlicher round as war reparations from Austria-Hungary at the end of World War I. It is believed that large quantities of 8x50R ammunition were acquired along with the weapons. These weapons were later issued in large numbers to Italian colonial troops; to ensure an adequate supply of ammunition the Italians themselves produced it beginning in the early 1920s. Cartridge cases were brass, loaded with solenite, and were Berdan primed; the 245 grain bullet had rounded ogive, a lead core, and jacketed in cupro nickel/clad steel or gilding metal, and muzzle velocity was 620 m/sec (2034 fps). Manufacturers included the Pirotecnico di Bologna, SMI, and BPD. ■

8mm French Lebel cartridge, made in Italy. (*Jon Cohen collection*)

8X50MMR LEBEL

A number of French origin weapons used by the Italians in both World Wars were chambered for this cartridge. It was a groundbreaking cartridge as it was the first smokeless cartridge to be adopted by any country. The two most widely used versions of this cartridge were the Balle D and the later Balle M; the Balle D had a 198 grain solid brass boat-tailed spitzer bullet, while the Balle M had a 232 grain jacketed lead core bullet. Muzzle velocities were 607 m/sec (1991 fps) for the Balle D and 488 m/sec (1601 fps) for the Balle M. Production of the Lebel round was undertaken in Italy in the 1920s and 1930s by the Pirotecnico di Bologna and SMI; the rounds produced in Italy had brass cases loaded with solenite, and a 197 grain boat-tailed lead core spitzer bullet clad in cupro-nickel clad steel. ■

MANNLICHER-CARCANO CLIP TYPES & VARIATIONS

The basic clip used for both the 6.5mm and 7.35mm cartridges was a simple clip that held six cartridges and could be inserted either end up into the rifle. Clips were made either of brass or of steel that was nickel coated, zinc coated, tin coated, or blued; a rare variation was made of stainless steel by the Pirotecnico di Bologna in 1940. Dimensions of the clips were 64.7 mm high (2.55"), 32.2 mm wide (1.27"), and 13.1 mm at the base (0.52"). Each side of the clip had a very large opening 44.2mm (1.74") by 17.8mm (0.7"), so that in effect the sides of the clip formed a rectangular frame. The cartridges were held in place by ribs pressed into the insides of the upper and lower side edges of the frame; the rib on the lower edge of the clip holds the rim of the cartridge, while the rib on the upper edge exerts a slight amount of pressure on the cartridge case to keep it in place. Markings on the outside bottom edge of the base reflected the inspector's code (on the left), and the producing factory and year (on the right); the presence of an X mark on the center connecting rib indicated that the clip had been used and recycled. Manufacturer's codes were B for Bologna, S-B for Società Italiana Generale per Munizioni e Armi (a subcontractor for Bologna), C for Capua, M for Milano, SMI or SMJ (on the left, in lieu of an inspector's code) for Campo Tizzoro, L.B.C. for Lèon Beaux, (on the left, in lieu of the inspector's code) LP for La Precisa of Teano (on the left, in lieu of the inspector's code),

Carcano clip markings, from top to bottom: RR 1936; RR 1935; M.U.G. 1942; LP 1950; LP 1935; LL 1936; INUF 1942; INUF 1943. (*Courtesy Ruggero Pettinelli*)

A six-round Carcano steel clip; although the most common type of clip was the steel clip, brass clips were also used to a limited extent. (*Author's collection*)

Images A & B Full 6.5mm clip, (A), and 7.35mm clip, (B). (*Author's collection*)

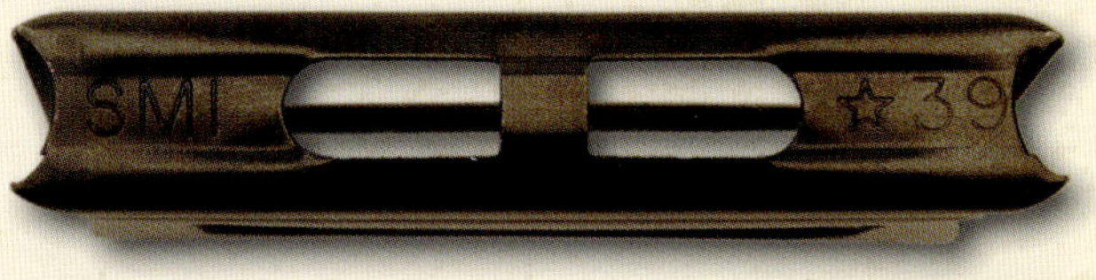

Markings on a 1939 SMI clip; placement and style of these markings are fairly typical. (*Author's collection*)

SMI 1936 brass clip and SMI 1939 steel clip. (*Author's collection*)

BPD (on the left) for Bombrini-Parodi-Delfino in Colleferro; codes for unknown manufacturers were INUF, LL and MUG. After the war, some clips were manufactured in the United States; these are recognizable because they are steel, lack any markings, and have openings on the sides that are smaller than those on the Italian clips.

A modified clip was developed for weapons chambered for the 7.92x57mm round; the clip was configured like the 6.5mm and 7.35mm clips, but was somewhat shorter and its ends were more angled than the standard Italian clips; due to the larger case of the 7.92 round, the clip had a capacity of only five rounds. A rarely encountered variant had a rib in the center opening; the rib looks very much like a stylized S rune associated with the SS, but this should in no way be construed or lead to the conclusion that either the clips or the 7.92mm Carcanos were issued to the SS.

Charger clips for the Breda Model 30 light machine gun held 10 rounds and were either brass or blued steel; they are easily recognizable because of a large sheet metal handle on the top of the charger. ■

INSPECTOR CODES ON CLIPS

AA Aldo Adamo; BP Boschesi Pietro; CA Cavalli Alfredo; LN Leggiatore Nicola; PN Pasarello Vincenzo; RM Rubino Mario; SL Scotti Luigi; ZG Zangari Gaetano. Unidentified inspector codes: ES, FP, LN, TR (Capua); S-B (possibly Scotti- Bologna), TM (Bologna); RR (possibly Milano).

A

B

Dull finish steel clip marked RR 36; the identity of RR remains unknown. (*Author's collection*)

Carcano clip markings, from top to bottom: SMI 1936; SMJ 1914 with X on connecting rib indicating that the clip has been recycled; BPD 1934 (brass); L.B.C. 1934; SL, Bologna 1894; S-B, Bologna 1918; E.S., Capua 1897 with X on connecting rib indicating that the clip had been recycled. (*Courtesy Ruggero Pettinelli*)

AMMUNITION PACKAGING

A 1917 box of Fiocchi 9mm Glisenti ammunition used with the Villar Perosa submachine gun. (*Museo della Meccanica e del Cuscinetto-Villar Perosa, via Renzo Turco*)

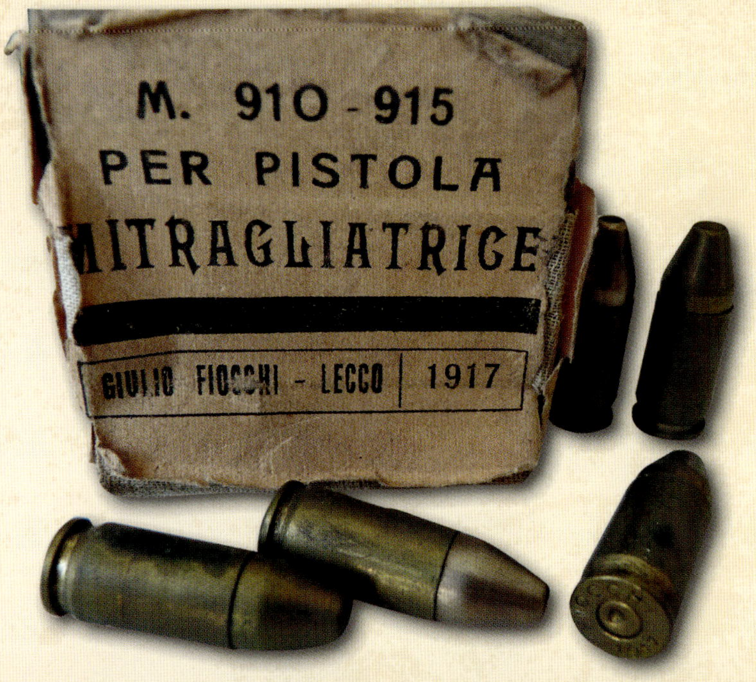

SMI Fornaci di Barga package, 1936. The label indicates use for Model 91 weapons and for machine guns. (*Author's collection*)

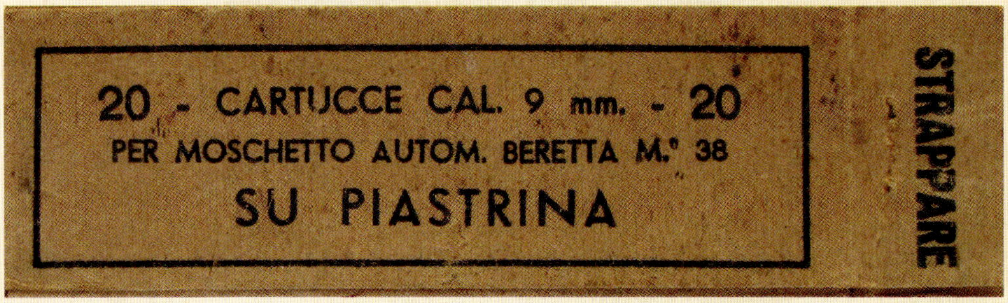

This box of 9mm submachine gun ammunition contains 20 rounds in two 10-round stripper clips. The word STRAPPARE on the tab indicates a pull or tear-off tab. (*Courtesy Ruggero Pettinelli*)

Carcano clips – both the 6.6mm and 7.35mm varieities – were packaged in cardboard boxes that each held three clips, for a total of eighteen rounds per box. The boxes measured 82mm high x 72mm wide x 44mm deep (about 3¼x2¾x1¾ inches). There were many variations in the coloring and construction of the boxes; colors included buff, brown, or greenish brown, but early boxes could be salmon or light orange. The top of the front edge had a semicircular area cut out to make opening the top of the box easier, and the top of the box itself had a front flap, or tongue, that folded down into the front of the body of the box; stapled to the front flap was a piece of cloth or hessian tape, or exceptionally, a piece of heavy string, which when pulled up would pull up and open the top flap. The front of the boxes were printed with information indicating the manufacturing establishment, the number of clips in the box (always 3), a description of the cartridges, the lot number and date of manufacture, and the type of powder in the cartridge. The information typically was printed directly on the cardboard itself, although in some instances a printed label was glued on the face of the box. This type of packaging continued well into the post-war years.

Packaging for pistol ammunition varied greatly by manufacturer and by type of ammunition. The size of the packaging was commensurate with the particular type of round (7.65mm, 9mm *corto*, 9mm Parabellum), and usually indicated the manufacturer, year of manufacture, ammunition caliber or type of weapon which the ammunition was for, and number of rounds in the box; other information could include the lot number and propellant type. Most

The inside of some boxes such as this 1936 Fornaci di Barga box were divided into three compartments. (*Author's collection*)

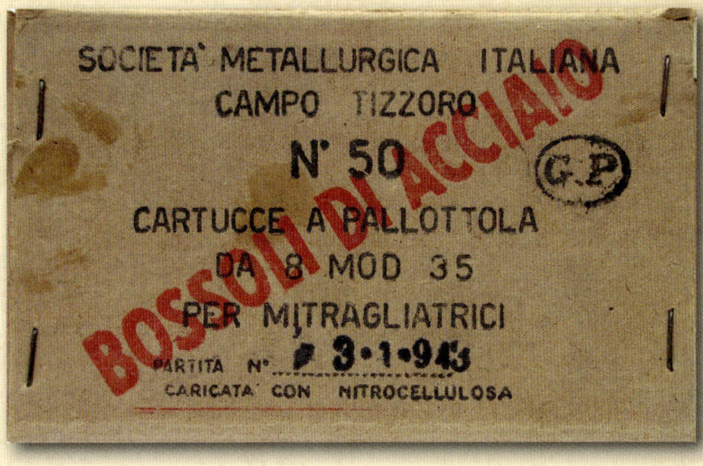

Fifty rounds of 8mm Breda machine gun ammunition. The BOSSOLI DI ACCIAO stamped in red indicates steel cased ammunition. (*Courtesy Ruggero Pettinelli*)

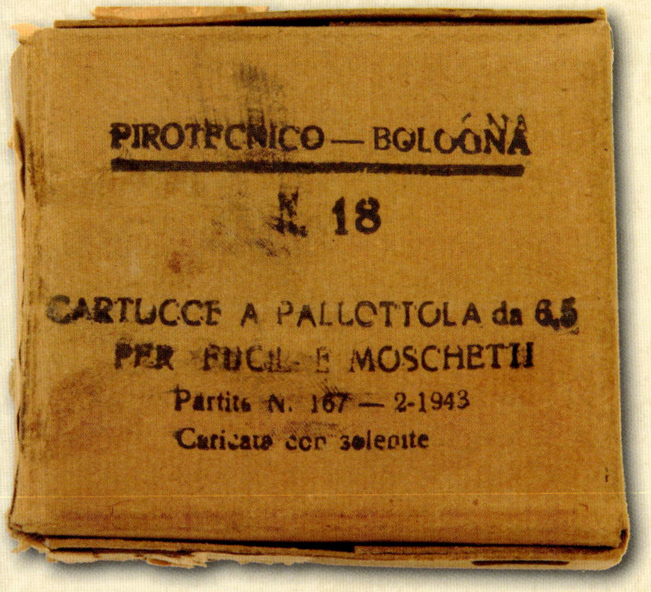

A package of 6.5mm cartridges from Pirotecnico di Bologna, 1943. The label on this package is unusual for three reasons: first, rather than indicating that it contains three clips, the information specified 18 rounds; second, the information is printed along the longer axis of the box rather than along its shorter axis, and third, the information is printed on the back of the box rather than on the front. (*Author's collection*)

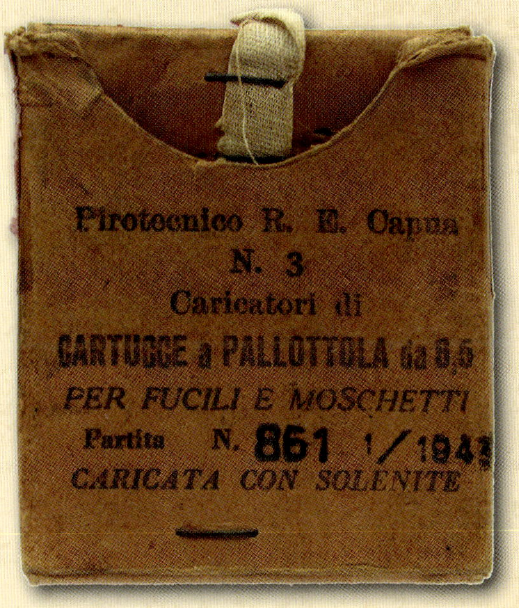

Capua package, 1943 6.5mm ball ammunition. (*Courtesy Ruggero Pettinelli*)

packages had the ammunition printed directly on the carboard box itself, although some had printed labels affixed to the boxes. Depending on the manufacturer, year, and type of ammunition, boxes could be white, grey, buff, brown, green, or blue or have a red label with white lettering or a grey label with black lettering. The 9mm 9M38 ammunition intended for the Beretta submachine guns was packaged in 10-round stripper clips, two stripper clips to a box.

Breda 8mm ammunition was packaged in buff colored cardboard boxes containing fifty rounds; the boxes were imprinted with information indicating the number of rounds (50) manufacturer, year of production, type of propellant, and lot number. Boxes containing steel cased ammunition were prominently marked with red lettering that indicated steel cases.

Ammunition for the Breda Model 37 machine gun was carried in a chest. Two different types of chest are reported, one which carried fifteen 20-round feed trays and one which carried twelve 20-round trays. The larger chest weighed 16.1 kg (35.5 lbs) with its full ammunition complement. The smaller capacity chest measuring 240mm (9.45") x 120mm (4.75") x 295mm (11.6") was very well made of wood and had metal reinforcing along the corners and edges. It was fitted with two fairly comfortable leather carrying handles affixed to the top of the chest and was divided into three compartments, each holding four 20-round feed trays. The feed trays themselves measured 265mm (10.4") by 90mm (3.5") and weighed .85 kg (1.85 lbs) loaded with 20 cartridges. ■

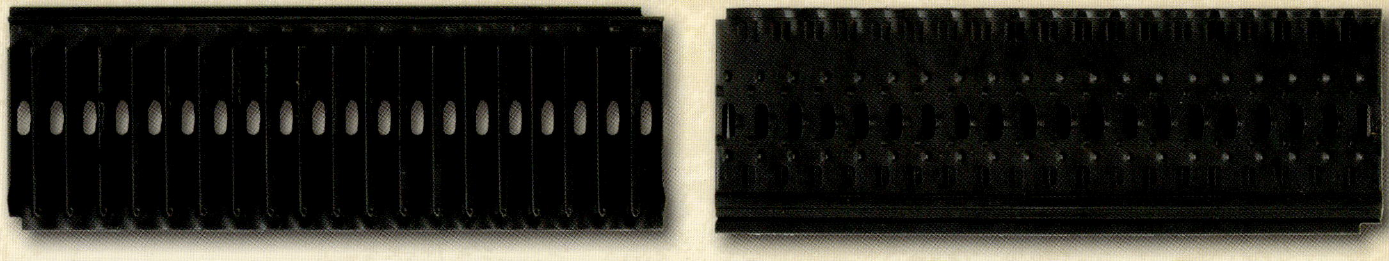

Top (left) and bottom (right) of 8mm Breda Model 37 feed trays. *(Author's collection)*

Breda ammunition chest with top opened viewed from above showing the three compartments for feed trays. *(Author's collection)*

Ammunition chest for 8mm Breda feed trays. The chest is divided into three compartments and holds a total of twelve 20-round feed trays. *(Author's collection)*

HEADSTAMPS

The following are the more common and most frequently encountered headstamp markings, but other variations of markings and placement can also be encountered.

PIROTECNICO DI BOLOGNA: Bologna headstamps do not reflect the caliber; the chief inspector's initials (surname and name) are at 12 o'clock, and the letter B (for Bologna) and the last two digits of the year of manufacture are at 6 o'clock; the B and the digits are separated by a dash.

PIROTECNICO DI CAPUA: Capua headstamps do not reflect the caliber; the chief inspector's initials (surname and name) are at 12 o'clock, and the letter C (for Capua) and the last two digits of the year of manufacture are at 6 o'clock; the C and the digits are separated by a dash. Post-war headstamps vary considerably and may contain the letters DCE at 12 o'clock, may lack the inspector's initials, or may be marked PEC or PECA (for Pirotecnico Esercito Capua).

PIROTECNICO DI TORINO: Torino headstamps do not reflect the caliber; the chief inspector's initials (surname and name) are at 12 o'clock, and the letter T (for Torino) and the last two digits of the year of

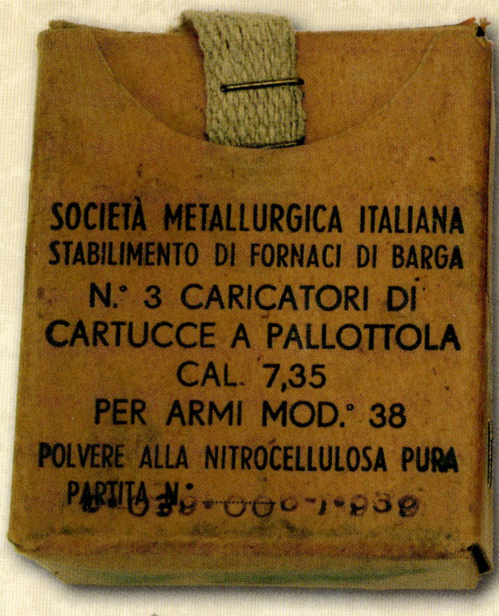

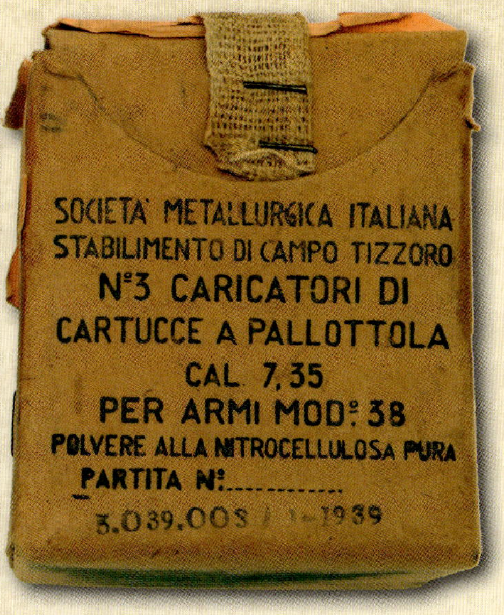

Two boxes of 7.35mm ammunition from two different SMI plants. The box on the left is from Fornaci di Barga, that on the right from Campo Tizzoro. Note the slight variations in lettering size and styles. (*Author's collection*)

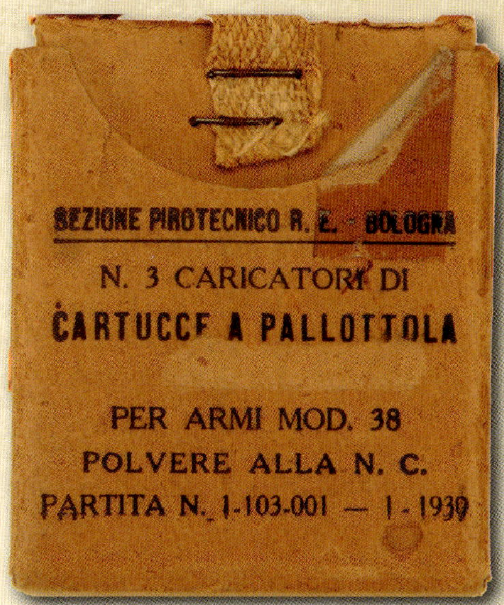

A 1939 package of ammunition from Bologna; for some reason, the caliber marking has been removed from the label. (*Author's collection*)

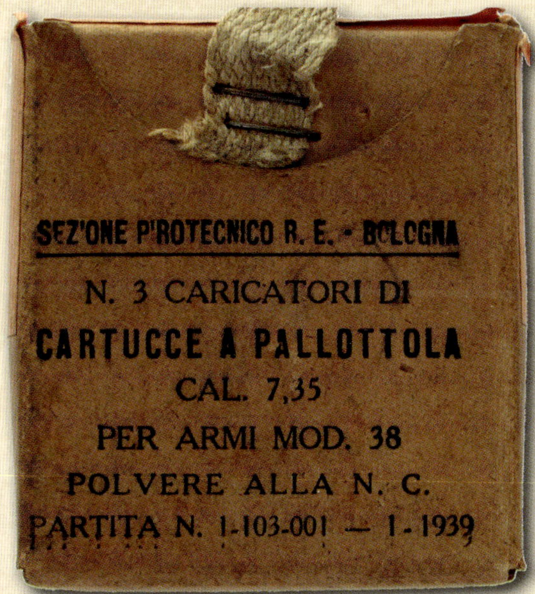

Bologna package 7.35mm ball ammunition, 1939. (*Author's collection*)

This factory sealed box of ammunition seems to have escaped the printing step to identify its contents as 6.5mm. The blank face of the box is shown, but the rear similarly is blank, as are the top and sides. (*Author's collection*)

manufacture are at 6 o'clock; the T and the digits are separated by a dash.

Lèon Beaux: Generally, LB or LBC at 12 o'clock, and date at 6 o'clock. After 1952 the caliber is also shown.

BOMBRINI PARODI DELFINO: Generally, BPD at 12 o'clock, and a two or three digit year of manufacture at 6 o'clock. Post-war headstamps (since 1952) also bear caliber markings.

GIULIO FIOCCHI: There is a wide variety of Fiocchi headstamps. The initials GFL, G.F.L., G*F*L*, G. FIOCCHI LECCO, or FIOCCHI are used in various positions to indicate the manufacturer; the date may be in two, three or four digits; caliber may or may not be indicated.

LA PRECISA: No information.

MARTIGNONI CARTUCCE: MCM at 12 o'clock, caliber (various styles of designation) at 6 o'clock.

SOCIETÀ METALLURGICA ITALIANA: Generally, the marking SMI or S.M.I. appears at the 12 o'clock position, and the date – generally the last three digits – at 6 o'clock. Variations can be encountered, especially after 1952 when the caliber is also indicated. ■

AMMUNITION MANUFACTURERS

The following list of manufacturers is believed to be complete, although details concerning physical locations and current use or status of the production facilities in some cases have proven impossible to determine. ■

GOVERNMENT AMMUNITION PRODUCTION FACILITIES

LABORATORIO PIROTECNICO DI BOLOGNA: The Laboratorio Pirotecnico di Bologna was built sometime around the year 1862 in an area south of the city center. Over the course of time the area became a rather large military complex, generally bounded by Viale Enrico Panzacchi to the north, Viale Castiglione to the east, Via delle Rose and Via Codivilla to the south, and Via San Mamolo to the west. In 1883, the Pirotenico employed 381 workers of whom 119 were women; by 1903 the census showed an increase to 1107 workers. The facility expanded exponentially to meet the need for ammunition in World War I and the labor force grew to 12,000, most of whom were women. In the late 1930s some thought was given to relocating the Pirotecnico for safety and security reasons as by now the premises were in close proximity to civilian housing and any explosion would be dangerous, and from a military security standpoint it was thought that the nearby bell tower of the church of San Michele in Bosco, which was a well known landmark, could provide an easy target reference point for bomber aircraft. However, with the beginning of the war these plans were abandoned. After the armistice was signed between Italy and the Allies in September 1943 the Pirotecnico came under German control and continued to produce ammunition until late-1944 when it was heavily damaged by Allied bombing; the surviving machinery was taken over by Baschieri & Pellagri, who resumed production at another location near Bologna, possibly at Via del Frullo in Marano del Castelnaso, west of Bologna. On 21 April 1945 the Pirotecnico was occupied by local partisan forces. In 1947, the former Pirotecnico premises assumed a new role as the ORMEC (Officina Riparazione Mezzi Corazzati, or Armored Vehicle Repair Workshops), and in 1978 became the Sta.Ve.Co. (Stabilimento Veicoli Corazzati, or Armored Vehicle Facility), retaining its role as an armored vehicle repair center. In 1990, its designation and function were again changed as the STAMOTO (Stabilimento Materiale per la Motorizzazione, or Vehicle Material Facility). The premises were closed as a military installation in 2003; as of 2013 the hope was to develop the area for residential or commercial use.

LABORATORIO PIROTECNICO DI CAPUA: The Laboratorio Pirotecnico di Capua, located in the old castle of Carlo V (Charles the Fifth) in Capua on the right bank of the Volturno River, is also known simply as the Pirotecnico di Capua. The main entrance to the Pirotecnico is on Via Appia. The origins of the premises occupied by the Pirotecnico date back to 1542 and to the fortress designed by Gian Giacomo dell'Acaya for Carlo V. Sometime around 1865 construction began on the site for a facility to produce ammunition for small arms and artillery. The facility produced ammunition through both World Wars; in 1943 part of the premises were destroyed by Allied bombing. The facility resumed production in 1946; ammunition produced at Capua included 9x19 Parabellum ball ammunition, .380 ball, 7.62mm NATO blank, 5.56mm blank, and possibly artillery ammunition as well. As of 2013 there was an arrangement between Capua and Giulio Fiocchi for the manufacture of military small arms ammunition at the Capua site, but further details are restricted due to security considerations.

LABORATORIO

PIROTECNICO DI TORINO: The Pirotecnico di Torino was established as early as 1582 during the reign of Emanuele Fliberto in order to avoid reliance on foreign suppliers of gunpowder, giving rise to the Regia Fabbrica delle Polveri e Raffineria dei Nitri (Royal Powder Factory and Nitrate Refinery). In 1673 plant machinery was modernized, and in 1754, by order of Carlo Emanuele II, the facility was further expanded. Additional land was acquired in 1767, and between 1775 and 1778 the facility was completely rebuilt; in 1815, under Vittorio Emanuele I, King of Sardinia, adjacent property was acquired and yet another expansion occurred. The north-south extension of the property, which in 2013 was generally bounded by Lungo Dora Agrigento to the north and Via Vittorio Andreis to the south, was 308 meters; the east-west extension, bounded by Via San Pietro in Vincoli to the west and Via Borgo Dora to the east, was 170 meters. On 26 April 1852 the powder works were largely destroyed by the explosion of 25,000 kilos of powder, leaving 23 dead; residential houses in the area were also severely damaged. Between 1862 and 1867 the original Pirotecnico facility was rebuilt by Giovanni Castellazzo and produced artillery carriages and subassemblies but no longer produced ammunition or explosives. It was heavily damaged in World War II, ceasing military activity in 1943. The property subsequently was transferred to the city of Torino and since 1983 has been occupied by Ser. Mi.G. (Servizio Missionario Giovani, Youth Missionary Service) and is now refrred to as L'Arsenale della Pace (The Arsenal of Peace).

PRIVATE AMMUNITION PRODUCTION FACILITIES

LÈON BEAUX: Sometime in the late-1890s, Lèon Beaux, a Frenchman, founded a company in Milan named Lèon Beaux et Cie. Shortly after 1900, the company was re-registered as Lèon Beaux srl. In 1923, the name changed to Lèon Beaux & Co. Società Franco-Italiana per la Fabbricazione delle Munizioni da Caccia, da Tiro, da Guerra ed Affini, and by 1924 had again changed to the somewhat abbreviated name of. Società Franco-Italiana per la Fabbricazione delle Munizioni da Caccia ed Affini – Lèon Beaux & C. 1932 brought yet another name change, to Società Italiana Munizioni Lèon Beaux & C. During both World Wars Beaux produced ammunition for the Italian armed forces. Beaux ceased producing ammunition in the early 1970s; although the company was registered in Milan and may have had corporate offices there, the manufacturing facility was physically located in Baranzate, slightly northwest of Milan. As of 2013, the Lèon Beaux premises in Baranzate, bounded by Via Trieste to the north, Via Milano to the west, and Via Fabio Filzi to the south, were abandoned.

BOMBRINI-PARODI-DELFINO (BPD): Bombrini-Parodi-Delfino, commonly referred to by the abbreviation BPD, owes its name to its founders, Giovanni Bombrini and Leopoldo Parodi-Delfino, who in 1912 founded a company in Colleferro, south of Rome, to produce explosives. During World War I it produced munitions for the Italian military and after the war diversified into fertilizers and cement. During World War II BPD again produced munitions, and after that war further diversified into chemicals, textiles, and mechanics. In 1968 BPD merged with SNIA-Viscosa and the chemical division was renamed SNIA-BPD. SNIA-BPD was engaged in developing missile solid fuels and in the 1980s developed a series of air-to-surface rockets designated as the Medusa system. In 1966 BPD became part of FIAT Avio; in 1988 FIAT acquired SIMMEL, which acquired the assets of BPD, and in 2007 SIMMEL became an operating company of the Chemring Group; SIMMEL produces ammunition in the 20mm and larger range.

GIULIO FIOCCHI: The firm of Fiocchi Munizioni was founded on 3 July 1876 in Lecco by Giulio Fiocchi, an accountant, who took over the operations of a plant in Lecco that was already producing ammunition. Fiocchi is the primary producer of pistol ammunition in Italy. During both World Wars Fiocchi produced military ammunition; in 1945 the Lecco plant was bombed by the Allies and production resumed in 1946. Fiocchi is known for high quality handgun ammunition, and in addition to the plant in Lecco Fiocchi also has manufacturing facilities in the U.S, the U.K., and Hungary. Fiocchi remains a family owned company. The plant is located at Via Santa Barbara 4, Lecco.

LA PRECISA: Information concerning the La Precisa ammunition works is very sparse. The year that it was founded is vague at best, but information suggests that it was at least as early as the 1920s and made radio sets for the civilian market, as well as possibly for military use. La Precisa was located in Teano, in the province of Caserta, and produced all types of ammunition including small arms ammunition during World War II, as indicated by the LP stamp on cartridge clips. Other firearms related products produced by La Precisa included rimfire starter gun caps and three-round clips for the Berthier 1907/15 rifle used by Italy as a stopgap measure during World War I. The factory premises located on Viale Ferrovia covered approximately 200,000 square meters (approximately 2,152,800 square feet), and consisted of some 200 buildings and sheds of varying size. During the post-war years La Precisa manufactured fuses for 105mm and 155mm artillery shells, as well as land mines and hand grenades. On 24 September 1964 an explosion in the fuze section killed five workers. It is not clear when the facility was closed, but as of 2013 the buildings were in a state of abandonment and disrepair.

MARTIGNONI CARTUCCE: Martignoni was founded in 1929 and is located in Molassana, Genova. Martignoni has produced pistol cartridges for military use, but headstamps in most cases were the same as those used on commercial ammunition. Current Martignoni production is devoted almost exclusively to shotgun ammunition. It currently trades under the name Nobel Sport Martignoni S.P.A., and is located at Via Geirato 86, Genova.

SOCIETÀ ANONIMA ITALIANA PER LA FABBRICAZIONE DELLA DINAMITE: The explosion of 1852 brought an end to ammunition production at the Pirotecnico di Torino. Until 1865, production of explosives and ammunition was a state monopoly, but on 5 June 1865 a new law brought that monopoly to an end. In 1872 the Nobel dynamite company established the Società Anonima Italiana per la

Fabbricazione della Dinamite, alternately referred to as the Società Anonima Italiana Dinamite Nobel. Nobel established a factory to produce explosives in the town of Avigliana, about 15 miles west of the city center of Torino. The first factory was established in the Valloja area of Avigliana, northwest of the city center; subsequently another factory was built at Allemandi, slightly to the southeast of the city center. Explosives produced at Avigliana were used largely for blasting railway tunnels in and between Italy and France, but powder for military use was also produced. Until 1882 Avigliana produced balistite powder for ammunition, and around 1896 it switched to production of solenite. Nobel Avigliana, known locally simply as *il dinamitificio* (the dynamite works), produced gunpowder for both the Army and Navy during both World Wars, but did not produce any small arms ammunition. The works were taken over by the Germans on 12 September 1943 but subsequently were the object of several attacks by Italian partisan forces. On 14 April 1945, the Allemandi works, whose precise location and physical layout had been provided to the Allies by the partisans, were completely destroyed by a British bombing raid. After World War II production of dynamite resumed on a limited scale at Valloja, and in November 1961 an explosion at the plant that killed one person and injured 22 others led to calls for closure of the plant, and in November 1965 all operations ceased at Avigliana. In September 2002, part of the Valloja premises was opened as the Ecomuseo del Dinamitificio Nobel, chronicling the history of the explosives plant. The area in which the Allemandi facility was located is now an exclusive golf course, the Golf Club Le Fronde.

SOCIETÀ ITALIANA GENERALE PER MUNIZIONI E ARMI (SIGMA): SIGMA was a subcontractor that produced ammunition for the Pirotecnico di Bologna during World War I. It was established on 6 November 1915 at Volta Casaralta, on the northern edge of Bologna, and ceased production in 1919. SIGMA clips and ammunition are identified by the letters S-B.

SOCIETÀ METALLURGICA ITALIANA (SMI): The Società Metallurgica Italiana (SMI) was founded in Florence in 1886 as a Franco-Italian venture, and began operations in Livorno in 1886. In 1902, SMI was acquired by the Orlando family which was involved heavily in shipbuilding, steel, communications and energy. SMI has evolved into KME Group, SpA; KME Group (as of 2013) has facilities in Italy, Germany, France, Spain and China, and is a worldwide leader involved in production of semi-finished metal goods, copper alloys, and high technology products.

SMI Campo Tizzoro: In 1911 SMI established a plant at Campo Tizzoro, north of Pistoia, to produce small arms and artillery ammunition for the Italian Army and Navy. The ammunition factory was the largest employer in Campo Tizzoro, and consisted of a sprawling complex centered on Via Orlando, the main thoroughfare in Campo Tizzoro. Just slightly to the northwest – a kilometer or less – was another ammunition production facilty known as Bardalone, which although referred to as a separate facility, would appear to have been in essence an extension of the Via Orlando facility. During both World Wars SMI Campo Tizzoro produced ammunition for the Italian military; following World War II about half of the production facilities at Campo Tizzoro were converted to civilian production of copper laminates and copper alloys for industrial use, and military munitions production continued until 2000. Production of civilian copper products ceased at Campo Tizzoro in 2005. The portion of the plant that manufactured ammunition has been sold to a consortium of small artisans and industrial firms, while the rest of the premises remain as property of SMI's successor, KME Group SpA. There are plans to open a small museum on the premises that chronicles the SMI history.

SMI Fornaci di Barga: In 1915 the Società Metallurgica Italiana built an ammunition production facility at Fornaci di Barga, in Lucca Province, to support the Italian war effort; the plant also produced ammunition during World War II. It is not certain when the plant at Fornaci di Barga ceased producing ammunition; as of 2013 it was engaged in working copper and alloys and also produces blanks for Euro coins. The facility is located at Via Repubblica 257 in Fornaci di Barga. ■

APPENDIX 7: ITALIAN SMALL ARMS MANUFACTURING FACILITIES

Historically, a very high percentage of Italian small arms manufacturing has been and remains concentrated in the province of Brescia in Italy's Lombardy region, more specifically, in and around the city of Brescia itself. This geographic concentration, although much smaller in extent, is comparable to that of the gun industry in New England in the United States that has a large concentration that runs for about eighty-five miles from Bridgeport, Connecticut, through New Haven, Hamden, and Hartford, up to Springfield and Chicopee in Massachusetts. Beginning prior to World War I, and through the end of World War II, large numbers of military small arms were manufactured in the Brescia area by a number of different firms, both government owned and private. Government arsenals included those at Brescia and Gardone Val Trompia, and among the private firms were Glisenti, Breda, the Fabbrica Nazionale d' Armi, Castelli (later Manifattura italiana d'Armi), and Breda in Brescia, and Beretta in Gardone Val Trompia (slightly north of Brescia), and Armaguerra in Cremona (south of Brescia). The area is still home to several of the same companies as well as a host of other smaller companies engaged in producing high quality sporting weapons.

The government also maintained a number of other arsenals, similar to Springfield Armory in the United States and the Royal Ordnance Factories (ROF) in England; the arsenal at Terni manufactured weapons from 1880 through World War II; the Rome arsenal production of the *modello 1891* was limited to the years 1917 and 1918 and in the 1920s became engaged in artillery repair; the armory at Torino, which had produced the *modello 1891* from 1893 to 1898, was sold off to private interests in 1906, and Torre Annunziata similarly had produced the *modello 1891* from 1893 to 1900 but did not engage in any small arms production during either of the World Wars.

English language publications, as well as some Italian publications, reflect sometimes incomplete and often confusing information on Italian small arms manufacturing facilities. This is in part due to the plethora of duplicate names for some of the same facilities or to similar names for different facilities. This book is believed to be the first publication in English or Italian to reflect the precise locations, to include street addresses where possible, of the various arms manufacturing facilities, as well as indicating the current status of premises formerly occupied by facilities no longer producing weapons. Unfortunately, there are still a few firms for which information is either incomplete or questionable to some extent, and the missing information seems to be unavailable from any source.

GOVERNMENT OWNED ARSENALS & ARMORIES

FABBRICA D'ARMI DI BRESCIA: The Arsenale di Brescia (Brescia Arsenal) had interesting and somewhat unusual origins. As far back as 1455 a group of Servite monks established the monastery of San Bartolomeo, located between Via Crispi and Via Moretto, in Brescia. In 1769 the explosion of the nearby powder mill damaged the monastery and the adjacent church of Sant'Alessandro, and in 1796 the church property was requisitioned by Napoleon for military use; beginning in 1812 the premises were employed in manufacturing small arms and became known as the Arsenale di Brescia. The manufacturing facility was renamed the Fabbrica d'Armi di Brescia in 1860. From 1895 through 1897 the arsenal produced the *fucile modello 1891*, production of the *moschetto mod. 1891* began in 1893 and continued until 1919, and from 1898 to 1919 it produced the *moschetto mod. 1891 per truppe special*. During World War II, the name of the facility was changed to Fabbrica d'Armi Regio Esercito (abbreviated as F.A.R.E, or FARE). On 2 March 1945 the facility was completely leveled by a heavy bomb raid by B-24 Liberators of the U.S. Army Air Force. After the war a military barracks complex was built on the site and named Caserma Serafino Gnutti; it housed the Headquarters and signal elements of the "Brescia" Mechanized Brigade from 1975 until the brigade was disbanded in 1991. It was closed as a military installation in 2009.

FABBRICA D'ARMI DI ROMA: This government arms facility was established in Rome on 14 September 1915 as a satellite facility (*sezione*) of the Regia Fabbrica d'Armi di Terni, and on 1 September 1916 became an independent facility designated the Officina di Costruzione di Artiglieria; the facility was located on the east bank of the Tiber River in the area of Via Falminia and Via Guido Reni. During World War I it became an important arms and munitions production facility producing small arms and artillery fuzes; the facility produced 244,977 Model 1891 rifles and converted 709,768 Vetterli Model 1870/87 rifles to 6.5mm configuration. In 1919 it was largely demobilized and the work force was scaled back to 3,000; production was restricted to fuzes and repair of small arms. Between the end of World War I and 1924 it engaged in repair of small arms and production of spare parts (including barrels); rifle stocks of weapons repaired in 1923 and 1924 bore the marking Fabbrica d'Armi di Roma. In 1920, the facility had been renamed the Fabbrica d'Armi di Roma, but soon after, in 1923, it became part of the Laboratorio di Precisione, the work force was reduced to about 1,000, and production was limited to fuzes. In 1925, part of the facility was ceded to Breda for the production of rifles and machine guns. On 1 January 1927 the military portion of the facility was redesignated as the Spolettificio Regio Esercito (Royal Army Fuze Works), with the work force further reduced to only 250. Sometime between 1935 and 1938 Breda moved out its part of the facility and moved to another location on the eastern outskirts of Rome; the newly expanded Spolettificio covered 45,000 square meters (about

485,000 square feet) and employed 1,500 workers. During World War II the facility produced artillery fuzes; the work force rose to about 3,500, most of which was female. It has not been possible to document or determine post-war activity and current status of the facility, but as of 2013 the facility is believed to exist as the Officina Costruzioni Artiglieria Roma (Rome Artillery Construction Workshop) engaged in repairing artillery associated optical equipment.

FABBRICA D'ARMI DI TERNI: Terni, located in the Italian region of Umbria, was selected as the site for an arms factory, among other reasons because of the Nera River that flowed through the town and the readily available abundant supply of lignite to fuel the furnaces. On 18 March 1874, a Royal Decree was issued authorizing the construction of an arms factory at Terni. On 2 May 1875, the first stone for the Fabbrica d'Armi di Terni was laid by the Minister of War, General Cesare Ricotti Magnani; the factory was designed by British engineers and was equipped with British designed and manufactured Greenwood gun-making machinery. The factory was inaugurated in 1880 and consisted of a main plant and support buildings as well as a 200 meter test range. The early work force came mainly from the government arms factories of Torino, Brescia and Torre Annunziata, and production of the Vetterli mod. 1870 rifle was begun, continuing until adoption of the Model 1891 Carcano which, beginning in 1892, was produced in large numbers at Terni. By March 1918, there were 7,172 workers at Terni of which more than 3,000 were women, working 12-hour shifts enabling production of 2,500 rifles per day. Between 1919 and 1921, the factory was almost without work due to a lack of orders, but then picked up the pace by repairing weapons. Between 1935 and 1940 almost all of the plant's machinery was replaced with Italian designed and built machinery. Terni was the major producer of rifles for the Italian Army in World War II; in 1940, employing three shifts and some 6,800 workers it was producing about 2,500 rifles daily. During the course of the war the factory suffered some 108 Allied bombings that caused numerous casualties among the work force; in September 1943, following the armistice between Italy and the Allies, the Germans transferred about 3,000 machine tools from Terni to the northern part of Italy held by the Germans. The Allies subsequently occupied the premises, finally leaving in 1946. Terni then became a repair facility, and in 1978 the factory's name was changed from the Fabbica Armi Esercito Terni (F.A.E.T.) to Stabilimento Militare dell'Armamento Leggero di Terni (S.M.A.L.T. – Terni Small Arms Military Factory), and in 2000, equipped with computer numeric controlled equipment, was renamed the Polo Mantenimento Armamento Leggero (P.M.A.L. – Small Arms Maintenance Center) to better reflect its role.

During World War I Terni produced the Model 1891 rifle, and during the inter-war period produced the *moschetto mod. 91* and *moschetto 91 TS* in 6.5mm, as well as the *moschetto 91/38* and the *moschetto 91/38 TS* in 7.35mm. During World War II, Terni produced a small number of Model 1891 rifles, as well as the *fucile modello 41* and the *fucile corto* in both 7.35mm and 6.5mm.

FABBRICA D'ARMI DI TORINO: Construction on a factory for producing small arms, located between Corso Ottone Rosai and Via Ceva in Valdocco, slightly south of the Dora Baltea River and northwest of the city center of Turin and now a part of the city itself, was begun in 1715, and by December 1715 the first building was completed. Between 1716 and 1720 the production facilities were greatly expanded, and between 1721 and 1722 work on the establishment was completed. The facility was devoted exclusively to the manufacture of small arms; by 1862 production reached 18,000 firearms and 15,000 edged weapons. Between 1893 and 1900 the armory manufactured the Carcano Model 1891 rifle, but the factory was shut down in 1902 and around 1906 the manufacturing complex was sold to Vandel & Co. and was subsequently used as an ironworks. Ferriere Piemontesi succeeded Vandel, and in 1917 was acquired by FIAT as part of its iron and steel arm. In 1927 these premises were converted to arms manufacturing, by establishing the FIAT-controlled subsidiary of Società Anonima Fabbrica Armi Torino (SAFAT). The SAFAT name, manufacturing rights and machinery were sold off to Breda in 1930, but the premises remained as FIAT property, and on 1 January 1978 became part of Teksid S.p.A.

REAL FABBRICA D'ARMI, TORRE ANNUNZIATA: During the reign of the House of Bourbon over the Kingdom of Naples, a facility was established at Torre Annunziata by King Charles of Bourbon as the first weapons factory in the kingdom –the Real Fabbrica d'Armi, or Royal Arms Factory – and began operations in 1761 under Lt. Col. Luca Ricci. Torre Annunziata is located southeast of the city of Naples, on the Bay of Naples, not far from Pompeii. The facility itself, whose original buildings were designed by Francesco Sabatini and completed by Ferdinando Fuga, is located on Piazza Paolo Morrone near the intersection of Via Dante and Via Parini and was built as a palazzo-style complex with a courtyard. From 1894 to 1900 the Torre Annunziata arsenal was engaged in producing the Model 91 rifle, but during both World Wars devoted production to other military items. Part of the premises of the original Real Fabbrica d'Armi now hosts a museum containing many of the weapons produced there; in 1977 the facility was designated the Stabilimento militare del munizionamento terrestre, Divisione spolette (Ground Munitions Military Establishment, Fuse Division), and in 1984 was renamed simply as the Stabilimento militare spolette (Military Fuze Factory). As of 2013 it was engaged in production of fuzes and hand grenades.

SEZIONE FABBRICA

D'ARMI REGIO ESERCITO (SFARE) GARDONE VAL TROMPIA: This government small arms facility, sometimes referred to as the Arsenale di Gardone Val Trompia, appears to have been built sometime around 1860 as a satellite facility of the Arsenale in Brescia and was located on Via Artigiani in Gardone Val Trompia. During World War I, in addition to producing some weapons, it was largely engaged in collecting and assembling parts for the *moschetto modello 1891* from small subcontractors in the Gardone area, which were then forwarded to the parent arsenal at Brescia or possibly to the government arsenal at Terni. Between 1914 and 1918, the work force grew from 260 to 3,790, and after the end of the war, when the arsenal at Brescia ceased activity, the facility at Gardone continued operations producing modest numbers of various versions of Model 1891 carbines until the late-1930s when the production pace again increased. The SFARE facility was located close to the Beretta factory. After the war the SFARE was engaged in repair and reconditioning of military small arms until the 1960s, when manufacturing operations ceased completely. As of 2013 only a small office remained on Via Artigiani, consisting of a staff that acted as liaison between the Italian Army and Beretta for matters dealing with military weapons produced by Beretta. ■

PRIVATELY OWNED ARMS MANUFACTURING FACILITIES

ARMAGUERRA: The Società Anonima Armaguerra was founded by an entrepreneur from Genoa, Francesco Ettore Nasturzio (1882-1963), whose interests included hunting and which apparently led to his decision to get into the arms business. Among other business interests Nasturzio owned the Società Anonima Banane Italiane (Italian Independent Banana Company) and a sawmill in Calabria. In November 1939 Nasturzio and Gino Revelli filed a patent for the design of a semi-automatic rifle designated the Revelli Model 1939; the patent was not actually granted until 1940. Cremona was selected as the location for the Armaguerra plant, which was built in the 1939-1940 timeframe specifically to produce the Revelli Model 1939 semi-automatic rifle chambered for the newly adopted 7.35x51mm cartridge. The Armaguerra company, however, had its corporate headquarters in Genoa – its official name was Armaguerra Genova Sa – and some parts of Armaguerra produced weapons bore the marking AG. The manufacturing plant, bounded by Via Seminario and Via Castellone in Cremona, measured 38,000 square meters (about 409,000 square feet) of which 14,550 (about 156,600 square feet) were covered. However, the timing of adoption of a rifle chambered for a new cartridge was not fortuitous and only a limited number of the Model 1939 were produced – possibly around 10,000 – in both 7.35mm and 6.5mm. Beginning in 1942 the production line was converted to production of the Model 41 bolt action rifle; a small number of Beretta Model 1935 pistols are also known to have been produced by Armaguerra in Cremona, and the prototype of the Oliani designed OG 42 and the miniscule production run of the Oliani OG 44 submachine guns were also produced by Armaguerra. At the height of production the factory is believed to have employed about 1,000 workers. Following the Armistice in 1943, small arms production continued under the Germans, with some of the production machinery being moved to tunnels along Lake Garda. There is some reason to believe that an Italian prototype of the Czech Cz Zk 391 semi-automatic rifle in 7.92x57mm, was produced at Armaguerra and that a production line for that rifle may have been at least partially completed, but this is unsubstantiated. The Zk 391 was a semi-automatic rifle with a ten-round detachable box magazine that in 1943 attracted the interest of Italian technical personnel, and apparently also caught the interest of the Germans who reportedly in 1944 attempted to begin production of the rifle at the Armaguerra factory, but little progress was made before the war ended. Shortly after the war ended in 1945 Nasturzio continued doing business, changing the company name from Società Anonima Armaguerra to Officine Meccaniche Cremonesi which manufactured small 50cc motors used on motorbikes, but in 1948 it went out of business. From 1949 to 1956, the premises were occupied by a company named ASPI, which made fire extinguishers and equipment for the garbage collection industry. In 1961 part of the old facilities were taken over by Boldrini, which manufactured heavy construction machinery there until it moved its operation to Milano in the 1970s. The last occupant of part of the premises was a stationery shop on the Via Seminario side, which closed in 1999. As of early-2013 the premises remained in a badly deteriorated state and had environmental problems related to the presence of asbestos in the old buildings.

Fabbrica d'Armi Pietro Beretta: The firm of Pietro Beretta has the enviable distinction of being the oldest firearm manufacturer in the world as well as being the oldest family run business in the world. It was founded in 1526 by gunmaker Maestro Bartolomeo Beretta of Gardone Val Trompia in the province of Brescia and has remained in the same location and belonged to the same family ever since. The town of Gardone Val Trompia is almost entirely devoted to gunmaking and the Beretta factory is the largest establishment in Gardone with its main plant located – not surprisingly – on Via Pietro Beretta. Beretta was a prime supplier of small arms for the Italian Army in both World Wars and continues to supply weapons to the Italian Army to this day. During World War II, Beretta was the foremost supplier of submachine guns – the excellent Beretta MAB 38 series – as well as of pistols to the *Regio Esercito*. It also produced rifles and carbines of the Model 1891 and Model 1938 families.

During World War II, except for the *fucile 41*, Beretta produced virtually every long arm in the Italian inventory, to include the *fucile modello 1891, moschetto modello 1891, moschetto modello 1891 per truppe speciali*, and *fucile corto mod. 38*. It also produced the Model 1934 and Model 1935 pistols, and the *moschetto automatico MAB 38* series of submachine guns.

VINCENZO BERNARDELLI: Documents date the beginning of Bernardelli as an arms manufacturer in Gardone Val Trompia to 1721, but it was not until 1865 that Vincenzo Bernardelli began to manufacture handguns for the army. In 1903 the company relocated to a larger facility. From 1930 to 1933 the company manufactured some 25,000 10.4mm Bodeo Model 1889 revolvers. During World War II the company manufactured artillery fuses and other military items, among them Bakelite oilers for submachine guns and rifles. In 1997 Vincenzo Bernardelli was forced into bankruptcy and its assets, brands and trademarks were acquired by the Turkish company Sarsilmaz. As of 2013, however, Sarsilmaz still produces and markets shotguns built in Torbole Casaglia, Brescia Province, under the Bernardelli name.

Società Italiana Ernesto Breda: Commonly referred to by its abbreviated form simply as Breda, this company was formed as a heavy machinery manufacturing company in 1886 in Milan by Ernesto Breda. Originally a manufacturer of locomotives and other railway equipment, Breda later expanded into aircraft and armaments manufacturing. Breda manufacturing operations were based in Brescia in the area bounded by Via Rose to the north, Via Lunga to the south and east, and Via Rampino to the west. In 1925, Breda established a separate arms manufacturing operation in Rome occupying a part of the Army artillery facility in the Via Flaminia/Via Guido Reni area that was devoted largely to production of fuzes but which had also produced small arms during World War II. Between 1927 and 1930, Breda's Rome facility produced the Mannlicher-Schönauer Model 1903/14 rifle for Greece as well as the Model 30 light machine gun; the Breda Model PG rifles were also produced at this location. In March 1930, Breda acquired the patents, manufacturing rights and machinery for making machine guns from FIAT, as well as acquiring the SAFAT name; SAFAT was a FIAT subsidiary located in Torino. FIAT, through SAFAT, had been Breda's chief competitor in the machine gun field in Italy. As a result of a desire expressed by Mussolini for a new facility to be dedicated exclusively to production of automatic weapons, on 1 December 1937 Breda purchased property consisting of 609 hectares (about 1,500 acres) in the Torre Gaia area on the eastern suburbs of Rome and south of the Via Casilina. Construction of what was to become known as Villaggio Breda began in early-1938 and by early-1939 the Breda arms manufacturing operations began to be transferred from the Via Guido Reni location to the new facility. On 27 May 1939, Mussolini visited the area and laid the cornerstone for a housing complex for the Breda workforce in the area generally bounded by Via Ambrogio Necchi on the north, Via Annibale Calzoni on the south, Via di Grotte Celoni on the west and Via Ercole Marelli on the east. During the war the facility produced a wide array of small, medium and heavy caliber automatic weapons as well as anti-aircraft guns and anti-tank guns. Production continued until at least 1943; the manufacturing facilities were closed after the war and the buildings converted to other uses. The radically downsized armaments sector has survived as Breda Meccanica Bresciana in Brescia, which now produces high quality shotguns.

CASTELLI: In 1900, Giuseppe Toschi and G. Castelli founded an arms company at Via Milano 24 in Brescia, and from 1900 to 1916 manufactured revolvers for the Italian Army. Toschi died in 1916, and beginning in 1917 G. Castelli continued producing weapons under the new name of Manifattura Italiana d'Armi (MIDA). In 1919, the company name changed to G.A. Castelli until about 1921, when Castelli's sons, Napoleone and Vittorio, took over operations resulting in another name change to N & V Castelli. For a period following the war the Castelli brothers engaged in the production of shotguns; Castelli also produced a very limited number of Model 91/28 TS carbines and Balilla carbines, probably in 1928. There is some indication that Castelli ceased arms production around 1928

FIAT: FIAT – the acronym for Fabbrica Italiana Automobili Torino, or Italian Automobile Works Torino – was founded in 1899 by a group of investors headed by Giovanni Agnelli. FIAT became, and remains, Italy's largest carmaker and has developed into a worldwide operation. Its headquarters and principal manufacturing facilities are located in Torino, more specifically, at the Mirafiori works. During World War I, FIAT developed the Model 1914 machine gun and during World War II it produced a wide array of military goods and equipment including tanks, wheeled military vehicles and aircraft, and also developed and produced a number of different types of machine guns under the SAFAT name (see separate entry). During World War I a FIAT subsidiary, Officine Villar Perosa (Villar

Perosa Works, located in Villar Perosa, southwest of Torino) produced the world's first submachine gun.

F.N.A (FABBRICA NAZIONALE D'ARMI), BRESCIA: F.N.A. Brescia is not to be confused with the Arsenale di Brescia, later renamed the Fabbrica d'Armi di Brescia, which was a government arsenal (see appropriate entry above). F.N.A. Brescia was a completely different privately owned facility, which was founded by Pietro Lorenzotti (see separate entry) in the early 1930s, but which became an incorporated company in 1936. A 1926 Pietro Lorenzotti catalogue indicates that although Lorenzotti had a retail outlet on Corso Magenta 18, he also had offices and a production facility at Via Rodolfo Vantini 1b, and a sketch shows the premises to be located at the intersection of Via Vantini and Viale Italia. In 1926 the facility had a covered area of 6,000 square meters (about 64,600 square feet), had a forge and stamping equipment, and was capable of producing everything from screws to sights to stocks. However, records indicate that the corporate address of F.N.A. was at Via Luigi Appolonio n. 21, Brescia; this address likely was for the F.N.A. administrative offices. Although the Lorenzotti facility on Via Vantini reportedly burned down in 1927, a manual for a training rifle produced by F.N.A. in 1931 gives the F.N.A. Brescia address as Via Vantini 5, so it seems reasonably certain that the facility was rebuilt by Lorenzotti and retained by F.N.A. as its manufacturing facility. In 1931, the former Lorenzotti premises at Via Vantini became known as the Fabbrica Nazionale d'Armi. Early F.N.A. guns still bore alphanumeric serial numbers with a PL (Pietro Lorenzotti) prefix. During World War II, F.N.A. produced the Model 1891 cavalry carbines and TS carbines, the Model 1938 family of rifles and carbines, the *moschetto Balilla*, the F.N.A. B 43 submachine gun and small numbers of the 9mm Sosso pistol, as well as some parts for other weapons such as the locking block for the Breda Model 1930 light machine gun and barrels for the Beretta Model 1935 pistol. It is interesting to note that small parts produced by F.N.A. tended not to be interchangeable with those of weapons from other producers. Following the war F.N.A. attempted unsuccessfully to produce and market a number of shotguns and modern military weapons, but by 1955 was forced to shut down its operations.

LUIGI FRANCHI: Despite the fact that Franchi is a quite familiar name in the Italian arms industry, surprisingly little is known of the company's background. The company was founded in 1868, presumably by Luigi Franchi, and is now part of Gruppo Beretta and is known primarily for its shotguns. Franchi originally was located in Brescia and remained a family business until 1957 when it was acquired by the SOCIMI industrial conglomerate; SOCIMI went bankrupt in 1993 and was acquired by Beretta Holdings. It has not been possible to document Franchi military production during World War I; during World War II Franchi produced parts for small arms, possibly including the receiver for the TZ 45 submachine gun, as well as producing bayonets. Shortly after the war Franchi was involved in converting 6.5mm carbines to 7.92mm for export to the Middle East. The Brescia manufacturing facility is believed to have been located at Via Calatafimi 17; current (2013) corporate address for Luigi Franchi is Via Artigiani 1, Gardone Val Trompia. Trademark applications in the 1980s reflected the Luigi Franchi location as Fornaci (Brescia Province), Italy.

Genar: What little information is available on this company leads only to speculation. During the post-war period Genar produced a number of submachine guns based directly on the wartime TZ-45, but the weapons were not commercially successful and the company ceased operations at an undetermined date. Genar had offices in Rome, but it is likely that any guns it did produce were manufactured elsewhere, probably in the Torino area. The Genar name has been linked with the MM 745 submachine gun designed by Aldo Zorzoli (one of the designers of the TZ-45), but it is unclear if the MM 745 predated the establishment of Genar itself. Genar's main office was in Rome, but it may have been the successor of the Società Anonima Meccanica Torinese, which had produced the TZ-45.

Siderurgica Glisenti Glisenti was a family owned ironworks that had its origins in the 14th century in the Valsabbia area near Brescia. Francesco Glisenti was born in 1822 and in 1859 he established a large establishment for producing military small arms at Villa Carcina, in Val Trompia, north of Brescia. The Carcina works were located on Via Italia, south of Via Ripe. In 1865, Glisenti received its first order for 50,000 rifles for the *Guardia Nazionale* (National Guard), followed by an order for 30,000 Chassepot rifles for France between 1867 and 1870. Beginning in 1874 Glisenti began to produce the Model 1874 revolver that had been adopted by the Italian Army; upon adoption of the Model 1898 Bodeo, Glisenti also manufactured that revolver. In 1898, Glisenti obtained a patent for the Glisenti-Gerosa semi-automatic pistol that closely resembled the Mauser C96, marking Glisenti's first tentative step towards developing a semi-automatic pistol. In 1900, the Glisenti holdings were established as the Siderurgica Glisenti; it is somewhat unclear, but it appears that at least part of the Glisenti holdings, those at Carcina, were known as the Manifattura Armi Glisenti. Subsequently, Glisenti developed the Model 1905/1906 pistol designed by Bethel Abiel Revelli, followed by the Model 1910 which also bore the Glisenti name. However, in March 1907, Glisenti sold its arms division to Metallurgica Bresciana già Tempini (MBT), and production of the Model 1910 and 1913 pistols took place at the MBT factory in Brescia. Following the sale of its arms manufacturing facilities, between 1907 and 1966 Siderurgica Glisenti was engaged in producing a broad range of metallurgical and mechanical products on a somewhat reduced scale. In 1966, as a result of a merger Glisenti, was renamed Glisenti Caster, and in 1974 became part of FIAT-Teksid. In 1980, in a further reorganization, the Fonderie Guido Glisenti was established at the old Villa Carcina location, which now produces nodular cast iron for industrial use.

EREDI GNUTTI METALLI: In 1860, Giacomo Gnutti established a foundry at Lumezzane, in the province of Brescia. Upon Giacomo's death in 1897 the company passed into the hands of his six sons (he also had two daughters), and over the years underwent a series of organizational and name changes. The Gnutti firm was engaged in the production of various types of swords but by World War I was also engaged in parts for rifles and other weapons. Between 1931 and 1933 Gnutti manufactured the Scotti Model X rifle. In about 1939, the company expanded its operations, acquiring additional premises in Lumezzane, and expanded operations to include manufacture of various types of fuzes, tripods, submachine guns and rifles, steel and light alloys. During World War II, among other items, Gnutti produced 45mm Brixia mortars and 81mm mortars. After the war, the company no longer produced weapons, and in 1950 assumed the name S.&A. Eredi Gnutti, Spa. Eredi Gnutti Metalli is now one of the main brass rod, copper and brass strip producers in Italy and Europe.

FRATELLI GRAZIAN: Little is known about the firm of Fratelli Grazian (Grazian Brothers), located in Verona, other than that it produced the *moschetto Balilla* (youth rifle). The *moschetto Balilla* produced by Fratelli Grazian was noted for extensive use of bronze parts, including the bolt and the bayonet. Markings on Fratelli Grazian youth rifles included the O.N.B. or G.I.L. crest on the receiver, the maker's name (GRAZIAN VERONA), the date in Arabic and Roman numerals, and the letters F.M.B. (presumably for *Fucile Modello Balilla*, Balilla Model Rifle) on the barrel. All efforts to determine the physical location of the manufacturing facility in or around Verona have been fruitless.

ISOTTA-FRASCHINI: The Isotta-Fraschini firm was founded in Milan on 27 January 1900 by Cesare Isotta and Vincenzo Fraschini as the Società Milanese Automobili Isotta, Fraschini & C. Isotta-Fraschini established a reputation for building racing cars, and in the 1920s developed as a luxury automobile manufacturer. During World War I, Isotta-Fraschini manufactured aircraft engines, and during World War II manufactured the 20/70 20mm cannon designed by Scotti, and also produced at least two prototype 8mm machine guns designed by Scotti in the 1930s as well as production models of a 7.7mm machine gun. The Albertini designed submachine gun that utilized extensive stampings was produced in the Isotta-Fraschini small arms plant in Cavaria, in the province of Varese, which was taken over by local partisan forces toward the end of the war. Current status or use of the plant was unable to be determined. Following the war Isotta-Fraschini specialized in design and manufacture of high performance diesel and marine engines. Its headquarters and manufacturing facilities, now branded as Isotta-Fraschini Motori S.p.A., are located in Bari.

PIETRO LORENZOTTI (BRESCIA): There are conflicting bits of information available about the Brescia firm of Pietro Lorenzotti. A 1926 catalog reflects that Pietro Lorenzotti had a sales outlet at Corso Magenta 18, Brescia and a production facility at Via Rodolfo Vantini 1b. It is very interesting that Corso Magenta is one of the streets (the other three being Corso Cavour, Via Moretto, and Via Francesco Crispi) that form the block in which the old Arsenale di Brescia – later the Fabbrica d'Armi di Brescia – was located. The Brescia location at Corso Magenta previously may have been a retail sales store for weapons produced by the Fabbrica Bresciana di Armi which had been founded in 1889 and was liquidated in 1911. Most sources indicate that Lorenzotti manufactured the *moschetto mod. 1891 per truppe speciali 91/28* from 1930 to 1931. In 1931 or 1932 the production facility was renamed as Fabbrica Nazionale Armi, Brescia and continued to manufacture the *moschetto per TS 91/28*, and later engaged in production of the Model 1938 family of rifles and carbines. It is unclear as to what happened to Lorenzotti after the war, although there are indications that his son Luigi inherited the business and manufactured shotguns until around 1980, or possibly even as late as 1990. What was left of Lorenzotti's operation was sold to Ceraia and Piccinali, who continued to sell guns with the Lorenzotti name until 1995, but that firm is now out of business as well. The premises at Corso Magenta 18/20 are now (2013) occupied by a leather goods shop (Pellicceria Pagano), but the occupants claim to be unaware of previous occupancy by Lorenzotti.

MIDA (MANIFATTURA ITALIANA D'ARMI) GIÁ TOSCHI E CASTELLI: The MIDA name is closely linked with that of the Castelli family (see Castelli entry above). MIDA was the successor to the firm of Toschi and Castelli who between 1900 and 1916 had produced the Model 1889 Bodeo revolver and the Model 1900 flare pistol. In 1917, following Toschi's death, the company name was changed to Manifattura italiana d'Armi (MIDA). During World War I, MIDA produced about 137,000 Model 1891 rifles as well as 172,000 Model 1889 revolvers. After the war, in 1919, the company name again changed, to G.A. Castelli, to change again in 1921 to N&V Castelli.

METALLURGICA BRESCIANA GIÁ TEMPINI: The Metallurgica Bresciana giá Tempini (commonly abbreviated as M.B.T. or MBT) was originally founded in 1884 under the name Tempini; the name was changed to Metallurgica Bresciana at a later, undetermined, date. In March 1907, MBT acquired the arms manufacturing segment of the Siderurgica Glisenti located in Carcina, north of Brescia, and subsequently produced the Glisenti Model 1910 and Brixia Model 1913 pistols at the MBT plant located in Brescia on Via Giovanni Tempini, just south of

Via Giulio Quinto Stefana and the Brescia cemetery. During World War I MBT was involved in production of artillery shells and other heavy armament and also produced the FIAT Model 1914 machine gun under license. In 1935, the Società Metallurgica Italiana (SMI) became a majority shareholder, but the MBT logo was retained. Metallurgica Bresciana manufactured the *moschetto mod. 1891 per TS* (91/28) in 1930, and also produced parts for the *tromboncino mod. 28* grenade launcher. In 1958, the company was completely merged with the Società Metallurgica Italiana; the Tempini family still operates in Brescia, manufacturing tiles for indoor and exterior use. Somewhere between 2005 and 2010 part of the old weapons manufacturing spaces located on Via Tempini were demolished, but some of the buildings were still standing as of 2013. SMI now (2013) trades under the name of KME Group.

OFFICINE VILLAR PEROSA: The origins of FIAT's Villar Perosa works trace back to 1906 when Roberto Incerti di Villar established the firm of RIV to produce ball bearings for the burgeoning Italian automobile industry; strong financial backing for RIV was provided by Giovanni Agnelli of FIAT. Sources differ as to the original location of RIV as being either on Corso Bramante or Via Carlo Marochetti in Torino, where Incerti previously had manufactured bicycles; in 1907 RIV transferred its operations to newly built facilities in Villar Perosa, outside of Pinerolo, southwest of Torino. The new facility, not surprisingly, became known as the Officine Villar Perosa (Villar Perosa Works), or O.V.P. In 1909, the establishment was taken over by Agnelli, and Incerti's participation in the venture ceased. During World War I, O.V.P. was involved in military production, and among other items produced bicycles (used mainly by the *bersaglieri*), gas tanks for trucks, artillery shells, and other military items. Beginning in 1914, O.V.P. began development of what would become the world's first submachine gun, the FIAT Model 1915. In 1919, the company's name changed to Società Anonima RIV Officine di Villar Perosa. RIV continued to grow and by the 1930s had established plants in France, Belgium, Argentina Germany and the Soviet Union. During World War II, on 3 January 1944 the Villar Perosa works were bombed heavily by USAAF B-17 bombers and rendered inoperable until the end of the war. Operations resumed in 1946, and in 1965 RIV became part of the SKF Group, the world's largest producer of ball bearings.

SAFAT: The Società Anonima Fabbrica Armi Torino (abbreviated as S.A.F.A.T. or SAFAT) was one of the chief rivals of Breda in the armaments field and was managed by Col. Revelli. SAFAT was located on the premises that had been the Arsenale di Torino (see separate entry), but which had been acquired by FIAT in 1917 as part of its iron and steel arm. In 1927, FIAT established the subsidiary of Società Anonima Fabbrica Armi Torino on the premises at Via Caserta for the primary purpose of developing and manufacturing machine guns. The buildings on Via Caserta, including those of the old arsenal, included seven rooms underground and 15 rooms or sheds above ground. The venture was rather short-lived, as after the Italian Army had decided to adopt the Breda Model 30 as its standard light machine gun over competing FIAT entries, on 25 March 1930 the SAFAT name, manufacturing rights and machinery were sold off to Breda, but the premises remained as FIAT property and on 1 January 1978 became part of Teksid S.p.A.

SOCIETÀ ANONIMA ARMI AUTOMATICHE SCOTTI: This company founded by Alfredo Scotti was not a manufacturing establishment *per se*, but was more in the nature of a coordinating and design bureau. Scotti himself was an energetic and resourceful entrepreneur who had extensive experience working within the Italian arms industry and is not known to have personally designed the Model X rifle or many of the other weapons that bear his name, but rather orchestrated the efforts of others who designed and produced the weapons. In 1931 Scotti set up the Società Anonima Armi Automatiche Scotti in Brescia, with offices at Via Silvio Pellico 24-26. Scotti brought together a loose association of firms engaged in the arms or mechanical industries, among them the Ditta Serafino e Andrea Gnutti of Lumezzane, which was active in producing swords and bayonets; the Società Anonima Napoleone e Vittorio Castelli of Brescia, (a successor of MIDA) which engaged in manufacturing firearms; the Metallurgica F.lli Polotti fu Santo of Lumezzane, which manufactured revolvers and knives; and the Officine Mecchaniche Antonio Grandi of Solbiate. It is not clear as to how all of these firms intereacted, or what the precise relationship was with Scotti. In the small arms field, in March 1931 Scotti unveiled the *carabina mod. T.S.* which appears to have been the first semi-automatic weapon offered by the Scotti consortium; this was sooon followed by the *fucile Scotti modello IX* and the almost identical *fucile Scotti modello X* which was produced in very limited numbers by Gnutti. Scotti had his name associated with a number and wide variety of semi-automatic weapons, most of which were machine guns or light automatic cannons; probably the most notable, and most widely produced weapon bearing the Scotti name was the 20mm anti-aircraft gun produced by Isotta-Fraschini during World War II. Although Isotta-Fraschini was not part of the original consortium that Scotti had organized, he later did develop a very strong relationship with that firm.

SOCIETÀ ANONIMA MECCANICA TORINESE (SAMT): Possibly also known as the Società Manifattura Meccanica Torinese, this company, of which little is known, may have produced the TZ 45 submachine gun and may have been formed specifically to manufacture the TZ 45. One lone source, a technical drawing of the TZ 45, indicates that the company's workshops were located at Piassasco (sic), and its head office was located at Via Monginevro 89 in Torino; As of 2013, the premises at 89 Via Monginevro were occupied by a jewelry shop, Gioellleria Babbini. Piassasco is a misspelling of Piossasco, a town located slightly southwest of Torino. Another source indicates that SAMT with production facilities in or near Torino and offices at Lungotevere dei Cenci 9/1 in Rome, produced the AZ 50 submachine gun – essentially the TZ 45 with slight modifications.

SOCIETÀ ITALIANA AVIAZIONE (S.I.A.): S.I.A. was founded in 1916 to produce military aircraft; between 1916 and 1918 it produced bombers of its own design as well as producing the British Farman MF.11 under license. In 1918, S.I.A. was acquired by FIAT and became FIAT Aviazione. It produced the S.I.A. aircraft machine gun as well as probably the Model 1928 light machine gun used in limited numbers during World War II. ■

APPENDIX 8: ITALIAN SMALL ARMS DESIGNERS

As can be seen from the information below, except for a handful of individuals, there is an appalling lack of background information on many Italian weapons designers. In some cases information is limited only to the designer's full name, and in one case, to only a surname, and to the gun or guns designed.

Giuseppe Albertini: Albertini was head of the Arms Division at Isotta-Fraschini during World War II and is credited with the design of the Isotta-Fraschini submachine gun. No other information available.

CARLO BODEO: Comparatively little is known about Carlo Bodeo; he likely was born in Naples, and is believed to have been employed by Glisenti during the period when that company produced the Model 1874 revolver, which presumably would account for his familiarity with that weapon. On 11 September 1886, Bodeo was granted a patent to replace the action of the Model 1874 revolver and is also credited with design of the Model 1889 revolver, which is often referred to as the Bodeo revolver rather than as the Model 1889. No other information available.

ROBERTO BORAGINE: A Major in the Italian Artillery Corps who was charged with developing the replacement for the Model 1891 rifle using the 7.35mm round developed in 1935. Boragine was in all likelihood assigned to the Direzione Superiore del Servizio Tecnico di Armi e Munizioni, or D.S.S.T.A.M., which was the Italian Army's technical service department that oversaw development of all army weapons and munitions. The result of his development work led to adoption of the Model 38 short rifle. No other information available.

SALVATORE CARCANO: Carcano was born in Bobbiate (Varese) 11 October 1827. In 1848, he fought against the Austrians during the First War of Independence, and in 1849 he moved to Piedmont. In 1852 he became an apprentice gunsmith at the Royal Arms Factory in Turin and began his long career as an inventor, designing and building machinery for producing barrels, bayonets, and other gun-related items. In 1858, he received a medal at the National Exhibition in Turin for his work. He later was issued a patent for a needle bolt system. In 1862, he was sent to Switzerland as an inspector for testing small arms, and in 1863 journeyed to Paris to test and purchase machinery for producing steel rifle barrels. In 1868, he was promoted to Chief Technician, First Class, at the Royal Arms Factory, Turin. In 1876, he patented a new sight system for rifles and carbines, and in 1891 the Italian government adopted the Model 1891 rifle, the true centerpiece of which was the bolt designed by Carcano. His name is also associated with a twin barrel machine gun that he invented. The father of twelve sons, he retired in 1896 as a Lieutenant Colonel, and died in Turin in 1903 at the age of 76.

SESTILIO FIORINI: Fiorini was head of the Breda Technical Department, dates undetermined, but presumably at least in the late-1920s and early-1930s, and was the designer of the Breda Model PG semi-automatic rifle. Although it cannot be confirmed, as head of the Breda Technical Department Fiorini may have been involved with or responsible for the design of either or both the Breda Model 30 light machine gun and the Breda Model 37 heavy machine gun. Between 1950 and 1960 Fiorini, still working for Breda, was granted four U.S. patents. These patents were U.S. 2523231, issued on 19 September 1950, for a mechanism for transforming continuous rotary motion into reciprocating motion; U.S. 2620851, issued on 9 December 1952, for a removable magazine extension; U.S. 2715356, issued on 16 August 1955 for a closing block with percussion safety for automatic guns, and U.S. 2951423, issued on 6 September 1960, for a magazine holder for the feeding of firearms, machine guns, cannons and the like.

TULLIO MARENGONI: Marengoni, Beretta's most prolific and well known gun designer, was born in 1881 and was hired by Pietro Beretta in 1904. From 1904 until 1915 Marengoni seems to have done little to distinguish himself from his contemporaries, but in 1915 his innate talent enabled him to break ground with his design of the Model 1915 semi-auto pistol for Beretta, the first of his many successful designs. In addition to his continuous improvement and refinement of a successive line of pistols that ultimately led to the legendary Model 1934 semi-auto pistol, Marengoni is credited with the concept and design of the highly successful Model 38 line of submachine guns. He is without question the most widely known and respected Italian gun designer of the period spanning both World Wars. Marengoni led the Beretta design team until his retirement in 1957; he died in 1965.

GIUSEPPE MASCARUCCI: Macarucci is credited with the design of the FIAT Model 1928 light machine gun. No other information is available.

GIOVANNI OLIANI: Oliani was an engineer for the Armaguerra factory in Cremona, responsible for the groundbreaking design of the OG 42 and OG 44 submachine guns. He may have been born in the Mantova area, possibly in Quingentole. No other information available.

GIUSEPPE PAVESI: Information on this designer is very tenuous at best. It is believed that Giuseppe Pavesi was the designer of the Pavesi Model 1938 and 1941 rifles. A patent was granted in May 1938 for an "automatic carbine" to a Giuseppe Pavesi, resident of Mantova, whose occupation was given as an armorer. No other information available.

UGO PAVESI: Ugo Pavesi was born in Novara on 17 July 1886. In 1909, he received a degree in mechanical engineering from the Torino Polytechnical College. In 1910 he joined forces with another young engineer, Giulio Tolotti, and they founded the "Moto Aratrice Brevetti Ingg. Pavesi & Tolotti" (Pavesi-Tolotti Mechanical Plow Company), with production facilities at Gomboloita, near Milan. During World War I the firm was engaged in military production of tractors, and in 1918 Pavesi entered into a partnership with the huge Ansaldo firm and established the company named "La Motomeccanica Brevetti Ing. Pavesi." During the 1920s and 1930s Pavesi designed and produced a number of agricultural and military tractors. Between at least 1928 through 1932 Pavesi military tractors, used as artillery prime movers, were produced by FIAT-Spa. Pavesi's role in development and production of weapons seems to have been limited to an arrangement with Bethel Revelli for production of the *moschetto automatico Pavesi-Revelli*, which was an adaptation of the Villar Perosa twin submachine gun arrangement. This partnership resulted in either a prototype only, or a very limited number of guns actually being produced.

BETHEL ABIEL REVELLI: Revelli is sometimes cited as Abiel Bethel Revelli. He was born in Sciolze, northeast of Torino, in 1864 and died in Torino in 1930. Revelli was a Major in the Italian artillery, and became known for designing a number of weapons, including the Villar Perosa, which was effectively the world's first submachine gun, for which he applied for the patent on 8 April 1914. He also designed the Model 1910 Glisenti semi-auto pistol, and the FIAT 1914, S.I.A. and FIAT 1926 machine guns. Revelli was assigned four U.S. patents, one of which, U.S. 1854062, issued on 12 April 1932, actually after he had died, was for an automatic rifle.

GINO REVELLI: Gino Revelli was the son of Bethel Abiel Revelli and was responsible for the design of the Revelli Model 1939 semi-automatic rifle, adopted by the Italian Army and produced in limited numbers at the Armaguerra factory in Cremona. No other information available.

SCALORI: Virtually nothing, to include his first name, is known about this individual who designed the F.N.A. B 43 submachine gun. The surname appears on only some examples of the F.N.A. B 43, and the Scalori S. 48, indicating that he was the patent holder for the weapon (Brevetto Scalori). No other information available.

ALFREDO SCOTTI: Scotti was born on 20 August 1878 in Verderio, in the province of Como, to a farming family. At about age fifeen he moved to Brescia and began working for a company named Palazzoli that made shotguns, and continued to work with other gun companies and associations until he founded his own design bureau in Brescia in 1931. Rather than being a designer in his own right, he was more of an organizer and coordinator of individuals and companies engaged in the design and production of weapons. Scotti had no production facilities of his own but worked closely in conjunction with Isotta-Fraschini in Milan, who produced many of the weapons he designed. His most lasting legacy is that of the 20mm Scotti 20/70 automatic cannon, produced in substantial numbers during the war, but he also designed a number of small arms, including the semi-automatic *fucile Scotti modello IX* and the *fucile Scotti modello X*, at least two prototype 8mm machine guns – one belt-fed and the other fed by a top-mounted box magazine – and the 7.7mm and 12.7mm Scotti aircraft machine guns manufactured by Isotta-Fraschini. Scotti weapons were characterized by a rotating bolt head actuated by a gas piston. Scotti died on 26 January 1950 in Gardone Riviera (on Lake Garda).

GIULIO SOSSO: Sosso was a gun designer and gunsmith born in Casale Monferrato on 29 September 1903. He became interested in firearms at an early age, and by age thirty had become somewhat obsessed with designing an ideal semi-automatic weapon. He maintained an office at Corso Francia 91 in Torino and his first pistol, which was the forerunner of the redesigned 9mm pistol offered to the Italian military, was marketed by Dott. Ing. Giovanni Deregibus whose office address was listed as Via Vittorio Emanuele 12, in Sosso's hometown of Casale

Monferrato. Sosso designed the 9mm Sosso pistol with a unique belt fed magazine for which he was granted two patents in the United States. He also offered his design to Walther in Germany, but it was not accepted. Despite, or perhaps because of, its unique design, the pistol never achieved either military or commercial success. Sosso also designed several long weapons, including a semi-automatic carbine and a submachine gun; a 1937 catalog for his earliest pistol indicated that a carbine that could fire three-round bursts was in the process of development, and that both a light machine gun and a heavy machinegun were also being contemplated. Sosso actually built a submachine gun, at least as a prototype, that reflected his seeming obsession with unique feed systems. Sosso applied for and was issued at least three patents in the United States. Patent number 2031433 was for an ammunition loading device with a chain conveyor for small arms, applied for on 19 June 1934 and granted on 18 February 1936; patent number 2086339 was for another type of endless belt magazine, applied for on 1 June 1936 and granted on 6 July 1937; the final patent, number 2251171, was for a sear mechanism for automatic pistols, applied for on 10 April 1937 and granted on 29 July 1941. Sosso also applied for a number of patents in Great Britain, including applications for an endless belt magazine, a sear mechanism, and a trigger mechanism. After the war he lived in his farmhouse near Casale Monferrato where he had a small gunsmith shop and where he maintained a fairly extensive collection of antique guns and swords. Sosso, who was unmarried, died on 29 March 1965 and was survived by a sister.

LT. COL TONON: Along with Aldo Zorzoli, Tonon designed the TZ 45 submachine gun. A lieutenant colonel in the *Regio Esercito*, Tonon – whose first name seems lost in the mists of history – was assigned to the SFARE, Gardone Val Trompia, presumably during the early- to mid-1940s. No other information available.

ALDO ZORZOLI: Aldo Zorzoli may have been the "senior" partner of the Tonon-Zorzoli team responsible for design of the TZ 45 submachine gun. Zorzoli, son of a high-ranking Lancia executive, had a lifelong interest in weapons, and had his own office in Torino. In addition to his part in the design of the TZ 45, Zorzoli is also credited with the design of the AZ 49 submachine gun (the AZ undoubtedly standing for Aldo Zorzoli) as well as a series of submachine guns produced by the Genar firm after the war. The predecessor of the Genar weapons was another Zorzoli design, the MM 745, produced during the final days of the war, probably by SAMT. ■

APPENDIX 9: CARCANO PRODUCTION SUMMARY TABLE

RIFLE OR CARBINE TOTAL PRODUCED

The following table is based on information in Di Giorgio and Pettinelli's book, *1891: Il fucile degli italiani*.

RIFLE OR CARBINE TOTAL PRODUCED

Model 1891 rifle 3,587,600
Model 91 carbine 789,000
Model 91/38 carbine, 7.35mm 215,000
Model 91/38 carbine, 6.5mm 1,618,000
Model 91 TS carbine 1,033,500
Model 91/38 TS carbine, 7.35mm 127,500
Model 91/38 TS carbine, 6.5mm 197,800
Model 38 short rifle, 7.35mm 301,900
Model 38 short rifle, 6.5mm 891,900
Model 41 rifle 928,000

APPENDIX 10: COLLECTOR'S NOTES

The collector market for military weapons, at least in the United States, tends to be dominated by German and U.S. weapons, followed by British and Japanese weapons. Except possibly for the Beretta Model 1934 and Model 1935 pistols, Italian weapons fall into a third tier status. As a general rule, Italian pistols and rifles are somewhat harder to find than are weapons of the countries previously mentioned, but as a corollary, they tend to be less expensive than those of other countries. Undoubtedly the most popular Italian weapons in the U.S. collector market are the Beretta Model 1934 and 1935 pistols, which tend to be in plentiful supply but which also command respectable prices. Pistols such as the Glisenti and Brixia, as well as the earlier Beretta pistols, are much scarcer and accordingly are relatively expensive. With respect to rifles, virtually all are from the Carcano family, but some variants are much more readily available than others. The Model 1891 rifle itself, which is the progenitor of all other Carcano types, is probably the least frequently encountered in the U.S. collector's marketplace, while the so-called cavalry carbine is much easier to find; the other early carbine types, such as the TS and 91/24 carbines, tend to fall somewhere in between in terms of availability. Interestingly, over an approximately six month long period during the course of writing this book, virtually every variant of the Carcano family, including Nazi marked carbines and scarce variants of the Model 38 short rifle, showed up on one of the major Internet gun auction sites. Pricewise, because of their relative scarcity on the U.S. market the Model 1891 rifles generally tend to be the most expensive of the Carcano family, and the cavalry carbines and Model 41 rifles the least expensive; naturally, condition and unique markings can exert a heavy influence on the price. Perhaps ironically the Balilla carbines, most of which fall into the non-gun category, command much higher prices than the actual Carcanos themselves and are considerably harder to find, especially in good condition. What might be considered a sub-category of Carcanos are the Model 38 short rifles, most of which found in the U.S. were imported from Finland and bear the Finnish Army "SA" stamp; these generally tend to be in better than average condition compared to Italian-issue rifles, not because of poor weapons maintenance practices by the Italians, but because the Model 38s were not used extensively by the Finns and consequently have very good to excellent bores, most bluing intact, and wood with little wear evident.

As this book hopefully will illustrate, there is a huge variety of Italian weapons that lend themselves to any number of collecting possibilities. Handgun collectors, even if for example focusing only on Beretta Model 1934 pistols, could build a collection based on year of manufacture and/or on service of issue (*Regio Esercito, Regia Marina, Regia Aeronautica*, as well as police marked and commercial pistols). Carcano collectors have the option of something as simple as one representative weapon of each type – Model 1891, cavalry carbine, TS carbine, 91/24 carbine, Model 41, Model 38 short rifle – or expand the collection by including various manufacturers, carbines chambered for both 6.5mm and 7.35mm, etc. Collecting all the variations of the Model 38 short rifle, for example, involves at least nine different variations, depending on manufacturer, date of manufacture and caliber. The possible permutations are almost limitless.

One positive aspect of collecting Italian weapons is that they are rarely subject to the manipulation or faking that is often encountered on high-end weapons, especially German and U.S., although there are some items to look for when collecting Italian weapons. Pistols tend to have more numbered parts than rifles; the Glisentis have at least six numbered parts in addition to the frame, and include the slide, receiver, barrel, side plate, trigger mechanism, and safety. Beretta pistols have the slide, frame and barrel numbered. A collector should pay particular attention to matching numbers on Italian pistols. Because of the relatively few parts stamped with serial numbers on Carcano rifles – the barrel, stock, and in early Model 1891 rifles, the bolt handle – there is little point or profit for a seller in trying to match numbers; it probably is more common to find matching barrel and stock numbers than not, although it seems that the Model 38 short rifles that passed through Finnish hands have a higher than average incidence of mismatched stocks. However, some sellers have been known to "enhance" Carcanos by refinishing them, sometimes almost completely, or to alter serial numbers in the hopes of passing a weapon off as a rarity. The more perfect or more unusual a 70 or 80 year-old Carcano looks, the more closely it should be examined prior to purchase.

The Carcano collector, however, should be wary of Carcanos bearing German markings; there are certainly legitimate examples of Carcanos seized by the Germans and appropriately marked, and these weapons command a premium both for advanced Carcano collectors as well as for collectors of German weapons. Unscrupulous individuals have been known to mark ordinary Carcanos with fake German markings, some of which are more convincing than others. The best advice when considering purchase of a

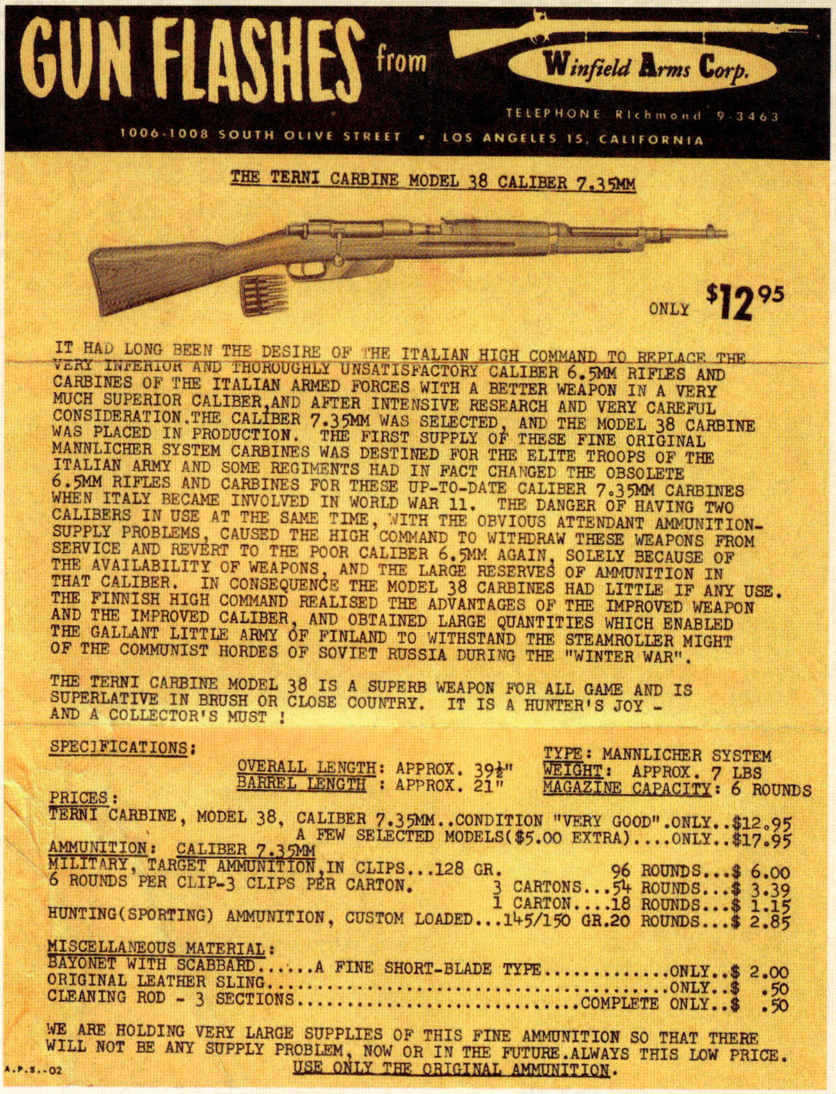
GUN FLASHES from Winfield Arms Corp.

TELEPHONE Richmond 9-3463

1006-1008 SOUTH OLIVE STREET • LOS ANGELES 15, CALIFORNIA

THE TERNI CARBINE MODEL 38 CALIBER 7.35MM

ONLY $12.95

IT HAD LONG BEEN THE DESIRE OF THE ITALIAN HIGH COMMAND TO REPLACE THE VERY INFERIOR AND THOROUGHLY UNSATISFACTORY CALIBER 6.5MM RIFLES AND CARBINES OF THE ITALIAN ARMED FORCES WITH A BETTER WEAPON IN A VERY MUCH SUPERIOR CALIBER, AND AFTER INTENSIVE RESEARCH AND VERY CAREFUL CONSIDERATION. THE CALIBER 7.35MM WAS SELECTED, AND THE MODEL 38 CARBINE WAS PLACED IN PRODUCTION. THE FIRST SUPPLY OF THESE FINE ORIGINAL MANNLICHER SYSTEM CARBINES WAS DESTINED FOR THE ELITE TROOPS OF THE ITALIAN ARMY AND SOME REGIMENTS HAD IN FACT CHANGED THE OBSOLETE 6.5MM RIFLES AND CARBINES FOR THESE UP-TO-DATE CALIBER 7.35MM CARBINES WHEN ITALY BECAME INVOLVED IN WORLD WAR 11. THE DANGER OF HAVING TWO CALIBERS IN USE AT THE SAME TIME, WITH THE OBVIOUS ATTENDANT AMMUNITION-SUPPLY PROBLEMS, CAUSED THE HIGH COMMAND TO WITHDRAW THESE WEAPONS FROM SERVICE AND REVERT TO THE POOR CALIBER 6.5MM AGAIN, SOLELY BECAUSE OF THE AVAILABILITY OF WEAPONS, AND THE LARGE RESERVES OF AMMUNITION IN THAT CALIBER. IN CONSEQUENCE THE MODEL 38 CARBINES HAD LITTLE IF ANY USE. THE FINNISH HIGH COMMAND REALISED THE ADVANTAGES OF THE IMPROVED WEAPON AND THE IMPROVED CALIBER, AND OBTAINED LARGE QUANTITIES WHICH ENABLED THE GALLANT LITTLE ARMY OF FINLAND TO WITHSTAND THE STEAMROLLER MIGHT OF THE COMMUNIST HORDES OF SOVIET RUSSIA DURING THE "WINTER WAR".

THE TERNI CARBINE MODEL 38 IS A SUPERB WEAPON FOR ALL GAME AND IS SUPERLATIVE IN BRUSH OR CLOSE COUNTRY. IT IS A HUNTER'S JOY - AND A COLLECTOR'S MUST !

SPECIFICATIONS:

OVERALL LENGTH: APPROX. 39½"
BARREL LENGTH : APPROX. 21"
TYPE: MANNLICHER SYSTEM
WEIGHT: APPROX. 7 LBS
MAGAZINE CAPACITY: 6 ROUNDS

PRICES:

TERNI CARBINE, MODEL 38, CALIBER 7.35MM..CONDITION "VERY GOOD".ONLY..$12.95
A FEW SELECTED MODELS($5.00 EXTRA)....ONLY..$17.95

AMMUNITION: CALIBER 7.35MM

MILITARY, TARGET AMMUNITION, IN CLIPS...128 GR. 96 ROUNDS...$ 6.00
6 ROUNDS PER CLIP-3 CLIPS PER CARTON. 3 CARTONS...54 ROUNDS...$ 3.39
1 CARTON....18 ROUNDS...$ 1.15
HUNTING(SPORTING) AMMUNITION, CUSTOM LOADED...145/150 GR.20 ROUNDS...$ 2.85

MISCELLANEOUS MATERIAL:

BAYONET WITH SCABBARD......A FINE SHORT-BLADE TYPE.............ONLY..$ 2.00
ORIGINAL LEATHER SLING....................................ONLY..$ .50
CLEANING ROD - 3 SECTIONS...........................COMPLETE ONLY..$ .50

WE ARE HOLDING VERY LARGE SUPPLIES OF THIS FINE AMMUNITION SO THAT THERE WILL NOT BE ANY SUPPLY PROBLEM, NOW OR IN THE FUTURE. ALWAYS THIS LOW PRICE.

USE ONLY THE ORIGINAL AMMUNITION.

A.P.S..02

This advertising sheet from the 1950s describes the Model 38 carbines offered for sale at would now be considered the unbelievably low price of $12.95, or $17.95 for specially selected examples. Similarly, the folding blade bayonet was offered for $2.00, and the sectional cleaning rod for $.50. By 2013 the latter two items had increased eighty fold or more. (*Author's collection*)

During the refurbishment process, stocks often were sanded and finished with a reddish-brown stain. The Model 41 rifle above carries the typical stained finish, while the 6.5mm Model 38 rifle below it has had the stain removed to reveal the natural finish that it would have had while in service. (*Author's collection*)

The stock of this early model moschetto TS was heavily sanded during the commercial refurbishment process, eliminating the stock cartouche and serial number. Portions of both the buttplate and the rear sling swivel are exposed because so much wood was removed by sanding. (*Author's collection*)

A Model 91/28 carbine with a barrel extension. It is not clear if the extension was added by the Bavarian users or if it was added to comply with U.S. import laws required to make it legal to import before 1968. The extension was merely a tube that fit over the muzzle. (*Author's collection*)

Carcano with German marking is to tread carefully and do as much research as possible to verify the authenticity of the piece.

During the 1950s and 1960s, large numbers of surplus Carcanos were imported into the United States. The primary importer at the time appears to have been a company named Crescent Firearms, a subsidiary of Adam Consolidated, based in New York City. In 1959 Adam Consolidated had contracted to purchase approximately 570,000 surplus Carcanos from the Italian Ministry of Defense and then approached Breda to refurbish the rifles. Breda was not interested and in May 1960 Adam Consolidated/Crescent Firearms then contracted with an individual named Luciano Riva to refurbish 150,000 rifles. For a variety of reasons, Riva was able to deliver only about 45,000 refurbished rifles by October 1960 (Adam/Crescent had failed to pay Riva in full for the guns already delivered). Adam/Crescent appears to have had an additional 80,000 rifles restored elsewhere, so it seems that something on the order of 125,000 Carcano rifles at a minimum were imported by Adam Consolidated/Crescent Firearms alone by the early-1960s. Other Carcanos were imported "as is" and were simply marked with an import stamp, normally on the barrel near the muzzle. Some Carcanos were imported by Century Arms International in the 1980s and were marked CAI St. Albans VT on the barrel with no apparent attempt at refurbishment. At least some of the CAI imports were Carcanos from the Albanian inventory; these generally are in relatively poor condition, although they may have been arsenal reblued by the Albanians; Albanian origin Carcanos also are likely to have

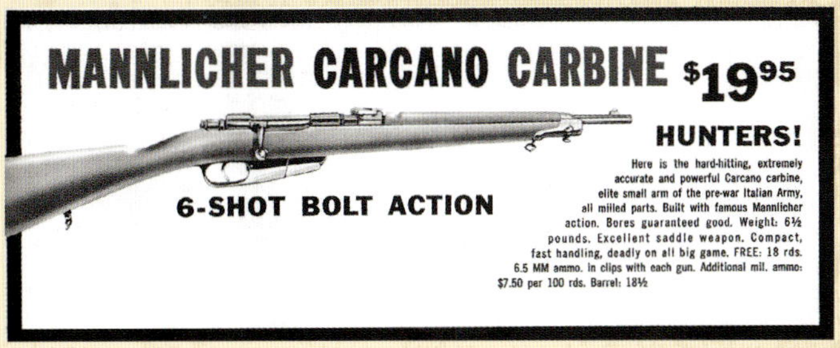

» Page from a 1950s Golden State Arms Corporation advertising brochure offering the early version of the moschetto per truppe speciali, with the transversal bayonet lug. In addition to being somewhat exaggerated by characterizing the carbine as the "elite small arm of the pre-war Italian Army," the reference to a "Mannlicher action" is inaccurate. (*Author's collection*)

« Markings on rifles imported to the United States in the early 1960s were altered; the caliber marking on the rear sight of this 6.5mm Model 38 short rifle has been partially obliterated, and the markings MADE IN ITALY and CALIBER 6.5 have been added on the receiver ring. The serial number, year of manufacture in Arabic and Roman numerals, and the manufacturer's name have been retained on the barrel. (*Author's collection*)

« This moschetto 91/24 bears an early import mark, MADE ITALY, on the receiver ring. It appears to have been imported in "as is" condition, without commercial or arsenal refurbishment. (*Author's collection*)

« A moschetto modello 1891 TS bearing a MADE IN ITALY import stamp on the receiver. (*Author's collection*)

mismatched stocks and other mismatched parts such as bent rather than straight bolts on Model 41 rifles, and the bolts may be blued as well. Springfield Sporters of Pennsylvania intentionally shortened the firing pins on 7.92mm Carcano conversions they sold because they judged them unsafe to fire. Shortly after the war an undetermined number of Carcanos had been refurbished by Italian government arsenals and also eventually found their way into the United States. Those refurbished by the Gardone arsenal were reblued, had their stocks sanded and refinished with a reddish-brown stain, were marked MADE ITALY on the barrel chamber, and had FAG and the date stamped on the buttstock; the marking MADE IN ITALY may also be encountered, but the two-word MADE ITALY marking is more frequently encountered.

It should be noted that some Model 1891 rifles had their barrel and forearm cut down during commercial refurbishments, resulting in a quasi-Model 1924 carbine; this "version" of the Carcano is known as the "Suprema." Because the barrel was shortened considerably the front barrel band and bayonet lug were eliminated, and the forearm likewise was cut to just ahead of the rear barrel band; the handguard was retained in its original form, and the bolt handle likewise was unaltered, retaining its straight configuration. Markings added to the chamber facets included MADE ITALY and CAL. 6.5; the stock was heavily sanded, eliminating the stock cartouche and serial number. Overall, this particular "conversion" is somewhat unattractive and has no particular collector value. ■

BIBLIOGRAPHY

BOOKS

Arendell, Russ. *Italy at War: Uniforms, Weapons, Equipment and Ephemera*. Lubbock, Texas: Arditi Books, 2010.

Arendell, Russ and Woodrum, Steve. *Italy's Battle Rifle: Story of the Mannlicher-Carcano Series of Rifles*. Lubbock, Texas: Arditi Books, 2012.

Bagnasco, Erminio and de Toro, Augusto. *The Littorio Class: Italy's Last and Largest Battleships* 1937-1948. Barnsley: Seaforth Publishing, 2011.

Balzi, Vittorio. *I mitra italiani 1915-1991*. Firenze: Editoriale Olimpia, Vallechi Editore S.p.A., 1992.

Benussi, Giuluio. *Armi portatili, artiglierie e semoventi del Regio Esercito italiano 1900-1943*. Milano: Intergest, 1975.

Bishop, Chris. *The Encyclopedia of Weapons of World War II*. New York: Barnes & Noble Books, 1998.

Bloomgarden, Henry S. *The Gun*. New York: Bantam Books, 1976.

Bogdanovic, Branko. *Serbian and Yugoslav Mauser Rifles*. Tustin, CA: North Cape Publications, Inc., 2005.

Chamberlain, Peter and Gander, Terry. *Machine Guns: WW 2 Fact Files*. London: Macdonald and Jane's, 1974.

Chinn, George M. *The Machine Gun. Volume I*. Washington, D.C., U.S. Government Printing Office, 1951.

Curami, Andrea., Ferrari, Paolo, and Rastelli, Achille. *Alle origini della Breda Meccanica Bresciana*. Brescia: Fondazione Negri, 2008.

Delpiano, Paolo Maria. *Viaggio intorno alla Dinamite Nobel*. Torino: Editris Duemila snc, 2011.

Di Giorgio, Bruno, and Pettinelli, Ruggero Filippo. *1891: il fucile degli italiani*. Pero: Edisport Editoriale, 2004.

Dolinek, Vladimir, Karlicky, Vladimir, and Vacha, Pavel. *Czech Firearms and Ammunition: History and Present*. Radix, 1995.

Gangarosa, Gene Jr. *Modern Beretta Firearms*. South Hackensack, New Jersey: Stoeger Publishing Company, 1994.

Hobbs, Richard. *The Carcano: Italy's Military Rifle*. Cameron Park, CA: 1996.

Hogg, Ian, and Weeks, John. *Military Small Arms of the Twentieth Century*, 7th Edition. Iola, Wisconsin: Gun Digest Books, 2000.

Law, Richard D. *Backbone of the Wehrmacht. The German K98k Rifle, 1934-1945*. Coburg, Ontario: 1993 Author's Revised Edition, 1992.

Marcianò, Emanuele, and Morin, Marco. *Dal Carcano al FAL*. Firenze: Editoriale Olimpia, 1974.

MAGAZINE ARTICLES

DIANA ARMI magazine, published by Editoriale Olimpia, Firenze. Issue number, subject, and pages indicated in the following list:

Novembre 1967. Il semiautomatico fantasma. Pages 23-28

Anno 2, N.1. ARMAGUERRA OG 44. Pages 26-32

Anno IV, N.4. Variara, un mitra alla macchia. Pages 29-35

Anno V, N.1. Breda 30. Pages 56-63

Anno V, N.2. La pistola automatica modello 1910. Pages 92-99

Anno VI, N.3. La rivoltella "89". Pages 37-45

Anno VI, N.4. La mitragliatrice FIAT '14. Pages 35-41

Anno V, N.5. Baionette militari in casa nostra. Pages 64-71

Anno VII, N.4. Il moschetto per ONB. Pages 74-76

Anno VII, N.12. La mitragliatrice FIAT mod. 35 cal. 8. Pages 66-71

No. 6, giugno 2002. Fucile semiautomatico Scotti cal. 6.5. Prima parte. Pages 140-145.

No. 7, luglio 2002. Fucile semiautomatico Scotti. Parte seconda. Pages 140-143.

Bobba, Vittorio. *Pistola Mitragliatrice Villar Perosa Mod. 1915*. tac armi, novembre 2000, pages 70-79.

Breternizer, Louis, and Skrobanek, Andreas. *Vom Motorpflug zur Pavesi-Revelli. Moschetto Automatico Kal. 9 mm mod. 915*. Bad Ems, Visier No 7-2008, pages 101-107.

Cappellano, Filippo. *Le pistole del Regio Esercito (1919-1943)*. Storia Militare n. 226 – Anno XX, luglio 2012.

Moss, John L. and Petrusic, Peter. *The 9mm Glisenti Cartridge*. IAA Journal, Issue 454, Mar/Apr 2007.

Moss, John L. and Petrusic, Peter. *The 7.65m/m Glisenti Cartridge*. IAA Journal, Issue 470, Nov/Dec 2009.

Scarlata, Paul. *Italy's Modello 1910 Glisenti Auto*. Guns and Ammo, Surplus Firearms magazine, October 2008, pages 106-113.

Scarlata, Paul. *Italy's Changeable Model 1891 Carcano*. Guns and Ammo, Surplus Firearms magazine, 2007, pages 14-24.

Springfield Armory Museum – Collection Record, Catalog Number SPAR 724; Rifle, Military – Italian Rifle model X Scotti-Brescia 6.5mm SN#2339

Marcianò, Emanuele, and Simoni, Adriano. *Le cinque vite della Glisenti 1910*. Parma: Ermanno Albertelli Editore, 2011.

McNab, Chris. *Twentieth Century Small Arms*. New York: Metro Books, 2001.

Menchini, Ugo. *Le pistole Beretta 1915/1974*. Firenze: Editoriale Olimpia, 1974.

Menchini, Ugo and Taviani, Pierluigi. *Pietro Beretta: Le automatiche/Automatic Pistols. I progetti anteguerra/The Pre-War Designs*. Firenze: Editoriale Olimpia, 1994.

Pettinelli, Ruggero Filippo. *Armi portatili e munizioni militari italiane 1870-1998*. Udine: Gaspari Editore, 2002.

Pignato, Nicola. *Armi della fanteria italiana nella seconda guerra mondiale*. Parma: Ermanno Albertelli Editore, 1971.

Pignato, Nicola, and Cappellano, Filippo. *Le armi della fanteria italiana (1919-1945)*. Milano: Storia Militare, 2008.

Rotasso, Gianrodolfo and Ruffo, Maurizio. *L'armamento individuale dell'esercito italiano dal 1861 al 1943*. Roma: Stato Maggiore dell'Esercito, Ufficio Storico, 1997.

Sacco, Sergio and Richetto, Gigi. *Il Dinamitificio Nobel di Avigliana*. Borgone Susa: Tipolto Melli, 2006.

Scarlata, Paul S. *Collecting Classic Bolt Action Military Rifles*. Lincoln, RI: Andrew Mowbray Publishers, 2001.

Simone, Gianfranco; Belogi, Ruggero; and Grimaldi, Alessio. *Il 91*. Milano: Editrice Ravizza, 1970.

Smith, W.H.B., and Smith, Joseph E. *Small Arms of the World*. Harrisburg, Pennsylvania: Stackpole Books, 1966.

Storia della artiglieria italiana, Parte IV (dal 1914 al 1920), Volume XI (dal 1917 al 1920), edited by the Biblioteca d'Artiglieria e Genio

Storia della artiglieria italiana, Parte V (dal 1920 al 1943), Volume XV (L'evoluzione dei concetti d'impiego del tiro, della tecnica e dei materiali), edited by the Biblioteca d'Artiglieria e Genio, Roma 1953

Walter, John. *Rifles of the World*, 2nd Edition. Iola, Wisconsin: Krause Publications, 1998.

Weaver, W. Darrin. *Desperate Measures: The Last-Ditch Weapons of the Nazi Volkssturm*. Coburg, Ontario: Collector Grade Publications Incorporated, 2005.

Wood, J.B. *Beretta Automatic Pistols: The Collector's and Shooter's Comprehensive Guide*. Harrisburg, Pennsylvania: Stackpole Books, 1985.

Zane, Marcello. *Eredi Gnutti Metalli 150o. 1860-2010*. Brescia: Negri Edizioni, 2010.

FACTORY BROCHURES

Typed description, disassembly and assembly instructions, furnished by Centro Storico Fiat: Mitragliatrice pesante FIAT mod. 1914, cal 6.5. Four pages, undated.

Mitragliatrice leggera FIAT mod. 1926, cal. 6.5. Five pages, undated

Mitragliatrice leggera FIAT mod. 1928, cal. 6.5. Eight pages, undated.

Mitragliatrice SIA. Brochure, printed by Officine Poligrafica Editrice Subalpina. Undated.

Mitra mod. 38 e derivati. Typed list and description prepared by Armi Beretta.

Fabbrica Bresciana d'Armi Pietro Lorenzotti. Catalogo Semestrale N. 32 – 1o Luglio 1926.

INTERNET SOURCES

www.cacciainfiera.it. *Storia della Fabbrica d'Armi del Esercito di Terni*, article by Brig. Gen. Guido Pesce.

www.il91.it This site is dedicated completely to the Carcano.

NOTES ON SELECTED BIBLIOGRAPHICAL SOURCES

Unquestionably the best book published on the 1891 Carcano is the 2007 book by Bruno DiGiorgio and Ruggero Filippo Pettinelli, *1891: il fucile degli italiani*. This book is a must for anyone seriously interested in the Carcano. It is superbly organized and lavishly illustrated, and covers almost anything and everything a historian or collector might want to know about the Carcano and its variants, markings, accessories, ammunition, and much more. The book is enhanced with a profusion of tables containing information on serial numbers, production dates by manufacturer, etc. Although it is in Italian, with a bit of effort most of the information should not be too difficult to understand for the English speaker. This book is likely the best book that ever will be published on the subject and is indispensable for a thorough understanding of the Carcano story.

For those unable to find or purchase the above mentioned book on the Carcano, an excellent Internet source is www.il91.it, which provides an exhaustive treatment, in Italian, of the modello 1891 and variants, with many superb photographs. This site also covers bayonets used with the mod. 91 and mod. 38, and has an extremely detailed and well organized section on markings, not available elsewhere, used by each of the armories and private manufacturers. Although the site is in Italian, as this book is being prepared for publication the site is also being translated into English.

Another excellent source for information on the *Carcano is Italy's Battle Rifle: Story of the Mannlicher-Carcano Series of Rifles* by Russ Arendell and Steve Woodrum, printed in 2012. The book contains a huge number of photographs, and although most are black and white, generally the quality is very good despite being printed on non-coated stock. It relies heavily on serial number tables and other information drawn from Di Giorgio and Pettinelli, and also copies a very extensive collection of Carcano markings as well as other information provided by Alberto Simonelli and Giovanni Chegia whose in-depth website, www.il91, is referenced above. This book is an essential reference work in English on the Carcano.

The Carcano: Italy's Military Rifle, self-published by Richard Hobbs, has been the standard English-language reference book on the Carcano since it came out in 1996. Hobbs, who would appear to be the premier Carcano collector in the United States, has done a generally creditable job of presenting a comprehensive account of the Carcano and associated items such as ammunition, bayonets, etc. The lack of photographs is offset to some extent by generally well done scale or line drawings. Overall, it is a good reference work, although subsequent research and documentation by both Italian and American sources have revealed some aspects of the book to be in error.

The best treatment of Beretta pistols is *Pietro Beretta: Le automatiche – Automatic Pistols* by Ugo Menchini and Pierluigi Taviani, published in 1994. The book has both Italian and English text and is a comprehensive, well written, well organized and lavishly illustrated treatment of all pre-war Beretta pistols. It is an absolute must as a reference work on this category of Italian weapons.

Two other books that deal with Beretta pistols are *Beretta Automatic Pistols: The Collector's and Shooter's Comprehensive Guide*, by J.B. Wood, and *Modern Beretta Firearms* by Gene Gangarosa Jr. The book by Wood covers Beretta pistols from their inception through the post-war period and provides a wealth of information; Gangarosa's book covers all of the Beretta pistols but focuses largely on the Model 92, and also covers Beretta rifles, shotguns and machine guns to some extent.

Another excellent book, although appealing to a much more limited audience, is the 2011 book by Emanuele Marcianò and Adriano Simoni, *Le cinque vite della Glisenti 1910*. It is a complete history of the Glisenti and Brixia pistols; the photography is absolutely incomparable.

Vittorio Balzi's *I mitra italiani 1915-1991*, published in 1992 and now almost impossible to find, is a thorough treatment of all Italian submachine guns from the first Villar Perosa through the beginning of the 1990s. This book traces the evolution and development of Italian submachine guns as well as providing extensive in-depth technical descriptions; some of the historical data has since been discovered to be erroneous and specifications tables are lacking, but overall, this is a worthwhile volume that limits itself to the specific field of Italian submachine guns. ■